The Great
Miss Lydia Becker

The Great Miss Lydia Becker

Joanna M. Williams

First published in Great Britain in 2022 by
Pen & Sword History
An imprint of
Pen & Sword Books Ltd
Yorkshire – Philadelphia

Copyright © Joanna M. Williams 2022

ISBN 978 1 39901 480 9

The right of Joanna M. Williams to be identified as Author of this work has been asserted by her in accordance with the Copyright, Designs and Patents Act 1988.

A CIP catalogue record for this book is
available from the British Library.

All rights reserved. No part of this book may be reproduced or transmitted in any form or by any means, electronic or mechanical including photocopying, recording or by any information storage and retrieval system, without permission from the Publisher in writing.

Typeset by Mac Style
Printed and bound by CPI Group (UK) Ltd, Croydon, CR0 4YY

Pen & Sword Books Limited incorporates the imprints of Atlas, Archaeology, Aviation, Discovery, Family History, Fiction, History, Maritime, Military, Military Classics, Politics, Select, Transport, True Crime, Air World, Frontline Publishing, Leo Cooper, Remember When, Seaforth Publishing, The Praetorian Press, Wharncliffe Local History, Wharncliffe Transport, Wharncliffe True Crime and White Owl.

For a complete list of Pen & Sword titles please contact

PEN & SWORD BOOKS LIMITED
47 Church Street, Barnsley, South Yorkshire, S70 2AS, England
E-mail: enquiries@pen-and-sword.co.uk
Website: www.pen-and-sword.co.uk

Or

PEN AND SWORD BOOKS
1950 Lawrence Rd, Havertown, PA 19083, USA
E-mail: Uspen-and-sword@casematepublishers.com
Website: www.penandswordbooks.com

To my daughters, Isobel, Helen and Miranda

Contents

Acknowledgements		viii
List of Figures		ix
Abbreviations		x
Introduction		xi
Chapter 1	Creation of a Feminist, 1827–67	1
Chapter 2	Emergence of the Suffragist Leader, 1867–8	33
Chapter 3	The Development of the Manchester Society	61
Chapter 4	Established Leader of the Women's Suffrage Movement, 1868–90	91
Chapter 5	The *Women's Suffrage Journal*, 1870–90	127
Chapter 6	The Women's Movement: A Multiplicity	138
Chapter 7	Local Government and the Isle of Man Franchise	160
Chapter 8	A Woman in a Man's World: the Manchester School Board	175
Chapter 9	Aspects of Becker's School Board Career	192
Chapter 10	The Bills for the Removal of the Electoral Disabilities of Women, 1870–80	216
Chapter 11	Lydia in London: The Third Reform Act and its Aftermath	231
Chapter 12	Death and Legacy	258
Conclusion		274
Notes		277
Select Bibliography		304
Index		308

Acknowledgements

I am deeply indebted to many who have helped me in this endeavour, particularly my publishers, Pen and Sword, who have been unfailingly helpful and supportive. My editor, Gaynor Haliday, has proved admirably patient and professional in helping me to refine and clarify the manuscript. The staff at Manchester Central Library; the John Rylands University of Manchester Library; the Women's Library at the London School of Economics; Girton College, Cambridge; the University of Nottingham Library; the University of Liverpool Library; the International Institute of Social History, Amsterdam; Chetham's Library, Manchester; Oldham Archives; Manchester Art Gallery; Fine and Country Real Estate Agents; and the George A. Smathers Library, University of Florida – have all provided invaluable assistance in accessing their archives or providing images. Should there be any unknown copyright holders of sources I have used unwittingly, they should kindly make themselves known to me. Many individuals have given generously of their time to answer my questions and I would like to thank particularly Emeritus Professor of Women's and Gender History June Purvis of the University of Portsmouth; Kelly-Ann Groves; Rev. Ian Rumsey; Andrew Simcock; the archivists of Manchester High School for Girls; and the University of Manchester Lydia Becker Institute of Immunology and Inflammation. My friends have been amazing in their help and interest in my work; most especially, Arja was wonderful in putting me up and feeding me during my London researches, and Pam most kindly read the manuscript and provided feedback and suggestions. My family, and in particular my husband, Ken, have given huge support. I could not have completed this biography without their love and belief that I could get there.

List of Figures

1. Lydia's first letter, aged 9
2. Moorside House
3. Photograph of Lydia Becker
4. Richard Pankhurst, 1893
5. The Free Trade Hall interior, c. 1865
6. Jacob Bright, 1876
7. The Mayor's Parlour, Manchester Town Hall
8. Lilly Maxwell
9. Clementia Taylor
10. Elizabeth Wolstenholme Elmy
11. Mangling done here
12. Jacob and Becca, 1870
13. An Ugly Rush
14. Josephine Butler
15. John Stuart Mill and Helen Taylor
16. Helen Blackburn
17. Caroline Ashurst Biggs
18. Frances Power Cobbe
19. Priscilla Bright McLaren
20. Lydia Becker 1873
21. Hanover Square meeting in London
22. Young Emmeline Pankhurst
23. Millicent Fawcett
24. 1876 – the Great Prize Fight
25. In at the finish
26. City Steeplechase
27. A Very Woman
28. Manchester Central Board School, opened 1884
29. Photograph of Lydia Becker in her black silk dress
30. Elizabeth Guinness portrait of Lydia Becker
31. Photograph of the Becker family grave

Abbreviations

BAAS British Association for the Advancement of Science
MNSWS Manchester National Society for Women's Suffrage
NAPSS National Association for the Promotion of Social Science
NSWS National Society for Women's Suffrage
NUWSS National Union of Women's Suffrage Societies
WSJ Women's Suffrage Journal
WSPU Women's Social and Political Union

Introduction

'Her life was, indeed, spent in working against the stream. The world owes much to those who dare to do what is unpopular.'
(Priscilla Bright McLaren)[1]

'The great Miss Lydia Becker ... a splendid character and a truly eloquent speaker', as described by the suffragette leader Emmeline Pankhurst, was the feisty driving force behind the early women's suffrage movement from 1867 to 1890. However, she is a figure about whom little is known today. Like most of the constitutional suffragists, she was written out of popular history in favour of the more spectacular suffragettes of the Women's Social and Political Union (WSPU). Yet ironically it was Lydia who first sparked a real commitment to the Cause in the 14-year-old Emmeline; in 1872, attending a meeting with her mother in Manchester, she was inspired by Becker's oratory, and 'left the meeting a conscious and confirmed suffragist'.[2]

The suffragettes did not appear out of nowhere; there had been a serious national campaign for women's emancipation in the preceding half-century, which made great headway in their parental, property, educational and vocational rights, and even in their political rights in terms of local government. Constitutional suffragists were a strong and vocal strand in this varied movement, and indeed they continued on into the twentieth century, campaigning peacefully until the vote was achieved for women. But the fact that the suffrage remained to be attained at the turn of the century allowed the more militant suffragettes to argue that the early campaigners had failed. Sylvia Pankhurst's disparaging comments on Lydia Becker in 1931 were an especially hostile example of this view. Whilst describing her as a 'remarkable' woman, she nevertheless claimed that Lydia possessed 'no remarkable gifts of intellect or oratory' and summarised her influence on the women's movement as 'on the whole a narrowing one'. Sylvia did concede that Lydia was the leader of the early suffrage movement, but attributed her success rather to the work for the society of her father, Richard Pankhurst.[3]

This biography will show that in fact any success ultimately gained by the twentieth-century suffragists of the WSPU and the more moderate suffragist groups, particularly the National Union of Women's Suffrage Societies (NUWSS) led by Millicent Fawcett, was made possible because they were 'standing on the shoulders' of others who had prepared the way for them. In the 1860s, the idea of middle-class women having any kind of role in the public sphere, gaining education and work skills, speaking in public, controlling their own lives and living independently of fathers or husbands was considered ridiculous. Any suggestion that women should have political rights was laughed out of parliament with licentious innuendo. By the end of the century, all this had changed; women were active in local government and campaigned in national elections, could access higher education, worked in offices and shops, were speaking routinely in meetings, had control of their own finances and could lead independent lives. And parliament was seriously discussing the prospect of giving them the vote.

All this was achieved through the combined efforts of a disparate group who have been designated 'feminists' by modern historiography. They included many men as well as women, were geographically scattered, and held widely differing views on aims and strategies. Nevertheless, they all shared a concern for the situation of women and the oppression they faced, and a focus on finding ways to remove the injustices and obstacles to their liberty. Whilst never a monolithic organisation, there were sufficient shared values to render the feminists of the nineteenth century an effective pressure group who shifted the social and political centre of gravity inexorably, if slowly, towards greater equality of the sexes. They not only changed the discourse, they also initiated strategies and policies which were continued on by later campaigners. These included public speaking to mass audiences; propaganda and publicity through advertising, posters, and journals; striking ideas like the contrasting of male criminals, who were enfranchised, with educated females, who were not; the rallying cry of 'no taxation without representation'; the use of legal precedents from earlier centuries to challenge judicial decisions; lobbying and petitioning parliament individually and in groups; even espousing what can be described as militant, though non-violent, resistance.

Feelings ran high amongst this earlier generation with regard to tactics and policy. Debate over whether to accept incremental gains and agitate initially for a vote for single women and widows, thus excluding married women, caused splits in the earlier period. And the uneasy relationship established between the suffragists and the Liberal Party in the 1890s was the outcome of a long-standing argument about whether the movement should be above politics, or whether it should hitch its wagon to one major party. Such matters occasioned conflicts which were every bit as acrimonious as those of the twentieth-century women's suffrage movement.

Lydia Becker represents a particularly neglected strand of this early British feminist history; the Manchester campaign for women's suffrage became a crucial part of the national movement under her leadership. She joined the women's movement when it was just beginning to find a voice, and was able to take advantage of the groundswell of feeling to seize the lead and try to direct the course of the agitation, at first in her native city, and very quickly right across the country. A mover and shaker amongst the early feminists, she was widely acknowledged, though not unchallenged, as the leader of the women's suffrage campaign for twenty years.

She did not come to political involvement until relatively late in life, when she was almost 40. She was unmarried, living at home with her widowed father, and trying to make her voice heard as a scientist. However, similarly to Emmeline Pankhurst, she was galvanised into action for women's rights when in October 1866 she attended a lecture. This was given at the National Association for the Promotion of Social Science (NAPSS) in Manchester by Barbara Leigh Smith Bodichon, then one of the most prominent feminists active in London, and she spoke on the need for female suffrage. Lydia was inspired; suddenly a whole new universe had been opened to her. She saw that there was a network of other people who were as dissatisfied as she with the limitations placed upon the lives and aspirations of women. Throwing herself into the Cause, she sought a role amongst the feminist campaigners, and soon produced her own writing on the topic of women's votes. So began her full-time campaign for women's rights, which continued unabated until her death at the age of 63 in 1890.

Like other feminists of the early period, Becker participated in a variety of agitations. Whilst she consistently argued that other feminist campaigns were side issues, which could only be fully resolved when women achieved votes on the same terms as men, she nevertheless involved herself in them with passion. She found common cause with Elizabeth Wolstenholme in the agitation for married women's property rights, and with Josephine Butler in defence of the interests of working women and in opposition to the Contagious Diseases Acts. Although it can be argued that Becker and other feminists had a middle-class view of women's issues, many of them were nevertheless ardent campaigners for women of every class. For twenty years, from its foundation until her death, she was the only woman on the Manchester School Board, and focused especially on improving and broadening the education of working-class girls and on better training and conditions for their female teachers.

She excelled in many aspects of campaigning. Her organisational abilities were superlative, and in an age when women did not speak in public she proved an excellent orator, travelling tirelessly around the country addressing packed audiences. She developed a sound understanding of parliament and its procedures, becoming the designated female suffrage lobbyist in the 1880s. Moreover, she edited and was the chief contributor to the *Women's Suffrage Journal* (*WSJ*) a major force in uniting women's campaigns across the United Kingdom and beyond. Her *de facto* leadership of the movement was fully recognised when, in 1881, she was invited to become secretary of the London society so that the movement could be led from the capital.

In 1867, Becker joined and extended a nationwide network of friends and allies who gave mutual support in 'the Cause' of women's rights, numbering among them Elizabeth Wolstenholme Elmy, Jacob and Ursula Bright, Richard Pankhurst, Josephine Butler, Priscilla Bright McLaren, Helen Blackburn, Caroline Ashurst Biggs, Frances Power Cobbe, Lilias Ashworth Hallett, Alice Scatcherd and Alice Wilson. To her closest friends she was affectionate and loyal, displaying a mischievous sense of humour with a beaming smile. But there was a personal cost to Lydia's high profile. She found the many cruel cartoons in the press and on placards, which caricatured her severe hairstyle and spectacles and impugned her femininity, extremely hurtful. Like Emily Davies, the women's educational reformer who became Lydia's mentor in the late 1860s, she took particular care always to be well dressed and to maintain the highest standards possible in her presentation.

Her single-minded devotion to the suffrage cause meant that she could be a demanding and unreasonable taskmaster who found it hard to tolerate dissent. As time went on, her approach became increasingly controversial; her methods could be high-handed and dictatorial. Then damaging disputes arose with those who had been staunch allies, over the issues of votes for married women and affiliation with the Liberal Party. There were also calls as early as the 1880s for uniting the campaign for female suffrage with that for universal suffrage. All these strategies were rejected by Becker, and the result was division and secession in the second half of the 1880s. And in parliament, despite the fact that it was by now widely believed that there was a majority in favour, lack of government support ensured that women's suffrage bills were excluded from consideration.

Many of Lydia's friends were lost in the turmoil of the 1880s, but others remained loyal and new allies were gained, notably the younger woman seen by many as her successor as suffragist leader: Millicent Garrett Fawcett. Feminist contemporaries, even some with whom she had clashed over policies and methods, recognised the value of her work and were devastated at her death in 1890. They mourned the loss of her 'guiding spirit' and acknowledged her as the head of the women's suffrage movement. History should also now take proper note of her contribution and rehabilitate her in the pantheon of outstanding women campaigners.

Chapter 1

Creation of a Feminist, 1827–67

The prevailing ideology surrounding the destiny of every middle-class woman in the nineteenth century was that she should marry, create a comfortable home for her husband, and bear him children. Whilst it is true that the ideal was never realised in many homes, it nevertheless had an important psychological impact on how women saw themselves, and on how they were perceived by men.[1] As journalist W.R. Greg put it in 1862, a woman's only true place was in 'embellishing the existence of others'.[2] Her sphere was around the domestic hearth, whilst that of a man was to be found in public life, out in the world. This ideology was enshrined in law: a woman was thought to have no need of her own property or rights, as she and her spouse were one legal entity, created by the common law doctrine of coverture. In the early part of the century she had no rights over her children; their father was their sole guardian. All her property and earnings came into the possession of her husband on marriage. She could not refuse conjugal rights – even her body was not her own. Indeed, the physical realities of being a woman were subject to an ideology that her normal state was weak and unhealthy. A healthy, energetic girl was not 'ladylike', so even this form of independence was strongly discouraged. Frailty was viewed as the inevitable consequence of her primary function of childbearing, and this extended to her mental capabilities, which were limited by nature so that all her energies could go into the furtherance of the species. The idea of public service or political rights for women was completely alien to these attitudes, and for much of the nineteenth century was dismissed by many, women as well as men, as arrant nonsense.

With the aim of producing girls who would make suitably biddable wives, many middle-class parents expected their daughters to suppress any wayward thoughts and speech. To do this, deceit was effectively socially prescribed from the earliest age, so that when the time came, a woman could hide any affections before marriage, for fear of premarital sex, conceal unseemly bodily functions such as menstruation, and once married, hide or feign sexual pleasure as it was argued that well brought up women had no carnal desires.[3] Girls were strictly controlled in their behaviour and correspondence, although some developed ways of circumventing this, such as using codes in speech and writing, or recruiting servants to pass on communications. The aim was a training in repression, concealment and self-censorship, with women being unable to acknowledge their true feelings or imaginings.

There was a key failing in the prevailing orthodoxy, however. Whilst most women did marry, a substantial proportion of middle-class girls did not, either through lack of opportunity or through choice. They remained spinsters and therefore failed to fulfil the role given to them by God, and the parlance of the age dubbed them 'redundant' or 'surplus' women. There was no place in society for such women. If they sought to work, it would be a rare employer who would be prepared to take them on. In any case, they usually lacked the required education and knowledge of the world; many middle-class parents thought women's education was unnecessary and even harmful, as a clever girl would not be attractive to potential husbands. They were brought up in the ways of a lady, learning how to embroider, paint, dance, sing and play the piano, by mothers or governesses who were as narrowly educated as they.

A young single woman of genteel background who fell on really hard times was forced to seek the only respectable work available – that of a governess, even though usually she could not offer her pupils much of an academic education. Her reputation, however, was safeguarded as she would form part of a household where her life would be supervised and controlled by her employers. For those who succeeded in finding a post, their position was often unenviable, if not unbearable. They belonged neither in the world of the servants, nor in that of their employers, and were forced into a lonely limbo where they could be friendless and isolated.

There were also many more such ladies than there were positions, and the plight of unemployed, poor but genteel, spinsters was desperate. The most vulnerable group were older spinsters who were left penniless and homeless on the death of aged parents, or the marriage of a brother. They were thrown into seeking work in their forties and fifties but, completely bereft of the necessary skills and knowledge, often had to rely on charity to survive at all.

The best an unmarried daughter could hope for would be to stay at home to care for ageing parents, or male members of the family such as brothers, and make herself useful, even indispensable, to the rest of the family, especially her married siblings and their offspring. Sometimes she had been identified early as the plain daughter who would not marry but remain at home, a permanent child. She could not go out unchaperoned, and no activity she might undertake could be more important than her familial duties. 'Unmarried daughters were ... expected to be invisible, doing good without thanks, forbearing to give advice, always to be available when needed.'[4] However, the status of such a woman was very low, due to the perception that she was a failure, and she was often regarded as a burden and a drain on the resources of her family, rather than a contributor to its success. Such women, not surprisingly, suffered from poor self-esteem which sometimes manifested itself in chronic illness, both physical and mental. The phenomenon of the lady who took to her bed with an ill-defined nervous disorder was common and attributed, not to suppression of the individual and her talents, but to the general frailty of the female sex, often in particular to 'hysteria': disease of her reproductive organs.[5]

Yet a few exceptional women created an alternative option for themselves which was not offered by society; they perceived that it might be possible for a single woman to live independently, as some widows who were provided for by their late husbands were able to do. Sometimes they came from unconventional families where they had been granted more freedom than was usual, and were encouraged by their father (more usually than by their mother) to develop their own interests and opinions; the Garrett sisters, Louisa, Elizabeth, Millicent, Rhoda and Agnes, were a prime example of this phenomenon. Some young women were even given an academic education by enlightened parents.[6]

There was a price to pay, however. The independent single woman was to some degree an outcast from the respectable middle class, and her choice of lifestyle was predicated on her having the financial wherewithal to sustain it. Many such women struggled to live on small pensions, or from meagre earnings from the very few occupations in which they might engage. They also risked being cut off, financially and emotionally, by disapproving friends and family. Ridicule of the spinster had a long history; the 'old maid' was either a flirt or a prurient prude, middle aged and ugly (as in the sisters in *Cinderella*). But the ridicule concealed a deeper fear that they were a threat to the social order.[7] Although the number of single women grew only in proportion with the general population, they were perceived as an increasing problem in the nineteenth century because of the actual numbers of impecunious single ladies.

However, with the efforts of concerned groups like the Kensington Society, new opportunities gradually opened up to them, such as in school teaching, nursing and office work. For those who were brave enough, there were the rewards of high-minded heroism and ambitions achieved, an escape from perpetual childhood, and self-development through celibacy, or sometimes very close female (and male) friendships, some of which became partnerships like that of Frances Power Cobbe and Mary Lloyd.[8] Ultimately such women achieved a powerful sense of self-worth. History has given them an identity as 'feminists,' which they shared with those men who supported their socially challenging aspirations.

Spinster daughter

Lydia Ernestine Becker was just such a spinster. She challenged the expectations of her family that she should confine herself to keeping house for her widowed father and being a surrogate mother to her younger brothers and sisters. Risking rejection, she broadened her horizons beyond the household in a range of activities which were increasingly outside the conventional parameters set by society for an unmarried lady. It is true that she remained for most of the time in the parental home until both parents were dead, in 1877, but she was an active campaigner from under her father's roof from 1867.

Lydia was born on 24 February 1827 in Cooper Street, Manchester, the first child of Mary and Hannibal Leigh Becker, and described by her fond godmother, Aunt Sophia, as 'the most beautiful child she ever saw'.[9] Her paternal grandfather, Ernest Hannibal Becker, was a naturalised German immigrant from Thuringia who had set up a manufacturing business supplying the cotton industry with dyes and other chemicals. In 1800 he married Lydia Kay Leigh. His success was manifested in his lease of the grand Foxdenton Hall at Chadderton, which remained the family seat for eighty years. Lydia's father, Hannibal Leigh Becker, was the eldest son. He married Mary Duncuft, daughter of a Hollinwood mill-owner, in 1826. Lydia Ernestine was born the following year and named after her paternal grandparents. Hannibal had gone into the family business and, perhaps to facilitate his involvement, Ernest lent him £600 with which he built himself and his young family a new home named Moorside near the works at Altham, whilst his younger brother, John Leigh, and his family resided at Foxdenton.[10]

Hannibal and Mary were living in Manchester at the time of Lydia's birth, but she spent a large part of her early years at Altham. Letters between her parents portray a loving couple who doted on their new baby; her father's letter to his wife on 7 October 1827 enjoined her to give 'our dear little babe' a kiss from him, and Mary wrote in April 1828 that 'our little Lydia is a great source of comfort and pleasure to us'.[11] The family moved to Reddish for thirteen years (c. 1837–50), when her father acquired a calico printing works there. It was from here that a 9-year-old Lydia wrote the first letter of what became a voluminous correspondence, telling her aunt about the cherry and pear trees and a wren building a nest in their garden.[12] Lydia apparently had a brief spell at boarding school in Everton (Liverpool), about which nothing is known, but otherwise she grew up in middle-class comfort, with all the conventional expectations, and was educated largely at home.[13]

Her later writings demonstrate that she perceived a lack of formal education as a key factor in the low status of women, and from the earliest years she did her best to remedy this defect in herself, reading widely in English literature and history, and having a special interest in science. When her brother Wilfred went off to university in 1868, she felt very keenly that she too should have been given that opportunity:

> I rejoice in his success, yet I have the conviction that had the same opportunities been placed within my reach … I could have done as much, and might now have occupied an assured position in the world, in a career honourable to myself, and useful to others, instead of being obscure, and helpless, with my intellectual powers crippled for want of knowledge of classics and mathematics and a mind half-starved for want of things I could have learned for myself … [14]

At the age of 41, having been encouraged by Richard Pankhurst, she began to consider formally studying Law, but feared that it 'would be terrible uphill work to begin now. I should have to learn Latin to begin with.'[15] Not surprisingly, in view of her total immersion in the suffrage cause by this date, this secret project came to nothing. In any case, the male bastion of the law at that time was unassailable, and perhaps this was a battle Lydia chose not to fight.[16] Yet an account in 1890 by Priscilla Bright McLaren confirms a general belief that Lydia would have made a very talented lawyer:

> A remark in one of the Memorial Articles on Miss Becker, saying that had she been a man she would have risen to a high position at the bar, if not even on the bench, reminded me of an incident connected with the Married Women's Property Bill. I accompanied her to the lobby of the House of Lords, as she wished to see the Earl of Shaftesbury about some flaw in the Bill. He came out, and Mr Russell Gurney came with him, who had been the chief promoter of the Bill. They both assured us that the Bill was as perfect as the House of Lords could make it. The light which fell upon the group was a thing to be remembered. It illumined Miss Becker's face, whilst those of our friendly legislators were thrown into shadow, and their expression harmonised with it, whilst she explained the matter to them. They stood silent for a moment, then looked very expressively at each other, and said, 'You are right, Miss Becker. Strange! we had neither of us seen this.'[17]

Altham was a beautiful place. There was a view of Pendle Hill from the house, and Lydia developed a great love of the countryside and the natural world. However, her time enjoying it was constricted by the demands of family life; her mother was constantly pregnant or nursing a new baby, and from the age of 7 or 8 Lydia was expected to take responsibility for her younger siblings. She saw her mother die of 'climacteric disease', which was related in the thinking of the era to menopausal problems and may have indicated depression, and pneumonia.[18] She was 47, and had born fifteen children in twenty-eight years, the last only seven months before her death. This may well have had an influence on Lydia's feelings about marriage and childbearing, and it certainly had an impact on her life in that she became the mother-figure for the family of eleven surviving siblings and their father in 1855.

Her sister Esther (Essie), born when Lydia was 8, recalled in old age that Lydia was very intelligent and that she was 'always a great reader'.

She had a big influence on her siblings' lives, teaching them to read and develop powers of observation, at which she was extremely adept. According to Esther, 'as a teacher her powers were remarkable; she seemed to go right down to the bottom of things, it all came out so clear to one's mind.' Lydia also

> always remembered what she read ... and had a wonderful way, too, of getting the kernel of a book in a very short time. Without reading through, she seized on the salient points, and knew more about it in an hour than I should have done after careful plodding through.

Such talents were to serve her well in her later career as a campaigner. But it was not all serious study. A young relative who was praised for her dancing attested to Lydia's gifts: 'Ah, who do you think taught me, why Lydia: from a spring-waltz to a plum pudding I would back Lydia against any woman in England.'[19]

In view of her usefulness to the family, which only increased with the number of children, and dramatically so with the death of their mother, it may be that Lydia was earmarked as the daughter who would remain at home and unmarried to care for the family. The fact that she suffered from ill-health and weaknesses tends to support this, even if it was not explicitly stated.[20] It is a moot point, though, whether the constrictions of conventional family life for a bright girl might have created, or exacerbated, her health issues.

She had a chronic back problem from at least her teens, and weakness in her hands and fingers which meant apparently that she could not properly master playing the piano, had poor handwriting and lacked general dexterity.[21] At 17 she was sent for around a year to Elgersburg, Thuringia in Germany for a cure at her father's cousin's hydropathic establishment. Her expansive letters reflected a lively interest in everything she saw on the two-week journey to reach it.[22] She was especially taken with the grandeur of the cathedral at Cologne, and preferred to sit on the top of the coach so that she would miss nothing, until 'a Frenchman who had placed himself next me began to make himself disagreeable squeezing my hand.' She accompanied her written descriptions with little drawings, such as one of a schloss from her bedroom window.[23]

At the *kurhaus*, she clearly felt a sense of liberation. Besides taking the waters, and improving in health, she learnt German from the local pastor and enjoyed the Christmas snow, when she fell out of a sledge. She took trips around the country to Leipzig, Dresden and other places about which she later corresponded enthusiastically with Lilias Ashworth Hallett.[24] Her doctor, Herman Piutti, wrote to her father that she had grown 'tall and stout', was keen in intellect and had an excellent memory, was reading and writing in German and playing the piano nicely, though limited by her back problems. She was also drawing very well and painting flowers on china, and often beat him at chess, a game which became a lifelong passion. Her mother expressed concern that she might have been outstaying her welcome, but Lydia clearly felt very at home, though interestingly she implied in a letter to her father that she was not always good at reading people. Significantly, Piutti mentioned that

> Lydia is the best-tempered girl I ever saw, which principally and partly arises from her activity of mind, which is always busy, time never hanging heavy on her hands. She is always interested for things around her and does all she can to increase her knowledge of things.[25]

Indeed, in letters home she showed an interest in matters beyond her immediate surroundings when she complained 'I miss the newspapers more than all the English comforts put together.'[26]

When she was brought home to Reddish by her uncle, John Leigh Becker, the family welcomed her with a giant bonfire. She was much changed; the experience of travel and freedom from family commitments had given her new perspectives. Intermittently, from January 1848 until August 1863 she kept a notebook which included quotations of poetry and scientific notes on fossils and birds. Very prominent were her thoughts on political events; she supported Morpeth's public health bill of 1848, believed in equal rights for Catholics, was against the draconian game laws of the day, and was a huge fan of free-trader Richard Cobden, whom she heard speak. She took a close interest in events in France, which she feared might lead to a general war in Europe and hoped England would not be dragged in. Revealingly, she already had radical ideas about politics: 'I am anxious to know if the French will have a republic if they are sufficiently enlightened. I hope they will and that it will last. The age of kings is going by.' However, she thought the French were too 'excitable and unsteady' to make it work. When Chartists were thought to be on their way to Altham, and later when the deposed French King Louis Philippe arrived in England, there was considerable excitement in the family. Esther recollected also that arguments about tariff reform and free trade raged amongst them: 'The stormy discussions connected with the Anti-Corn Law League were reproduced in miniature in our juvenile circle.'[27]

Despite such political awareness, Lydia otherwise inhabited a rural bubble, where she seemingly remained unaware of the nascent feminism emerging in the wider world. Women like educational reformer Emily Davies, advocate of equal opportunities for women at work Barbara Leigh Smith (Bodichon), and political economist and social theorist Harriet Martineau, all of whom who expressed dissatisfaction with the lot of women, do not appear to have impinged upon her consciousness at all. When, in Manchester at Bodichon's 1866 NAPSS lecture, she was suddenly confronted with this new universe. It changed her life in many ways, not least her relationship with her family, which now ceased to be the sole focus of her life.

Lydia's feelings towards her family were always very warm and close, and she was proud of their success. Yet happiness was marred by troubles which eventually led to the move in 1865 from rural Altham to industrial Manchester:

> There is no doubt about us being a remarkably distinguished family, and we may congratulate one another on our abilities, whilst we condole with each other on the ill fortune that has pursued us, and from the shadow of which some of us will never emerge.[28]

The family had returned to Altham from Reddish in 1850, and Lydia's last fifteen years there were marked by some painful events. The loss of her mother in 1855, with the attendant heavy burden of duty which fell on her, was a devastating blow. In the depths of winter, she recorded her feelings in her notebook: 'It is winter also in my heart. Four weeks today our dear mother was finally removed from our sight. Oh how long it seems more and more I miss her …' The death of her brother Ernest in Brazil in 1857, aged 22 (unlike three other siblings who had died in infancy) seems to have affected her so badly that she would never allow it to be mentioned.

Esther hinted at further difficulties: 'Other troubles, many and bitter, followed ...' In 1855 there was clearly some financial issue; Lydia wrote to her aunt on 23 March that their father had told them they must cut household expenses, and so two servants had been given notice. This meant that Lydia was to take on a greater role in looking after the large family, but she felt that this was too much for her physically. Accordingly, she and her sister Mary began looking for situations as governesses. Anticipating opposition from her aunt due to the 'coming down in the world', she argued that at a salary of £40 a year (which might even rise to the dizzy heights of £80 plus her washing, as in the case of a Miss Mitchell, a governess of her acquaintance) would give them independence and greater financial benefit than remaining at home doing the servants' work. Also, she had observed governesses of her acquaintance who seemed well off and were treated with 'great kindness and respect'. She enjoyed teaching and believed she could be equal to the task, having taught local girls to read and write.

> I believe it is one of the best things that could happen to me ... employment is what I have long wanted; something to occupy my mind when I could feel that day by day I had done my work and accomplished something. To set myself hard at work in study required [sic] more energy and determination than I possess amidst the distractions and constantly recurring occupations of a position in a large family yet I have often felt as if my life was passing away without purpose; I could not have gone without being obliged but now that I see it is for the best I am glad.[29]

The governess project came to nothing, it seems, and by 1858 Lydia, in place of her mother, was supervising Mary's wedding preparations.[30] The lack of money may well have been exacerbated further by the decline or temporary collapse of Hannibal Leigh Becker's business in the 1860s. The American Civil War of 1861–5, which disrupted Manchester's raw cotton supplies, resulted in the 'Cotton Famine' in Lancashire, with widespread hardship and even starvation amongst the workers. For companies like the Beckers', dependent on orders from cotton manufacturers, this spelled disaster. Hannibal apparently ceased chemical manufacturing for a period. In 1865, the family left their beautiful house at Altham and went to live in smoky Manchester at 11 Grove Street, Ardwick.

Life in rural Reddish and Altham had been very quiet, and there does not appear to have been any attempt to find a husband for Lydia in her most marriageable years from 18 to her late twenties. She clearly had a full-time job in bringing up her siblings, and was also much occupied in scientific studies, particularly botany. The option of marriage might have been more realistic once the family had moved to salubrious Ardwick, but she was by then at the advanced age of 38.

There may, however, have been one possible suitor, according to Sylvia Pankhurst. When Lydia came to the women's suffrage movement in the later 1860s at the age of 40, and began in earnest her long campaign, she was ably assisted by a bright lawyer seven years her junior: Richard Marsden Pankhurst. Sylvia reported in 1931, 'Her confident reliance upon his aid ... caused many observers to anticipate a romance which never materialized ...' And in letters to her brother (John) Leigh, Lydia confided 'I like Dr Pankhurst – he is a clever little man with plenty to say – and some strange ideas – it is refreshing to meet with people whose actions get out of the ordinary groove.'[31] It could be, however, that Lydia simply held him in high regard for the valuable work he undoubtedly carried out for the suffrage movement, and did not perceive him as a potential husband. Nevertheless, rumours of an attachment continued, and even as late as 1883 during an election meeting, in response to a rhetorical question 'who is Dr Pankhurst?' a heckler called out 'Lydia Becker's sweetheart.'[32] But of course, he was by then married to Emmeline Pankhurst.

Trained to take on a domestic role, Lydia perceived work in the home as at least equal in value to that of a male wage-earner:

> The peculiar duties of women are quite as important as the peculiar duties of men and make quite as great demands on the energies of those who perform them – they ought therefore to receive equal acknowledgement in the shape of personal independence – political privileges, honours, rewards, and last, though not least – pay.
>
> I think it a mistake to assume that the man who works for the wages on which his family live – bears the whole burden of their maintenance. The wife, who works all day in family and household duties contributes an equal share to the family income by setting the man free from them.[33]

This did not preclude a view that, when equality prevailed and just laws existed, marriage could be a very happy condition. Unlike her later friend, Frances Power Cobbe, Lydia was probably not a spinster by her own choice.[34] It seems unlikely that she ever received an offer of marriage; in 1868 she discussed the hypothetical case that she might receive one, and gave the impression that had she done so she would have accepted it, as long as her suitor was prepared to treat her as an equal, a concept which she elucidated elsewhere:

> Husband and wife should be co-ordinate and co-equal, each owing to the other entire personal service and devotion, their obligations being strictly reciprocal and mutual. In a happy marriage, there is no question of 'obedience' or which shall be 'paramount' …[35]

Indeed, according to Priscilla Bright McLaren in 1890, Lydia is even said to have replied in 1874 to a married woman who was pressing her claim to a vote, 'My dear friend, a really good husband is worth a hundred votes.' And Sylvia Pankhurst claimed that 'in some argument with Mrs Pankhurst' she had expostulated that 'Married women have all the plums of life!'[36]

By 1871, still living in Grove Street, Ardwick, Hannibal was recorded in the census as no longer a 'manufacturing chemist and farmer' (1861), but as an 'agent (refuses to give full information)'; he had clearly come down in the world, though at his death in 1877 he was again noted as a manufacturing chemist.[37] The household over which Lydia still presided now consisted of Hannibal and two unmarried brothers in their twenties; Arthur, a professor of music, and Wilfred, an Oxford undergraduate.[38] There were also two Backhouse cousins, Sarah, 31 with no occupation listed, but who from at least 1872 was Lydia's 'coadjutor' in the Manchester National Society for Women's Suffrage (MNSWS) office, and Norah, 19 and described as an 'artist painting'. They were still sufficiently well off to employ two domestic servants.

Lydia continued to take her family duties seriously, and later on, even in the midst of her campaigning, she apparently had a sewing machine in her lodgings, on which she made clothes for them. Priscilla Bright McLaren at their first meeting reported that Lydia had been cutting out garments for all the family when she called on her.[39] She worried about her siblings, and when her brother, John Leigh, moved to work as a doctor in Australia, she wrote urging him to not to overtax his health, advising him to take the suffragist MP Jacob Bright (who had a 'weak chest') as a model for looking after himself. She reported on his replies to her Aunt Backhouse, noting in 1868 that he was in good spirits in Queensland, but thought it seemed 'a God forsaken country'. Attempts were made to advise him how to handle competition in his medical practice, and she recommended that he concentrate on doing his job well instead of worrying about what other people thought.[40] She also confided in him her hopes and fears for her campaigns. During the 'Persons' campaign of 1868, she wrote: 'We are leaving our mark on the civilisation of this age … not of our country alone, but of the world.'[41] It must have been a great blow when he died in Queensland aged only 32.[42]

She was not averse to using her political friendships to benefit her siblings either. When Wilfred, her junior by twenty-three years, applied for the Fishmonger's Scholarship so that he could go up to Oxford, she asked Jacob Bright to speak to the MP for Bridport who had it in his gift, pointing out that 'I would not ask anyone's interest for him if I did not know him to be entirely deserving of what his friends can do for him in the matter.' Wilfred was granted the £30 a year as a result.[43]

Although her father spoke well of Lydia's domestic efforts, it seems that they sometimes had a difficult relationship. In this, Lydia had experience in common with some other feminists, notably Frances Power Cobbe and Emily Davies. When in Germany, she had written that 'there has been little of the confidence of friends between us, but I hope this separation may be the means of bringing us nearer together.'[44] Once living in Manchester, it is often claimed that Hannibal disapproved of his daughter's involvement in the women's campaign (though he did cash for her the cheques she received as donations).[45] Although his father, Ernest, had been a Liberal, Hannibal inclined towards the Conservatives, and it did not please him that his eldest daughter in the early years of her campaigning favoured the Liberals as the party most likely to support female suffrage. Yet Priscilla McLaren recorded that when taking tea with Lydia at her father's house:

> I was struck with the close affectionate sympathy which seemed to bind the family together, and with the pride with which the father regarded Lydia. He pointed to a picture of her and her sister taken

together when girls; the one of Lydia was not quite finished, 'because,' he said, 'I would not allow the painter to put another stroke to it lest he should spoil the likeness.' As I was leaving, he said, 'I wish you to know that all the good there is in my children they have got from their mother.' I could never forget the love which brightened Miss Becker's eyes that evening.[46]

Nevertheless, it may well have been due to differences with Hannibal that Lydia spent a lot of time staying at the home of fellow suffrage campaigners Jacob and Ursula Bright in Alderley Edge, such as in 1867, when she seems to have spent most of June there.[47] Around the end of September 1867, she took the daring step of finding lodgings in Carter Street in Greenheys, Manchester, and wrote home to her father 'It was an important step – one which involved grave consequences and has exposed us all to much comment on its singularity …'[48] Her tone in this letter was decidedly exasperated, and it was occasioned by her father's wish to move house and persuade her to return under his roof. However, she had clearly committed to the move; 'On the faith of it I have entered into serious responsibilities …' Nevertheless, by the time of the census of 1871 she was back in Grove Street, possibly due to financial problems, as she had told Mary Stephens soon after moving into Carter Street that she had 'neither bed, couch nor chair where I can get complete rest' and that she could just about manage, with nothing to spare.[49] She had very little income; a small remuneration as secretary of the MNSWS, and earnings from articles she managed to get published. Furthermore, as the campaign developed she had heavy costs to meet. There was also a social issue; she explained to her friend Sarah Ann Jackson that landlords 'are accustomed to let their rooms to gentlemen and find that it is too much trouble to attend to the needs of a lady'. Her Carter Street landlady wanted to let a back room to a gentleman, but

> she finds that gentlemen object to come to places where other lodgers are ladies – she says the room has been let <u>three times</u> – and gone off – on that ground. You can imagine that the idea of a mixed lot of lodgers is <u>excessively disagreeable</u> to me – though I have never experienced the slightest actual annoyance. Then you know my <u>address</u> is public property – it has to be provided for reference all over England – and it does not do to be perpetually changing.

For my own respectability and the honour of the Society – I must have a permanent resting place from which I cannot be driven at the will of others. These considerations make a house seem a <u>necessity</u> – the difficulties, and they are enormous, are to be considered only in the light of things to be overcome. I have so many difficulties and troubles crowding on me just now that I cannot tell what is going to come of them all.[50]

The death of Lydia's father in 1877, whilst it occasioned sadness and disrupted what had by then become a busy speaking schedule, opened up the prospect of greater freedom, which expressed itself in her removal at last to her own house, firstly to Humboldt Villas on Withington Road, then 155 Shrewsbury Street in Chorlton-on-Medlock. This was a very bold move for an unmarried lady, and must have been a real challenge at the age of 50. Throughout the rest of her life, Lydia struggled to maintain herself and carry out the work of her campaigns, and often wished she were rich like some of her fellow campaigners so that she might do more for the Cause.

In 1881, she branched out further when she took on the role of general secretary for the National Society for Women's Suffrage (NSWS) in the London and Central district. She did not want to be a salaried employee, but agreed to a consideration of £200 a year. This post required residence in London for the parliamentary session, allowing a few days a month in Manchester. Lydia took up lodgings at 15 Langham Street, and became a well-known lobbyist in the Houses of Parliament.[51] She was still in straitened circumstances, and forced to seek further sources of money, such as in 1884, when she attended the conference of the NAPSS held that year in Montreal, Canada, and persuaded the editor of the *Manchester Examiner and Times* to pay her for descriptive letters sent back reporting in detail on the meetings, whilst she stayed with relatives to cut costs.[52]

Lydia thus established herself as an independent woman and had shaken off the restraints of her upbringing and middle-class expectation. She had lamented the position of middle-class women as 'nobodies', who 'if they act for themselves … lose caste!'[53] Yet she had now proven that this could be changed. However, in doing so she had seriously threatened the established order, and the response in sections of the press was a series of political cartoons in which she and her colleagues were portrayed as strident, ugly and unladylike. The jibes hit home, and in a letter to Josephine Butler, campaigner against the Contagious Diseases Acts, she expressed her 'horror of newspapers', and her avoidance of seeing them.[54] She pushed on with her efforts, regardless.

Science and gender

Lydia had taken the opportunity of a rural upbringing to develop a deep interest in the natural world. In the observations she carried out, with the techniques she developed for drying and preserving flowers, and in her artistic efforts to record them in detail, she was following a path designated suitable for a respectable girl. Indeed, her uncle, John Leigh Becker, a well-respected physician and chemist in Manchester scientific circles, in the 1850s encouraged her in observing and recording the local flora and recommended books to help her become more systematic. He did not perceive this primarily as a scientific endeavour for her, avowing that it was 'a charming study for a young lady', and even better 'your Papa has discovered that it adds very much to the interest of a walk'. When he recommended a book on botany by a Mrs Seer it was as 'a most charming work, full of incident, information, poetry and beautiful thoughts'. Nevertheless, he and Lydia corresponded on botanical matters and exchanged seeds and specimens, and he introduced her to a wide network of male-dominated academic debate. She was eager to be scientific and exact in every aspect of her studies and joined a watercolour class at Altham to enhance her recording. It may have been around this time that she made paintings of the red campion, *Lychnis dioica*, on the panels of the sitting room door at Moorside.[55]

Esther recalled that 'Her pleasure in botany was intense, and her knowledge of it thorough and complete.'[56] In 1862, having devised a method of drying plants quickly under pressure and heat so that they kept their colour, Lydia won a gold medal at the South Kensington Horticultural Society national competition for the best collection of wild plants made within a year. She went on to write *Botany for Novices*, which was privately published with the help of her family.[57] It was part of a genre of women's writing which aimed to make scientific knowledge accessible to those who were excluded, particularly women and children, though she mentioned no specific audience, and she did not reveal her gender, being identified as 'LEB'. The volume explained simply the classification of plants, expressed in the clear prose for which she was noted in her later speeches and writings. But Lydia broke from the tradition of female writing in abandoning the Linnaean system of classification, which linked plants to contemporary concepts of social hierarchy, such as references to 'husband' and 'wife' plants raising floral 'children', and validated traditional female roles by showing their reflection in the natural order. Instead she adopted the more intellectual natural system of male botanists. She also emphasised the importance of even the most seemingly minor study to encourage her readers to participate actively in research: 'in nature, nothing is trivial or unimportant, the smallest and most ephemeral of beings owes its origins to the working of the same laws, and the force of the same Power that produces the greatest and mightiest on earth.'[58] Lydia produced a second beginners' guide on another passion, *Stargazing for Novices*, but this remained unpublished, probably because the circulation of her first guide had not been extensive.[59]

Despite her supposed physical frailties, she was extremely active in digging up and collecting specimens, even with the limitations of mid-Victorian female clothing and footwear, and observed the local plant life minutely in all seasons and weathers.[60] The love of botany stayed with her all her life, and fellow suffragist Jessie Boucherett said that her ideal happiness was a small house in the country near Manchester with a garden and a 'donkey chair'.[61] When out for a drive she identified the flowers they passed, and when she finally set up in her own house in Shrewsbury Street her great joy was a little conservatory. In London in the 1880s, she liked nothing better than to take a break in Kew Gardens, and in her office there were always flowers.

Not only did she spend long hours in her earlier years in the lanes and fields of Lancashire studying flowers and observing the stars, but she also engaged, as far as was possible, with the latest scientific thinking, notably corresponding with Charles Darwin.[62] Fourteen of her letters survive in the Darwin archive, from 1863 to 1877, with two of the great man's replies. Lydia first approached him in May 1863, when she sent him red campion flowers, requesting his opinion on an unusual feature – a hermaphrodite variation. Her letters were intense and detailed, as that of 23 May demonstrates:

> On receipt of your second letter this morning I went into the wood and examined 137 plants of Lychnis, taking them indiscriminately, though I do not pretend to have examined all I saw. The plants were of four kinds, viz
>
> 1 Male flowers of the usual type small pale yellow anthers 56
> 2 Female flower do. with long spreading pistils 25
> 3 Hermaphrodites having large dark purple anthers and dark purple anthers and short straight upright pistils 31
> 4 Male flowers with stamens like those of the hermaphrodite 25
>
> I searched in vain for a female flower with pistils like the hermaphrodite or an hermaphrodite with pistils like the female flower. this [sic] suggests the query Can [sic] the long spreading pistils be an adaptation or a struggle to catch the pollen wafted from a distant flower, a provision needless in the hermaphrodite which has an abundant supply close at hand.

She hoped she had discovered a new variety, but Darwin believed that the mutations she observed were the result of a fungal disease of the plant. A lively correspondence ensued, with Lydia sending Darwin many samples of flowers, seeds and roots, and asking further questions which showed her attempts to reconcile her observations with his latest botanical articles. He seems to have been as engaged in the investigation as she was; he highlighted and annotated parts of her letters and responded courteously to all her queries and suggestions, sending her copies of his own writings on the subject. In effect the correspondence amounted to a joint investigation of the plant's morphology.

Her observations also appeared in the work of other male scientists; Charles Joseph Ashfield read a paper to the Historic Society of Lancashire and Cheshire 'On the Flora of Preston and the Neighbourhood' in December 1864. He acknowledged throughout, his indebtedness to 'Miss Becker ... for much of the information ... particularly with regard to the habitats of those two interesting plants, the *Impatiens noli-me-tangere* and the *Colchicum autumnale*.'[63] Others of her correspondents included Charles Babington, professor of botany at Cambridge, and later Alfred Russel Wallace, the distinguished naturalist and evolutionary theorist. It is clear that she was eager to be recognised as a serious scientist, despite the prejudices of the day which asserted that a woman could only ever be a dilettante in such a field.

It seems that science and a love of nature also informed her personal beliefs. They are rarely mentioned in the extant archives, but she was in fact something of a 'freethinker' and it was in a letter to her friend Mary Johnson that she opened up on the topic. In terms very reminiscent of the then popular notions of Theosophy, she compared belief to the ocean:

> Differing creeds – or even the opposition between creed and no creed – seem to me to bear the same relation to truth that the shifting and restless waves do to the vast silent ocean – little eminences – lashed into prominence by the breath of the moment, and subsiding as they rose. I do not fix my soul on any one of shifting creeds – but those who do are yet in the great ocean and at will of its everlasting fountains though this wave may seem to them greater than the ocean! It may appear as difficult to some persons to realise the fact that all forms of doctrine are of this unstable, fleeting nature as it does to others that the dry land undulates like the ocean – that it is a moving, restless surface as surely as the sea is, though it undulates so slowly that to us, creatures of a day, it seems at rest – yet we know that 'The hills are shadows, and they flow from form to form, and nothing stands. They melt like mist – the solid lands, like clouds they shape themselves and go.'
>
> And so it is with all the forms in which human thought moulds itself. Yet amid all these changes the undying spirit moves upwards and onwards towards a future whose possibilities none can limit or foresee.

In a further missive she elucidated:

> I wonder why you should have troubled about my being a supposed 'rationalist'? I have not the faintest notion what the word conveys to other people ... I do not assent to any proposition which is not either learned by direct consciousness or capable of logical proof ... I believe that all nature is one.

However, in an age when formal religious observance was strongly associated with respectability, an admission of these unconventional views could have seriously damaged her reputation, so they were reserved only for private correspondence and discussion. Moreover, she stressed her respect for genuinely held religious views: 'I would not drag away any support from anyone ... where faith is a real thing ...'[64] Priscilla Bright McLaren also revealed an ambivalence in Lydia's beliefs when she recalled how she had 'more than once' said that 'in earnest work she felt she was carrying out her baptismal vows, and that this thought gave her much nervous power ...'[65]

When the family moved to Manchester the practical study of flowers had to end, as Lydia wrote to Darwin:

> I have not been able to pursue my study of the *Lychnis* flowers nor my endeavours to penetrate the mystery of their alteration in form, for since then we have ceased to reside in the country and now, surrounded by acres of bricks and mortar—and an atmosphere laden with coal smoke, I have no opportunity of watching living plants.

Instead she took this as a chance to expand her theoretical scientific knowledge, and may have joined the Ray Society once she went to London, as she apparently had access to its library. Despite the fact that on 12 December 1865 Lydia's prize-winning plant collection was put on show by the Manchester Scientific Students' Association, her attempts to join scientific bodies in the city, the most notable of which was the Literary and Philosophical Society, met a brick wall as their all-male ethos was resolutely defended. She therefore decided to start her own 'Ladies' Literary Society' which, contrary to its name, was to focus especially on scientific issues. When she asked Darwin to send her one of his pamphlets for discussion at the opening meeting, she made the exclusion of women from such knowledge clear:

> Of course we are not so unreasonable as to desire that you should write anything specially for us, but I think it possible you may have by you a copy of some paper such as that on the *Linum* which you have communicated to the learned societies but which is unknown and inaccessible to us unless through your kindness.[66]

Her speech at the inaugural meeting on 30 January 1867, in a room provided by the Manchester Royal Institution, was tactful in its attempt to defer to male superiority and dominance in knowledge; Lydia was well aware of the constraints on her interested audience.[67] Nevertheless, she offered them a productive alternative to their isolation at home in undertaking their own scientific study of 'loved and familiar objects'. She was able to use the example of Darwin himself, who, during a period of illness, had studied climbing plants from his sickbed. She made it clear that women were not trying to compete with men, or do their own groundbreaking studies, but wanted to sit at the feet of scholars and scientists and learn from them. Although if, in the process, they were able to do some modest investigation themselves, just as she had been wont to do, it would be valuable in its own small way. The speech was an extremely important step for Lydia personally, as it was the first time she had addressed an audience – an occupation which she was to make very much her own.

The plan was that at each meeting a learned paper would be read, such as that on climbing plants provided by Darwin (he had also provided papers on 'Dimorphic condition in *Primula*' and probably 'Three forms of *Lythrum salicaria*'), then the ladies would discuss it, asking questions and stating opinions and arguments. It started quite well, although Lydia was somewhat disappointed with the turnout. Perhaps the members were less than enthused by her own gloomy talk against the use of evergreens for Christmas decorations, which she feared caused the destruction of wild holly trees and mistletoe; she proposed the use of artificial greenery, which would have the added bonus of providing employment for women to make it.[68] There were enough members to allow the purchase of a small library, but the society did not survive long, perhaps because Lydia's energies were soon diverted into the women's suffrage campaign.

The society brought Lydia to public notice, however, as her controversial lectures there on social issues led to increasing notoriety. As well as corresponding with Darwin, she read his works avidly and was very taken by his theory of natural selection. On sending him a copy of *Botany for Novices* she stated that he had 'made plain for future explorers – the path in which henceforward they must all proceed'.[69] She was thinking of herself amongst those explorers and in 1868 she presented a revolutionary new idea about female intelligence to the Ladies' Literary Society in her paper 'Is there any Specific Distinction between Male and Female Intellect?' Her case, going against received medical and social wisdom of the time, was that the differences between the intellectual achievements of men and women were culturally determined.

A strong argument has been made by Tina Gianquitto that Lydia came to this view through her study of *Lychnis* and her understanding of evolutionary theory. She began to apply 'biological principles to social constructs'. If plants could mutate, from single-sex females to hermaphrodites, due to the outside agency of a parasitic fungus, then external factors might also affect human development. This was extended in 'On Some Supposed Differences in the Minds of Men and Women with Regard to Educational Necessities', where she showed that women had been denied opportunities to develop their intellect (as her own early life demonstrated) and argued that, with equal education to men, such distinctions would eventually disappear. Basing her views on her studies of *Lychnis* and following Darwin, she believed that even fixed categories, such as biological gender, were fluid in evolutionary terms. She clearly saw the potential of science to challenge conventional views on female intellectual inferiority.

In 1868, Lydia broke several taboos of Victorian society by addressing a male-dominated institution, the British Association for the Advancement of Science (BAAS) at its Norwich conference. The BAAS, founded in 1831, had only ever admitted women grudgingly, but by 1868 they did have access to all parts of the annual conference, if they were accompanied by a man. Although it was generally considered unseemly for a woman to speak in public, Lydia was invited to give her paper 'Is there any Specific Distinction between Male and Female Intellect?' Having caught the attention of the Manchester Anthropological Society, she had presented it at their monthly meeting and caused a 'quite a commotion', and was naively surprised at the stir it elicited:

> I was quite unprepared for the amount of attention which the subject of my paper seems to have excited, and the only thing which causes me to hesitate about giving it circulation beyond the members of the Society for which it was written is the feeling that I have not done justice to the subject.

It was clearly a reassurance and pleasure to her that in an article just published by a rising star of the London National Society for Women's Suffrage, Millicent Fawcett, she found a like-minded colleague: 'I should say her opinion about the ideology of male-female intellect exactly coincides with mine.'[70] And there were others, notably Emily Davies, who thought that the differences between the sexes were exaggerated and that their common humanity was far more significant.[71]

The BAAS saw that the topic had great potential for debate in the Economics and Statistics Section of their conference at Norwich, which was the area where the very few female lecturers were allowed to speak – usually on subjects related to geography, travel and ethnology. It was viewed as the least scientific section and therefore suitable for ladies. Nevertheless, one commentator noted that the 'Section of Economic Science is hardly the one in which we should expect a lady to shine'. Having scraped together the funds to attend for the week, Lydia spoke to a full house; the audience was anticipating lively debates on women's supposed intellectual inferiority, and her demand for co-educational opportunities for females. The same commentator allowed that: 'Miss Becker took it by storm, and carried everything with her. The very title of her paper was a challenge.'

Her idea that the human mind had no sex made a huge impact on such an audience, and she reinforced her point cogently, arguing that 'there is no distinction between the intellects of men and women corresponding to, and dependent on, the special organization of their bodies.' She proposed that 'female' minds could be found in 'male' bodies, and vice versa, and that the differences between the sexes were a response to environmental and cultural conditions. Like stunted plants, women had been 'pent in a small corner' with no access to light and no possibility for growth. She attributed the entire concept of 'separate spheres', of the outside world for men and the home for women, to this condition. She also argued that there were as many variations within each sex as there were between the sexes; it was a matter of individual, rather than sexual, difference. In the printed version of the speech, she quoted the case of women who cross-dressed in order to take on the role of men in the armed forces, and in this was echoing Darwin's idea that 'the potentiality for change is borne by the individual'.

The audience responded with frequent laughter, not all sympathetic, and applause, and she 'resumed her seat amid loud cheers'. The next speakers found it hard to gain attention as 'the interest excited by Miss Becker's paper was so great that it was found impossible for [them] to secure the attention of the section.' There was a storm of debate and criticism in the press, in homes, and in private correspondence. Lydia, 'wonderfully amazed at the great success of my paper ... and the attention it excited', was invited to address the Nottingham Philosophical Society and the Hull Literary Institute on the back of it. This last was a very prestigious event, as she was billed alongside university professors Phillips and Huxley.[72] The novelist George Eliot (Mary Ann Evans) wrote to Emily Davies, who was also a correspondent of Lydia Becker, that 'a young physician, an Oxford man of scientific bent, who came to see us on Sunday spoke of Miss Becker's paper as "brilliant", and thought it likely to do good.'

But this was an unusual view; most reviewers rejected her arguments out of hand, notably in *The Times*, the *Pall Mall Gazette* and the *Saturday Review*. Lydia was particularly incensed that many reports 'completely misrepresented' the import of her words, and she argued very sensibly that 'if these papers had answered what I actually said instead of what they chose to fancy that I meant, their criticisms would have been more valuable.' The worst attacks were personal, aimed at humiliation, and questioned her femininity. The satirical press took great delight in doubting Lydia's sex, claiming that she did not use a side-saddle to ride a horse, referring to her as a 'person' and an 'Amazon'. A letter to the *Stroud Journal* began 'I read somewhere ... that there are now three sexes – masculine, feminine, and Miss Becker.' Further, a reviewer for the *Journal of the Anthropological Society of London* commented: 'A woman with a masculine mind, is as anomalous a creature, as a woman with man's breasts, a man's pelvis, a man's muscular leg, or a man's beard.' Such a woman, he asserted, 'is unnatural and repulsive'. Even the boys of the London Merchant Taylor's School in their winter entertainment performed a scene inspired by Becker which looked forward to a time 'when, 1876 at the latest, man shall be dethroned and woman take the initiative in politics, in love – in everything'.[73] Lydia became aware that she must be very cautious about her self-presentation.

Despite this, the BAAS Norwich conference liberated Lydia in several ways. She wrote about it in great detail to her brother Leigh, in Australia, recounting an excursion to Cromer in a company which included Joseph Hoare, the Tory candidate as MP for Manchester, who very courteously drove her in his carriage all afternoon along the cliffs. She also delighted in dropping the names of eminent scientists whom she encountered, notably Sir James Simpson the discoverer of chloroform, Henry Bates of the Royal Geographical Society and Alfred Russel Wallace, who had collaborated with Darwin on his theory of natural selection. There is an indication of enthusiasm for the British Empire, which she expressed much more publicly in the 1880s, in her account of meeting a 'very friendly' Colonel Sir Arthur P. Hayes, 'the hero of Magdala', who came to hear her and listened 'with the greatest attention'.[74] She was thrilled and bemused after the delivery of her paper to find that she had become a 'distinguished visitor', and accordingly took advantage of the presence of Dundee photographer, James Valentine, to have four portraits taken of herself which she proceeded to distribute to supporters.

Perhaps thus emboldened, she battled on for women at the BAAS and in 1869 took a stand on the issue of the ladies' tickets, which were only available to those accompanying a male relative. She presented to the council a memorial that they should be the same as those for ordinary members and associates. She also demanded to know whether ladies were eligible to be elected to the sectional committees for each of the areas covered by the conference, as well as to the general and other committees. The council reluctantly conceded that there was no official bar to ladies, but it was just not 'done', and the practice did not in fact change till 1913. It was an early lesson for Lydia on the trials of putting the feminist case; it was clear that established practice was a huge obstacle in gaining full access for women to yet another institution.[75]

In the same year, at Exeter Lydia addressed the prestigious Botany and Zoology Section of the BAAS, not normally open to women speakers, on her study of *Lychnis*. She made use of her correspondence with Darwin and his theory of pangenesis, published in 1868, in support of her argument, but she also was confident enough to disagree with his interpretation of her observations. She explained how via pangenesis both male and female 'gemmules' were to be found in every individual *Lychnis* plant, and how, whereas Darwin believed the female reproductive organ in hermaphrodite specimens was 'compensatory', being produced for the accommodation of the parasitical fungus by which they were attacked, she believed it was the male organ which had this role. It took several years for this to become accepted in scientific circles, as it flew in the face not only of the Darwin's theory, but also of the male-dominated concept of the world.

On the basis of extensive research, as evidenced in her 1868 Letter Book, Lydia also published 'On the Study of Science by Women' in the *Contemporary Review*, applying her theory of the absence of gender in the human brain to the realm of education. Universalising her own experience, she advocated the academic study of science for women to save them from lives of 'intellectual vacuity'. The scientific societies and universities should be open to them so that life's stream might be populated with 'fish worth catching' instead of with 'minnows and sticklebacks'.[76]

It may have been the case that by putting forward her views on gender, Lydia helped to push the medical and scientific establishment into tightening up their definitions of male and female. This led to a polarisation of the debate, by reducing women to reproductive vessels. The divide was deepened when Darwin, in *The Descent of Man* in 1871, began to argue that natural selection had produced female inferiority, both physically and intellectually. His work now overtly supported the idea that reproduction was the natural and immutable purpose of women.[77] Confirming existing prejudices as it did, this became a widely accepted rationalisation of continued female oppression, including the dismissal of the desirability of female education on the same terms as that offered to men.

Lydia never challenged this aspect of Darwin's theories openly; she left that to others, such as the American Antoinette Brown Blackwell. All the same, she turned away from evolutionary theory in her campaigning and explored other approaches in her arguments. However, her interest in science continued; she went on to attend the BAAS until the end of her life, and gave in total five lectures at its conferences, which in 1868 she described as 'the one great treat of the year for me'.[78] Moreover, in 1881 she joined the Anthropological Institute in London and in 1884 was listed amongst the 'gentlemen' of the Manchester Geographical Society committee, which, under the chairmanship of the feminist Reverend Samuel Steinthal, had just decided to admit women members.[79] Her conversation sometimes reflected her continuing commitment to science, although conversing intelligently with an anti-suffragist (such people were nicknamed 'antis') could also serve as an undercover tactic for winning over the opposition in the women's suffrage debate, as Priscilla Bright McLaren hinted:

Hers was not a one-sided mind. At a brilliant reception given in Hyde Park Gardens by our friend Mrs Thomas Taylor, a gentleman adverse [sic] to women's suffrage was requested by our hostess to take Miss Becker down to supper. On returning to the drawing room he thanked Mrs Taylor for the pleasure he had had. It had not been the ordeal he expected. He had not heard one word about women's suffrage, but much that was interesting about science.[80]

Throughout her life, Lydia was devoted to scientific study in all its variety. At the BAAS in 1876 she attended a lecture on the fashionable topic of spiritualism. She commented in the discussion that she had witnessed what today would be termed 'the paranormal' – a trance – and that it should be further investigated. She also concerned herself with the environment, particularly noxious fumes and smoke in industrial Manchester. Then in 1880 she became a committee member of the newly formed Manchester branch of the St John's Ambulance.[81] Even in the maelstrom of defeat after the Third Reform Act, when she was busy regrouping the supporters of women's suffrage in 1885, she found time to write to Alfred Russel Wallace on the subject of beetles.[82] And she said that, had it not been for the suffragist cause, she would have dedicated herself to natural science, and she looked forward to the achievement of women's suffrage so that she could go back to this first love. In recent years, the University of Manchester has commemorated her scientific achievements and aspirations by establishing the Lydia Becker Institute of Immunology and Inflammation; she would no doubt have been delighted.

Political awakening

When the Beckers moved to Manchester in 1865 it was a city renowned for its vibrancy and innovation. In the early part of the century it had been the 'shock city' of the industrial revolution and at the cutting edge of social, technological and commercial change. The Chartist movement of the 1830s and 1840s had found strong support there, and it was still closely associated with radicalism; in 1868 the first Trades Union Congress was held in the city.

In October 1866, it hosted the NAPSS, a relatively new organisation, and Lydia, keen to enjoy the intellectual challenges offered, was to be found among the audience. Unlike the BAAS, it welcomed women as full members and even encouraged them to offer papers. An influential founder member was Barbara Leigh Smith Bodichon, a cousin of Florence Nightingale. At Manchester, Bodichon presented the first ever paper on women's suffrage, although it was actually read by a male supporter. 'Reasons for the Enfranchisement of Women', argued that any unenfranchised group would be ignored by those in power, and since some women paid taxes they should be represented. It also contended that the participation of women in the political process would add to their sense of public spirit, and end their wasteful confinement to the home; society was losing out on the practical experience women had to offer.[83]

Although the paper was not printed in the transactions of the society, reflecting a low assessment of its importance, it made a huge impression on Lydia Becker. Bodichon had mentioned that four months earlier there had been a petition for women's suffrage presented to parliament by John Stuart Mill. This was apparently the first Lydia knew of it, and she immediately regretted that her name was not on it; there had been 1,499 signatures and she wished that hers had been the 1,500th.[84] To judge by the speed and intensity with which she now became involved at the heart of the embryonic Manchester women's suffrage group, it is clear that she suddenly perceived a whole new universe of people who shared her dissatisfaction with the norms and expectations pertaining to women, and she was immensely excited at the prospect of joining them.

She offered her services to the London committee set up to gather a new petition, and began a correspondence with Emily Davies who became her mentor and friend – addressing her first letter to Lydia in January 1867 as 'madam' but by February as 'My dear Miss Becker'.[85] She provided her with another petition to be signed by Manchester's women householders, who might be presumed to be the group who would be enfranchised. Lydia demonstrated her commitment by returning it with signatures and a request for further forms and Davies advised her that a new Manchester committee chaired by the Liberal Jacob Bright had met on 11 January 1867 at the home of Dr Louis Borchardt. When the group met again a month later, they were joined by a further six, including Lydia Becker.[86] Her evident enthusiasm, and the confidence that she possessed the requisite skills of organisation with an ability to write clearly, concisely and persuasively, resulted in her appointment as secretary to the new Manchester women's suffrage committee, which included some prominent Manchester figures, including Dr Richard Pankhurst, Mr and Mrs Jacob Bright, Mr and Mrs Max Kyllmann, and Rev. Samuel Steinthal. It was the start of a lifelong commitment, and she began as she meant to go on, writing letters all over the place to solicit support. Showing an early appreciation of the value of publicity, her missive of 26 February to the Manchester MP Edward James, with his guardedly positive reply, was published at her request in the *Manchester Guardian* on 7 March.[87]

Even before this, Lydia had sent to Emily Davies her first article on the subject, named simply 'Female Suffrage'. It had impressed her mentor so strongly, containing 'so much good sense expressed in a somewhat playful form, and so little indignation ...', that she had submitted it for publication in the *Contemporary Review*, edited by a member of the London committee, Dean Alford. She had advised Lydia on a few minor revisions, in particular of an overly honest remark: 'the sentence in which you say that we cannot tell without trying whether women would use their votes better or worse than men'. And she warned her to be circumspect, a lesson Lydia took to heart in all her writings for publication:

> In women especially, the slightest appearance of being angry or contemptuous, offends, and provokes opposition ... It is I suppose a general rule that in all controversy, a tone of exaggerated courtesy, is best, but I am sure it is as regards women. People notice our manner more than our arguments ... Sarcasm, unless it be of the tenderest sort ... will not be endured from women.[88]

Whilst the article did not contain any new arguments, reflecting much of what Bodichon had said at the NAPSS, it was 'fresh and clear' in its tone, and it demonstrated Lydia's logical and scientific manner of analysis. It also represented the basis of her argument for women's suffrage for the rest of her career. She began by explaining why the issue had been hitherto little addressed, and summed up the prevailing attitudes:

> It has been assumed that the male sex, by a sort of divine right, has the exclusive privilege of directing the affairs of the community; and any serious claim made by the other half of the human race, to a share in controlling its destinies, has been met, not by argument showing the groundlessness or inexpediency of the demand but by a refusal to entertain it, as if it were something intrinsically absurd.[89]

She went on to clarify that a major argument against those challenging the *status quo* was that it was just not 'done' for women to vote, and that in any case they had no desire to do so. Her answer to this was that the petitions presented showed that many women of high distinction did in fact want that right. Since it was accepted that women could hold opinions, she asked why they should not be allowed to express them, when men who may not be clever, learned, or otherwise able *were* allowed. Anyone who considered women should not have opinions was failing to recognise the fact that British women were not sequestered from the world, and therefore could not but have views of their own. Moreover, women, who paid the same taxes, were not represented as men were.

But, she argued, men, who held the power to change things, did not ask women seriously whether they wished to have the franchise. Instead they adopted a bantering tone with leading questions, designed to make women, brought up to a submissive role, provide the response they desired:

> If we do not hear much of such discontent as may exist, it must be remembered that women are naturally shy at expressing any sentiments liable to draw upon them the disapprobation or ridicule of their male friends ...

To those who opined that women should make their opinions known indirectly through the votes of male relatives, she claimed that this effectively nullified those opinions as they could be ignored, and even if the male voter agreed with them, they added nothing to his one vote. Enfranchising some women would change things for all women:

> Every woman in the land would have an immediate accession of personal dignity ... Though she might not happen to possess the requisite qualification for a vote, personal exclusion from political power would lose its sting, for it would cease to imply presumed mental incapacity for its exercise ... It is to this feeling, and not to any unworthy desire to interfere in party squabbles, that the movement of women for enfranchisement is to be attributed.

The objection that women should not face the roughness of the polling station was countered in that this was not necessarily a typical problem; in Manchester, elections were orderly because they were taken very seriously. In any case, such a state of affairs would be unpleasant for men of refinement, and was nowhere acceptable. It could be avoided by the use of polling papers (a secret ballot), and anyway women might exercise a 'softening influence over [the] rougher elements'. Moreover, nobody was obliged to vote if they did not want to do so. It was argued that women were too busy with domestic affairs to cope with political knowledge and voting as well, but Lydia pointed out that men too had busy lives, and yet still managed to exercise their political rights. She strayed into the area of the meaning of 'representative government' to support her point, arguing that the duty of the voter was only to know sufficient to use their vote intelligently, and thereafter to leave the minutiae of policy to those elected to deal with it full-time.

Despite all this, Lydia's hopes for women as stated in 1867 were in some ways quite limited. She did not question the domestic role as woman's primary sphere, and accordingly she also answered fears that voting women would lead to women MPs, by saying that this was a ridiculous idea and using the comparison of a medieval tournament:

> It may be admitted that the personal participation of woman in the active struggles of parliamentary life, would be as incongruous as would have been her appearance armed in the lists, where of old her fate was oft-times decided, without therefore believing that it is necessary to the preservation of her womanly character, to deprive her judgement of all voice in the selection of the champion to whose efforts the interests of herself and those dear to her are confided.

Comparing women with clergymen, who whilst they could vote could not become MPs, she put the point that if it worked for them, why not for women? It is unclear whether she really believed that there should be no women MPs, or whether this was a tactical response, avoiding the more extreme idea in order to placate opposition from those who might be won over to the more limited proposal.

Lydia rounded off her arguments with examples of laws over which women had no control, but which regulated their lives to their disadvantage: most notably the rules of coverture 'which gives to the husband of a woman who marries without a settlement [under the Law of Equity], the power of spending any money she may possess, or even of leaving it away from her in his will'. She ended resoundingly:

'Women have nothing to do with politics' is a mere assertion, founded on sentimental, not on scientific grounds. It may be true, it may be false; it is a proposition fairly open to dispute. But though this proposition may be doubted, there is no doubt at all about its converse. It may be denied that women have anything to do with politics; it cannot be denied that politics have a great deal to do with women.

The article appeared in March 1867 and provoked a great interest in the identity of this 'Miss Becker'. So impressed were the suffragists that they published it as a ten-page pamphlet and distributed it widely. Much of the rhetoric was echoed through the decades into the campaigns of the twentieth century.[90] The name of Lydia Becker became known across the nation. She began to galvanise the movement in Manchester, and by August 1867 had organised the MNSWS. She had passed nearly two-thirds of her life in obscurity in rural Lancashire, leading an existence which she felt was aimless and unfulfilled. In Manchester, city of radicalism, vibrancy and change, she found new purpose and outlets for her energies and interests at the age of 40. She went on to become a household name across Britain, by general agreement the effective leader of the women's suffrage movement until her death in 1890.

Chapter 2

Emergence of the Suffragist Leader, 1867–8

On 26 November 1867, a remarkable event occurred in Manchester: a woman voted in a parliamentary by-election, called on the death of one of the city's two MPs, Edward James. Mrs Lilly Maxwell was a Scottish widow, a retired domestic servant who owned a crockery shop in Ludlow Street.[1] Her name had mysteriously appeared on the voters' register, and had escaped questioning by the overseer responsible for the ward. How it got on the list is unknown; the supporters of women's suffrage said that it must have been assumed that Lilly Maxwell was a man, but that begs the question of who registered her in the first place. *The Times* was convinced that it was a deep plot by the suffragists to insinuate women into the electoral process by stealth. Lydia Becker, by now secretary to the MNSWS, wrote to the newspaper denying any such implication.[2]

When the Manchester suffragists were made aware of the situation, it is claimed only a few days before the vote, Mrs Maxwell was cultivated by Becker, who wrote to the local papers describing her as

> a widow who keeps a small shop in a quiet street in Manchester. She supports herself and pays her own rates and taxes out of her earnings. She has no man to influence or be influenced by, and she has very decided political principles …'[3]

According to a letter from Lydia Becker to Mary Smith of Carlisle, Mrs Maxwell was at first reluctant to vote: 'She was rather timid at first – and I believe I should never have got her to come, only that she was so strongly in favour of Mr [Jacob] Bright.' Indeed, she apparently stated that if she had twenty votes, she would cast them all for that pro-suffrage Liberal candidate. Together with another member of the Manchester committee, Lydia went with Mrs Maxwell to Bright's committee room, and from there the ladies were escorted to Chorlton-on-Medlock Town Hall by several gentlemen, presumably to ensure that they came to no harm in the potentially rowdy atmosphere of the poll. Since Lilly Maxwell was on the list of electors and had been unchallenged, the returning officer had no option but to allow her to participate. In fact, according to Helen Blackburn, a devoted supporter of Lydia Becker, Mrs Maxwell was given three cheers by all the voters in the room, even those who did not support Bright, and their behaviour was impeccable – even better than would be found 'at a public concert or in a fashionable chapel'.[4]

Of course, even if Blackburn's account can be fully trusted, written as it was from Becker's own story, it seems likely that not all the voters present were actually suffragists, but were happy to have their day livened up by what at the time would have been the bizarre sight of a female standing in a polling station and publicly recording her vote. Those same men who cheered might well have taken a rather different view if there had been a hundred women exercising the right. Indeed, it was certainly not an enthusiasm shared by everyone. In a letter to Ursula Bright, Lydia reported the shocking remarks of one of the overseers whom she visited the following May in an effort to get women registered to vote in the forthcoming general election:

> [He said] suppose a horse or a dog sent in a claim they would not be bound to publish it! And it is not the first time I have heard the comparison made – and women classed not even with felons and idiots, but as regards voting, with the brute creation!

The offending overseer went on to assert 'that the polling clerk had no more right to <u>enter</u> Lilly Maxwell's name on the list, than if she had been a dog!'[5]

When Bright, the successful by-election candidate, made his acceptance speech from the steps of Manchester Town Hall he commented on Maxwell's participation; it was the first time he had known a woman to vote since 1832, and there was a moral in this: 'This woman is a hardworking honest person, who pays her rates as you do ... if any woman should possess a vote, it is precisely such a one as she.'[6] And Lilly's deed was immortalised in *Punch* in punning verse, foreseeing that she would be the first of many women voters:

> And when in the course of the ages,
> Which in good time all good measures bring,
> Our *femmes soles* [single or widowed women], like birds out of cages

Released, on the register sing,
Once doves, henceforth eagles, they press,
Let a Bright Lilly badge deck their chignons,
And be clan-Maxwell tartan their dress.⁷

Maxwell's fame spread even to the United States, whence the American suffragist Susan B. Anthony wrote to her and sent her papers to read via Lydia; the latter was keen to save herself the trouble of delivering them all the time, and furnished the American with Lilly's address at 17 Cowgill Street, Chorlton-on-Medlock.⁸

Becker was, in principle, in favour of universal suffrage, but Jane Rendall has argued that the focus on Lilly Maxwell as the respectable householder who was effectively a single woman led on to the entrenchment of the movement in attempts to gain the vote for such women, rather than for all women or even all adults. It was a path which held a more immediate attraction, as a first step, but later on it caused splits over the position of married women which weakened the whole movement. Lydia's writings show that she did not go into this unthinkingly, but had a rational basis for her strategies:

> I certainly agree with you that women, as women, ought to vote – but that principle is not acknowledged yet in the case of men, and I do not see that we can ask for women more than men have … My own personal opinion as to the right of suffrage carries it further than I have ever heard any other person advocate. I am for universal suffrage. I would enact that the right should be forfeited on conviction of crime – but for nothing else …

What Lydia meant by 'universal suffrage' was really revolutionary, even for the modern reader, as she went on to advocate the vote for children as a right given to them at birth. They would exercise their right 'as soon as ever the child chose'. She equated this with other 'rights', such as that of walking, and referred to the possibility of the franchise being exercised by 12 and 13 year olds. This idiosyncratic opinion is perhaps not as bizarre as might be thought, in that Lydia was expressing a very modern belief that the vote was not a privilege, as had hitherto been the overwhelmingly dominant view, but was a right to which all were entitled because they were members of society. She confirmed this explicitly a few months later: 'The representatives derive their power from the suffrages of the people – they do not "grant" the power of electing them to the people.'[9]

Lilly's vote, although at the time an aberration, and indeed not strictly admissible under the 1832 Reform Act, which had made it explicit that the franchise was limited to 'male persons', clearly achieved what Lydia and her colleagues had hoped.[10] It showed that a woman could vote and wanted to vote, and that furthermore the world did not come to a catastrophic end as a result. Lydia wrote to Susan B. Anthony that this was a moral victory: 'though the fact of her voting had no legal effect, the moral effect can, I think hardly be overrated'.[11] It had proven to be quite a simple and unthreatening action to take one woman to the poll; just how much more difficult it was going to be to replicate this for the thousands of women householders who were excluded from the franchise purely by reason of their sex would become apparent over the next decades.

Precursors, J.S. Mill and the first petitions

Agitation for women's rights at an informal and unorganised level can be traced back at least as far as the writings of Mary Wollstonecraft in 1792, and the baton was taken up in the first half of the nineteenth century by Chartists and radical Unitarians. In 1832, MP Henry Hunt had introduced a petition, the time-honoured way to influence the legislators, to grant the vote to unmarried women who met the property requirements in the 1832 Great Reform Act. However, for the first time, parliament explicitly limited the franchise to 'male persons'. Taking the demand a step further, in 1851 Anne Knight, a Quaker, helped set up the Sheffield Female Political Association, and presented a women's suffrage petition to the House of Lords.

The organised women's movement originated in London at 19 Langham Place and was led by Barbara Bodichon and Bessie Rayner Parkes.[12] From 1858 they produced the *English Woman's Journal*, the first publication to deal with matters particularly of concern to women, and established the Married Women's Property committee to agitate for a change in the laws of coverture.[13] Not surprisingly, they were also interested in other aspects of women's rights. Some of those active in Langham Place, notably Barbara Bodichon, Jessie Boucherett and Emily Davies, participated in the Kensington Society, established in 1865 to promote women's education and training. They focused especially on the plight of single middle-class women who found themselves without income, and also without the skills and opportunities to earn a living. On a practical level, their headquarters became a sort of job and training centre for women in law copying, bookkeeping and clerking. And by late 1865 they were also discussing the possibility of franchise extension to women, and formed a women's suffrage association in London.

The mid-1860s were altogether remarkable for the growing campaign for women's rights, even in parliament itself. The election of 1865 had produced a new MP who became recognised as the leading parliamentary voice for women's suffrage: John Stuart Mill, Liberal MP for Westminster. Having put the issue at the heart of his election campaign, he was approached by Barbara Bodichon to present a women's petition to the House of Commons in 1866, when the Liberals were trying to pass a reform bill which was intended to extend the electorate to include some upper working-class men. He was clearly much encouraged in his endeavour when, having asked for a hundred names in support of women's suffrage, on 7 June 1866 he received the petition with 1,499 signatures.[14] However, the Liberal bill was defeated.

Mill was a distinguished philosopher and political economist whose writings were hugely influential. On the woman question he was a noted theorist, as exemplified in *The Subjection of Women* (1869), in which he posited the central oppressive relationship as that of marriage, even though he still believed it was the normal state for women. His advocacy of female suffrage was based on the educational and moral effects it would bring, but he saw no need for women actually to participate in the struggle to achieve it, and if they did, then they should take care to be decorous and restrained, and if possible, married. He believed that once women had gained full citizenship through the vote, they would influence legislation and benefit from a rise in status which would help prevent domestic violence and sexual subordination. For him the suffrage was the paramount issue for feminism.[15]

It was soon after Mill's presentation of the women's petition that Lydia Becker became aware of events in parliament and sought to involve herself in the suffrage movement by writing to Emily Davies in London, asking how she could help. Elizabeth Wolstenholme, the headmistress and proprietor of a private girls' school, had several months earlier established the Manchester Committee for the Enfranchisement of Women, and as its secretary had gathered 300 signatures for the parliamentary petition of 1866. She was put in touch with Becker and they became close friends. Happy to surrender her post to allow herself time to develop her educational interests, Wolstenholme gave the Manchester minute book to Becker and she became the committee's secretary.[16]

Although London was then leading the way in campaigning for divers women's rights, Lydia was throughout convinced that the suffrage was the fundamental and crucial issue. She had had no connection with, or even it seems any awareness of, the organisations which had sprung up in the metropolis. Far away in smoky Manchester, she did not engage with Langham Place or the Kensington Society, primarily concerned as they were with what she considered to be 'branch' issues, which diverted attention and effort away from the 'root' cause of women's plight: their lack of political power. When she burst onto the Manchester scene she was eager to prove her worth; her life acquired a focus and value that it had hitherto been lacking. The chance to join the fight for a vote, and conveniently in Manchester, was grabbed with joyful enthusiasm as the panacea for the struggles of all women.

Meanwhile, the Conservatives, led by Lord Derby and Benjamin Disraeli, in an attempt to outdo the Liberals, introduced their own reform bill in March 1867. Becker, since February a dynamic force amongst the Manchester suffragists, threw herself into the effort of raising further petitions to parliament; one for Manchester women householders and one for the general public.[17] Lists of likely signatories were drawn up, notable figures were canvassed and petition forms were distributed to anyone who might be willing to circulate them amongst friends, family, neighbours and colleagues. Lydia made long-term contacts in London with Jessie Boucherett, Francis Power Cobbe and Helen Taylor, J.S. Mill's stepdaughter, though her relationship with the latter quickly became very thorny. Jessie Boucherett, for one, was highly impressed with the new activist: 'How well the Manchester petition has been managed! It is wonderful that Miss Becker should have got so many signatures in so short a time.'[18]

Mill proposed an amendment to the Conservative bill, replacing the word 'man' with 'person', which would in effect give women a vote on the same terms as men – that is, subject to a property qualification.[19] When the Colchester MP, Edward Karslake, objected that he had not met one woman in Essex who agreed with women's suffrage, Lydia Becker, along with Helen Taylor and Frances Power Cobbe, who over the years became Lydia's close friend, raised a petition in Colchester signed by 129 women; on 25 July a presumably chastened Karslake presented it to the Commons.[20] However, in May, Mill's amendment had been voted down by 196 to 73 votes in the Commons, whilst the main bill succeeded and on 15 August 1867 enfranchised around a million working-class men.

The inception of the Manchester National Society for Women's Suffrage

The events in parliament created a surge of support for the Cause, and it is touchingly naive that Lydia believed the battle was almost over:

> I must make a vigorous effort to beg for money in Manchester, to go on. I do believe that if we are thoroughly bent on our point, and play our cards well, we may see women voting at the next election, and I am quite sure that if they do not vote then it will be the last general election from which they will be excluded.[21]

But it was an unrelenting strain to get there, and right from the start Lydia's efforts were so gargantuan that she seems to have been often ill. As early as February 1867, Emily Davies had expressed concern about her: 'I am afraid you are not very strong', and in March 'I hope you have recovered from the painful ailment from which you were suffering a short time since. You will want a good rest when this work [the petitions] is over.'[22]

In fact, once the petitions had been presented, Lydia immediately turned her attention to establishing a properly organised society in Manchester. From the Alderley Edge home of Jacob and Ursula Bright in June she corresponded with the Unitarian minister, Samuel Steinthal, who later became treasurer of the Manchester Society. Lydia, probably with the support of the Brights, was clearly making the running; whilst Steinthal was more relaxed about the urgency of forming a body with a proper constitution, a formal committee and a list of members, she drew up a draft constitution and pushed for a public meeting to 'strike while the iron is hot'. Her tone to Steinthal was decidedly bossy: 'unless you can show some very convincing reason against ... I propose to summon the committee for this purpose on [Wednesday next].'[23] Interestingly, the meeting could not be held at Dr Borchardt's, as previously, 'as they are having their annual cleaning' – clearly a mammoth event – 'so the meeting is to be at my father's house.' A surprising decision in view of her parent's supposed opposition to her campaigning activities.

Rejecting the phrase 'Woman Suffrage', the title of the new society was by August established as the 'Manchester National Society for Women's Suffrage', and its goal was to achieve the vote for women on the same property terms as for men. This would apply only to widows and spinsters; although married women were not explicitly excluded, they were in effect not included because of the prevailing doctrine of coverture, which prevented them owning any property. Around the same time, similar societies were set up by feminist campaigners in Edinburgh, Birmingham and Bristol.

The role of male suffragists became extremely significant for Lydia Becker, and they were prominent in the newly formed Manchester Society. It may seem ironic that, whilst she was honorary secretary to the new society, Jacob Bright, MP for Manchester, was its president. Lydia was firmly committed throughout her life to the notion that committees of any kind were most effective when they included both sexes. In the early years, she depended heavily on male campaigners for moral and practical support. She met John Stuart Mill in July 1867 and often quoted him in her letters as someone whose opinion she valued. Moreover, it was the male activists of the Manchester Society on whom she heavily relied in these early years. She and Lilly Maxwell had been escorted to the poll by several of them, and when the first large women's suffrage meeting was held in Manchester on 14 April 1868, Lydia was reassured to find that Rev. Steinthal supported her 'like a brick' by sitting behind her on the platform, so that she could literally turn to him for advice.

Jacob Bright also sat at her side all evening, and she was very pleased when he took his place 'in his nice kind way'.[24] As that year wore on, Lydia's opinion of Jacob became extremely high, even bordering on adoration. Indeed, a few months later she wrote comparing Jacob favourably with his much better known and more distinguished brother, John, the famous anti-corn law and male franchise campaigner:

> The younger brother [Jacob] seems to be to be of a far higher nature that the other [John] ... his mind seems so balanced and harmonious, and he is so thoroughly just, gentle and good... John Bright is regarded with enthusiastic admiration by his friends and supporters, Jacob Bright is <u>beloved</u>.[25]

Characteristics which would today be called 'being in touch with his feminine side' and his physical frailty would have put Jacob at a disadvantage in the male rough and tumble of Victorian politics. Indeed, Lydia worried that his exertions in the election campaign in the autumn of 1868 might exacerbate his weak chest. She continued in private to make comparisons:

> He is not so powerful either physically or intellectually as his brother John, but in some things surpasses him. His mind is so evenly balanced that he never seems carried away unduly in any direction. Mr J.S. Mill remarked to me that his mind was freer than his brother's and I think he has a higher nature. He unites the virtues that adorn both sexes, and is a perfectly womanly – as well as a perfectly manly – man. Before I knew him, I had a perverse prejudice against him, merely as John Bright's brother, but no prejudice could withstand the influence of his gentleness and goodness.[26]

Having been invited to listen to his speech for the 1868 general election in Ursula Bright's box in the Free Trade Hall, she admitted 'I have a presentiment that his speech will not be quite what I want it to be. I generally like his speeches better when I read than when I hear them ...' She was delighted when it turned out to be 'dignified and statesmanlike', in contrast to those of the other Manchester Liberal candidates; Mr Bazley was 'dry' and Mr Jones 'full of claptrap'! She elucidated a week later in a letter to Ursula that she had not liked one section, touching on Christianity because it was vague, but exclaimed 'I only mention this to prove that I can be critical!!!!' The rest 'was delightful' because 'free from passion and prejudice ... eminently rational and humane' with 'no blunder or blemish in the language' and with a 'superiority of spirit'. His voice seemed 'to have gained strength, while losing none of its beauty'.[27] She was so impressed by his speeches as a candidate that she thought they should be collected 'as a great exposition of Liberal policies'.[28] He had become an MP in November 1867, and was already making himself known in parliament, where Lydia jokingly referred to him as her personal agent. 'He has a great influence ... I feel that though I have no vote, I have a very efficient representative in the House of Commons.'[29] In her extremely long letter to Susan B. Anthony, the American women's rights activist, she continued her encomium:

> The name of Jacob Bright ought to be a household word among all women. He is, I believe, the only English candidate except Mr Mill who has included women's suffrage among those articles of his political creed on which he takes his stand in his formal address to his constituents ... In January 1867 five persons met to form the Manchester committee for the enfranchisement of women. Jacob Bright was one of these. He took the chair, and under his auspices the Society originated which has since effected so much. He did not take a very active part in the immediate operations, but he lent us the support of his name and influence, and never shrank from anything which he could do to help us ... If John Bright deserves honour and gratitude from men, Jacob Bright deserves yet more from women.[30]

She referred to an aspect of Jacob Bright's difficulties which she shared with him, in that he frequently featured in satirical cartoons as an unmanly man and was derided because of his espousal of the women's cause. She asserted that this lessened his standing in the Liberal Party, and his election chances. 'But none of these things moved him.' The cartoons focused particularly on the relationship between Becker and Bright. One, showing her beating him with a birch whilst he pushes two small children in a perambulator labelled 'Only women's rights', was occasioned by the Persons campaign which the MNSWS pursued avidly in the spring and summer of 1868.[31]

The 'Persons campaign'

When, in 1868, it was expected that the minority Conservative government would call an election soon, the Manchester Society began to prepare. As early as this, Lydia was hopeful that a Liberal victory would bring rapid success for the suffragists, though she was always realistic about the depth of their commitment: 'I do not believe that the Liberal Party as a party care a straw for the interests and wishes of women, or will stir a step to do them justice ... However, I expect a different spirit will come over them soon.'[32] In an empirical way, she understood what modern feminist writers have identified as a serious barrier to women's emancipation under any liberal regime; the 'extent to which women's exclusion from citizenship was an integral part of liberal democratic citizenship at the outset'.[33] She perceived William Gladstone, the Liberal leader, as 'the Arch Enemy', although she conceded that he 'is scrupulous and would not tell a lie'. Because of his known opposition to women's votes she hoped that a movement to oust him from his seat in South Lancashire would succeed. Indeed, 'If my power were equal to my will, he would not re-enter the House till he had learned one lesson from his great rival.'[34]

This was of course a reference to that other titan of the Victorian age, Benjamin Disraeli, leader of the Conservatives and prime minister. Ironically, although the majority of his party opposed women's votes, he had told J.S. Mill the previous year that he 'was in favour of the principle of female suffrage'. However, he reportedly went on to admit that he could not vote for it 'on account of his colleagues, but he was working for it, inside the cabinet'. Lydia was well aware that 'Dizzy' was a problematic ally; she wrote to her sister, Esther, with gossip from Jacob Bright that it was 'supposed the Premier finds the strain on him so great that he maintains himself with stimulants, and certainly during his speeches, he drinks a great deal of something that is not water!'[35] Moreover, she stated her perception that he was 'unscrupulous and will tell any amount of lies, and wear a mask all his life to accomplish his purposes'. Nevertheless, she believed he had 'earnest convictions' and 'the courage to propose and the ability to carry the measures he approves of'.

Two months earlier, she had expressed a desire for Disraeli to remain in power until Jacob's brother, John, who was a radical Liberal but was unsympathetic towards women's suffrage, was in a position to take over the leadership of the Liberal Party. Her assessment betrays somewhat wishful thinking for a party still dominated by the traditionally minded landed aristocracy, and in any case she sadly underestimated the strength of John Bright's hostility to her cause:

> He [John Bright] is a far greater man than Gladstone. And when the reformed Parliament comes into power he seems the natural leader

of the popular party ... I don't think his wishes are exactly with our side any more than Gladstone. But when the issue is put for his decision justice carries the day and his vote gives weight.[36]

She seems to have been disabused of her illusions quite quickly; in a letter three months later, she noted that John Bright was slow to support a married women's property bill as he was 'an inveterate Tory', an opinion which she had adopted from a conversation with Mill.[37]

The researches of another vital male supporter of women's suffrage, the young barrister Richard Pankhurst, and his colleague Thomas Chisholm Anstey, in 1868 inspired a new tactic to allow women to vote. Anstey had uncovered documentary evidence to prove that women had voted in the distant past, and published his findings using the example of Anne Clifford, Countess of Dorset (d. 1676).[38] Furthermore, Lord Brougham's Act of 1850 had declared that any use of the term 'man' in legislation applied by default to women too, unless they were explicitly excluded. Applying this to the 1867 Reform Act, it was argued logically by the lawyers, and accordingly by Lydia, that if the ratepayer clauses applying to 'men' also applied to women (as everyone agreed), then the clauses in the same Act which referred to 'men' voting likewise applied to women.

Lydia and the committee decided to bypass conventional thinking and make use of the legal loopholes Anstey and Pankhurst had unearthed. Armed with the arguments they provided and taking note of the example of Lilly Maxwell, who had been enabled to vote by the fact of her registration on the electoral registers, Lydia in great excitement began a campaign all over the country to persuade all eligible women (with the requisite property) to submit a claim for registration to the overseers. The work of petitioning, so beloved of the London Society, was put on the back burner for this radical challenge, known as the Persons campaign.

Her first move was to visit the Manchester overseers, and she explained to Helen Taylor in December 1867 that she had asked them to put all the women ratepayers on the voters register:

> I saw the official today, he was utterly incredulous as to the possibility of women being enfranchised by the new Act and the Town Clerk, who happened to come in, expressed the same opinion. But neither had even heard of Mr Anstey's argument and both promised me that they would carefully study it, and the overseer said if he had the

smallest doubt, personally as to the effect of the new Act on women's right to vote, he should give the women the benefit of it, and include them all in his original list.[39]

She, nevertheless, was dubious as to whether he would actually do this, even if he agreed in principle, and therefore planned a public meeting for 14 April to launch the campaign officially, as 'A question is never considered one of practical politics till advocates appeal to public opinion in this way.'[40] This would be a landmark, as the first ever public meeting in the history of the women's movement addressed by women.

To test out the reception they might expect, on 11 February Lydia and Alice Wilson went to the Manchester Liberal Reform Club, where the National Reform Union was holding its conference under the chairmanship of Alice's father, George Wilson. Towards the end of the meeting, to the surprise of the men gathered, Alice stood up and asked for their assent to a resolution that 'no householder rated for the relief of the poor ought to be excluded from the franchise'. This was, of course, in effect a demand for women's suffrage. They must have been relieved and gratified that the assembly reacted with unanimous cheering. The verdict was that Alice had overturned the belief that women could not speak calmly, briefly and with 'political tact'.

Although she was ably supported in a speech given by Jacob Bright, the paternal affection of the chairman could not overrule the constitution of the National Reform Union, which stated its purpose was to 'obtain such an extension of the franchise ... on every male person rated ... for the relief of the poor'. Lydia reported to Helen Taylor in London that she was annoyed that they had been too far from the platform to realise that, according to Jacob Bright, a gentleman was in fact proposing to support the women by recommending that the word 'male' be removed from the organisation's programme. Unaware, Alice had withdrawn her resolution.[41]

However, their reception did raise even higher the hope that women's suffrage would soon be achieved. In a letter to a more circumspect Jacob Bright of 27 March, Lydia reproached him for his lack of faith:

> You make me sad by telling me that the time is distant when we shall win. You should leave that for the enemy, it ... is so disheartening from a friend ... if we make up our minds that we are going to win as

soon as we can, we may find the end sooner than we think. Things move faster than they did three years ago.⁴²

She was clearly buoyed up by the more favourable reactions she had encountered and wrote to one of the April meeting's speakers, Miss Anne Robertson from Dublin, on 30 March:

> I expect we shall make a great sensation with our meeting – it will be, we believe, the first, which has been held on the subject ... As far as we have had the means of testing the minds of Manchester people on our question, we have met with hearty approval and people say we shall no doubt carry our resolutions.⁴³

She was even more encouraged when she heard that the famous nursing reformer, Florence Nightingale, had declared her support for the movement:

> Is it not glorious that Florence Nightingale has joined our Society? It must take a very hard-hearted M.P. to say no when she asks for a vote. I should think even Mr Gladstone might be brought to reason if she were to try to convert him.⁴⁴

With such affirmations of support, on 14 April the MNSWS addressed a crowded audience in the Free Trade Hall assembly room and opened up a forum for the discussion of a variety of women's issues. In a remarkable innovation, women appeared on the platform advocating the political cause – a clear challenge to the concept of 'separate spheres' – although a man did chair the gathering in the person of H.D. Pochin, Mayor of Salford. Other men who attended to support the women included Jacob Bright, Thomas Potter (ex-Mayor of Manchester), Richard Pankhurst and Archdeacon Sandford, but it was noticeable that no representatives from other societies were prepared to appear, highlighting the fact that this was a risky enterprise.

Three resolutions were proposed by women, of whom the first was Lydia, asking for the women's right to vote 'on the same condition as it is or may be [given] to men', the wording adopted by the MNSWS in their constitution. Agnes Pochin of Salford and Anne Robertson of Dublin moved resolutions supporting friends of emancipation in parliament, and urging women with the necessary qualifications to put their names on the electoral register. The public was surprised at how capably the women spoke, and it was reported, somewhat condescendingly and grudgingly, that 'resolutions were proposed ... exactly as if it were a real meeting'. There was particular admiration for Becker's performance; she had fulfilled 'the duty she undertook, as like the real thing as it could be'. The meeting put the Manchester Society on the political map, and it was even known abroad; a newspaper in Milan published a report on 21 April.[45]

In the true spirit of Manchester radicalism, beneath the official resolutions ran an undercurrent of rebellion, and Becker's address made the greatest impact, ending with a demand for 'a nation of free women as well as free men'.[46] Indeed, there was even stronger evidence of a nascent militancy in her private letters around this time. The burning political question of the day was how to deal with Irish nationalism, which the previous year had taken the form of murderous attacks by Fenians in London and Manchester. Lydia took a great interest in the debate, and she drew parallels between Ireland and the women's suffrage cause. Writing to Jacob Bright, she took heart from the emancipation of Irish Catholics in 1829, though she was later to be sadly disabused of her faith in Queen Victoria:

> Fortunately we have not a bigoted sovereign to contend with, as in the last great concession of justice to the Catholic population of Ireland and if we had, the obstacle would but be as great as in those days.[47]

In a letter to Esther later the same month, Lydia was much exercised by Fenian violence and, still drawing a parallel, whilst condemning 'such wicked deeds' she trenchantly observed:

> But more melancholy to me than these occurrences is the fact that it <u>needs</u> deeds of bloodshed or violence before the British Government can be roused to do justice. But for ... Fenianism [we should have] no disestablishment of the Irish [Anglican] church. The imperial sin lies at the door of those who lamely acquiesce in public wrongs ... till somebody is provoked to an act of resistance or crime.[48]

This extreme and arguably prescient view was reserved only for the eyes of her closest allies, and never given public utterance. She often, however, referred to the struggle for the franchise as a 'battle' and used warlike metaphors. On writing to her friend Josephine Butler, Liverpool campaigner against the invidious Contagious Diseases Acts, she expressed the need to 'cut fearlessly into people's prejudices ... Our object is to <u>kill</u> people's prejudices against women doing certain things – why then would we fear to <u>wound</u> that which we want to <u>kill</u>!'[49]

Becker hoped to apply the model adopted for the Persons campaign by the Manchester Society to the other regional groups, as well as to London. Accordingly, she encouraged the secretary of the newly founded Birmingham Suffrage Society, Mary Johnson, to hold a public meeting in that city, at which Lydia was asked to speak. Being unused at this stage to public speaking, her approach to this gathering was hesitant:

> It is nervous work, and I cannot help feeling the meeting will get into a mess some way ... I am thankful to say they have given up the great hall, and will have the Exchange rooms holding 600 persons. That is quite enough – especially with lady speakers.

It is unclear whether limiting the room size was due to a belief that the audience would be small, or because women speakers might be daunted by a giant hall and have trouble making themselves heard. In spite of her misgivings, Lydia saw the advantages of her own participation. 'Our success ought to be at once an encouragement and an incentive to such a step. Our resolution will then have been moved by Manchester, seconded by Birmingham, and must be accepted by the country.' Indeed, she admitted 'I rather enjoy this sense of power in having made the country listen to what I have got to say.' After a successful event, she was excited and elated enough to stay up, writing to Ursula Bright 'Late as it is, I must write to tell you of the triumphant scenes at the Birmingham meeting.'[50]

It was not all business; Lydia was feeling in need of friendship at this time, perhaps because she did not have much family support. She quickly developed a strong affection for Mary Johnson, originating from her stay at the latter's home during the Birmingham conference, and strengthened by her admiration for Mary's effectiveness as a leader and organiser. She sent Mary a trinket as a present, and wrote about her to her friend, Elizabeth Wolstenholme: 'I like her so much – she is a clever and charming girl – very frank and inspiring in her ways and will prove an invaluable acquisition to our band of workers.'[51] Writing to Mary herself, she was open about her feelings, despite the novelty of their acquaintance:

'I feel much flattered by the way you look to me. I have never had an elder sister or brother – or any one near me to lean on ... But <u>sympathy</u> is what one longs for – it is the sunshine of the heart!' Ten days later she revealed that she had not been able to stave off depression:

> Tell me dear, do you ever feel disconnected and out of heart? That is rather my case just now – perhaps as reaction[?] from the efforts we have been making lately. I do not mean out of heart regarding our cause – that is making rapid progress. It is purely a personal feeling – I hope it will go away in a day or two.

Likewise in July to Dr Pankhurst she explained that she was subject to lows: 'I never do believe that anything that will make me very happy will really come to pass!'[52]

This mental state was not the only health issue she faced around this time. In April she had fallen sick with a debilitating illness, a condition to which she was prone throughout her life. She attributed its cause to 'over-fatigue' due to overwork. Writing to her Bowdon friend, Sarah Anne Jackson, she explained that her strength had entirely collapsed, and that she was a 'prisoner' in the house because she could not walk the length of the street. She was also worried that she could not get her spring wardrobe ready, and that her sitting room 'feels desperately to want its "spring dressing" – it smells frowsy and dingy'. The next day she reported that she could not get out of her chair without collapsing and was unable to afford a carriage to go anywhere. Clearly in desperation, she penned a letter to Jessie Boucherett, founder of the Society for Promoting the Employment of Women, in London explaining her situation and asking whether there might be financial help from the 'Mission Fund', but she may not have posted this letter as it is crossed out in her letter book. There was also around this time a problem with her eyes, with lines appearing from time to time in her vision, which she treated as of scientific interest – 'It would be interesting to experiment on other near-sighted eyes.' By November the eye problem had settled down, but she was finding that she needed spectacles more often for reading, and blamed this on too much writing. It may be that she managed to consult a doctor, but to no good effect; in a letter later in the year she wrote at length about the horrors of falling 'into the hands of a doctor who believes in starvation'.[53] This may account for the slowness of her general recovery, which took several weeks.

Her friends rallied round. As Lydia had requested, Sarah Anne offered her house in leafy Bowdon as a respite, but she only stayed a day or two, as it was due to be spring cleaned and she did not want to inconvenience the maid. She accepted Elizabeth Wolstenholme's offer of a week's stay at her home in Congleton in May, and more immediately spent a weekend at Alderley Edge with Ursula Bright. Later in April she was still low: 'I feel almost overwhelmed with work, and my strength wretchedly feeble. If I were strong or rich, I could do so much!'[54]

However, there was little let-up in the stream of missives through which she attempted to maintain her role at a crucial time for the movement. The Persons campaign was now underway. It necessitated ensuring the inclusion of women ratepayers on the registers, which were to be drawn up in August 1868, in preparation for an election called for December. The system was that a potential elector had to register with the overseers of their township. In normal circumstances the claim was allowed, but if considered unsound or challenged it would be referred to a barrister for review and decision. Lydia and her committee set an initial target of finding 2,000 Manchester women to sign up, and not only put advertisements in the newspapers, but also formed deputations to prepare the ground by visiting the local overseers in person. They encouraged the other suffrage societies to do the same.[55]

The parliamentary borough of Manchester comprised eight townships, of which Manchester itself was the pre-eminent. Lydia accordingly arranged to meet the Manchester township overseers in person to try to smooth the path of those women who she hoped would register. She did not know what to expect and when she found that Rev. Steinthal, who was supposed to have been present, was delayed in London, she was put 'in a fright' that she would 'make a mess of it without him'. Indeed she wrote reproaching him for his absence: 'Dismay is the only word that can convey my feeling on finding that you would not be present at our interview with the overseers ... Dr Pankhurst, Miss Alice Wilson and I had it all to ourselves.' Richard Pankhurst was as yet an unknown quantity, but Lydia was delighted to find that he ably led the discussion and put forward the legal arguments most cogently, to the extent that the chairman of the overseers confessed that they had 'opened his eyes', as Lydia excitedly reported in every letter she penned around this time.[56]

She was not alone in feeling the strain; in a letter to Mary Johnson on 20 June she expressed concern that too much was being asked of the male suffragists, especially of Richard Pankhurst, of whom she said 'I am sadly afraid that we are taking too much from him ... He seems to be my main stay on the committee now ...' She developed this theme in her letter to Josephine Butler two weeks later:

> He has a good deal of home pressure to withstand in following up his own convictions. His father, whom I accidentally encountered, told me he had no sympathy with our cause – said he wished his son had nothing to do with us, and said his mother is quite wild about him. But there is no half-heartedness about the son – he has gone into the work heart and soul – and borne himself bravely ... [57]

The suggestion by Sylvia Pankhurst that there was some romantic feeling on Lydia's part towards Richard, which seems to have had some local currency, may perhaps be borne out by her letter to him of 24 May 1868. Lydia is known to have written only a very few missives employing such high-flown sentiments, addressed only to those with whom she felt great sympathy, and in this case they were expressed in praise of Dr Pankhurst's additions to their report on the overseers meeting. He had demonstrated that their aim was

> the full recognition of the principle that every human soul is an independent kingdom – nay, a universe over which the individual soul is sovereign – The notion that anyone owes subjection or subordination to another is fatal to the higher life of both ruler and subject. Freedom and equality not only do not prevent self devotion to the welfare of others but seem essential to it – essential also to that enlightened and voluntary obedience which is the only safeguard against anarchy, the only guarantee for the maintenance of peace and order in the commonwealth.[58]

He had certainly brought out the philosopher in her!

Whatever her feelings about Dr Pankhurst, Lydia certainly found him fascinating and wrote about him to many of her correspondents. She noted to Jessie Boucherett on the same day that 'He is clever and original – and will do our cause good service', but qualified this with the caveat that 'He has some odd notions, and to hear him talk you would think he despised our sex utterly.' And to Josephine Butler she confided, 'The oddest part of the matter is that he pretends to despise women, and says they are men's natural enemies!!' Indeed, he seems to have offended Lydia on at least one occasion by using the phrase 'woman's reason' in an apparently disparaging manner. But she forgave him, whilst making herself quite clear: 'We shall not think more about the expression ... you will never feel tempted, I am sure, to use it again ...'[59] He had also been very critical of Elizabeth Wolstenholme, who Lydia believed should stick to her opinions and not be overwhelmed by him. 'I do not quite understand your sudden collapse and readiness to give in to Dr Pankhurst.' He was an independent thinker, even criticising the great and revered J.S. Mill, calling his amendment of 1867 'a fatal blunder' because it implicitly admitted what Pankhurst and Anstey sought to disprove: that the Reform Act as it stood was a legal obstacle to women's suffrage because 'man' meant a male person only. To Sarah Anne Jackson she related that she had visited him in his office, but been unable to get away:

> He is a very clever little man – with some most extraordinary sentiments about life in general and women in particular – and so much to say on them that it is really dangerous to venture into his den. I called at his chambers on Friday to give him a paper and intended to stay five minutes, and found it impossible to escape under two hours! I wonder what you would make of him! [60]

Lydia's attachment to Pankhurst was very closely linked to her conviction that the work they were engaged in was going to change history, and she was buoyed up and empowered by this sense of destiny. She wrote to her brother Leigh in Australia:

> I feel that we are making history, and that the movement in which we are engaged, and which is making progress far beyond the expectations of those who started it, will have a very important influence on the future of our country. My own share in it might gratify a more ambitious person, and I confess to enjoying the sense of power produced by finding my opinion and statements so widely published and commented on. It is satisfactory to find people ready to listen to what one has got to say.[61]

However, there was a setback in store; the Manchester overseers refused to put the women onto the register and their secretary doubted their eligibility, and pointed out that he would be liable to a £50 fine if he included ineligible persons, whereas if he excluded an eligible person there was no such penalty. In Chorlton-on-Medlock township the electoral right was denied, according to Richard Pankhurst, on the grounds that 'women were in a state of perpetual infancy and perpetual mental imbecility'. Even more disappointingly, the Ardwick overseers, who had at first received the deputation very positively, resolved to follow suit.[62] It was a salutary warning that the road would not be smooth. When 400 circulars were sent out to overseers all over the country, there was little response. Perhaps not surprisingly, Lydia reported 'I feel a great weight of responsibility just now – I am so anxious that all should be done rightly at this important juncture.'[63] On the same day, her frustration and eagerness to get the suffrage message across was obvious in her letter to Richard Pankhurst:

> We ought to din it into people's ears, proclaim it from the housetops, and claim it in our hundreds and thousands. How wicked it is to feel so dumb and powerless, when so much has to be done, and the golden moments are slipping away! I am quite oppressed by the thought.[64]

Yet there was encouragement from some quarters. The clerk for the Manchester district of Hulme, Mr Tozer, agreed to give Lydia a list of all the women ratepayers in the township so that she could ask for the whole group to be put on the list of claimants to vote, 'without putting us to the labour and expense of a piecemeal canvass!! ... Please be discreet about this for it is not strictly regular ...' And there was room for rejoicing in Salford, where the mayor and Mrs Pochin, ardent suffragists, used their influence to good effect in favour of the women's registration. Lydia Becker, characteristically upbeat in public at least, described their success as 'a great triumph for Manchester policy'.[65] In some places, such as Farnworth, the overseers did not respond to Lydia's circular, but went ahead and put the women on their registers anyway. Eventually, she also received news that in London there had been successes; she complained that the information they had sent was vague and incomplete, but took heart that 'The single fact that women have actually been placed on the register of electors, will have more effect in making people think they ought to vote, than all Mr Mill's logic – and all Mr Fawcett's and Mr Bright's opinions that way.'[66]

The committee planned a campaign of visiting those women eligible in Manchester, all 7,000 of them, individually in their homes, with the purpose of getting them to apply for registration regardless. Paid canvassers, led by a Mr Rogers, were recruited to help in the effort. They were highly successful, and 5,750 women agreed to participate, who then had to be re-visited with forms and given help to complete them. It is conceivable that more might have been garnered, but Lydia ran out of money completely and was forced to stop the canvass. Of those women who signed up, a few were dismissed out of hand by the overseers. Most were passed on for review by revising barristers, who not surprisingly felt suddenly inundated; they normally dealt with only a handful of cases. A few names though did slip through the net and were allowed to remain on the registers; those women had the right to vote.

As the day approached when the revising barrister for Manchester would hold his court to decide on most of the claims, Lydia stepped up her preparations. She briefed the women's counsel, Mr Cobbett, placed advertisements in the local papers exhorting all women to attend the hearing, put up placards all over the town, and herself called on many women begging them to come. Although she was fully aware of the likely outcome, she tried in public to focus on the positive, but inwardly she was full of trepidation:

> It will be an immense gain if the court is full of eager listeners, and will impress the Barristers with a sense of their responsibility and the seriousness of the case ... It will shew that we have no notion of being 'smiled out of court' as Dr Pankhurst said we should be ... and if we lose tomorrow defeat will be the next best thing to victory.
> ... The women of Manchester mean – in the language of *The Times* about Lilly Maxwell – to 'make female suffrage an accomplished fact' next election 'to carry by storm a British polling booth, and plant the standard of women's rights in the heart of the British Constitution'. You must forgive a little bravado – just to keep up my spirits against the reverse we are going to have tomorrow.[67]

Mr John Hosack, revising barrister for the borough of Manchester, as she had predicted, disallowed the women's claims. She had noted beforehand that he had illegally struck off women registered in Salford even though they had not been challenged, so his attitude was not in doubt. The court was full of interested parties, and the discussion went on for two and a half hours. Richard Pankhurst was present, as Lydia reported: 'I saw Dr Pankhurst filing his nails in the court – and I know that if he only had the chance he would have sprung on the Barrister like a tiger and "had his blood" as he says. Did not I long to see him at it!!'[68]

The hearing was reported in detail in the press. Lydia Becker, 'a bold leader', made a determined stand to force Hosack to allow all the claims to go to appeal, 'to show that the women claimants in all these townships are thoroughly earnest in the matter'. *The Times* cynically questioned whether it proved rather 'that their patroness is persistent'.[69] Lydia had foreseen the outcome of the Manchester judgement as early as July when the canvass was still in progress, but she believed that the work would in any case not be in vain. Indeed she was aware that *The Times* 'seemed surprised that there were so many qualified women' and claimed that the public had been 'seriously impressed' and therefore went on to propose:

> Suppose we should lose in the courts, we should want a bill brought in next session and we should want Mr Bright to make a speech for us. Now if he could say 'There are 6,000 women ratepayers in the township of Manchester and 4000 of these claimed their votes in the registration courts['] it seems to me that would be a fact which would be impossible to gainsay and it is well worth the expenditure necessary to obtain it.[70]

Appeals to the High Court, for which Lydia had agitated so strongly, were allowed, but in the event she and the Brights had misgivings as to whether it was wise to pursue them, probably due to the high financial cost. They had to be submitted quickly, with the election looming, and there was little time for proper consideration. Lydia accepted that she should have planned more carefully for the possible outcomes of the revising court, to ensure that the committee's reaction might be more measured. As it happened, the doubters were overruled by a vote in the Manchester committee taking the advice of Richard Pankhurst, and the appeals went ahead.[71] Lydia gratefully felt relieved of the responsibility for making the decision, and afterwards pointed out to Ursula Bright that stopping at this point might well have demoralised the committee. With trepidation, she prepared for another defeat, but with the hope that at least one of the appeal court judges might decide in the women's favour: 'If so, such a decision, even if overruled by a majority, would be <u>complete</u> justification in the eyes of all the world – of the legal position we have assumed and a most powerful weapon in agitation.'[72]

Shortly before the High Court hearing, on 30 October the MNSWS held its very first AGM in Manchester Town Hall, chaired by Philippine Kyllmann, a prominent member of the committee.[73] This was a bold move as there had been worries that it would be ill-attended and the society would look foolish, but the meeting was packed with supporters, much to the delight of the committee. Even the presentation to Philippine of a parcel of old stockings for mending, with a silly note suggesting that this was the proper business of women, did not dampen the jubilation at the success of the gathering.[74] Encouraged and buoyant, they faced the High Court in early November.[75]

The opportunity to appeal was taken up by 5,346 women represented by the case of Mary Abbott, alongside another test case centred on the claim for a South Lancashire county vote by Philippine Kyllmann. Meanwhile, Lydia asked the press to publish news of female registrations which had been allowed in other areas, to encourage those women who could vote to press on; at Cockermouth, Sebergham, Winterton, Ormskirk and Finsbury, for example, well over fifty women had their claims allowed by revising barristers.[76]

When the appeal of Manchester householder Mary Abbott, known as the case of Chorlton v. Lings, was heard by Lord Chief Justice Bovill and Justices Willes, Keating and Byles, Lydia was present in the public gallery, and the court was packed with lawyers interested in the outcome.[77] Sir John Coleridge, QC, assisted by Richard Pankhurst, presented the women's case very ably, citing all the legal arguments. There was a possibility that the judges would not pronounce before the general election, and in that case there were plans for the Manchester claimants to vote under a loophole in the 1832 Reform Act by which they could present themselves at the poll and the polling clerks were bound to accept them, but making a mark to distinguish theirs from the undisputed votes.[78]

In the event, judgement came too quickly for this to occur. As expected, the logic and justice of the case fell on deaf ears, and the judges unanimously rejected the claims on the grounds of decorum, and the privilege of the female sex not to be bothered and discomfited by the rigours of politics and the rough and tumble of polling. Lydia, having foreseen the strong possibility that the judges would rule against, immediately sent a telegram to the Manchester activists which said cryptically 'Post your letters'. Eight hundred letters had been handwritten, ready to post out to all the electoral candidates, asking them to support female suffrage. This kept the matter in the public eye, and alerted those about to enter parliament to the determination and assiduity of the campaigners.

Lydia was encouraged by vocal support for women's suffrage from a redoubtable South Lancashire noblewoman and landowner, Lady Anne Scarisbrick, who had successfully registered to vote in the county election, along with twenty-seven female tenants. Becker found it ironic that Gladstone, reputedly so hostile to women's political involvement that he maintained 'that it is very improper for women to come to listen to the debate in the House of Commons, or even to read the newspapers', would have 'coals of fire heaped on his head' in the election, when Lady Anne and her tenants voted for him.[79]

However, there was a price to pay for the failed legal challenge. It caused dissent in the Manchester committee because, although an appeal had been put out for donations to defray the expense of the hearing 'as the question is one of national importance', the MNSWS was financially embarrassed by the cost of the action. Becker, convinced of the justice of the Cause, did not hesitate to seek financial support wherever she could get it. She asked for money from John Stuart Mill and his stepdaughter Helen Taylor in October 1868. However, Philippine Kyllmann, now the Manchester treasurer, whose county (Lancashire) vote had been the test case in the High Court, and her sister-in-law, Mathilde (the previous MNSWS treasurer) were mortified, and resigned from the Manchester organisation.[80]

Fourteen women in Manchester and sixteen in Salford, who had been allowed to register, were unaffected by the court ruling. Lydia Becker approached each one of them personally, and twenty-four local women did vote in the 1868 election. The Hulme voters were typical, and Lydia wrote in detail to Ursula Bright and Miss Robertson about the work she carried out with Alice Wilson to bring them to the poll. At first the women were very shy, but were soon persuaded:

They extended in <u>grade</u> from well-to-do shopkeepers down to one miserably poor creature, who did not possess bonnet and shawl to cover her ragged gown, but who <u>borrowed</u> one to come and vote. I had a great deal of difficulty in inducing some of them to vote – it seemed strange to them – there were timid, and could not believe they had a right to do so ...

One old lady, who resolutely declined going to the poll when I urged it on general grounds, at last asked me for whom I wanted her to vote and when I said I left that quite to herself and asked her which she preferred, she said she wanted 'the old men' to get in and asked if I thought they were safe. I said yes, certainly, but they would not get in, unless their friends who were on the register went up and voted for them and that if I had a vote I would walk ten miles to give it to Mr Bright. The notion of supporting and helping the 'old members' shook her disinclination to go to the poll – and I believe she will be induced to come with us, solely by her feeling of allegiance to them.[81]

They were each accompanied in turn by Lydia, using a carriage and a pair of greys put at her disposal for the occasion by a Liberal gentleman. In a letter to Jessie Boucherett, she reported that the local Conservatives were annoyed as the women she had taken all voted Liberal. When a Tory agent objected, she had informed him that she knew of one woman who would vote Conservative, if he would like to go and fetch her. He did so, using the carriage of Conservative candidate Hugh Birley, and Lydia was gleeful that he had thus tied himself to the principle of female suffrage. Unable personally to escort the Salford female voters, she was delighted that both the Tory and the Liberal committees pledged to look after them – especially as 'I am perfectly aware that a voter must not enter a cab!! on election day', for fear of being forced to vote against their own inclinations. Six Manchester women also voted in the Lancashire county election.

When the results were known, Lydia's personal preference for the Liberals was somewhat disappointed, in that the Tories were triumphant in Lancashire.[82] Gladstone's loss of his South Lancashire seat was a mixed blessing; he was forced to stand for Greenwich instead. The loss of his Westminster seat by suffrage leader John Stuart Mill to the newsagent W.H. Smith, whose campaign was said by *The Times* to have been extremely corrupt, was 'a terrible loss, but I do not regard it as a fatal blow'. Lydia reported to Susan B. Anthony 'we have lost our leader', having received the news in a telegram at the Free Trade Hall passed on to her by Jacob Bright. However, she was not entirely surprised, as she had got wind of it when in Westminster earlier in the year. And she was deeply consoled by the fact that in Jacob Bright they had a Mancunian on whom 'the mantle had fallen': 'He would have been a sound efficient lieutenant of Mr Mill – and if he will be captain, he can lead us on to victory.'[83] Bright was returned with Thomas Bazley for Manchester, along with Conservative Hugh Birley.

Lydia sat up half the night writing letters in great excitement to all her friends. She had been instrumental in breaking the rule that women could not vote in general elections, and was uplifted that 'Great enthusiasm was manifested by the people, and we were everywhere received with deafening cheers – our cause is very popular in Manchester.'[84] She estimated from a report in the *Daily News* that perhaps 1,000 women countrywide had successfully registered to vote, which she felt was symptomatic of a huge advance 'with giant strides'.[85]

Moreover, Lydia had been eagerly collecting in pledges of support from prospective MPs in the new Commons; she reported that ninety were forthcoming, which was an increase of twelve over the previous parliament. Jacob Bright agreed to lead the women's suffrage group in the legislature, and discussion began within the Manchester committee as to how to extend the movement, dismissing the possibility of introducing an amendment to the 1867 Reform Act, in favour of a private members' bill for women's suffrage. The claims of over 5,500 women in Manchester to vote in 1868, and a great petition to be gathered, were to form the basis of the argument.[86]

Lydia Becker very quickly established herself at the forefront of suffragist campaigning in the late 1860s. By the end of May 1868 she was being introduced by Mayor Pochin of Salford, a keen suffragist himself, at a supper for the Peel Park Exhibition in Salford as 'one of Manchester's notabilities'.[87] She had high hopes that the irrefutable arguments she and her colleagues put forward would win the day in the near future. Recognising that women needed to break out of their conventional norms, she determinedly led the way in organising, speaking and challenging in the name of women's rights, particularly with regard to the franchise. She braved the barbs of opponents, both men and women, who dismissed her as an untypical, unfeminine woman, and gritted her teeth in the face of ridicule in articles and cartoons. She held fast to a firm belief in the ultimate victory of logical argument, and set out to develop the women's campaign to convey it more effectively.

Chapter 3

The Development of the Manchester Society

However massive her personal effort, Lydia Becker could not run the women's suffrage agitation alone, and her clear recognition of this fact had led her to push the Manchester committee to establish as quickly as possible the MNSWS, and to do her utmost to encourage like-minded people to set up parallel organisations all over Britain. It was not enough just to set up machinery and a committee, however; the new body needed foot soldiers to gather signatures for petitions, help run meetings, lobby MPs by letter, and above all provide finance for the furtherance of what became known as 'the Cause'. Lydia as secretary of the dynamic Manchester Society spearheaded all such initiatives, co-ordinating efforts with London and other major centres, even visiting small towns to encourage and oversee the embryonic women's movement wherever a seed could be sown. The Manchester Society held its AGMs in the mayor's parlour of the town hall, and its discussions were reported in the influential local press, thus ensuring that their activities and achievements were maintained in the public eye. In the nature of things, and particularly in the light of the big personalities and passionately held views involved, there were fall-outs within the movement, and from the start there was a particular difficulty between the London and Manchester societies which was never fully resolved. The aspirations of the secretary of the Manchester committee to dominate the movement meant that it was the most vibrant promoter of the women's cause, but also that the road was fraught with rivalries and enmity.

Rules and tactics of the MNSWS

From its first meeting, the aim of the MNSWS was set out clearly and continued to be stated under the heading of 'Rules' in every annual report thereafter: it was 'to obtain for Women the Right of Voting for Members of Parliament on the same conditions as it is, or may be, granted to men.'

The rules went on to explain that membership would be dependent on the members' approval of the society's objects, and their payment of an annual subscription, which was set at one shilling in 1868, but amended from 1869 to 'any amount' so that the net was cast as widely as possible. The AGM would receive a report and a statement of accounts, and would appoint an executive committee, from which a secretary and a treasurer would be chosen by the committee. The committee or twenty-five ordinary members could call a special general meeting to discuss a particular subject, which had to be cited in the notice for the meeting. These rules could only be altered by a general meeting, and a month's notice was required for any rule change.[1]

By the end of 1868, the Manchester executive committee boasted seventeen members, of whom ten were women. The president was MP Jacob Bright; the early feminists welcomed the support of men to give the movement clout and confidence. Bright was an assiduous campaigner in the House for women's rights, but was unable to participate in the day-to-day running of the organisation. Its treasurer was (briefly) Mathilde then Philippine Kyllmann, but as there was no prohibition on male office-holders, from 1869 Rev. Samuel Steinthal took over the role. With Jacob and Ursula Bright, Richard Pankhurst and Lydia Becker herself, he was one of the most significant figures in the early years and his voice was influential in decision-making. The personnel of the executive committee remained fairly constant, with notable exceptions, over the next eighteen years, though in 1886 it was augmented by the inclusion of eight MPs, and further so in 1889 when there were eleven. However, until at least the early 1880s, when she began to spend a large part of her time in London, it was Lydia as secretary who dominated it, aiming (usually successfully) to direct its policy, organising its activities and carrying out the lion's share of the work.

The new organisation's tactics were also set out in every annual report for the benefit of members, who were strongly encouraged to participate in any way they could.[2] They were first enjoined to collect signatures for petitions to parliament, and to bring up the question of women's suffrage with MPs whenever they appeared before their constituents, as well as writing letters to them if the issue was broached in the House. When an election occurred, they should especially quiz the candidates on their attitude to women's suffrage, and at all times strive to ensure facts and arguments were published by the local press. The use of placards was also regularly adopted in large towns either locally, as during the Manchester High Court hearing in 1868, or nationally, as for the election of 1874. Should members discover anything or anyone useful to the society, they were to communicate such information to the secretary, Lydia Becker. They were expected to seek out new members, and if a few people were to be found in the same place, to set up a new local branch.

By the mid-1870s, the leadership had also realised that it would be a huge boost to gain the support of whichever party was in government. In January 1874, for instance, the Birmingham Society held a conference at which a memorial to Liberal Prime Minister Gladstone, drawn up by the Manchester committee, was adopted for the whole movement. It stressed how women's lack of suffrage in national elections was by then an anomaly, as women had many other political roles, and how the current law was particularly unjust to female taxpayers and women disadvantaged in work by laws which allowed male closed-shops. When an election was declared very soon afterwards, a copy of the memorial was sent to every candidate in England and Wales. Other similar memorials to party leaders followed. Yet although it could be argued that the movement was aware of the problems of attempting to add amendments to government bills and of the weaknesses of private members' bills, it proved impossible to convince enough leading politicians that women's suffrage was not only desirable but should also be a priority, as Gladstone's reply to Becker in July 1874 made clear.[3]

Measures adopted by the suffragists at the start of the 1870s were continued in parliament throughout the decade. A sympathetic MP was selected to present the Women's Electoral Disabilities Bill almost every year; up to 1874 this was Jacob Bright. When he lost his seat in that year, his place was taken by Conservative MP William Forsyth leading a cross-party group of MPs. Jacob Bright briefly resumed the role on his return to parliament in a by-election in 1876, but due to conflicts within the society from 1878 it was taken over initially by Liberal MP Leonard Courtney.

Petitions continued to be raised throughout with considerable success, to support the proposals being put before parliament. They reached their peak in 1874 with 430,343 signatures and in her annual report Lydia noted that these 'greatly exceed those for any other object'. Many of them arose from public meetings which were held every year all over the country; Lydia was a prolific speaker, as her list of engagements in 1874 demonstrates. She addressed a huge gathering in the Manchester Free Trade Hall, followed up by meetings all over the north and Wales between February and May, and in the autumn she toured Yorkshire. But whereas the meetings generally continued, and were augmented by a programme of summer events at 'watering places' such as Llandudno, Harrogate, and Scarborough, petitions had declined to a mere 35,000 signatures by 1879 as the movement began to lose momentum for a while, and faith in private members' bills was challenged.[4]

Membership and finances

Lydia perceived the importance of recruitment right from the start. She produced a prodigious amount of propaganda aimed at attracting members, starting with her article 'Female Suffrage'. By the later 1870s, the Manchester AGM was being attended by 600–700 people, mostly women, demonstrating the society's success in acquiring subscribers. From the start, it had boasted members from all parts of the UK, stretching from Devon to Dundee. Those who joined paid a subscription and to encourage others their names were listed, with the amount they paid, in the annual reports. Some opted for anonymity and chose titles which expressed their motivation: 'One of many Educated Women deeply interested in the cause'; 'A Father of seven daughters'; 'A Well-robbed, Well-crushed, and Effectually Suppressed Wife'; 'A Friend to justice'; 'a White Slave'; and 'Not an Enemy'.

The subscription list increased with encouraging speed: in its first two years alone it quadrupled and, although it slowed at times, growth continued into the 1880s. It reached a peak in 1883 with well over 900 subscribers, many of whom gave generously. The largest reported amount was a hefty £150, the smallest 1 shilling. Recruitment was hugely boosted by public meetings, at which activists, often led by Becker herself, spoke and elicited signatures for petitions and new members were admitted; the lecture tours of 1874 hugely boosted the membership, for instance, and a fund set up to pay for the 'demonstration' of 1880 found 287 donors who together provided over £170.[5]

Other funds came from extra donations, some of them large ones from wealthy individuals such as Jessie Boucherett, John Stuart Mill, Helen Taylor and Jacob Bright. In 1869, in view of the decision to bring in a bill the following year to remove the electoral disabilities of women, it was agreed by the committee that £5,000 was required over the next five years. A drive was instituted to raise the funds from wealthy supporters, initiated by five ladies and gentlemen who had each provided £100. Rich donors were generous, contributing the huge sum of £1,200 to the Cause in just one month of 1872. Sometimes a donation came with strings; in 1883 Mr R.B. Kennett offered a donation of £500 if others would give a further £1,000. On this occasion, the society failed to raise the latter sum, but Mr Kennett paid up regardless.[6] There were also occasions where wealthy patrons had the power to hinder efforts, as Priscilla Bright McLaren related in 1878:

> She [Alice Scatcherd of Leeds] and Miss Becker had a most successful meeting at Harrogate where Miss Becker won golden opinions – quite transcending herself on the occasion. We wish to get up a similar lecture at Ilkley but they are so poor they can't do it without J. Thomasson's leave and help – he has been applied to – but I do not know if he will come to the rescue – as he actually prevented a meeting being held at Blackpool on account of the expense! The very place to catch Lancashire and Yorkshire ladies who will not go to meetings in their own towns – and who live often in country places. He is very good at giving, but I think he ought to have helped such efforts.[7]

Manchester's income fluctuated with the fortunes of the Cause; in 1868 it started at a modest £229 12s 8d per annum, and by 1873 had reached a high of £2,499 11s 9d.[8] It was never as rich as the London Society, and it never attained this level again. Thereafter the finances gradually declined, due very much to splits which developed with regard to policy and tactics; the Jacob Brights, for instance, ceased their generous donations from 1874 after their quarrel with Lydia over married women's votes.[9]

Frequently, the society had to operate in a hand to mouth manner, which entailed Lydia writing begging letters when funds could not meet expenses. In June 1868, for instance she had reported that she needed £100 to continue with the Persons campaign, and when she ran out of money it had to stop. When Mary Johnson became secretary of the Birmingham Society, she wrote to her: 'You will have to practise the art of begging: It is very unpleasant at first but one gets used to it after the receipt of a few cheques and postal orders!'[10] Lydia even managed to laugh at her own efforts to squeeze money out of sympathisers, as she recounted in a letter to Richard Pankhurst:

> I went to collect a subscription promised me by Mr Binney, solicitor and F.R.S. I was amused at his fright, for he had forgotten how much he had promised me – he is one of those rich people who look at both sides of a penny – and his suspense was something ludicrously touching. I told him I hoped he would give me more than he had promised; and when I revealed that his liability was only five shillings he cried, 'I'll give you ten' with an alacrity which showed how his imagination had run on to alarming possibilities. I ought to have got at least £1 out of the situation, but am burdened with a conscience, an article a secretary ought to get rid of with all convenient speed.[11]

Money also came in from soirées and appeals. In 1871–2 it was decided to hold a bazaar to raise £500. Mrs J.P. Thomasson undertook to guarantee that amount with her contacts, but even this sum was thought to be too little and appeals were made at the AGM for 'increased pecuniary support'. Similar efforts were made in subsequent years; after the AGM in 1874 there was entertainment at a cost of 2*s* 6*d* per ticket. Coffee in the mayor's parlour at 7 p.m. was accompanied by a piano recital, followed by some short addresses and a *conversazione* at 9 p.m.[12]

Despite these efforts, by 1886 the society had 'liabilities' to the tune of over £200, and from then on was struggling with little success to eliminate these debts. With the stresses and confusions of the later 1880s, by 1887 the finances had reached a parlous state. A public appeal was made through the press for the raising of £500 above and beyond normal subscriptions to meet the shortfall and enable work to continue. The problem was not alleviated by a move in 1888 to offices in Queen's Chambers on John Dalton Street, considered by Frances Power Cobbe to be 'comparatively poor and exceedingly noisy'. In 1889, it was openly stated in the *WSJ* that a post-AGM sale of work was to raise funds to pay the debt off. After Lydia's death, it was admitted that this debt had 'long weighed upon the committee'.¹³ Funding the movement was never an easy task, and in Lydia's last few years it had become again necessary, as in the early days, to cut back the work of campaigning, though she may have been cushioned from the impact of this decline due to her focus by this time on the National Society and its efforts in parliament.

Lydia Becker as secretary

For Lydia Becker, women's suffrage was far more than a campaign. Symptomatic of her approach, she refused to have the sums paid to her by the society noted in the accounts as a 'salary' – she acted as a labour of love, and the money was paid only as a 'grant' to enable her to continue to do so. Ironically, it could be argued that by not accepting that it was paid work, she was playing into the hands of opponents of feminism, who regarded women who were paid as not respectable.¹⁴ In a letter of November 1868, she explained to her sceptical brother, Leigh, how she saw her role:

> I attribute your want of sympathy with our movement rather to a want of appreciation of the benefits it is destined to confer – primarily on women – and secondly on mankind ... rather than to want of sympathy with the object of trying to improve the condition of society and the world ... When any very great and important movement is in its infancy – those in most intimate personal relation with its features are often the last to perceive the magnitude of the events that are ripening under their eyes. Names connected with great events in the past history of civilisation now stand out with prominence – like mountain peaks ... But while they lived, they were not so prominent among others who surrounded them, especially while their work was young and their ideas yet undeveloped – such it is with our movement ... we are leaving our mark on the civilisation of this age, and making an epoch in the history, not of our own country alone, but of the world. This language may sound inflated to you now – and much <u>may</u> happen to prevent its ever attaining significance. But if I live – and can keep my head above water – I will make them [sic] prophetic and as Jacob Bright said of his brother – 'and to our family name, a place in the records of our time'.¹⁵

High-flown rhetoric aside, Lydia, as the Manchester committee's most dynamic member, had also of necessity to learn quickly the art of organising and running a society. It was not easy; liberalism – which set the tone of much discussion – prized individual conscience, rather than collective will. This meant that every decision had to be weighed and judged by each individual before they could act, and led to splits and disagreements. Lydia did her best to counter this by being as bossy as she dared. As Jessie Boucherett remembered in 1890:

> Miss Becker was an honest, straightforward worker. She held her opinions very strongly and would urge them with impetuosity and determination, and she sometimes gave offence by so doing; but whether she were bringing forward a measure she approved, or opposing one of which she disapproved, her conduct was always open and fair. She would, if she could, bring over to her opinion those who differed from her by hard reasoning, and if she could not do so, she would try to defeat them by an honest majority. If she failed in this, she would submit in silence, and, though grieved at the failure of what she considered to be the best plan, she would yet try heartily and loyally to make the less good plan succeed.[16]

Lydia's advice to Mary Johnson, secretary in Birmingham, revealed her methods clearly:

> Never go to a committee for an instruction ... Think out carefully a decided plan, put it in the form of one set of resolutions – ask them to assent ... you may very likely find that some modification, possibly improvement may suggest itself in committee ... you must be its leader, by exercising decision and firmness and tact ... People are generally so helpless and find such difficulty in making up their minds they are really thankful to be told what to do![17]

This approach was risky, however, and on occasion she pushed it too far. A dispute late in 1868 with committee members Philippine and Mathilde Kyllmann demonstrated how she could ruffle feathers, and that she had enemies as well as staunch supporters. It also revealed the depth of her insecurity and her vulnerability when she encountered hostility; it is evident from her letters that the dispute badly affected her confidence and nerves.

Relations with Philippine Kyllmann had been cordial earlier in 1868; Philippine wrote to Helen Taylor that Miss Becker was 'a very earnest woman' and that the work she had been doing in the Ladies' Literary Society was 'an invaluable thing'.[18] The goodwill continued to the end of October at the AGM, when Philippine occupied the chair to good effect.[19] However, the ill-feeling which exploded in mid-November was not without precedent; Lydia made it clear in her correspondence with friends that she had experienced hostility from the two Kyllmann ladies on previous occasions, such as when she had summoned a committee meeting at Mrs Bright's house in Alderley Edge, a good way outside Manchester, to which they had reacted with violent indignation. They appear to have been trying to challenge and limit Lydia's power, but with little success. Philippine wrote as much to Helen Taylor in London: 'I long feared that the great latitude left to our Secretary would bring us some day into trouble.' As they were French ladies who had married into a German family, relations may have been soured by Lydia's preference for English women to run the society, expressed on several occasions, which was highly ironic considering her own origins.[20]

On 14 November, the Kyllmanns came to her home in what can only be described as a fury about something in Lydia's correspondence, though they were not specific as to exactly what. In her letter to Ursula Bright, she described them as 'viragos', who threatened resignation from the committee if they did not get satisfaction in the form of a vote of confidence against her. Feeling that she would not get a fair hearing from them, she had resolved to say nothing, and informed them that she 'altogether denied their right to come to my rooms' and would speak only to the whole committee, when she would read out all her correspondence. She clearly felt extremely vulnerable, but nevertheless hopeful of the committee's support:

> It is quite certain, however, that they [the Kyllmanns] regard me with extreme suspicion, and that every word I say is instantly seized upon, and made a matter for fresh accusation. They are the only members of the committee who have not given me the most generous and indulgent support in all the efforts I have made to further our cause … and if … there is to be instituted a feeling of mistrust and suspicion I shall wither under it, and my powers become completely paralysed.

I have hitherto felt that the committee not only collectively, but individually, with the exception of these two, had, without pledging themselves to approval in detail of all that I had said or done, such a general confidence in my ability and discretion that they could give me complete and individual support ... [21]

After a day to consider the attack, its origin seems to have dawned on her – that they strongly objected to a letter she had unilaterally written in October to Helen Taylor and J.S. Mill. She had asked for financial help to pay the legal costs of the High Court Appeal, reminding them that in the summer they had offered to guarantee £100 of the expenses. Perhaps, as Philippine feared, Lydia had been hoping that Mill's friendship with the recently deceased Max Kyllmann, Philippine's husband, might make them kindly disposed to help defray the costs of her test case in the High Court. Lydia took comfort, however, that 'as the application resulted in an accession of £60 to our treasury I think the committee have no reason to quarrel with that'. In fact, the Mills were becoming disillusioned with the Manchester committee and had stipulated that £50 of the money should be earmarked for Philippine's own freeholder case. Philippine's letters to Helen Taylor give her side of the story.[22] She received the £50 completely out of the blue, and nothing was said in the committee about it having been solicited in 'a begging letter' by Becker – this came out only in passing. She then realised that Lydia had acted entirely alone and that the committee was unaware that she had written. Philippine felt her name had been used without her permission, exploiting her friendship with Mill and Taylor.

Lydia told Jacob Bright that she believed Philippine, at this time treasurer to the Manchester committee, might be planning to offer to return the donation to Mr Mill, which Lydia feared would insult him. Although this was denied, on 2 December Philippine did indeed send the Mills a personal cheque for £50. Taylor wrote back that they had assumed that Becker had written with the approval of the committee and were surprised that she had not consulted them, but they refused to accept the repayment offered, as long as it went as intended to help Philippine with her own costs.

Meanwhile, martialling her defences, immediately after the Kyllmanns' dramatic visit Lydia wrote to Mrs Bright asking that she and her husband arrive punctually at the next committee meeting to get in first and ensure that Jacob would be elected as chairman because he would see that there was 'fair play' and 'in his hands I shall feel perfectly safe'. She was hopeful that the two Kyllmann ladies would resign, and make her life easier, and tried to persuade Ursula Bright to take over as treasurer, as she thought 'it is much better to have a lady', rather than asking Mr Steinthal.[23] She also asked her other friends to attend in her support – including Richard Pankhurst.

Philippine proposed a resolution that all Lydia's letters must be seen by the committee, but this was resisted by 'some of our public men as unreasonable and ridiculous and was met on the part of the Secretary with a threat to resign'. By the time this meeting was over, Lydia was feeling less besieged but still anxious. The blessed Jacob had worked his magic to make things 'go right': 'It was worth enduring all the pain to have such an experience of his goodness, to feel the influence of a mind so fine … it was like listening to an exquisite piece of music whose fine and noble harmonies come through the deepest chords of the heart,' she wrote.

Mr Steinthal, rather more prosaically, had offered to act as arbiter in the dispute, and Lydia agreed to place herself in his hands, confident that 'the difficulty in our committee will now be happily settled', though the knowledge that he was to call in on her with a proposition gave her a sleepless night. On 28 November, she resolved to call on Mr Steinthal, and 'after a long hard fight', in which the gentleman was friendly and sympathetic throughout (but made it clear that if she did not comply with his proposals she would cause a serious split and destroy the committee), Lydia agreed to do what he asked at the next meeting. This entailed making available all her letters written in the committee's name, which seems to have allowed matters to be smoothed over, avoiding a disastrous split.[24]

Lydia had sufficiently recovered from the Kyllmann onslaught to step back and admit that the wrong was not all on one side, though unbeknownst to her Philippine had not been honest about her offer of repayment to the Mills:

> What a strange scene we had at the meeting, and was it not a pity that such a ridiculous disturbance should have been made where

there was nothing to find fault with at all ... I may perhaps have done Mrs Max Kyllmann great injustice by saying to Mr Bright that I feared she might say something to Mr Mill about returning his money – I had no right to say so – the only thing that made me think she could was that she said in the committee meeting that she thought the money ought to be returned if it should appear that it was given out of friendship to her. That was before she heard the correspondence we had. I had no right to assume that she would be guilty of the gross breach of trust as making any suggestion as to returning the money – and I am very sorry I hinted at such a notion to Mr Bright. Dr Pankhurst says she seems as if she thought she had a vested interest in Mr Mill!!

Accordingly, Lydia had written a courteous official note to Philippine as treasurer asking her to bring £119 to the next meeting so that the appeal court costs could be paid, but 'I do not know on what terms I stand with her personally.'

Unwilling to lose Becker, their greatest and most active campaigner, and no doubt also mindful of the potentially massive workload in attempting to carry on without her, the Brights and most of the committee had supported her and defeated the Kyllmanns' attack. Unsurprisingly, Philippine Kyllmann's next letter to Helen Taylor in London demonstrated that she was still unhappy:

It seemed to me ... most undesirable that so much should be left to the entire discretion of a Secretary, but all I could obtain was that all letters written in the name of the Committee should be copied. All those received were of course to be read to us, but in presence of the general feeling, to attempt any more would have been useless, and with the exception of the two last letters to you, which I insisted on being read, I do not think that any has been seen by the Committee.[25]

Philippine did not take the situation lying down, and she and her sister-in-law resigned from the Manchester suffrage committee, no doubt much to Lydia's relief. The following year Philippine summed up her feelings to Helen Taylor:

Supported as the secretary is, in everything by Mr and Mrs Bright ... My opinion of her is such that I will no longer have my name on any committee in which she works. I have for that reason withdrawn from the MWP [Married Women's Property] Society, for the very qualities which I thoroughly appreciated combined with the other points of her character make her in my eyes the most dangerous person.[26]

All this discussion took place at 28 Jackson's Row, Manchester, the MNSWS's home until 1888 when the headquarters were moved to John Dalton Street. A small but devoted group, which included some paid office staff, worked there. From at least 1879, Lydia's deputy as secretary was Sarah Backhouse, her cousin, and in addition a Mrs McCormick was paid as 'organising agent' to travel the country setting up meetings, as well as working in the Manchester office. But there is no doubt that Becker herself took on the lion's share of the decision-making, insisting that everything they produced must look ultra-professional. She tested out the circulars to women ratepayers for the election of 1868 on her sister Esther: '

> I had a great deal of trouble before I got them right, but now I hope they are intelligible to the meanest capacity. I tested them by giving them to my sister … she did it right – which was satisfactory!'[27]

Indeed, her missives looked so good that in Chevening, Kent the circular to overseers requesting them to put women ratepayers on the voting lists was mistaken for an official communication and was obeyed, much to the annoyance of the hostile Liberal agent.[28] To facilitate the production of literature, a decision was made to invest in a duplicating press, which was a boon; but even this was a stressful business as when Lydia braved the all-male preserve of the supplier 'they were highly amused and slightly contemptuous over my ignorance, but of course some things do not come by instinct … I only wish we had it from the beginning, it would have made an interesting record of the work that has been done …'[29]

The press was also a vital tool in the armoury, and Lydia spent much time in building up contacts with local editors and reporters; the doings of the society were reported in important local papers, notably the liberal *Manchester Guardian* and *Manchester Examiner and Times,* and the Tory *Manchester Courier,* as well as in satirical magazines such as the *City Jackdaw.* She even on occasion addressed missives to the editor of *The*

Times. And of course Becker eventually decided that the movement needed its own organ as the *Englishwoman's Review*, founded by Jessie Boucherett in 1866, was insufficient for the needs of the suffrage campaign, and so in 1870 the *Women's Suffrage Journal* was born. And it was Lydia who edited it and was its major contributor.

Lydia learnt from the experience of other movements the techniques needed to keep up momentum; the Anti-Corn Law League's use of petition, public meetings and lobbying, funded by soirées and dinners as well as subscriptions, was emulated closely. As John Gorst reorganised the Conservative party and its local machinery to take account of the mass electorate created by the Second Reform Act in 1867, setting up local committees in every important town, the same methods were adopted in the women's suffrage movement. Under Becker's aegis, evangelism extended out from Manchester, and the country was informally divided into six regions based on six key conurbations; Manchester (North of the Trent and North Wales under Becker and in Leeds, Alice Scatcherd), Birmingham (under Mary Johnson and Eliza Sturge), London (Caroline Ashurst Biggs), Bristol and South Wales (Helen Blackburn and Lilias Ashworth Hallett), Edinburgh (Priscilla Bright McLaren) and Dublin (Anne Robertson).[30]

Perhaps because of her strong relationship with Mary Johnson, of these major societies it was Birmingham in which Lydia appears to have to have taken the keenest interest. They were in close contact, with Lydia advising Mary minutely on procedures and tactics, and sending sample letters to copy. This aspect of their relationship was very similar to Lydia's own contacts with Emily Davies in 1867, and it reveals much about how she managed the Manchester Society. In her inimitable way, Lydia advocated a characteristically single-minded approach: 'If Mrs Tyndall is the only objector there can be no difficulty in getting her outvoted – you must never be afraid to take a vote – on any question. So do your best to secure a fair discussion and then take a vote on it.'

On the other hand, she also advised Mary to choose her battles wisely, responding in the negative to her friend's appeal that she would reply to an opponent of women medical practitioners in *The Times* by arguing 'It is a wretched production not worth the labour of answering – the man has a low mind, incapable of comprehending the dignity of a woman's nature' and it was 'not worth the powder and shot …' She thought that if she succeeded it would 'not be by firing random shots at chance foes, but by well-aimed, carefully planted missiles'.

She avowed that her aim was to enable the Birmingham Society to 'stand alone and to become <u>independent</u>'. Then, betraying an interesting sense of her own superiority as a leader, she enjoined Mary to be careful of local sensibilities: 'Take counsel from your new committee – you must not let them get hold of the notion that you receive your inspiration from Manchester.' During the Persons campaign she added to her other injunctions that it was beneficial to recruit influential people in the local area to help spread the network of contacts, and if the response to an approach was doubtful, she explained that it was necessary to 'win them over' (or bludgeon them into submission!) with a full exposition of the legal case for women to vote. She did not leave Mary to her own devices, however, and after counselling the use of a deputation to visit the overseers, asked her to send her the names of those included on it so that she could give her opinion on the selection.[31]

The Bristol Society was less satisfactory, at least at the start. In 1868, Becker complained that they were ineffectual in their efforts during the Persons campaign, and initially attributed this to the influence of Professor Francis William Newman, who was 'always making difficulties'. When he went away, she had hopes that the vice-secretary would carry out her plans more effectively, and believed that the committee was 'moving more vigorously now' but was put out to receive a 'maddening' letter indicating that the Bristol committee did not believe a canvass would work. She was hugely exasperated: 'I could throw the letter at their head, and slap them all around!! It can't be <u>all</u> Newman's fault, after all!'[32]

Cordial relations with Edinburgh were established early on when Priscilla Bright McLaren visited Lydia in Manchester, and similarly the influence of Anne Robertson allowed for co-operation with Dublin. But it was in England and Wales that Lydia was personally most active and that the MNSWS was most directly effective.

AGMs and annual reports

The MNSWS held its AGM in late autumn every year from 1868, and Becker regularly wrote and presented a report on the activities undertaken during the preceding year. Several venues had been mooted for the initial gathering in 1868, including the Memorial Hall in Albert Square and a small meeting at Dr Borchardt's, but Mr Steinthal's idea of using the mayor's parlour in the town hall was finally adopted and continued to be so every year. This prestigious venue enhanced the standing of the society, especially as it meant they sometimes met under the chairmanship of the Mayor of Manchester.[33]

At the first AGM, on 30 October 1868, Lydia was worried that the numbers attending would not justify the use of such a notable setting. It seems that the burden of organising everything fell largely on her. Although she had distributed 500 tickets, she was aware that some key people were not planning to attend: Elizabeth Wolstenholme, for instance, who would have brought many others with her, was ill. It did not help that an important committee meeting a week before was so poorly attended that Lydia could not proceed with arrangements. She feared that 'the public mind is full of other things just now' and cited the concert season and the forthcoming election as diversions which might result in a poor turnout and give ammunition to 'the enemy'.[34] It may equally be that Lydia's dominance over the committee discouraged other members from taking responsibility upon themselves.

The meeting took place shortly before the 1868 general election and during the Persons campaign. It was noted by the *Manchester Guardian*, which remarked that although most of those attending were women, apart from Lydia's lengthy report the only other woman to speak was the chairperson, Philippine Kyllmann, who volunteered just a few comments. The paper regretted that most of the talking was done by male suffragists, the Liberal candidates Jacob Bright and Ernest Jones, and Richard Pankhurst. The views of the paper were ahead of their time in implying that 'Miss Becker and some of her stronger sisters' would one day become MPs, and praising Lydia's style as highly suited to parliamentary debate, as it was 'matter-of-fact, businesslike, and to the point, contrasting in all three respects very favourably with the speeches delivered by the male champions of her cause ...'[35]

Lydia was delighted with the meeting, which 'was a glorious success'. She had stated to several correspondents beforehand that she would be happy with a turnout of fifty persons, but in the event the meeting was packed. Having secured Josephine Butler as chair, she had been deeply disappointed that she could not attend as she was unwell. Yet her reservations about the alternative chairmanship of Philippine Kyllmann, although she 'would be a good president', proved unfounded. Despite the fact that Lydia regretted that 'we could not have an Englishwoman in the chair', she conceded that Mrs Kyllmann was a 'very efficient president' over a crowded room with good speeches which were appreciated by the audience. Even more encouraging, though in the event misleading, was a missive from the Liberal leader:

> Mr Gladstone's note was read – it shews he is just beginning to think about the matter – I hope Lady Scarisbrick and her tenants will give him some practical proof of the view of women voters – perhaps their being on the register has done something to open his eyes.[36]

Regarding the women's campaign in some ways as a war, Lydia saw her report for the first Manchester AGM as a most effective 'missile'.[37] The annual report was always an impressive piece of propaganda. The upbeat and encouraging attitude which emerged in her less private correspondence was reflected and enlarged in her accounts of the achievements of the society for each year. There was no hint of the turmoil which went on behind the scenes; the row between Becker and the Kyllmanns which threatened to break up the committee in 1868 is nowhere mentioned, except that the two sisters-in-law quietly disappeared from the committee by the report of 1869. The annoyance which Lydia felt with the London committee, and the power struggle which went on between the committees of Manchester and the metropolis, is completely absent from the version of events in the official record. The furious row between Becker and the Brights, Wolstenholme and Richard Pankhurst over the exclusion of married women from the bill proposed by Forsyth in 1874 is passed over in silence.[38]

What was there in abundance, stultifyingly boring to all those not intimately concerned with the minutiae of political analysis, was a detailed and multi-faceted breakdown of all the results of the campaigning. Lydia's number crunching was worthy, impressive and used to furnish further ammunition to the supporters of the Cause. Most notably, votes in the Commons were interpreted according to political party, type of constituency and area of the UK, every petition presented was noted in detail, with its origins and presenting MP, and lectures were enumerated and assessed as the means of spreading the word and rallying increasing numbers to the Cause.

In her annual report of 1869, praised at the AGM by Conservative MP for Salford, William Charley, as 'an historic State document', Lydia harked back to Chorlton v Lings, the High Court legal case which had stated in law that women could not vote in general elections. Nevertheless, her tone was optimistic as she recorded the momentous fact that women had actually voted in the general election of December 1868. She explained how this demonstrated 'that the incapacity of women was purely theoretical, and that they were both able and willing to exercise the suffrage whenever the legal disability was removed'. She also pointed out that both political parties in Manchester supported the women in voting.

However, she reserved her greatest triumph for the advent of the municipal franchise for women, granted in 1869 to female ratepayers in municipal corporations, such as Manchester.[39] In the annual report, she was not slow to claim this victory for her own committee, as it 'would not have been obtained without the efforts and influence of the Manchester Society, on which the entire work outside of Parliament, devolved'.[40] The committee had carried out research into the proportion of women voters in England and Wales, allowing Lydia to cite some statistics. Ending on a note of high optimism she stated:

> The principle of women's suffrage in popular elections having been thus formally recognised by the legislature, and proof having been afforded that women value and use the franchise conferred upon them, the extension of this principle to the parliamentary suffrage seems only a question of time.[41]

Charley also noted the 'great services' of Lydia as an 'energetic and able' secretary, who 'quite rained petitions on him during the last session'.

Her subsequent reports up to 1872 continued to furnish increasingly detailed analysis of the voting in municipal elections, including comparisons between male and female voting numbers in both proportionate and absolute terms, though it did not help when town clerks like the one at Southport failed to enumerate the women, noting laconically that there were 'a goodly number. The number who polled surprised us all.'[42] However, the advent of the secret ballot in 1872 put a stop to this aspect of the number crunching, perhaps much to the relief of those who were less than enthused by the plethora of statistics.

It was also at the 1869 AGM that Richard Pankhurst successfully moved that, in the light of the progress made in the municipal franchise, a bill to remove the remaining disabilities of women should be introduced into the next parliament of 1870 by MPs Jacob Bright, Sir Charles Dilke and Peter Rylands. It was clear from Bright's response that he hoped such a bill would succeed within a year. Disappointingly, the report for 1870 noted that the bill had been lost in committee by 126, as well as that 170 MPs had voted or paired in support. It went on to cite a figure of 134,561 signatures on 120 petitions presented to parliament in support of the bill, which were listed with details of the origin and organiser of each one and the number of signatures. Indeed, every year from 1869 the report included similar information with the purpose of spurring on those engaged in the canvassing of petitions. The 1870 report also noted the inauguration of the *WSJ* under Becker's editorship and subsequent reports included a paragraph on the progress and achievements of the *Journal*.[43]

By the AGM of 1871 there was a need to boost morale, as the Women's Disabilities Bill had now failed twice with no decrease in the votes against; accordingly Lydia noted that although the majority against the bill was sixty-nine, the five great towns with three MPs gave 'undivided support' to the bill, which was the case for no other issue. This had to be qualified, however; in fact one of their votes was given against 'under a mistake' and two more 'were neutral'. Nevertheless, the town councils of seven towns (having been circulated by Lydia personally) had petitioned in favour of the bill. Lydia proceeded to give a full analysis of the voting across the whole of the Commons. The key point she wished to stress was that the votes in favour had risen from 94 to 151. Moreover, she claimed that Gladstone had moved from being strongly hostile, to seeming to approve the principle of the bill by abstaining, whilst the leader of the Conservative opposition, Benjamin Disraeli, had voted in favour. A similar format of reporting was followed in subsequent AGMs.

Lydia went on to suggest that a conference held in London had been so successful that a national demonstration should be held of representatives from all over the UK; it would meet in London when parliament was in session to support the bill when it was again proposed. Manchester had already sounded out the other societies and received 'assurances of approbation'.[44] The upshot was the long-awaited establishment of the Central Committee.

MNSWS relations with the London Society and the Central Committee, 1867–81

The attempt to amend the Second Reform Act by J.S. Mill, MP for Westminster, in 1867, had meant that to begin with London was at the forefront of the women's suffrage movement. The role of Manchester was played down; Elizabeth Wolstenholme always claimed that there had been a women's suffrage committee in Manchester, of which she was secretary, from October 1865, before London properly organised.[45] But later histories of the movement ignored this and dated the Manchester Society from 1867, after the London Society had been formed.

After the failure of Mill's attempt to include women in the franchise, on 6 July 1867 Becker visited London and met him at his home in Blackheath to discuss a proposal from Helen Taylor, Mill's stepdaughter, to unite the existing committees of London, Manchester, Bristol and Edinburgh into one organisation. It would have a general committee consisting of members who had published writings advocating women's suffrage, three people who had contributed 10 shillings to their local committee, and others elected by the existing members. This general committee would appoint executive committees in each town.[46] It seems that the London committee was aware that Lydia and the Manchester committee might have their own ideas about this. As early as 17 June, Clementia (Mentia) Taylor, secretary of the London committee, wrote to Helen Taylor informing her that Frances Power Cobbe was planning a lunch for them all, including Lydia Becker, and advised 'before arranging matters with Miss Becker ... have your own Executive Committee ready'.[47]

Two days before her visit, Lydia wrote to Taylor to arrange to meet her in the Ladies' Waiting Room at Euston; she would be recognisable in a 'violet serge dress and jacket, black hat and spectacles'. It was already clear that she and her committee were wary of London's intentions, and she had submitted a draft of her own view for the way forward to Taylor:

> I shall be very glad to have the opportunity of consulting with you as to the course of action to be taken by our committee. No doubt the four centres should each work independently collecting their own funds and through their own general and executive committees. But I do not quite understand from your note what is the bond of union you propose between the different centres. It should be one which,

while securing the advantage of concert and co-operation and mutual communication, should leave each centre free to work in the mode best adapted to the locality in which they are engaged. Should we form four independent societies? Or a National Society with four centres? If the latter should there be a general central committee? All these details want arranging. The suggested rules issued by our committee are merely tentative and can be modified to any extent.[48]

Despite some feelings of caution, at this stage relations between the two great centres of the suffrage movement were superficially cordial, and indeed the Mills had become members of the Manchester Society. Lydia wrote to Taylor of her delight at being entertained at their home: 'I have wished I could express to you something of the feeling with which I appreciated the privilege you and Mr Mill conferred upon me.'[49] Lydia was soon invited by Helen Taylor with Frances Power Cobbe to help get up the petition in Colchester which would disprove MP Karslake's claim that no women in Essex wanted the franchise, and she eagerly accepted, with the caveat that she was unable to pay her own travelling costs. Fortunately, Taylor had been alerted to her pecuniary difficulties by Jessie Boucherett and seems to have offered to pay her expenses. Once there, Lydia tackled the task with her usual energy and reported from the Red Lion Hotel that she was gathering signatures with some difficulty because 'I have found many who approve of the principle too timid to sign', although she had found that an individual approach could be effective. The petition was presented bearing 129 signatures. She also resolved to form a new suffrage committee in the town and was able to get a nucleus of four local ladies to effect this.[50]

In a letter to Lydia on 19 July, Mentia Taylor was keen to elicit a reassurance that they were all going to join together in one society.[51] By contrast, it appears that the Manchester committee was reluctant to go any further than co-operation from the position of separate societies and committees, failing to see what would be gained from a greater amalgamation. Lydia wrote to Helen Taylor explaining the position and requesting some concrete ideas for a constitution and the benefits which Manchester, currently 'perfectly satisfied with its own independent position', would gain.[52] When Taylor responded with a proposal for the Manchester committee to consider, it was sufficiently reassured and agreed to join the new National Society for Women's Suffrage. It would have a national roll of members, but retain the separate identities of the component parts 'with independent centres of action', separate constitutions, executives and funds.[53]

The National Society was viewed by Becker as a body which could give an umbrella of authority for campaigns, wherever they were to be carried out. In correspondence with London she furnished the example of Preston in Lancashire; whereas the Manchester Society could not really campaign there because it belonged to another conurbation, a National Society could do so. She also floated her idea that England should be divided into spheres of influence; London would have the south, Bristol the west, Birmingham the midlands, and Manchester the north. But she did not support the idea of joint finances, and was keen to show that her own proposals, which she had worked out in detail, were only for the purpose of concerted efforts, such as the Persons campaign. [54]

So it was that a very loose federation was to become the hallmark of the early suffragist movement. It has been claimed that this was a manifestation of a conscious rejection of male values, which modelled a hierarchical power structure with a dominant leader at the top; but it seems to have been at least as much a result of a power struggle between London and Manchester.[55] Although in her 1868 report to the MNSWS Becker claimed London had adopted her plan for separate entities to work in concert, in reality the London committee was reluctant. From their point of view, the meeting between Lydia and the Mills of July 1867 had been aimed at establishing one committee led by London, but Manchester had effectively rejected the capital's claim to primacy, and begun attempts to dominate the movement everywhere. This clash was symptomatic of the development of a serious rivalry between London and Manchester for the leadership of the movement. Lydia made it clear to the London committee that 'the only concert I propose is the concert of authority', although she did her best to avoid annoying and alienating them, recognising that she needed their support.[56]

The Mills soon began to regard Becker and her committee with distaste, especially in the light of the Kyllmann affair.[57] This was not the first time that money had become a divisive issue. In August 1867, Lydia had written to Helen Taylor explaining that Manchester lacked funds, whereas the London committee was, she pointed out, very rich.

Certainly it is true that even ordinary members in London were expected to pay a subscription of 1 shilling, whereas in Manchester it was fixed in 1868 at 'any amount' because even that was beyond the means of some. Philippine Kyllmann later confirmed that Manchester found difficulty in raising subscriptions, due to the lack of support amongst the 'upper class' and also 'a reluctance to apply to the class who can ill afford them'.[58]

What must have rankled especially with Taylor was that Becker went on to cite figures which she believed proved that Manchester was far more efficient than London in its use of resources. In particular, she pointed out the costly inefficiency of London's canvassing for signatures by post, as compared to a paid agent, Mrs Knott in Bolton, who at a cost of £3 for ten days acquired 132 signatures and the nucleus of a committee. To annoy her correspondent even further, Lydia referred to the words of J.S. Mill that 'he intended to divide his support between the funds of the London and Manchester committees'. She hoped that he would help her out, and enquired whether he still regarded himself equally connected with both London and Manchester.[59] Taylor put paid to her hopes in a letter of 31 October 1867, when Manchester was considering whether to focus on getting women onto the voting lists, rather than raising further petitions:

> We do not understand how it happens that the Manchester Committee with as rich or richer members than we have in London, after declining to do anything towards petitioning, in order to reserve its funds for testing the existing state of the law, should still be in such difficulties and want of money as to have to apply to the London Committee for help. Whatever is the cause of this state of things it is much to be regretted as it must cripple the exertions of the Manchester Committee, since it cannot be expected that the London [Committee] will be willing often to contribute much towards the work in the direction of which it is permitted no voice. If the London is to take upon itself the pecuniary burdens of a mother-committee I imagine it will wish also to have the weight and influence of one.[60]

Lydia was quick to retort that there was never any intention of asking the London committee for help, 'nor do we regard it in any way as a mother-committee. It has co-operated with us loyally and effectively where our policy has agreed ...' Any suggestion that Manchester was less than equal, if not the superior partner, was firmly rebutted.[61]

The decision of the Manchester committee to pursue the Persons campaign further pushed the Mills into opposition. To begin with they seemed to be in favour; in September 1867, before the idea had taken any concrete form, Lydia wrote to Taylor: 'I am very pleased that you approve of women making claims under the new Act before the overseers and revising barrister.' But at this time she assured her that there would be no question of pursuing the matter into the higher courts 'without the full concurrence and advice of the leaders of the movement'. This was sufficiently vague as to allow the Mills to believe she meant them. She rather disingenuously ended 'Indeed I do not know anyone who would be likely to be able to bear the cost of expensive litigation.'[62] In the event, of course, the views of the Mills were ignored by the decision of the Manchester committee to take the test cases to the High Court, but she still applied to them for financial support.

Increasingly, Manchester went its own way in terms of strategy. After the Manchester by-election of 1867, Miss Knott had struggled to get signatures for a women's suffrage petition from sympathisers in Stockport because they said there was no point in signing when Lilly Maxwell had shown that women could in fact vote. Argument raged in the Manchester committee about the value of petitioning, a policy much favoured in London; Mr Steinthal, proving the strongest opponent, argued that it was only worth doing when it was in support of a bill in parliament. Once Chisholm Anstey's idea that the 1867 Reform Act actually enfranchised women was adopted by Manchester the clamour against petitions became even louder, as Lydia explained to Helen Taylor in a letter of 3 November 1867:

> It has been as much a matter of regret to us as to them [the London committee], that there should have been a divergence of opinion with regard to petitioning. We have, however, seen no reason to repent of the course we took. We should have found it hard to answer the question 'why, if you are convinced that the existing law is in your favour, did you petition for a change?' This would have been a legal and a moral issue. They [campaigners] find it hard enough 'to convince people that we <u>really believe</u> the law is in our favour'.[63]

In spite of this, the Manchester committee decided to continue petitioning until the law had been tested and policy was agreed. Lydia was keen to get Helen Taylor on board, and invited her to attend a public meeting planned for the following year, but there was no positive response. In the new year of 1868, the Manchester committee, at a well-attended meeting chaired by Jacob Bright, resolved to stop petitioning and instead to focus on increasing the membership; this would save £2–3 a week which could be re-directed. Lydia claimed to Taylor that she had taken a neutral stance, and was merely bowing to the will of the meeting. However, she admitted:

> It seems to me that when we find practical men like Mr Jacob Bright and Mr Rusden ... well acquainted with Manchester and accustomed to take a leading part in political movements, seriously of opinion that our question has advanced beyond the stage of petitioning and prepared to take their stand on the existing state of the law – this is a step forwards which causes me great satisfaction.[64]

Accordingly Lydia, attempting to exert her own and Manchester's leadership, in May 1868, began to pester the London committee, and particularly its secretary, Mentia Taylor, with the aim of ensuring their participation in the Persons campaign. She was very aware that the London group were sensitive and could be easily deterred, so to begin with she tried to influence them through the friendship of Rev. Steinthal with Mentia. She stressed to Ursula Bright that 'We must not do anything to annoy the London committee.'[65] Despite this, when she tried to put into effect her idea of concerted action, Helen Taylor wrote in June saying that it was the view of Mill and herself that this was not a good time to try to put women on the electoral registers. To which Lydia retorted in a letter to Ursula Bright 'I have not the slightest intention of allowing our course of action to be governed from London ...'[66]

As the Persons campaign got underway in Manchester, she became increasingly critical in her letters of London's slowness to act. 'It is a great pity the London committee did not spend the energy on getting women's claims that they have done in the petition.' When Mentia eventually did consent to join in with the Persons campaign in London, she wanted to send her paid canvassers to visit the overseers instead of going in person, claiming that 'a personal interview could not be arranged'. Lydia dismissed the idea as 'undignified and ridiculous' and thought they should at least *try* to arrange an interview in person. She also found fault with their relations with the Birmingham Society:

> Miss Johnson's account of the Birmingham committee ... does not quite agree with Mrs Taylor's claim to having set them to work ... Miss Johnson told me ... she would have had her committee properly organised months ago – that Mrs Taylor kept writing to her but did not tell her what to do. So the credit of having set Birmingham to work belongs to Manchester ... If they [London] will not help we must do as well as we can without them.'[67]

It may be significant that the London Society, without consultation, used the title of National Society in its own circular about participation in the Persons campaign in London in May 1868. Lydia picked up on this immediately and wrote to Mary Johnson in Birmingham. 'Mrs Taylor has done a very strange thing – no doubt inadvertently' and requesting Mary to change the title on any circulars in her possession to 'London National Society'. It may be that this was all part of an attempt by London to re-establish the capital's position, wresting the initiative from Manchester, by arrogating to themselves the title of simply National Society as the supposedly natural leaders of the movement. Lydia clearly suspected that this was the case: 'If Mrs Taylor aspires to be the leader of the movement, why doesn't she lead? Instead of lagging behind Manchester.'

She also wrote 'to remonstrate' with them about something 'very objectionable' in the circular; it recommended application to the 'Liberal registration agents'. This was in direct opposition to Becker's own avowed and lifelong policy that the suffrage movement should be above party politics; she wrote later 'Any woman is a political friend of mine who will support the cause which I hold to be the one measure most important to this world and political life of the nation.' London's recommendation made them 'guilty of a gross breach of faith'.[68]

The Kyllmann affair thus served to widen an existing breach between Becker and London. By December 1868, Taylor was telling Philippine that she and Mill had been shown 'studied discourtesy' by Manchester, not only over the requests for money but also by the insult of sending Mill a mere circular, along with 800 other parliamentary candidates, asking whether he would vote for women's suffrage and informing him that a bill was to be brought in the next parliament. She ended with a direct criticism, clearly aimed at Becker: 'There is so much that is unsatisfactory for some time past about the management of the [Manchester committee] that we feel that we had better not be concerned in it for the present.'[69] The Mills resigned their membership.

The tone of the two societies was markedly different: the London group favoured 'gradualism', whereas Manchester preferred activism and even confrontation. Manchester held large conferences, and encouraged the other provincial suffrage societies to do the same, but London preferred small drawing-room meetings. The London Society was run on a top-down model, and in contrast to Manchester, the committee and the members had no control over the executive, which Lydia disparagingly referred to as 'a self-elected irresponsible body'.[70] Mill, hugely influential in London, was mostly focused on the spread of ideas; his distinguished work *The Subjection of Women,* published in 1869, was a notable example of his approach. By contrast, although Becker produced written works, they were much more modest and she set far greater store by tangible achievements.

Mill did not consider single women suitable for prominence in the suffrage campaign and believed it was important to show that 'the championship of woman's cause is not confined to women who have no qualifications for success in the more beaten track [marriage]'.[71] He feared, with some justification, that female suffragists were regarded as unfeminine, and too many of them were 'old maids'. It was apparently at his insistence that the secretary of the London Society must be a married woman, and also that at meetings only attractive and docile-looking women should be allowed in the front row; any who appeared 'strong-minded' were obliged to sit at the rear of the hall.[72] It is certainly true that the married London secretary Mentia Taylor was no Lydia Becker; in late May 1868 the latter complained that Mentia had

> sent me a very imperfect report of the [London] conference. Instead of writing out plainly all the resolutions agreed to ... she has merely made notes on the proposals ... so I have great difficulty in finding out the drift of what was agreed to – and then, it is a question of interpretation. She really is not businesslike.[73]

As the 1868 Persons campaign developed, the support of London was only ever very half-hearted; in early June Lydia exclaimed in a letter to Ursula

Bright, 'The Bristol committee have three claims – you say that London has three – What can they have been about? I have already ninety-seven for Manchester.' When she wrote to Jessie Boucherett on 13 September she was full of righteous indignation about the incomplete and confusing information and data on the campaign furnished by Caroline Biggs from the capital:

> It is one of the more important and responsible parts of the duty of a secretary to collect and publish accurate and complete information and to send it to the secretaries of other centres for publication in their districts, and this duty seems but lamely performed in London. Perhaps you can (but not as from me!!) give a hint to that effect.[74]

London submitted relatively few claims for women ratepayers to vote and avoided holding public meetings, for fear of provoking greater opposition.[75] Lydia and the Manchester Society took the view that the best defence was more agitation: 'Our parliamentary friends must keep a sharp look out, and if a hostile move be threatened we must <u>instantly</u> have a public meeting to protest.' She made no concession to the reservations of the London group and wrote to Ursula Bright: 'The London Committee seem to think that the movement can be profited by avoiding publicity and wish to agitate in a modest and retiring manner. They will have to follow our lead on that point as they have done on everything else.' The Manchester committee's success in Salford was contrasted with the recalcitrance of London: 'They never would have done anything in the way of attacking the overseers if we had not made them …' She expressed relief that Ursula Bright, living in London with her MP husband, Jacob, was able to attend the meetings of the London committee, so that she could there represent Manchester, and pass on Lydia's attempts to instruct them how to proceed in the campaign.[76]

She justified her attitude in a letter to Mary Johnson by arguing that the London group was unrealistic: 'The fault consists in the fact that they absolutely forget, or do not know, that the majority of the people of England have yet to be led to see the propriety of giving women any rights at all.'[77] The upshot was that in the 1868 election campaign 500 candidates were lobbied by activists led from Manchester; the women's campaign there was achieving its aim of becoming a major irritant and maintaining a high profile for the Cause.

In the afterglow of the 1868 election, when so many women had claimed their votes, a great petition was proposed by Manchester in support of a Women's Electoral Disabilities Bill and the committee was eager to enlist the participation of the whole country, making it a clear policy to work with the other committees. They found London less than enthusiastic, and Lydia wrote to Jessie Boucherett, by now her source on the doings of the London committee:

> I am greatly astonished by your saying that the London Committee do not intend to petition. I repeat your query, what do they intend to do instead? It seems very unfortunate that last year, when they had the far more effective measure of agitation – in collecting a great number of claims they should have neglected that, and wasted their strength in petitioning, and now – when the petition seems the only thing, they should think of giving it up.[78]

In 1870, Manchester planned to send a deputation of ladies to see Prime Minister Gladstone, in support of the Women's Disabilities Bill before parliament. Although Mill opposed this because it might simply arouse more hostility, he conceded that the Cause had made 'immense progress' since 1867 and had become

> a serious matter ... We may count among our gains, the tone of exasperation which has succeeded to that of mockery in the Saturday Review, Pall Mall Gazette, etc., which is at once a sign that they feel us to be getting on, and a help, by the resentment which their insolence arouses in women.[79]

The Manchester Society, including Lydia Becker, and those of the London Society who were disillusioned with the softly-softly approach dictated by Mill and Helen Taylor united in November 1871 to set up a 'Central Committee' which held its first general NSWS meeting in January 1872, chaired by Jacob Bright.[80] Precipitated by the failure of the first two Women's Disabilities bills, it was ostensibly, according to Rev. Steinthal to be 'simply the instrument by which that public opinion which is created in the provinces can be brought efficiently to bear in a concentrated form upon the House of Commons'.[81] Its founders were delighted to have the support of Harriet Martineau, Mary Somerville and Florence Nightingale, but important elements in the London Society failed to back it, notably Mill and Taylor, and Millicent Garrett Fawcett. They particularly objected to the new committee's support of Josephine Butler's campaign against the Contagious Diseases Acts.[82] Its focus on matters considered unseemly for respectable women, that is the forcible testing and treatment for venereal disease of women thought to be prostitutes, was considered by them to be bringing the suffrage movement into disrepute. There were mutual criticisms between the two sides with Mill and Taylor increasingly hostile, referring to the northern 'radical' suffragists as 'the obnoxious set'. Because London failed to participate in the Central Committee until 1876/7 it lost what little command of the movement it had managed to retain.

Lydia, a member of the Central Executive Committee from the start, did not often attend the weekly meetings in London (between 3 February 1875 and 12 April 1877 there were seventy-three, of which she is recorded at five). Nevertheless, she made it her business to be present whenever there was a pressing matter which required action, and participated fully, now and then taking the chair, more often moving resolutions, joining sub-committees, and planning and attending public meetings such as the one at St George's Hall on 13 May 1876. On 27 May the same year, she made sure she was present to read out a letter from William Forsyth MP, in which he resigned from his role as proponent of the women's vote in the Commons, and to participate in the vital discussion as to his successor. In this committee she made allies and renewed friendships with Frances Power Cobbe, Caroline Biggs, Helen Blackburn and Lilias Ashworth, as well as her long-standing correspondent Jessie Boucherett.[83]

The death of Mill in 1873, though he was much mourned, was arguably by then a sideshow as the organisation had moved on without him. The Central Committee co-ordinated parliamentary activity and lobbying, helped to form provincial and local committees, was a centre for the collection and diffusion of information, raised funds, and helped to meet the costs of the *WSJ*. Its executive committee boasted several MPs and had considerable clout; its general committee included not only suffragists, but also figures from the women's education movement and the BAAS. Ultimately, there was a rapprochement with the London group, aided especially by Helen Blackburn, who became secretary of the Central Committee in 1874, and from 1876 performed the same office for a finally unified body.[84]

Chapter 4

Established Leader of the Women's Suffrage Movement, 1868–90

In the 1870s, Lydia established herself as the effective leader of the suffrage movement, despite her regional official position as the secretary of the MNSWS. In this decade she exerted the leadership of Manchester over the whole movement. By sheer force of personality and passion for 'the Cause' she attracted both admiration and opprobrium. A wide network of friendships was developed amongst feminists across the country on which Lydia relied for moral and practical support. She strongly believed that the vote was close to being achieved, a view shared by many supporters; the examples of local government and later the Isle of Man would, they felt sure, convince doubters of the wisdom of such a measure. In the wake of excitement at the admission of women to municipal politics, Lydia and her colleagues spent the 1870s bombarding politicians with letters and petitions to support the Women's Electoral Disabilities bills which were introduced every year apart from 1874. Most of the rest of her time, she travelled around the northern region giving lectures, and addressed meetings all over the country but especially in London. Emmeline Pankhurst, in her memoir, recalled that 'The movement was very much alive in the early seventies, nowhere more so than in Manchester, where it was organised by a group of extraordinary men and women.' Moreover, she described Becker in complimentary terms as 'the Susan B. Anthony of the English movement'.[1] Lydia's pre-eminence was recognised and extended in the 1880s when the London Society invited her to take on a key role in the capital as their secretary and parliamentary lobbyist, openly acknowledging that she would lend their organisation the authority to lead the movement.

Leader and friend

Martin Pugh has, however, argued that one reason the early suffrage movement did not in the end achieve more was that its leadership was lacking. Lydia Becker, whom he acknowledges as up to 1890 probably 'the most influential single individual in the movement … an indefatigable, intellectually tough but slightly academic advocate of the vote', was in his view ultimately uncharismatic. Pugh does concede, however, that she had a 'thorough grasp of parliamentary procedure, mastery of detail, and persistence in dealing with politicians', all of which made her 'formidable', but she was 'not flamboyant'.[2]

He further contends that because the movement had several significant leaders, of whom Becker was the foremost, it lacked the strength of a single, overarching figure to dominate its development. However, Philippa Levine argues that the early feminists opted for a different model of political organisation, which did not follow the pattern set by male hierarchies, using networks of support and a diffused leadership. Whilst this may be valid, the implication that as a result 'no power struggles ever disfigured the movement' is demonstrably untrue, as the conflicts already discussed show.[3] Lydia's determination, right from the beginning, to establish any national society under her own control illustrates that she fully understood the need for co-ordinated action. But there was an ongoing power struggle, between Becker and the Manchester Society on the one hand, and the London Society on the other, for dominance of the movement. And it can be strongly argued that Becker was winning that contest.[4]

However, there were clearly some features of Lydia's personality which alienated potential supporters. Those who did not know her well may have gained the impression that she was stern, unbending and overly intellectual in her leadership style. She was also passionate about her beliefs and sometimes caused offence by urging them vehemently. Her close ally Helen Blackburn noted that she could be irritable and hasty, being impatient of 'fussiness' and indifferent to petty matters. Anyone who exhibited 'deceit or underhand dealing' was not tolerated; people who were 'weak' felt overpowered by her, and the 'over-zealous' who presumably offended by acting unilaterally and without her approval were put in their place.[5] Her conflict in 1868 with the Kyllmanns illustrates her domineering approach, and it is notable that she made no concession to the fact that Philippine had been widowed shortly before this affair exploded, and was left in uncertain circumstances with two small children.[6] And Lydia certainly did not suffer fools gladly, referring to the Mayor of Manchester as a 'stupid ass' when he refused to sign a married women's property petition.[7]

It may be surmised that the root of at least some of her impatience was her own immense and self-imposed workload, which she referred to as 'the mountain'. Her letters in 1868 display a strong sense of her own inadequacy to carry out the work necessary: 'I feel as if I ought to read all the local papers in the kingdom to take advantage of what turns up, but with only one pair of eyes and hands how limited we are …'[8] Moreover, there was a consistent vein of self-doubt and vulnerability in her leadership, as is shown by her defensiveness in the Kyllmann affair the same year. Such desperate emotional reliance on people such as the Brights and Richard Pankhurst at times of conflict may have been somewhat off-putting.

Perennial concerns about finance likewise would not have helped her mood. The small sums she received from the MNSWS, such as £40 in 1868, were quite insufficient for the endeavours she undertook, and in a letter to Mary Johnson she noted that she had two canvassers working for her who were achieving about ninety claims to vote a day from the women householders they visited, but she had run out of money to fund them. Nevertheless, 'I am continuing in faith this week … I cannot find it in my heart to stop them till I have made another desperate effort.'[9] She wanted to be regarded as offering her endeavours as a 'labour of love', and wished 'very much that circumstance enabled me to dispense with the assistance and generosity afforded by the committee'.[10] She noted that she could have had a position as a teacher and earned £50 a year, but 'I could not forsake the work on which I am engaged.'[11] She struggled to afford the conferences of the BAAS and the NAPSS, which were one of her greatest pleasures in life: 'It is horrid to be stopped for want of money so perpetually. If women had a fair chance in this world, that would probably not have been my lot.'[12] Her sister, Esther, recalled her view that 'Everyone ought to have an intellectual region, independent of the troubles and trials of the daily life – a region of calm enjoyment to which he could sometimes retreat, and experience a happiness independent of outward things.'[13]

Journalism and writing helped to some extent to mitigate her lack of money. Her knowledge of German came in useful, as in April 1868 she received £2 for translating an article into English for the *Englishwoman's Review*, and in July the *Review* also paid her the same sum for her article on male and female intellect.[14] Preparing her paper for the BAAS conference at Norwich was 'desperately hard work', and to deliver it she had to find 7s 6d a night for her accommodation, which she could not afford. She therefore persuaded the editor of the *Manchester Examiner and Times* to pay her as a special correspondent for the week of the conference, and with the extra work she covered her expenses.[15] Similarly in 1884, when she went to Montreal in Canada to attend the BAAS, she was commissioned again to write reports for the paper and was thus able to finance her trip. It is perhaps revealing of the significance to her of this employment, that in the school board election of the following year she described herself in the nominations as a 'journalist'.[16]

Relatives and friends also helped. They provided accommodation during her visit to Canada, for instance, and from time to time she benefited from their legacies. By 1890, she had an income from interest on £240 bequeathed by her Aunt Charlotte Becker (often anglicised to Backhouse), and in 1887 she received the sum of £50 in the will of Elizabeth Heywood of the MNSWS.[17] In spite of this, throughout her life Lydia expressed the view that her funds were insufficient to allow her to achieve everything she would wish for the Cause.

Many of her family were not particularly supportive of her political commitments, as she mentioned in her letters to them, but it did not stop her giving them her latest political news, such was her enthusiasm. To her brother Leigh in Australia, for instance, although she stated that she did not think he would be interested in her activities, and tried to focus on events such as an attempt to assassinate the Duke of Edinburgh and the wreck of the Duncan Dunbar, in the end she could not resist a disquisition on the merits of Jacob Bright in forwarding the Married Women's Property Bill.[18] There were exceptions, however. Her younger sister, Esther, supported her campaigns, and was detailed in 1868 to save news cuttings on the women's suffrage question, as well as to sell tickets for a meeting in Bury and persuade a sympathetic bookseller to do likewise. She was clearly a close confidante. It seems that Lydia attempted to involve Esther more deeply in the women's rights movement. In 1868, she suggested forcefully, but apparently unsuccessfully, that she should apply for the vacant position of secretary to the women's higher education committee, which was paid at £40–50 a year. This would allow her to live at home, free up her time, and bring her into contact with 'many nice people'. It was Esther who copied Lydia's early letters for posterity and wrote her own memoir of her 'big sister' to go with them; much that is known of their youth was preserved thanks to her.[19] In addition, their aunt, Mrs Backhouse, who had previously been involved in organising a petition, was instructed by Lydia how to go about it again, and their relations seem to have continued to be very cordial, even though on this occasion her aunt seems to have declined. Most significantly, Lydia's relative Sarah Backhouse worked with her from 1872 and was her secretary in the Manchester office by at least 1879, proving a staunch support through thick and thin until Lydia's final journey on the continent in 1890.[20]

When she joined the embryonic feminist movement, Becker soon established within and beyond it a network of colleagues, friends and supporters. She made new contacts, such as Mary Johnson, Jessie Boucherett and Frances Power Cobbe, through her travels when attending committees and conferences and addressing meetings. And she maintained relationships by occasional visits, but more often by writing enormous numbers of letters. Her letter book of March to November 1868, with copies of well over 200 missives, provides a deep insight into her thoughts and her relationships. Many other such sources of evidence have been lost; her letters to Elizabeth Wolstenholme Elmy were, by the latter's account, very numerous, but they have mostly not survived.[21] The network grew as the campaigns progressed and provided a huge degree of mutual support between feminists who felt isolated in their unconventional beliefs. Indeed, in the leader of the first edition of the *WSJ*, Lydia explained that the *Journal*'s purpose was to reach out to 'every isolated well-wisher.'[22] This was surely drawn from her own early experiences.

Her extensive correspondence, whilst often providing solace and encouragement, also added to her burdens. She must have spent hours each day engaged in composing letters, if the 1868 letter book is anything to go by. Blackburn reported that Lydia never wrote anything in haste, but 'with great care and consideration'.[23] She kept a copy of every missive and expected others to do the same; in December 1868 she criticised

Professor Newman of the Bristol committee for failing in this regard. He protested that this would be too onerous and that he would have to employ a secretary. He also hinted that Lydia was intolerant of others, and warned her that impulsiveness and small errors must be allowed because too much supervision of a colleague 'will tend to break his or her spirit ... We are of different constitution, and cannot always agree ... I keep no copy of this letter ...' he wrote, provocatively.[24]

Many of her correspondents were far-flung, as contact was maintained with suffragist groups established all over the United Kingdom, including in Dublin, Belfast and Edinburgh. In an attempt to build bridges between the different regional branches of the movement, and to reduce her own load, Lydia tried to put other leaders in touch with each other. In 1868, for instance, she wanted a letter from Isabella Tod of Belfast to be sent to Anne Robertson of Dublin so that they could work together. Moreover, as early as November 1868 she was in transatlantic contact with Susan B. Anthony, the American suffragist, proudly expressing the opinion that 'Our cause is very popular in Manchester.'[25]

Whilst it seems that to outsiders Lydia could appear aloof, even intimidating, towards friends and colleagues she was warm and generous. Helen Blackburn, a close associate of Becker and co-worker with her in the Central Committee gave a personal and overwhelmingly positive view, reflecting how many fellow-suffragists perceived her at the time. What shone through was an all-consuming passion for her work in 'the Cause'; she had a 'wealth of sympathy with suffering and wrong' and had 'massive force of purpose'. With high expectations of herself and also of those with whom she worked, she let them get on with their allotted tasks and appreciated their achievements.[26]

Many of Lydia's colleagues in the Cause became valued friends. She often sat up late into the night, particularly when she needed to share her experiences, writing long letters to those such as Ursula and Jacob Bright, who in the early years were staunch allies on the Manchester committee. Lydia spent much time at their home in Alderley Edge – 'I always <u>rest</u> so charmingly with them.' A very happy day was passed with the Brights and George and Josephine Butler in the autumn of 1868 and her account demonstrates that she did allow herself days off from time to time:

> It was a heavenly autumn day – we had a long drive through some of the loveliest parts of Cheshire to a quaint country village – I was

seated between my two dear friends Mrs Butler and Mrs Jacob Bright. I did not care to talk. I gave myself up to dreamy happiness. It was one of those rare and precious bits of one's life, which come but seldom – and are remembered like angels' visits.[27]

As a frequent visitor to the Bright home she became intimate with the whole family and wrote to her sister, Esther, about their new baby, which she described as 'a perfect beauty. I never saw such a little darling. It looks so sweet tempered and intelligent.' She confided her innermost feelings to women friends like Ursula:

I get very weary sometimes ... the worst time for me is when I waken early in the morning – I often feel quite wretched then, but fresher after I get up and then feel quite strong. When I am anxious or perplexed, or see obstacles in our path, all my physical strength seems to collapse, but it comes again when matters brighten up. It does me good to know that you approve of what we are doing.[28]

She also had a particularly fruitful political friendship with Jacob himself, whom she hugely admired, and enjoyed hearing from him detailed accounts of debates in the Commons and snippets of Westminster gossip. On 9 September 1868, she was able to reciprocate when she reported in detail to him a discussion she had with her paid canvasser, Mr Rogers. She warned that an Irish attack on a political meeting in Manchester had led Rogers and many others to abandon their support for the Liberals, and therefore for Jacob Bright, because of the party's espousal of Gladstone's policy of disestablishing the Irish Church. There was now no sympathy for the 'Papists'. She feared that this could be disastrous to Liberal electoral prospects in the constituency in the forthcoming election.[29]

She expressed intense affection for other feminists who shared her preoccupations. In June 1868, she reported that she had spent a few days in Congleton with Elizabeth Wolstenholme and Jessie Boucherett, who she noted was 'very agreeable and amusing and I think we all three enjoyed ourselves very much. We made up our minds that there must be a grand gathering of friends when we have the annual meeting of our Society,' in which Mary Johnson of Birmingham and the Irish campaigner Anne Robertson would be included.[30] There is also evidence that she invited friends to her home: Elizabeth Wolstenholme, for instance, was asked on at least two occasions in 1868.[31]

Josephine Butler, rescuer of Liverpool prostitutes and leader of the campaign against the Contagious Diseases Acts, was a cherished correspondent whose letters were 'pearls'. When Butler sent her a bonnet and other gifts, Lydia was thrilled and responded in language which revealed a longing for love and nurturing:

> They are lovely – and seemed to bring an atmosphere of your presence and taste with them. The bonnet is not only perfect in itself, but <u>suits</u> me – you must have seen me in it! ... coming from you they are priceless! They come to me with the sacredness of a mother's gifts for it seems to me as if I might be your <u>child</u> – not in years of course – for I suppose you may be younger than me – but you are a wife and mother and have had a far wider and deeper range of experience than I, who have led a secluded and subdued life – so it seems to me always, as if I must sit at your feet like a child.

By October 1868, she was desperately eager to persuade Butler to move her efforts over to the suffrage question, perceiving that her 'weapons of womanly grace and beauty' could overcome 'the monster that blocks our path, as none other that I know of is capable of doing'. Then she turned up the heat and argued that philanthropic works such as Butler's were 'palliative' only, appealing to her to focus on the roots of the problem, political power for women, 'the better and higher way'. Bringing in the big guns for a religious woman like Josephine, she cited the case of the early Christian female martyrs, who fought against prejudice and had never been forgotten. And she did not give up – again in November she was writing equally forcefully and fulsomely that Butler should leave the philanthropy to lesser mortals and devote herself to the higher cause.

It is perhaps unsurprising that Josephine experienced serious irritations when they worked too closely together, though by late 1873 she admitted privately in a letter to her friend Miss Priestman that she had revised her thinking on the importance of the suffrage question, if not on the shortcomings of Miss Becker:

> I feel more and more anxious to get women's suffrage ... very soon. Cogitations have led me to feel and fear that we shall shortly be utterly swamped if we don't get it, and that it is a more <u>urgent</u> matter than I once thought. I should like to see it worked by some of our best people – and not left to be <u>too much represented </u>by poor dear

Miss Becker – to whom we owe a great debt of gratitude, but who has not the gift of <u>winning.</u>

But we <u>cannot</u> drop the repeal [of the Contagious Diseases Acts] work. I try now to join the two as much as possible tho' it <u>does</u> annoy some people.[32]

During the Persons campaign, Lydia was fulsome in her praise of her Birmingham friend and protégé, Mary Johnson: 'You are doing splendidly! It is most encouraging to hear of such well-directed energy – If we had <u>you</u> in every large town what a demonstration we should have!' After the defeat in the Revision Courts, she wrote 'dear girl – your bright fresh spirit is like a breath of mountain air to me …'[33] Indeed, whilst Elizabeth Wolstenholme and Josephine Butler were usually addressed as 'Dear Friend', Mary Johnson became 'My dear Mary' and they agreed never to address each other as 'the odious "Miss".' It was probably a great disappointment to her that Mary married in 1870 and resigned from the secretaryship of the Birmingham Society, being succeeded by the equally successful Eliza Sturge, with whom there seems to have been only a business relationship.[34]

By the 1880s, a close correspondence had developed with Frances Power Cobbe, a London Society suffragist of Conservative persuasions, who perceived the more humorous, affectionate and vulnerable side of Lydia, and described

> a vein of softness and gentleness in her inner nature for which, I imagine, few people give her sufficient credit. It was very commonly imagined that Miss Becker was of a combative disposition; a sort of Valkyria of the political battlefield, who enjoyed the war for its own sake. Nothing could be further from the truth.[35]

They shared a strong dislike of the Liberal leader, William Gladstone, whom Cobbe described as 'the evil genius of our sex – and of our country'. Lydia proved a discreet friend and keeper of secrets for Frances, who confided from her home in Wales that she was contemplating writing her autobiography, and signed off her letter with 'Ever yours, dear Lydia Becker'.[36]

Becker also clearly developed very friendly relations with London's Lilias Ashworth Hallett and her aunt, Edinburgh's Priscilla Bright

McLaren. The latter related an incident in their early years which demonstrated Lydia's affection and need of friends:

> She was leaving Edinburgh one afternoon when a drawing-room meeting was to be held at the house of our friend Bailie Cranston. She missed the train, and we begged her to come back to our meeting, but she said her box was packed and she had not the wherewithal to appear. I lent her a lace fichu, which she smilingly said was so becoming that she asked if she might take it home. In a few days she returned it, saying she could not keep it, but that I should find in one corner a little *forget-me-not* which she had worked upon it.[37]

And Priscilla remembered her special smile: 'She had a thoughtful face, but it lighted up with that peculiar beaming expression, which all will remember, when anything deeply interested her.'[38]

Lydia's friendships often flourished or languished depending on whether there was agreement or conflict over policy and strategy. Although in 1868 Lydia had expressed the sentiment that the best friends were old friends, many of her earlier close relationships turned sour as the franchise struggle became protracted. She and Elizabeth Wolstenholme finally fell out in 1874 over Lydia's reluctant but pragmatic acceptance that married women should be explicitly excluded from the suffrage bill presented by Conservative MP William Forsyth. This also caused trouble with Richard Pankhurst and the Jacob Brights, compounded by an argument about Elizabeth Wolstenholme's 'free love' arrangement with Ben Elmy.[39] There was discord in the 1880s over proposals to affiliate with the Liberal Party, which Becker strongly opposed. She found herself again at odds with the Brights, and Priscilla Bright McLaren wrote to Helen Priestman Bright Clark referring to 'cat and dog work' between Ursula and Lydia. Priscilla herself, who tried to act as a conciliator, expressed disquiet at the overweening influence of Becker over the London-based Central Committee in the mid-1880s. And Lydia was also in conflict on these issues with the Pankhursts; there were further splits in the movement.[40]

However, she retained the support and sympathy of many with whom she worked from other regions of the UK, some of whom were contributors to the final, memorial issue of the *WSJ* in August 1890. Notables such as Priscilla Bright McLaren (Edinburgh), Leonard Courtney (MP for

Liskeard, Cornwall), Frances Power Cobbe, Lilias Ashworth Hallett, Jessie Boucherett and Millicent Fawcett (all of London and the Central Committee) wrote about her achievements and their personal memories of her. At the same time, several of them also referred to her divisive tendencies and her impatience with those who took issue with her tactics.

The alienation from several of her closest friends of the earlier years of campaigning was a great sorrow to Lydia, and Priscilla Bright McLaren noted 'I have often been touched by the heart-sorrow of our friend when we have alluded to the friction which some of these differences of opinion and action have caused.' She sought solace with those friends remaining, and also, as Power Cobbe and Bright McLaren recalled on her death, she invested her need for affection in animal companions:

> Once Miss Becker consulted me about the purchase of a dog to be her own companion. I begged her to come and take luncheon with me in Hereford Square, so that we might go together afterwards to the Battersea Home and see if there were to be found one to please her ... When, a little later, we had chosen a pretty Black-and-tan at the Home, and were walking back through Battersea Gardens, I noticed the gentle and tender way with which – a stranger to dogs as she evidently was – she led the creature by her side, and encouraged it by her caresses to fawn on her.
>
> She said, 'I could not live without beautiful things to look upon, and something to love,' and rising from the table she fetched a little bird from the bedroom, saying, 'I must have my little loving companion near me to give it something, or its little heart will pine.'[41]

In compensation for the loss of old allies, one singularly significant relationship began to blossom. In the 1880s, there was a growing closeness between Lydia Becker and the future leader of the suffragist movement, Millicent Fawcett, who was twenty years her junior. As early as October 1885, at a time when there was trouble brewing within the movement and Lydia was experiencing opposition, they were corresponding on intimate terms. Millicent had asked Lydia how old she was, and the reply was warm:

> I thank you for your kind letter. I do not know how to express my feelings about this kindness and purpose to exert on my behalf ... I was 58 last birthday. I have the feeling that I could do ten years more good work to the franchise cause ...

By February 1887 they were exchanging gifts. Millicent had sent Lydia a box of spring flowers and a root of winter hellebore; the latter returned the compliment with some dried flowers on a card. When splits in the movement led to bitter rifts in friendships, Fawcett was always to be found in the Becker camp.[42]

Orator

In the aftermath of the Persons campaign of 1868, money was needed to keep the effort going and Lydia had in mind a grand lecture tour to publicise the case for women's suffrage and recruit members. Ursula Bright promised she would find some affluent friends who could be prevailed upon to guarantee £100 each to help finance the tour. Local committees were set up to get names on a further petition and acquire donations, and in the spring of 1869 Lydia Becker was able to undertake her first speaking tour all over the north of England.[43] This was a remarkably brave thing to do at that time. Indeed, Martin Pugh has gone so far as to designate Lydia and other women who followed the trail she thus blazed as 'militants' because they spoke to mixed audiences of women and men, something which was considered then to be verging on immoral.[44] The *Saturday Review,* an inveterate but by no means isolated opponent, in 1870 memorably dubbed such feminist campaigners with the unpleasant nickname, the 'Shrieking Sisterhood'.[45] Undaunted, Lydia's subject was 'The Claims of Women to Representation in the House of Commons', covering both electoral rights and education. She set off accompanied by the faithful Alice Wilson of the MNSWS committee.

Her venture into public speaking had in fact begun two years before; at the BAAS in 1867 she had risked a remark in a post-lecture discussion in the Natural History section. It was well received and applauded, so she recalled that she thought to herself 'if women will just quietly do what they feel they can do and make no fuss – they may do so much with approval. But self-consciousness and artificial timidity stand in the way.'[46] She had tested out her theory at the suffrage meeting in the Free Trade Hall in April 1868 when she read from a script. She faced criticism for speaking from both men and women, and even from her non-suffragist Bowdon friend, Sarah Anne Jackson. The latter was especially exercised by the participation in the meeting of married women with families;

the Mayoress of Salford, Mrs Pochin, came in for particular censure. Miss Jackson argued that such women were going against Scripture, notably the authority of St Paul. In her reply, Lydia put it that actually Mrs Pochin had obeyed her suffragist husband in speaking, and was therefore on the right side of Paul's teaching. She pointed out that in fact Scripture was contradictory on the issue, and remarked that the 'dear old Archdeacon [Sandford] ... said he would not have missed it for anything ... he expressed great delight at their oratory ...'[47] Not at all concerned by the danger to her immortal soul, therefore, but a little daunted by the exposure, a month later when she was invited to address the meeting in Birmingham, Lydia nervously accepted: 'They have just fixed the Birmingham meeting for Friday next – I am dismayed by an intimation that they can't do without me as an orator! I shall consequently be obliged to say a few words in support of one of the resolutions ...' [48]

To some degree emboldened by her success at the BAAS in Norwich, she nevertheless began with small-scale public lectures in the following spring of 1869. They were held in schoolrooms or institutes, with male suffragists to bolster support and prevent serious disturbance. At Cheetham Hill schoolroom in Manchester on 15 April 1869, a Mr Benson ridiculed her speech, but was put in his place by committee member Thomas Chorlton; at Longsight, a Mr Lakin proposed an amendment to the women's suffrage resolution that 'the extension of the suffrage to women was absolutely unnecessary, unwise and impolitic', but Councillor Robert Rumney squashed both Lakin and the amendment.[49]

As she began her 1869 northern speaking tour, Lydia worried that her voice was insufficiently strong to carry, and that she would not acquit herself well. Indeed, her nerves caused her to be at first overly serious and unsmiling. She also appeared singularly unbending because of back pain. Nevertheless, she was not short of audiences; women speakers were a great novelty, and the curious flocked to see the strange phenomenon. They were intrigued to see the hair and dress of such an 'unfeminine' woman. She wore black silk and had her hair coiled and plaited on the top of her head, scraped back most severely, the ensemble being completed by steel-rimmed spectacles. Like many other feminists, Lydia was all too aware that she would be judged, and always emphasised the importance of suitable dress and demeanour. However, even the anti-suffrage press were grudgingly admiring: 'she dresses with considerable neatness

... Evidently an educated lady, she expresses her thoughts with much correctness and thought. She has no gesticulation, however, although the expression of her features is suited to the word.' Her sincerity too made a favourable impression as 'Her large eyes increase in size as she portrays the wrongs of womankind and turns the tables upon the lords of the creation', but the same writer also felt that her voice was too weak and she relied too much on her manuscript.[50]

She made her first address in Leeds at the Mechanics Institute, where she was well received, but still self-critical in a letter to a Miss Holland:

> I am bewildered, puzzled, unnerved and dissatisfied about my lecture, and unable to see my way clearly to mend matters, while the time is very short for any improvement. I believe I should do much better speaking than reading, but have not sufficient practice to make it safe to trust to mere notes for the *piece de resistance* of the evening; my only chance is to trust to a discussion, to something being said that will give me the opportunity to reply. Learning a lecture by heart is quite out of the question. My peculiar nervous organization makes such a feat absolutely impossible.[51]

Nevertheless, with experience, over time she acquired the technique of speaking from notes and would not be deflected from her point. In 1872 she also demonstrated an ability to put down hecklers with wit: a drunken youth was effectively dealt with as a 'specimen of a class of individuals who conclusively proved their incapacity to govern women by showing their utter incapacity to govern themselves'.[52] Her speeches were sometimes very fruitful, as in Carlisle, where a new branch resulted under an energetic Miss Mary Smith, which Lydia expected would become 'an effective centre of operations for the North of England'.[53]

It took years for women to be accepted as fit to be engaging in public oratory. Some in the movement, notably J.S. Mill, had misgivings about intellectual spinsters such as Becker speaking at meetings and creating an undesirable image of suffragists.[54] But her dignity and composure, combined with a sensitivity and depth of feeling when she discussed issues of domestic violence, such as her speech in Bradford in 1881 concerning the case of a woman brutally murdered by her husband, won over many supporters. She impressed with her intellectual ability and knowledge of her subject, and her clarity and perception of the salient points were frequently praised. She thought that Josephine Butler was the model to aim for – an elegant, cultured and natural woman, who also happened to be married with children. Lydia tried to persuade her to speak more for the suffrage, pointing out: 'But if ladies – <u>real ladies</u> – of refinement, and culture, and position – will break the spell – people will soon become accustomed to the novelty [of women speaking] and tumult subside as hastily as it arose.'[55]

At the opposite end of the spectrum, another speaker whom Lydia, and others such as Priscilla McLaren in Scotland, promoted and from 1879 paid as an employee for the Cause, was Jessie Craigen.[56] A fascinating character, Jessie came from obscure, working-class origins. She spoke for the suffragists, but also for several other causes, notably in opposition to the Contagious Diseases Acts and vivisection and in favour of Irish nationalism. Indeed she was something of a loose cannon, and was prone to veer off one subject into another in the same speech, which did not endear her to her middle-class suffragist employers. Yet she knew how to work an audience, and appealed especially to working-class listeners. The American suffragist Elizabeth Cady Stanton described her as 'One of the greatest orators I have ever heard ... fearless in speaking out her convictions, and some of the passages of her speech might be justly described as "logic on fire"'.[57]

At an important Free Trade Hall meeting in 1880, Craigen inspired the audience with 'a voice that pealed like a sonorous bell over the vast multitude ... till everyone had risen from their seats in one united burst of cheering'. This was all the more remarkable because at that time female audiences tended to sit in silence and their applause was very restrained. In St George's Hall, Bradford in 1881, 3,000 women entered in a subdued manner and 'extraordinary quietness prevailed not only during the interval of waiting, but while the speeches were being delivered' and conversations were whispered 'which in the aggregate produced a curious effect, more like the rustling of leaves in a wood'. The women were unsure how to applaud; clapping was timid and spasmodic and very few cheered.[58]

Craigen was employed by Becker specifically because of her appeal to working-class women, but her image was unfortunate; she was a 'heavy, uncouth figure', unrestrained and passionate, unkempt and ill-dressed. For a time there was an attempt to spruce her up with silk dresses and lavender kid gloves, but to no avail. She took herself off, alone except for her little dog, Tiny, on tours of docks and factories and was briefly imprisoned as an activist, possibly after some disorder. Periodically, Lydia received petitions from her, which according to Helen Blackburn were 'very genuine and very dirty'. Craigen's employment by the suffragists ceased in the mid-1880s, when the movement could no longer afford to pay her, and she died in obscurity in 1899.

As time went on, Lydia developed into a renowned speaker, who led where others, often initially inexpert and over-long, followed. In addition to a punishing schedule of suffragist addresses all over the country, the MNSWS also launched an initiative for the summer months in 1872, when Lydia visited 'places of fashionable resort' such as Blackpool, Morecambe, Ambleside, Buxton, Chester, Caernarfon, Llandudno and Scarborough, to rally holidaymakers to the Cause. It was hoped that women who would be reluctant to attend in their home towns might be persuaded to do so when away from the normal restraints. She put herself in other situations where she might be expected to speak formally, particularly at the AGMs of the MNSWS. When elected to the new Manchester School Board from 1870 she spoke, not only at elections, but also at prize-givings and school inaugurations. In October 1880, her reputation as a speaker merited an invitation to address a literary subject; the Beard Memorial Union heard her on 'The Heroines of Sir Walter Scott', showing her propensity to adapt her own agenda to her listeners' interests. She extolled the many virtues of women as delineated by Scott, but in particular she focused on their strength. She put it that the quality was usually ascribed to men, but that the writer demonstrated that 'there were brave women as well as timid men'. Personally exemplifying the point that 'strength of mind and independence of character' were not exclusively male virtues, Lydia battled through the speech despite a heavy cold.[59]

She continued to address the BAAS from time to time, following up her 1868 and 1869 lectures on the human brain and the *Lychnis* plant. At Edinburgh in 1871, she spoke on women's employment, demanding equal pay, and the *Daily News* reported that 'it was the most interesting paper read anywhere today.' She was described as 'a hard hitter; but her missiles are facts; it is only occasionally that she drops, in her quiet, telling way, a sarcasm with a bitter, keen edge to it.'[60] The next year she addressed the Oxford audience on the education of girls in Manchester elementary schools. In all such cases, she was dependent for her opportunity to speak on the sympathy of male secretaries or presidents of the BAAS sections, who considered her a valuable contributor to their conferences, as her papers were consistently controversial and gave rise to much debate. In 1871 at Edinburgh, she was even asked to be patroness to the closing ball, which amused her: 'This is the first time I have ever been asked to do anything that was popular.'[61]

The family diary kept by the Beckers in 1873 gives a taste of how extensive her speaking commitments could be. She was recorded away from Manchester for about ninety days of the year; from January to June she travelled every month around the north of England and also visited Oxford and London. From 29 July to 16 August she was on a lecture tour which commenced in Blackpool. Having rested up at Alderley Edge with the Jacob Brights, she was off again on 20 to 23 August again visiting Chester and North Wales. So demanding was her schedule that she was concerned that she had not been able to replenish her wardrobe, something which was very close to her heart.[62]

The ultimate sign of women's progress as public speakers was, ironically, the all-female meeting, a symbol of the desire of women to express their views independently of men. The first such gatherings, advertised through the local press, were held for the benefit of women in Manchester who had been given the vote in municipal elections in 1869. Lydia perceived that many women needed information and advice to enable them to exercise their right, and in 1878 in St Luke's ward she began a series of talks for women.[63] The meeting brought her support, particularly from working-class women; she reported her feelings to Priscilla McLaren in 1879:

> It has been a new life to me to know and feel the strength there is in those women – when many fall away from us and leaders desert us; but in those women there is a force which, gathered together, led, organized and made manifest, is enough to lead us to victory. It has given me such a feeling of strength and happiness. I know the comfort in this hour will pass away, and the clouds gather again over my spirit; but I trust that the knowledge of what there is in these women around me, and the sense of their support in our work, will be a source of strength which will not pass away.[64]

The success of the all-women meetings for local elections inspired the Manchester Society to hold the much larger national suffragist demonstration in the Free Trade Hall in Manchester on 3 February 1880, which was most unusual in being for women, organised by women and addressed by women. Lydia was very nervous that she had taken on too much, as Helen Blackburn recorded:

> The attempt to fill that immense building by an appeal to one-half of the population, and that the stay-at-home half, was an undertaking that might well make her tremble at her own conception. So strong were her doubts that, two or three days before the event, she went to the hall to see whether, if need be, some portions might be screened off.[65]

She need not have worried. The hall was so packed that an overflow meeting had to be held in the Memorial Hall in Albert Square. In a reversal of the usual practice, men were only allowed to attend in the galleries. In the chair was the Edinburgh suffragist Priscilla McLaren, sister of Jacob Bright, supported by 'Miss Becker and a number of other Manchester ladies'. The liberal *Manchester Times* called Lydia a liberator: 'perhaps six centuries hence Miss Becker will be revered as the Moses or Simon de Montfort of her sex.'[66] There were letters of solidarity from Ireland, and a simultaneous meeting was held at Downpatrick. The resolution, carried unanimously by acclamation, was intended to build on the success of women as voters in local elections, citing their experience in support of their claim for the national franchise. A deputation was chosen to present it to Benjamin Disraeli, Lord Beaconsfield, the prime minister:

> It desired that the franchise should be extended to women before another general election, so that in consulting the judgement of the nation their opinion might be heard and have due weight in questions affecting their interest and well-being as taxpayers and subjects of the Crown.[67]

As was frequently the pattern, where Manchester led the other cities followed, and similar meetings were held in London, Bristol, Birmingham, Bradford, Glasgow and Edinburgh. On each occasion Lydia was a key organiser and a leading speaker. And everywhere she addressed full halls of thousands of women.[68]

From 1870, other women were encouraged to embark on speaking engagements, notably Alice Scatcherd from Leeds, and the redoubtable Jessie Craigen. Women began to be invited to speak at the great party conferences, such as the Leeds Liberal Conference in 1873 when Helen Bright Clark and Jane Cobden, daughters of the famous leaders of the Anti-Corn Law League, featured.[69] The progress of women orators, and of Becker in particular, was pointed up by the comments of one Councillor Eaton in the Crewe Corn Exchange in 1878. In his introduction as chairman he harked back to the first occasion when Lydia had spoken there in 1870. At that time she had described the venue as 'not the most comfortable place in creation', and this may have been due at least in part to the reception her lecture received. According to Mr Eaton, in 1870:

> Considerable amusement was created in the minds of some gentlemen who asked whether they were going to advocate sending ladies to Parliament ... the difference between the large audience now [in 1878] assembled and the small one on that occasion showed that the question had been making an advance, and that it was not now considered such a very outré thing to advocate what men called the rights of women. (applause)[70]

By 1879, Lydia Becker was fully recognised as the leader of the national movement; the *City Jackdaw* teased that she was 'a public man of whom Manchester has reason to be proud'.[71] She shared platforms with mayors, leading educationalists and MPs, which helped to raise the status of the women's movement. She spoke not only about women's rights but about wider issues, particularly temperance, co-operation, girls' education and the needs of the poor. Nevertheless, she was not always taken as seriously as she would have liked, even by supporters, as Frances Mary Sterling recalled in a letter in 1941 to Ray Strachey:

> My first suffrage meeting at St James Hall [London] was a real sight – Becker to make the chief speech (and a magnificent one too, from a voice like a peacock) boiled down and poured into tight black satin (tight to bursting point), and hair scragged off a hideous forehead and Miss Blackburn and Miss Biggs one each side of the platform (Miss Biggs in grey ringlets) holding up a long banner with a noble sentiment on it. Oh! my, oh! my! That you could have been there to

see – But it was a good and enthusiastic meeting – it must have been to have weathered such a sight! We laughed over it for years after, at home.[72]

Perhaps the frustrations and weariness of campaigning were beginning to show by the end of the 1870s. Lydia had taken on a very demanding schedule of speaking; for example, in 1879 there were women's suffrage measures in parliament and school board elections in Manchester and she faced the delivery of up to four speeches in a single evening. The young David Lloyd George, who heard her speak at Porthmadog in 1879, noted tersely that 'she was rather sarcastic'.[73]

Becker was one of those responsible for bringing women successfully into the arena of public speaking, thereby challenging the doctrine of 'separate spheres' and changing attitudes. This achievement has suffered from a lack of recognition by history because the militants of the WSPU demoted the suffragist style of oratory – organised, lengthy, reasoned and indoors – in favour of outdoor rallies and disruption. The hard-won acceptance of women as public speakers suffered a temporary setback. Like many aspects of the work done by Lydia Becker to further women's rights, her role in normalising female oratory was minimised and forgotten in the maelstrom of suffragette activism. Even so, many who heard Becker, like Emmeline Pankhurst, later in life recalled how she had influenced them. In 1925, Judge Atherley-Jones paid tribute to her influence:

> I owe the origin of my political life to a pioneer of the Woman Suffrage movement – Miss Lydia Becker, of Manchester. It was the time when the cause, under the inspiring influence of John Stuart Mill, was attracting public attention. She inspired me, though then a very young boy, with an indignant sense of the political degradation of women.[74]

Tactician

In terms of the tactics of the suffrage cause, the aim was to have a committee in every town, not just in the great metropolises.[75] Lydia used the example of her work setting up a committee in Colchester in 1867 to try to persuade Helen Taylor, who was doubtful because of the cost, of the value of such activity in challenging electoral candidates.[76] By the end of 1872, there were sixty-six societies, and the number continued to grow. Her commitment to the foundation of new committees meant personal involvement in many cases, and Joan E. Parker has documented in detail the effort put in to start a new group in Hyde, a few miles east of Manchester.[77] Twice in January 1879, Becker asked Jessie Craigen, maverick speaker of the movement, to lecture there. The following August, Lydia too spoke to an – unusually – open-air meeting of two or three thousand people in heavy rain from the back of a 'lurry'. When Hyde became a municipal corporation, she circulated the potential women voters and ran meetings, which proved overwhelmingly popular, to educate them politically. Finally, in October 1881, the Hyde Women's Suffrage Society was founded, and even then Lydia kept in close touch and attended its AGMs when possible. And Hyde was not an isolated example.

One benefit of setting up such local committees was that they would work to acquire signatures for petitions, which in themselves were perceived as 'an educational process' with 'exceptional value'. They would also put pressure on MPs and candidates in elections. Helped by the growing organisation, and the advent of the *WSJ*, the petitions burgeoned from over 60,000 signatures before 1870 to a maximum of over 430,000 in 1874.[78] However, disillusion and fatigue with this approach eventually set in, as MPs began to question whether their size was more due to the assiduity of the campaigners than to the enthusiasm of the signatories. Such views began to take their toll especially in the mid-1880s, as Caroline Biggs admitted when she wrote in 1884 for the *WSJ*, even though Lydia was determined to press on.[79]

The suffragists adopted the full panoply of traditional tactics to make their voice heard. Such means had been extremely effective in agitation to abolish slavery and repeal the Corn Laws and many middle- and upper-class women had gained a political education in such campaigns. So it was that, alongside the petitions, they took the route of public meetings, letter-writing to individuals and bodies such as local councils, drawing-room meetings, lobbying MPs and deputations to ministers. The NSWS remained a loose confederation of societies all over the UK, with periodic combined efforts to raise support, and it maintained a strong belief in the power of logic, persuasion and moral force to convince sufficient MPs and Lords to support a vote for women's suffrage in parliament.

Behind the scenes, it was often Lydia Becker herself who was driving the movement on in the direction she believed most beneficial. To take one instance, a letter of 1869 demonstrates that she worked assiduously to ensure that a deputation to ministers (on the municipal vote) was effective, even though in the press reports she did not figure prominently:

> Please multiply copies of the enclosed and send them to all the ladies who would be likely to form part of the deputation. Put especial pressure on Miss Cobbe [Frances Power Cobbe of the London Society] and Miss Sturge [Birmingham] – we <u>must</u> have them, at any price ... It is not necessary that the ladies who join this deputation should all be prepared to speak. If there are one or two speakers it will be enough. The rest support by their presence ... Please send copies of this letter to Mrs Butler, and ask her to do what she can among the London ladies. I have written to her by this post. I will write to all those whose names you gave me ... with all the urgency I can, but do you please write after as you are better acquainted with them.[80]

On a broader front, Lydia developed a knowledge and understanding of the wider political landscape, including the rules of parliamentary procedure. Leonard Courtney noted in 1890 that

> She showed all the qualities which make up a director of political movements – an idealist in her aims, a realist in her appreciation and management of means ... She had at her command the comparatively poor art of Parliamentary procedure which not a few members of Parliament never succeed in mastering.[81]

She had strong views on government and party policy. In 1868, for instance, with regard to Liberal policy as framed by Gladstone for the election campaign, she expressed doubts as to the advisability of his Irish Church disestablishment policy: 'To stake the fall of the Liberal Party on the single question of the Irish Church is like trying to make a pyramid stand on its apex.' Her view was that the campaign should be fought on general policy, and the Irish Church could have been quietly disposed of. As it was, Gladstone had aroused opposition, when he ought to 'raise the Liberal standard on measures for lightening the burdens of the people – for promoting their wealth and happiness, and the means of moral and intellectual advancement for every member of the community', within which she of course included women.[82]

In the 1870s, the dilemma for suffragists was whether to hope for a further reform bill and to piggyback it with a female suffrage amendment, as Mill had tried to do in 1867, or whether to bring in a private members' bill. Since there was no further reform bill in the offing until late in the decade, the latter course was chosen. So from 1870, the whole thrust of the suffrage campaign was targeted to persuade the legislature that they should pass a women's suffrage Act. The default reaction in parliament to any such proposal was typified in 1873: Earl Percy mocked the idea of a female prime minister 'busy with her accouchement [giving birth]'; another MP remarked he 'did not like to see women enter into competition with dancing dogs, to show their wonderful powers in doing things which it is not expected they will do'.[83]

Many suffragists, though by no means all, were Liberal in their personal inclinations. This is certainly true of Lydia Becker, until the mid-1880s at any rate. All the same, she was aware right from the start that the Liberal Party was not just going to pass an Act unless it suited it; she hoped, however, that MPs could be persuaded.[84] But, in the absence of practical support from the leadership of either political party, it was bound to be an uphill task; of 109 private members' bills in 1879, for instance, only 17 were passed.[85] When Lydia realised that the MPs of Gladstone's party could not be relied upon, she began to cultivate the Conservatives in parliament. Indeed, after the Liberals opted for Irish Home Rule as a policy in 1886 she changed her personal allegiance to the Conservatives, and was amongst those who nominated the Tory, Captain Rose, in the Lancashire County Council election of 1889, and encouraged women electors to support him.[86]

In an attempt to win over more MPs, in 1874 Becker had reluctantly agreed to William Forsyth's introduction of a bill which specifically excluded married women.[87] She was showing her pragmatism and tried to persuade campaigners that this was a first instalment only. Even so, it was a huge and permanent stumbling block for some in the movement and led to irreparable splits. Winning over MPs in any case proved very slippery. It was particularly disappointing when Sir Thomas Bazley, MP for Manchester, changed sides and joined the opposition in the summer of 1875. According to letters published by Becker in the press, he explained his defection by citing abuses against the privilege of voting in local elections by women. He referred to claims that municipal women voters had been compromised by plying them with drink before taking them to the poll. Lydia requested evidence of this, and produced her own documents to prove the contrary, but these were damaging allegations.[88]

Other MPs disappointed in other ways. Some would agree to support a suffrage bill, but, when the vote came, failed to do so. This was particularly the case once William Gladstone, the massively influential leader of the Liberals, made it eminently clear in 1870 that he was not in favour of the female franchise bill.[89] Many of the campaigners, Lydia Becker among them, blamed him for its failure. But at the heart of the matter was the development of parties, and the increasing significance of party politics. However sound the suffrage arguments were, most MPs chose to vote according to the interests, as they perceived them, of their own party and their own careers. Only slowly did it dawn on the campaigners that these matters were not incidental or easily overcome, but central to the thinking of MPs.

In 1881, in a momentous departure, Lydia was appointed as the secretary of the London and Central Committee, and moved to live for a large part of the time in London digs. Already well-versed in all the fine details of parliamentary procedure, she now began to attend the Commons regularly. By 1885 she had become the committee's parliamentary agent.[90] With her support, a group of sympathetic MPs was formed in June 1887 to discuss strategy in the House; she was not admitted to their deliberations, and Helen Blackburn recorded how she had to wait in the corridor for them to bring her their minutes.[91] Despite this humiliating circumstance, she did feel she was making headway, and by the later 1880s it was not a Commons majority which was believed to be stopping the passage of a bill, but the government's dominance of business; for them women's suffrage was far from a priority.

Lydia remained wedded to the established tactics. She failed to perceive what others began to understand: that the new rules of the parliamentary game required a different strategy. The developing significance of party politics and the crucial need to harness the support of one or other of the main parties was for Lydia trumped by her conviction that the suffrage movement should be above party. This approach was increasingly criticised. Many suffragists argued the need for affiliation with the Women's Liberal

Federation, and thereby with the Liberal Party itself. Finally, at the end of 1888 there came a split in which Lydia, alongside Millicent Fawcett, remained steadfastly non-party (the College Street group), whilst a larger group (the Parliament Street group) allied themselves with the Liberals. On top of this setback, the following year those who wanted married women specifically included in suffrage bills also broke away and formed their own Women's Franchise League. The tactics which had seemed to serve the movement so well now seemed to be outdated and limiting.[92] Despite this, no less a person than Christabel Pankhurst in her inter-war account of the suffragette movement paid tribute to the work of Becker as a strategist: 'Miss Becker's gift of strategy was remarkable, and if the woman's vote could have been peaceably gained, her statecraft would have won it.'[93]

Image: figure of fun and fashionista

Vexation was frequently occasioned by the attacks and ridicule Becker suffered in the hostile and satirical press, nevertheless, she was not daunted from continuing the fight. As Leonard Courtney MP put it in 1890, 'Miss Becker knew what it was to be laughed at, without being thereby diverted from her path.'[94] One feature of Becker's campaigning which gave rise to ridicule was an early attempt to remove gendered vocabulary. The word 'chairman' was at issue, though in fact many women chairpersons preferred the traditional male term. Lydia saw an opportunity for humour in the attempt to avoid supposedly gendered language in the word 'manifesto'. In 1882, John Slagg, MP for Manchester, spoke in a school board election and referred to an earlier such occasion when he had stood with Becker:

> We issued a manifesto – when I use the expression manifesto I must really make some little apology to Miss Becker, because in a celebrated instance, after that expression was made use of in regard to the proclamation of a lady, she insisted that a lady could not issue a 'manifesto', that it must be a 'woman festo' (Laughter), I am prepared then to say that we issued a 'manifesto' and a woman festo.[95]

It was not all good-natured joshing. Becker featured right from the start in unpleasant anti-suffrage cartoons in which she was characterised by her style of dress and her spectacles. She and her supporters were presented as strident harridans, ugly, scruffy and showing an unladylike ankle in their physical attempts to beat Jacob Bright into obedience, or to break down the door of the legislature. Non-suffragist women were shown averting their eyes in embarrassment from their antics. Bright himself did not escape; he was portrayed as a dishevelled, browbeaten and effeminate man, carrying out tasks ascribed conventionally to women, such as pushing a pram. Lydia was usually armed – with a birch for beating Jacob, or even with boxing gloves, about to punch John Bright in 1876 for his anti-suffrage speech. In one 1874 cartoon, Jacob is shown riding a donkey labelled 'Schoolmistress Backer', who wears spectacles and has a lace collar; this referred to the election, in which Bright lost his seat (which he recovered in 1876).[96] This was echoed elsewhere; there was even a racehorse at this time named 'Miss Becker'. Understandably, Lydia tried to avoid seeing such jibes, and did not thank those who thought fit to tell her about them: 'I will forgive the person who says a disagreeable thing about me, but I will not forgive the person who comes and tells it me, for that means mischief.'[97]

It was because they were so open to ridicule that Lydia, very much in tune with the educationalist Emily Davies, her early mentor, believed that it was vital that suffragist women were well presented and ladylike.[98] Philippa Levine notes that the prettiest and best-dressed women were highly valued and placed in the front row at meetings.[99] As early as 1868 when Lydia was quite seriously ill, she was very concerned that she was 'as regards clothes … running to seed in a messy manner, for want of time, money and energy!'[100] Certainly, when audiences arrived at her speaking engagements they expected to see a badly dressed, manly figure, and were pleasantly surprised at how presentable she and most of the other suffragist speakers were. It was perhaps partly for this reason that she staunchly and famously defended the use of 'stays' against the advocates of 'rational dress' at the BAAS on more than one occasion. More than this, she loved clothes and fashion, as the drawings of bonnets in her papers illustrate.[101] She was nevertheless critical of the trade in feathers at the 1876 BAAS conference:

> She would like to see ladies educated up to a truer feeling for the preservation of feathered songsters, instead of wearing humming bees and other small birds of like value in their bonnets. She would like

to see them more disposed to adopt as ornaments, ostrich feathers, or the wings of fowl or birds expressly reared for their plumage.[102]

This passion for wild feathered friends was stirred during her first BAAS conference at Norwich, when at Northropp Hall near Cromer on an organised excursion she first saw a colony of parrots living wild – 'a lovely sight' – on which Mr Charles Buxton read a paper. Lydia was so excited she wrote in detail to inform Darwin about the colony.[103]

At the Aberdeen conference of the NAPSS of 1877, Lydia joined in the discussion on workers' modes of dress, which in a rather rambling statement led her to attribute a British lack of a sense of beauty to 'coal smoke, chemical vapours, and ascetic and gloomy opinions on religious matters'. She did, however, believe that 'the love of dress in women itself was to be regarded as evidencing a sense of beauty, and should not meet with denunciation at the hands of men as it did'. She thought that if women were to act as men seemed to think they should, the men would soon be glad to have 'all the finery' back again.[104] She approved of the saying of a French man, that a well-dressed lady had a sense of inward tranquillity which religion could not bestow. The *Manchester Courier* had some fun with this: 'Who would not go some way to see Miss Lydia Becker in the costume which so interiorly delights a lady well dressed?' The paper went on to warn her to be ready to be censured by a bishop for her daring sentiment.[105]

Going against the views of other feminists, who in 1881 founded the Rational Dress Society, by the 1880s she was speaking at the BAAS as an 'out and out defender of the corsets', against criticism of the garment.[106] This caused jubilation in the fashion magazines; *The World of Fashion* complimented her on her common sense on 'this important subject'. The arguments in favour of the corset stated that it gave the female figure comfort and support: 'A woman so provided feels braced up and trim – "ready for anything" …' It went on to put it that some 'gentle compression is an advantage to the female figure'. It may be that the lifelong back pain, from which Lydia seems to have suffered, influenced her view in favour of the support afforded by stays, which were in effect a sort of exo-skeleton. In the *Sanitary Record* Becker claimed that wearing skirts required a firm waistband to which they could be attached, but she went on to admit that

> The real foundation on which all modes of women's costume must rest is neither the actual form of the body nor that of any antique statues, but rather that of the little figures in the toy Noah's ark … The creature to be dressed is in the form of a woman down to her waist, and then simply a cone. The graceful contours of body and limbs, with the ideal lines of beauty which delight the mind in contemplating the masterpieces of ancient art, are extinguished under this simple cone, and it is upon this cone that artists in dress have to mould graceful and becoming costumes.

The corset was a foundation for the dress, and it should be 'well-modelled and comfortably laced', with no attempt to reduce the waist too far. The weight of clothes should be reduced as much as possible, with fewer underskirts, and rest on the hips, rather than on the shoulders. The dress should be as short as would be consistent 'with an agreeable and presentable appearance', and women could attain this ideal 'without recourse to the revolutionary proposals which some dress reformers desire them to adopt'.[107] This was, of course, a reference to the dreaded 'rational dress' campaign, which led Helen Taylor, for example, daringly to wear trousers. However, in the *WSJ* Becker introduced a novel and more dramatic justification: 'A new benefit of corsets is shown by the incidents of a trial for attempted murder at the last Manchester assizes. The man tried to shoot his wife with a pistol. The bullet entered her back, but her corsets prevented it from entering her chest and killing her.' One manufacturer of stays in Austria was so impressed by her advocacy that he sent a pair, which were put on display at a sale of work following the AGM of the MNSWS in the following November.[108]

In 1874, Lydia found herself represented in a display of waxworks in the Manchester Free Trade Hall, alongside figures as disparate as the royal family, the Bishop of Manchester, the Emperor of Russia and Henry VIII and his wives. She may well have been content to appear in such illustrious and historically significant company, a vindication of her struggle to be taken seriously and recognised as an important figure in the public eye.[109] She continued to be long-recognised as a fashionable lady; Lydia would have been gratified to know that in a 'Pageant of Dress' in 1932 her green silk gown was included as a model of later nineteenth-century fashion.[110]

The feminism of Lydia Becker

Since feminism was not even coined as a concept until the early twentieth century, it is hardly surprising that those described by historians as feminists in the nineteenth varied hugely in their beliefs about the position of women. There was agreement amongst them that women were subject to oppression, that their condition was socially constructed and not divinely ordained, and that they were both a biological sex and a social grouping. There was, however, considerable disagreement as to the basis and nature of the oppression, and how to reform it.[111] Lydia Becker, therefore, like everyone else, had her own idiosyncratic take on the 'woman question', which had been formed initially by the experiences of her life up to the age of 40, and subsequently by the knowledge and attitudes she adopted during her campaigning career. So far as the sources show, she was not noticeably influenced by feminist reading and theories. Whilst Elizabeth Wolstenholme esteemed the notorious Mary Wollstonecraft, and Millicent Garrett Fawcett was full of admiration for the writings of J.S. Mill, Lydia's views were far more the product of empirical experience and, early on, scientific reading.[112]

Once launched on her feminist campaigning career, she gave herself to it wholeheartedly. Like Davies, she was organised and punctilious in her record keeping and used her correspondence (of which she kept copies) to drive forward the current cause.[113] Whilst she wrote occasional articles for circulation, and numerous letters to newspapers, most of her compositions were originally in the form of speeches delivered in the BAAS and the NAPSS. With the advent of the *WSJ* her writing became far more prolific, as she was not only the *Journal*'s editor but also its main contributor. Yet unlike those of Millicent Fawcett or Josephine Butler, hers were not theoretical works, but practical discourses on current grievances and developments. Becker was, in the early years, on the radical wing of agitation, believing from the start in the desirability and effectiveness of large meetings and other forms of vocal campaigning, rejected by feminists such as Davies and Cobbe as their 'good taste might be questionable'.[114] In both her speeches and her writings she shared with Cobbe and Fawcett a tendency for ridicule and irony, which was relished by supporters, but greatly annoyed detractors.[115]

Her childhood and youth, spent as they were within a loving but conventional family, gave impetus to several strands in her thinking.

She was acutely aware of the role of wives and mothers, having seen her own mother survive pregnancy after pregnancy and the death of several children, only to die at the age of 47.[116] Her view of marriage right from the start of her public career was that wives brought just as much to a marriage as husbands: their contribution was unpaid labour in keeping the household running and caring for the children. She went so far, indeed, as to suggest that their labour should be paid.[117] As a spinster, she apparently willingly went on caring for her father and brothers well into late middle age, making clothes for them even as she was running suffrage campaigns. She found marriage an attractive prospect, but only providing any prospective husband was prepared to recognise her as an equal. Arguing in favour of the vote for married women, she pointed out that it seemed highly undesirable that women should lose any possible future right to vote on their marriage. When later she supported bills before parliament which specifically excluded married women from the vote, she did so in a spirit of reluctant practicality. Like many contemporary feminists, notably her friend Frances Power Cobbe, she was not against the domestic role of women *per se*, but believed that women could perform it alongside their participation in public life.[118] Her support of the married women's property campaign was of a piece with her belief that the rights of women should be equal with those of men, even when their roles within marriage might constitute what were termed 'separate spheres'.

On the other hand, whereas many Victorian feminists accepted that there were innate differences between men and women, not only physically, but also psychologically and in terms of values, Becker was somewhat unusual in believing that male and female brains were the same, and that any differences were a product of a lack of mental and educational nurturing in women.[119] She explained to Richard Pankhurst how she thought men did not understand the feelings of women about the franchise because they mistakenly believed women were different from them: 'Women feel it as a matter of political life and death. I believe men think women do not feel at all, at least that women do not feel as men would, if they were similarly treated.'[120]

She arrived at this view through her scientific studies of plants and her reading of Darwin's *On the Origin of Species* (1859). Her view, though not necessarily its basis in scientific study, was shared by Emily Davies, and like Davies, Becker did not generally enter into any adulation of femininity or motherhood, although she made an exception for Josephine Butler, whom she regarded as a perfect model of womanhood.[121] She spelled out unequivocally in a letter that it was necessary for the women's movement to recruit women whose

> own domestic bliss is perfect ... However miserable a woman may be, if she makes that the ground of agitation for an amelioration of the condition of her sex – though she is undoubtedly right in doing so, yet it may be said that self-seeking is at the bottom of her efforts. But when women who have nothing to ask for, so far as they personally are concerned, exert themselves in the cause of their suffering sisters, the voice of reproach is silenced.

Butler was, in Becker's eyes, the ultimate model of this sort of selflessness.[122]

Like many feminists she sought the support of other women who shared her preoccupations, and having joined a ready-made network in the embryonic suffrage movement in 1867, she immediately began to build on it and added close friends and allies. Whilst contact was often established and continued by letters, she enriched relationships with personal meetings. As has been seen, early friends included Elizabeth Wolstenholme, with whom Lydia stayed in Congleton, the Jacob Brights who invited her for long periods to their home in Alderley Edge, and Mary Johnson in Birmingham with whose family she stayed for the first Birmingham suffrage meeting in 1868. Josephine Butler was adored and held up as an ideal of womanhood, but the relationship was not without friction and Butler described frustration with Becker who had 'not the gift of winning'.[123] One friendship which became lifelong was that with Frances Power Cobbe, and in later years, Lydia established a very cordial relationship with Millicent Garrett Fawcett.[124]

Becker's own lack of formal education and regret that she had no opportunity to attend university might have led to an expectation that she would join Emily Davies and others in their campaign for higher education for women. Indeed she joined the North of England Council for Promoting the Higher Education for Women, of which the much-admired Josephine Butler was president.[125] But whilst she was certainly in sympathy with the aims of the organisation, it was on the poorest girls in society that she focused her educational efforts through her participation on the Manchester School Board. For these pupils she echoed Davies in her demand that the same education be offered to girls as was then offered to boys.[126] Her work on the board was unusual amongst the leading feminists of the 1870s; although Elizabeth Garrett Anderson and Emily Davies were elected to London school boards, this was not a major element of their activity, whereas Becker was extremely committed and assiduous in her performance and extension of the role.[127]

This reflected a much stronger interest in the plight of working-class women than most other feminists exhibited. Whilst Cobbe and Butler proposed to do good to them, and Davies, conscious of her own superior status, largely ignored them, Lydia Becker made it her business to find out about their lives, talking to them about the problems of running a family without control of the finances, asking them to sign petitions for the Married Women's Property campaign or supporting the vote for ordinary women.[128] It is true that in 1868 she expressed a naive view that working-class women were like women of the upper class in that she thought they were their own agents. That delusion was soon dispelled by her experiences. On the school board she investigated the reasons why parents failed to send their children, and especially their daughters, to school, and developed a profound sympathy for their plight, when children had to mind siblings or work so that the family could eat.[129]

This awareness may have led her to support Josephine Butler in campaigns in the 1880s to prevent government legislation to 'protect' women at work, notably at the pit-head; such laws had rather the effect of keeping women out of better-paid employment, to the benefit of men. Lydia even concerned herself with the issues surrounding domestic service, the largest employer of working-class women. She opposed the increasingly domestic curriculum offered to girls in board schools, designed as they were to prepare pupils for life as a servant. In so far as she might accept an element of domestic education, she put it that it should apply equally to boys, who should learn to 'darn their own socks and cook their own chops'. Mostly, though, she contended that the education offered to all children should be academic and relevant to an understanding of the world, and in particular of science. In this way, humanity would progress more quickly with the benefit of input from all, rather than from just the privileged male half who gained an academic training.[130]

In the eyes of society, at the bottom of the social heap was the prostitute. Lydia was in sympathy with the agitation led by her friend Josephine Butler to gain the repeal of the Contagious Diseases Acts of the 1860s, which allowed the police to subject women suspected of prostitution to an examination for sexually transmitted diseases: if found to be infected, they were put in a 'lock-hospital' to be treated. She became treasurer of the Ladies National Association, set up to agitate in favour of repeal. However, Becker was cognisant of the fact that many regarded this whole area as unsuitable for the involvement of respectable women, and due to this and friction with Josephine Butler she ceased to be active in the campaign by the mid-1870s. So toxic was the connection that this was the only really significant feminist campaign which was not openly aired in the *WSJ*.[131]

Later, in the 1880s, when many feminists like Millicent Garrett Fawcett became deeply committed to purity campaigns and the Vigilance Association, which challenged the sexual double standard whereby it was accepted that men would be sexually promiscuous but women must be 'pure', Lydia was not a party to that agitation.[132] Indeed she does not appear to have made much in general of the view of other feminists like Josephine Butler that women are naturally more moral and religious than men, and that therefore they should be given political power to change the world by moral regeneration.[133] The whole tenor of her belief was that a far more important reason was that they were equal in intellect to men, and also needed to defend themselves against a system which oppressed them through laws made by men, elected by men.

Yet she did not reject men, indeed she enjoyed their company and throughout her public life stoutly argued that they were needed in the women's movement. Like Emily Davies, her early mentor, Becker opined that men and women should be friends and colleagues, meeting as equals.[134] J.S. Mill believed that ideally only men should campaign for a women's vote; Josephine Butler wanted only women to do so.[135] Lydia was happy to take men's advice, be defended by them at meetings, and in the same way that she adored the charismatic Josephine Butler as a model of beauty and womanhood, she also set Richard Pankhurst and Jacob Bright on a pedestal as exemplars of men who possessed fine feelings, and even had a 'feminine' side. Her ideal committee for any organisation, be it a trade union for seamstresses or a school trust, was one which included a balance of both men and women.[136] And of course, for any reform to occur, the support of men in parliament was vital.

Many feminists pinned their hopes on the Liberal Party as the bastion of individual freedom; that surely was to be extended to women.[137] Lydia was more cynical – although inclined to that persuasion, she voiced a belief that the Liberals would not pass reforms benefiting women unless they benefited the party too.[138] Yet she hoped they might be persuaded by reasoned argument to see that a women's vote was not only right, but also expedient. Eventually, she perceived that this might not be feasible, and indeed it has been pointed out by Barbara Caine that Liberal values took no account of the needs or wishes of women. Further, Laura Mayhall has argued that the whole Liberal concept of citizenship was defined as male.[139] Her move in the end to the Conservatives, which must have been much to the delight of Conservative evangelist Frances Power Cobbe, was born of disillusion, and an apparently sudden onset of belief in empire, perhaps as the purveyor of British values which, whilst wanting, were at least less oppressive to women than customs in the subject nations, such as suttee, which were regarded with horror by English feminists.[140]

But it was the men who ruled the empire, who made the laws, who sat in parliament, who held the key to changing the position of women. So, along with J.S. Mill and later Millicent Fawcett, Lydia believed that the only way to achieve the changes which women required was to gain a foothold in the electoral system, in the form of votes for women in national elections.[141] For her, unlike Elizabeth Wolstenholme Elmy or Josephine Butler, both of whom she tried to persuade to abandon their own campaigns in favour of the suffrage cause, the key to everything was the vote. However, whereas for most suffragists the right to vote was a matter of legal equality based on property, Becker's view was much more radical than that. She secretly harboured an unusual opinion that a vote was a natural right for everyone who was living in the state and accordingly as early as 1868 privately expressed her support for universal suffrage. Even more radically, her concept was so broad as to even include children's votes.[142]

In the later 1880s, Becker's brand of feminism was less and less comfortable with what had become a new radicalism in the movement; the incrementalism and non-party approach she had adopted was increasingly challenged and undermined. It has been noted how Davies and Cobbe both withdrew from feminist campaigning when it moved away from its early roots; there is every sign that Lydia Becker, had she lived into the 1890s and even more so into the twentieth century, would have reacted in a similar way.[143] Certainly she was vehemently opposed to new ideas such as 'rational dress', although the 'new woman' ethos of the twentieth century would have appealed in other ways, particularly in attitudes to work and education. Her lack of interest in 'purity' suggests that she may have been less outraged than some by the new sexual attitudes which attended the concept in its more radical forms.[144]

In the 1880s she decisively rejected the rising cry for affiliation to a political party, usually the Liberals, and although she desired to win the vote for married women she had become convinced that this could not yet be achieved, but that it might be possible for single women.[145] The fact that at the BAAS she spoke out against socialism, would indicate that she would have been even less open to the idea of affiliation with a socialist Labour Party, which was adopted by the NUWSS in 1912.[146] Indeed, there is strong evidence that Millicent Fawcett, as president of the NUWSS, only accepted it because Labour was the only party formally to espouse the women's vote; it was younger women in the organisation, notably Catherine Marshall and Kathleen Courtney, who had pushed forward this agenda. For Lydia, making common cause with those agitating for universal suffrage, although she would have been in sympathy with it as with the married women's vote, would probably have been rejected on the grounds that it was too radical a move to be achieved all at once. It is perhaps true to say that Lydia Becker was always a radical in ambition, but became a constitutionalist and moderate in strategy. As it was, her death in 1890 allowed her effectively to leave the stage when she still had much of her influence in the movement, and saved her from even worse heartache than she experienced in her last few years.

It has been argued by Pugh, with some justification, that as a leader Lydia Becker had by the end of her life become a divisive figure.[147] However, there can be no doubt that, once she had found what she considered a real purpose, she was the most dedicated of suffragist leaders. She suffered from bouts of illness which appear to have been brought on by exhaustion, but there was little let-up and as soon as possible she was back on the campaign trail. She was perhaps not the most attractive of companions for those who were less than obsessed with the justice of the Cause, or who diverged from her in their opinion as to how it should be pursued. Although she did not come across in her public persona as a woman who could laugh at herself or who engaged in light-hearted pursuits, in fact she did both, and forged many loyal and lasting relationships across the country. The most telling point about the period of her leadership is that, whereas in 1867 the issue of women's suffrage was a matter for ribald jokes in parliament, by the end of the 1880s it was being seriously discussed as a matter proper for the attention of the greatest body in the land. She and her fellow-workers in the suffrage movement had prepared the ground for the leaders of the future, notably Millicent Fawcett and Emmeline Pankhurst, to build on the foundations they had laid.

Chapter 5

The *Women's Suffrage Journal*, 1870–90

A key aspect of Becker's leadership of the movement was the distinction she acquired through the unifying influence of the *WSJ*. The women's movement at the start of 1870 was still very fragmented, and the only journal which reflected its activities, usually in a non-political manner, was Jessie Boucherett's *Englishwoman's Review*, produced in London. Although grateful for the exposure which the *Review* afforded to the suffrage movement, Lydia was also aware of its limitations. She expressed concern in July 1868 that it had misrepresented the Birmingham suffrage meeting of the preceding month, and that it was financed at a loss by the wealthy Jessie Boucherett: 'The *Review* might be very useful to us, as our organ, but it cannot be properly effective till it becomes self-supporting.'[1]

It may be that she was also motivated to inaugurate her own publication by her dissatisfaction with the established press, about which she complained in her letters. Her only recourse in the early days had been to try to ensure they included notices about suffrage events; when Florence Nightingale declared her support, Lydia sent the news around the Manchester and Leeds papers 'and it will soon be all over the country and will do us a world of good'.[2] This was immensely time consuming; on 1 June, for instance, she noted that 'I have been very busy all day writing to the papers.'[3] The results were not always satisfactory; the Birmingham meeting of early May 1868 is a case in point. To begin with, her father informed her that the Manchester *City News* referred to Lydia as 'Miss Becker of Birmingham'. Then she noted that 'the Birmingham reporter made nonsense of many of the speeches.'[4] During the Persons campaign she was again annoyed to see that the *Pall Mall Gazette* muddled up Salford and Manchester.[5] Even her own work was not handled satisfactorily; she was exercised to find that the Manchester journal *Free Lance* had published a paper she had submitted without either sending her the proofs for checking or telling her that the article would be included. She had had no opportunity to correct mistakes and was mortified that the paper appeared in a state which she found unacceptable, so she vowed she would send them no further work unless they could communicate in a satisfactory manner with her.[6] She must have felt that she could do better herself.

The plan for an organ for the suffrage movement had apparently been discussed for a while by Misses Becker and Boucherett. Indeed, as early as August 1868, Lydia had it in mind, but she dismissed the idea at this point because it would be too hard to enlist sufficient subscribers and too costly to rent rooms in a central location for it. She wrote to Susan B. Anthony in October: 'We have no special organ – but the ordinary London and other journals discuss our question so freely that we hardly need one.' The idea was not abandoned, however, and in November she had clearly floated the idea amongst possible subscribers:

> I could not get many subscriptions to such a magazine – half a crown would be the extent. If the number fixed on by the Publisher is not hopelessly large, the best plan would be to have a prospectus printed stating the plan and giving all particulars – and if that were extensively circulated, it might procure the number needed. I should think Miss Robertson [of the Dublin Society] might be engaged to write a story for it.[7]

She consulted sympathetic Manchester men with experience in the field, such as Henry Dunckley, editor of the *Manchester Examiner and Times*, and journalist Alexander Ireland. Her aspiration to make the journal a completely female enterprise, like Emily Faithfull's Victoria Press and the *Englishwoman's Review*, attests to her awareness of the work of other feminists and her desire to emulate them.[8]

Spurred by the advent of the first Women's Disabilities Bill, and despite her own difficulties of time, money and effort, Lydia finally resolved to establish a monthly journal with the aim of keeping activists across the whole country in touch, particularly with the campaigns of the radical Manchester Society. Not that she found writing easy: 'When I have written anything I feel disgusted with it, and think it silly ... and try to forget that I have perpetrated it ...'[9] This was especially the case when it came to papers for presentation and publication. In 1868 she poured out her troubles to Mary Johnson:

> Writing is a slow and painful process to me – thoughts form themselves in my mind, and trickle out slowly, then the right word does not always come when it is wanted, then when the idea is formed expression has to be selected, and the sentences placed in order so as to present the thought with the greatest clearness and grace until this comes out as I feel that it <u>ought</u> to come out, I am never satisfied, and I have sometimes spent hours over a single paragraph.

But she took comfort in the thought that she was not alone in this, as she had heard that it was the same with 'the greatest minds', including that of Mr Mill.[10]

As editor of the new journal, then called the *Journal of the MNSWS*, she wrote in its first edition in March 1870 that its purpose was 'to extend to every isolated well-wisher the firm grasp of an outstretched hand'.[11] It must be said that, as both editor and main contributor, the *Journal* was also the vehicle for Lydia's own preoccupations and her personal version of feminism. It was radical and wide ranging, and its most significant achievement was to unite what was, effectively, a federation of women's societies across the whole of Britain, informing women everywhere of what was being attempted and gained for women. Her correspondents included those who felt alone in their sympathies for women's rights; she hoped to bolster their resolve and also to help them find like-minded companions. Certainly, the young Emmeline Goulden (later Pankhurst) remembered reading the *WSJ* at home even before she attended her first suffrage meeting and heard Becker speak.[12] The *Journal* also served to forge strong links between the societies which sprang up in the different regions of the country, to facilitate understanding between them and to effect concerted action.

Becker fully recognised that publicity for the Cause was another crucial part of the publication's purpose. As early as 1868, during the Persons campaign she wrote to Jessie Boucherett that it was vital to inform the public that women had the right to vote under the Second Reform Act, as 'publicity is our greatest safeguard'. She reinforced this on 1 April with criticism of her friend's account, in the *Englishwoman's Review*, of the Reform Union conference at which Alice Wilson had been bold enough to speak up for the women's vote. Attributing the mistake to a 'slip of the pen' she pointedly objected that

> You say the <u>majority</u> of the audience cheered enthusiastically ... Now the fact was that the meeting was completely unanimous in the most enthusiastic expression of approbation – and not content with the ordinary cheering, at the end of the [speech?] every man in room [sic] was on his feet in response ...[13]

To Mary Johnson in Birmingham she explained

> The more communications you can get into papers the better – our great bid now is to make the public mind thoroughly familiar with the conception of women voters – it is like a young horse which 'shies' at a novel sight, but when it is coaxed to <u>look</u> at the 'hobgoblin' – it finds it to be altogether harmless.[14]

It was Lydia Becker's stamp which was the unifying factor in the enterprise of the *WSJ*; as Blackburn put it, it was carried on by her 'with loving care and strenuous exactness during the rest of her life'. She described it as 'like a child' to her.[15] It was guarded jealously from any interference and Lydia was keen to maintain a hard-earned reputation for excellent journalism. Reviews praised the *Journal* as 'well-written and conducted with great spirit and enterprise' and 'a clever advocate of the movement reflecting much credit on the editorship'. When Lydia died, her supporters decided to cease publication, ostensibly because they wanted it to be wholly her achievement, but probably also because no one felt able to continue the massive effort and expense she had put into each edition.

Income, costs and production

At 1*d* per copy, or an annual subscription of 1*s* 6*d*, the *WSJ* was good value for money. The *Englishwoman's Review* was kept afloat by the private wealth of Jessie Boucherett, but Lydia had no such luxury. The new publication had to become self-supporting, though this was not entirely the case until November 1877; by then it was doing so well from subscriptions and advertising that in 1878 a separate bank account was opened for it.[16] A wide subscription was essential, especially as every member of both Houses of Parliament received his complimentary copy, and it had always been considered worthwhile to send one to the editor of every UK newspaper because many of them published extracts from the

Journal and thereby gave it added circulation. In 1877–8 it was decided also to provide free copies to libraries, literary institutions, mechanics institutes, political and other clubs, co-operatives, debating societies and reading and newsrooms.

The *Journal* was expensive to produce. As early as December 1869, in an attempt to address this, a meeting in the Manchester Memorial Hall, at which Rev. Steinthal and Richard Pankhurst were present, discussed one possibility of forming a limited liability company of female workers on co-operative lines. Then there was debate about the price of labour between the suffragists and the male printers' union, fearful of a reduction in wages, which the latter eventually won.[17] A printer's estimate quoted £17 5s for 5,000 copies and £2 3s for each additional thousand. It required a high circulation just to break even, and to maximise its popularity Lydia, not only its editor but also its business manager, ensured that she got her money's worth. The resulting publication was very professional in appearance and demonstrated great attention to detail and accuracy.

In September 1870, it was re-named the *Women's Suffrage Journal*, symbolising the fact that it was not just a Manchester organ, but national in its content and its readership, far outstripping the circulation of the *Englishwoman's Review*. Commercial advertising began to be solicited, and the first was a whole-page spread for a labour-saving device for the housewife, the Willcox and Gibbs sewing machine.

The *WSJ* varied in number of pages, reaching a hefty twenty-nine in July 1877. Fifteen thousand copies were produced and to offset the costs there was a greater number of small advertisements thought to be of interest to women readers, such as Reckitt's Paris Blue (for washing), Benger's Food (for babies) and Fenning's Children's Powders. ('Do not let your child die!') By the late 1880s, more labour-saving devices were included, notably Bradford's Vowel A1 washing machine and mangle – 'My wife would not part with the Vowel A1 on any account, as she can do the whole of the washing for seven of us in about three hours, without trouble, and without wearing the clothes.' Lydia was also exercised in thinking up new gimmicks to attract and keep readers; in 1880, a monthly calendar was introduced, listing events important to women, such as the term dates of the all-female Girton College at Cambridge and the anniversary of the founding of the women-only Victoria Press. There were also competitions with a 5-shilling prize and publication in the *Journal*, such as the one for the best anagram from the sentence 'The nineteenth-century ladies who do not want to vote.' This was won by Helen Blackburn, Lydia's colleague on the Central Committee, with 'Denote when counted a very thin total, then 'tis too new.' Another offering came from Barbara Bodichon with an even more arcane 'The worthy inane noodles that veto it we needn't count.'[18]

Although the annual reports of the MNSWS recorded excellent progress in the circulation of the *WSJ* in the 1870s, after 1878 there were no further references in the subsequent reports, and when it was next mentioned in 1889 it is clear that the society no longer owned the organ. The *Journal*'s funds had been separated from those of the committee, and it was explained that 'The pecuniary responsibility for the production of the *Journal* now rests solely with the proprietors, your Committee being merely purchasers of the number of copies required by them for sale and circulation.'[19]

In the report of 1890, following the death of Lydia Becker, it is stated that in fact she had been its proprietor 'for some time'.[20] It seems possible that the *Journal* had been struggling after 1884, much like the rest of the activities of the society, and that Lydia had taken it on to save it from being closed down by the committee. The final, commemorative issue of August 1890 was produced by Helen Blackburn with finance from the ever generous Jessie Boucherett.

Contributors

Lydia Becker was not only the *Journal*'s business manager and editor, but also its main contributor. In particular she wrote the leaders, which were models of plain speaking and common sense, but also reflected her own views on events. As Marion Holmes recorded, they demonstrated her political acumen and 'a knowledge of Parliamentary procedure rare even amongst old Parliamentarians'.[21] In addition, she made the extensive selection of articles from other publications and re-wrote some in her own words with a detailed commentary. On top of this, she collated all the statistics and lists of meetings, speakers and societies on a monthly basis, and included detailed reports of some of the lectures delivered.

Others who provided occasional material were trusted allies, notably Helen Blackburn, and perhaps most importantly Caroline Biggs, editor of the *Englishwoman's Review*. These two women were entrusted with the production of the *Journal* in September and October 1884 when Lydia travelled to Canada to attend the conference of the BAAS. It must have been a hard decision for her to relinquish control this way, but she had clearly decided that it was well worthwhile. She was compensated to some degree by the opportunity to visit relatives there, but more significantly, she had been commissioned to send back articles to the *Manchester Examiner and Times*, at a time when it was reported in the *WSJ* that the Canadian prime minister, Sir John Macdonald, had introduced provisions for women's suffrage in an electoral bill before Canada's parliament. Eleven ladies from the BAAS signed an address of thanks to him, amongst them Lydia Becker. Moreover, Lydia's international profile was enhanced when she provided an interview, then a novel form of newspaper reporting, to the *Montreal Star*, which was reported verbatim in the *Journal*.[22]

What she actually made of the work of Biggs and Blackburn is not known, but the editorial produced by Caroline Biggs for September was notably pessimistic when compared to Lydia's own unflagging optimism in all her public pronouncements about the women's cause. The article began by referring to the recent parliamentary session as the 'Session of failures' and went on to declare that it had been 'barren ... in which the interest has centred chiefly round one point, and that point has not been achieved'. This point of course was the women's vote – not only in the Third Reform Act, but also in the London Government Bill. She continued with further downbeat comments about the lack of meetings in the past month: 'It will be almost a relief to our readers, for whom such numerous meetings have been chronicled through the past winter and summer, that during the month which has just gone by no meetings have been held.' She appeared again to have a greater comprehension of the wearisome nature of the relentless pursuit of the suffrage for the average member of the rank and file than the single-minded Lydia, when she admitted that petitioning was discouraging when it seemed to have no impact:

> It is at all times a toilsome proceeding, and when undertaken year after year with the knowledge that each time Parliament has rejected the prayer, and that Sisyphus-like we must begin to roll up our stone from the bottom of the hill again, we are not surprised that many have discontinued petitioning from discouragement.[23]

Although there was room for some encouragement, and developments were noted in France with regard to equality in the divorce laws, and Norway where higher education and professional opportunities had been opened up to women, it must have been a relief to readers when Lydia resumed the reins and the overall tone was notably more uplifting.[24]

Topics

The *WSJ* was 'an unbroken record of every step of the [suffrage] movement for the twenty years during which it was carried on'.[25] As well as the leading articles, it conveyed information on proposed meetings all over the country, issued instructions as to how to complete petition forms, and advised on committee procedure. It reported the complete text of suffrage bills, and in a forthright manner recounted parliamentary debates and division lists, so that a reader would know how the local MP voted. In July 1870, for example, the *Journal* reported in full the debate on the Women's Disabilities Bill, and Lydia wrote her own reply to the 'anti' who cited Don Quixote's Dulcinea as a model of womanhood.[26] The letters to and from MPs were printed so that their views could be transparent. Suffrage societies sent in reports of their meetings for publication, and there was coverage of the AGMs of all the key societies and the Central Committee itself. Books and articles were reviewed and offered for sale. A large number of relevant extracts from the national and international press were included. Like any self-respecting organ, it also boasted a letters section and obituaries, and even occasional poetic works like the pastiche on Shakespeare's *Hamlet* from the *Boston Women's Journal*, 'A Man's Soliloquy on Voting', which commenced 'To vote or not to vote, that is the question ...'[27]

The *WSJ* reported not only on the suffrage campaign, but on many subjects relating to women, notably women's property rights and women's work. There were articles dealing with the workings of the Married Women's Property Acts, such as 'Can a Wife prosecute her Husband under the Married Women's Property Act?' and related issues like the law on intestacy as it affected women. On occasion there were requests for help with publicising other campaigns, and despite the rift in their friendship in 1874, nine years later Elizabeth Wolstenholme Elmy was writing to Becker asking her to promote the arguments for the right of women to have custody and guardianship of their children.[28] Discrimination in employment was addressed with comparisons of wages paid to men and women. When the government proposed to cut the working hours of women from ten to nine hours a day, Lydia, through the *Journal*, opposed this, fearing the amount of work would not be cut accordingly:

> In these things it is the pace that kills ... Mr Mundella's Bill allows one hour for dinner, and it is intended that no other meal shall be taken during the nine hours' working day. A Scotch working man gets two meals and two hours of time out of his work hours. An Englishwoman, even if she is a nursing mother, is to have only one meal and one hour of rest during the whole of her outdoor working day.

She pointed out that whereas a man could come home from work and relax, it was otherwise for his wife:

> It may be fairly said that she is working in some way or other from rising in the morning until going to rest at night ... and men are asking Parliament to limit the hours of women's remunerative labour in order that they may have more time, not for 'play', but for domestic work.[29]

In December 1870, the *Journal* drew attention to the plight of women farmers who were denied membership of the Royal Agricultural Society and therefore missed out on its benefits. Even the woman who won a competition for the best-managed farm was barred. Then in 1872, it reported the controversy over women employed in the civil service, when the Postmaster General permitted women to be clerks in the Post Office Savings Bank and there was a public outcry. The *Journal* also noted the Didot firm in France, which trained women printers, and there were numerous accounts of women demonstrating unusual skill or courage.[30]

Other issues which affected ordinary women were addressed, dealing with cases of domestic abuse, hardship and starvation. So great were the crimes against women that there were monthly reports from 1878 on 'Wife Torture', an area which was especially the concern of Lydia's friend Frances Power Cobbe, who had written a monograph that year under the same title.[31] 'A Wife Chained to the Floor' and 'A Wife Burned to Death' featured in 1878. Not to mention the description of a wife sale in Rawtenstall, Lancashire.[32] The activities of the Vigilance Association received similar attention in the 1870s.[33] There was even support for the Mourning Reform Association, calling for less extravagant mourning clothes and a shorter period than was then customarily expected.[34]

On the other hand, one campaign which did not receive the coverage which might have been expected was that against the Contagious Diseases Acts. Whilst an original member of the Ladies National Association committee as its treasurer, Lydia was probably wary of the damage to the suffrage cause which could be perpetrated by this agitation. It was a topic widely considered unsuitable for the consideration of respectable women. Accordingly, references in the *Journal* were oblique; in 1871 she mentioned 'recent oppressive legislation' and when the Acts were repealed she noted 'It is beyond the province of this *Journal* to enter into any details respecting legislation on this painful subject.'[35]

The *Journal*'s subject matter was not confined to Britain. It included extracts from other newspapers on events concerning women all over the world, such as the USA, India, Burma, Afghanistan, New Zealand, South Africa, Canada, France, Germany, Russia and Italy. Lydia referred in her letters to newscuttings which had been sent to her, and it seems that many of them ended up as extracts in the *Journal*. Some were on the achievements of individual women, such as 'Native Lady Lawyers and Doctors in India', but others related specifically to women's suffrage, like 'Practical Results of Women's Suffrage in Wyoming'.[36] Then there was the speech which Mary Carpenter sent for inclusion by the anti-slavery campaigner, Frederick Douglass, who had 'lately married ... a white lady who is also an earnest advocate of Women's Suffrage'.[37] On occasion there were notices of international events, such as the *Congrès International du Droit des Femmes* in Paris of July 1878.[38] Moreover, the *Journal* was distributed abroad, particularly to North America where Lydia had prominent contacts such as Susan B. Anthony and Elizabeth Cady Stanton.

Not everyone appreciated its virtues. Joseph Chamberlain, Liberal MP for Birmingham, noted of his free copy that it was 'a truly awful periodical ... It was full of scathing denunciation of his sex, and he never rose from its perusal without a most depressing sense of inferiority.'[39] There were also jibes in other organs of the press; in 1878 it was referred to as 'that Manchester organ of the stronger-minded members of the weaker-bodied sex'.[40]

Cessation

In the second half of the 1880s, alongside the general decline in support for the suffrage movement, the *Journal* was reduced in size to its original eight pages. Financing the publication and monthly deadlines had always put huge pressure on Lydia, and the burden that she took on in the *WSJ* was so great that on her death there was no one willing to grasp the baton and carry on the publication. It was acknowledged that 'The work of conducting it is one demanding a rare union of ability with devotion and self-sacrifice ...'[41] Readers were referred henceforth by the Central Committee of the NSWS to the *Englishwoman's Review,* in which its proprietor undertook to include a section on the suffrage. The black-bordered final edition of the *WSJ*, of August 1890, was produced by Becker's colleagues from material she had already prepared, with the addition of tributes from colleagues, family and friends. The staff of the *Journal* sent this message to its readers:

> For twenty years and four months this Journal has received the impress of one hand and one mind, so that its long row of volumes form one continuous work, and now when that careful hand is laid low and the energies of that far-seeing mind are carried beyond our mortal ken, it would seem fitting to close these pages where Miss Becker left them, that so the Journal shall be wholly hers, nor suffer by any change to any less experienced hand or any mind less comprehensive.[42]

Whatever the virtues and failings of the *WSJ*, it had played a central role in drawing together the disparate feminist groups around Britain. Its cessation left a vacuum which would not be filled until the advent of the suffragette organ, *Votes for Women* in 1907.

Chapter 6

The Women's Movement: A Multiplicity

Whilst by the end of the nineteenth century attention in the women's movement was focused on the right to vote in national elections, in the 1860s and 1870s it had many strands, including married women's rights, education for women, employment opportunities, trade union membership, repeal of the Contagious Diseases Acts, and even birth control; the suffrage was just one amongst many. The average number of campaigns undertaken by a woman campaigner in this period has been calculated at 2.5. As other areas progressed and much was achieved to alleviate social and economic grievances, the suffrage gained in prominence.[1] Although she was committed from the start to women's suffrage, Lydia was also very active in the campaigns for the rights of married women and working women. This evolved into support for the Vigilance Association in defence of civil rights particularly as they applied to women, although when the association was re-founded in 1885 as a vehicle for the 'purity' campaign, Lydia did not continue her association.

The Married Women's Property Acts

In the mid-century, the Common Law considered a husband to be his wife's legal representative, and also her moral guardian. His sanctions were legally limited from the seventeenth century to admonition and confinement, but it was traditionally believed that it was acceptable to beat a wife as long as the stick used was no thicker than his thumb. The law also assumed a husband would provide for his family, but there was no legal way this could be enforced.[2]

Many women were increasingly aware of their predicament, by which they lost all independence and individuality on marriage, under the Common Law. Those with wealth were sometimes protected from the worst effects of this 'coverture' by using the Law of Equity to draw up a deed of trusteeship.[3] This secured money and property for the sole use of the wife, but it was still usually controlled by male trustees, and only a small proportion of married women were thus protected. Women with no money did not have this option available to them, and indeed there were many middle-class women who were unprotected by any pre-nuptial settlement. For such women, a husband's control of their money and property, whether inherited or earned, meant the man could use it as he liked, and could even abandon his wife taking all her money with him. This was doubly disastrous because of the inability of most middle-class women to earn their own living, due to a lack of education and training.

Because the right to vote was based on property ownership, this also meant that suffragist campaigns to gain the vote for women on the same terms as it was held by men in effect would leave married women unenfranchised. Suffrage campaigners were well aware of this, and many of them were highly sympathetic to the agitation led by Elizabeth Wolstenholme to persuade parliament to pass a married women's property act to give women control and ownership of their own money. Even were this to be achieved, other aspects of the law of coverture would still stand and could prevent married women from having the same rights as their husbands, including that of voting.

It was not only women who were unhappy about the laws governing married women and their property; lawyers in the Law Amendment Society and the NAPSS were also perturbed about the confusion of an outmoded legal system, and regarded the married women's property laws as in need of reform as part of a wider policy.[4] A commission on the law reported in 1869 and began a thoroughgoing rationalisation of the legal system. There was sympathy for the plight of married women whose husbands misused their power over them, though there was less concern about married women in relationships which were not considered abusive.

A women's campaign to reform the laws on married women's property had been founded by Barbara Leigh Smith (later Bodichon) when she set up a committee to collect evidence of the sufferings caused by the current law, and to present the arguments for reform.[5] In the time-honoured way, a petition with 26,000 signatures was gathered to submit to parliament on 14 March 1856. This was followed up by a public meeting in London, sponsored by the Law Amendment Society.

In the 1857 Matrimonial Causes Act, matrimonial matters were transferred from the ecclesiastical to the secular courts, which brought the option of divorce into the reach of the middle classes, though on terms which discriminated against women. Whereas a man had only to prove infidelity, a woman had to prove cruelty or some other 'aggravated enormity' as well; this was, and is, notoriously difficult to achieve.[6] The Act also provided that a divorced or separated woman had the same rights to property gained after the event as a single woman, and protected the property of deserted wives from their husbands. A divorced woman's rights over her children were now to be decided by the new Divorce Court, abrogating the Common Law rights of fathers over children.[7]

The passage of this Act hindered attempts to introduce a Married Women's Property Bill (which would give women control of their own property and earnings) at the same time, and the campaign languished for some years. It was revived when John Stuart Mill spoke about the issue and a committee, led by Elizabeth Wolstenholme and Jessie Boucherett, was set up in April 1868 in Manchester to steer a bill through parliament. The committee was joined as its treasurer by Lydia Becker, a close friend of Wolstenholme, and her ally in the suffrage cause, Richard Pankhurst. The heavyweights, Jacob and Ursula Bright were recruited. Becker distributed Boucherett's pamphlet on married women's property law, wrote letters and advised on tactics, which included the usual petitioning, writing to MPs, and collecting anecdotal evidence of cases of hardship as a result of the current law, such as Lydia's story of a laundress who could not put her earnings into a bank because this would allow her husband access to them.[8]

A petition raised in Manchester boasted over 5,000 signatures, collected by Becker and her paid canvassers and volunteers, in an attempt 'to bombard the house [of Commons] with a fire of petitions'. Although she admitted that it was easier to acquire signatures for the married women's property petition than for the franchise ones, it was still not as straightforward as it might seem; many women were afraid to sign because of the disapproval of husbands, families and friends, which might lead to social ostracism. Lydia's voluminous 1868 letter book shows her sterling effort to gather signatures, and she was proud to have acquired the signature of Mr Leigh, the Manchester Officer of Health, though the mayor had refused 'on the ground that "married women would give themselves airs" if the law were changed'. He was not alone in his opposition. *The Times* newspaper objected that even if a reform were effected, a man would still be liable to support his wife but a wife might refuse to contribute out of her own property to the support of the household and children. Lydia Becker was ready with a riposte that a wife received support in return for her wifely duties; whilst even a cook got a wage, a wife was paid nothing. She also went so far as to point out in a letter to the paper that the Married Women's Property Bill, if passed, would possibly hamper the cause of women's suffrage because MPs would thereby 'without affecting the justice of the claim of women to representation, destroy one of the strongest reasons for pressing it'.[9]

Becker was very keen to gain the support of working-class women, who she believed were eager to sign, and employed Mr and Mrs Poole and Mrs Young as paid canvassers with this purpose. This approach had its own problems; she periodically ran out of money to pay them, and work had to cease until funds were forthcoming. Moreover, many poor women in areas like Rochdale were illiterate and made only their mark. Lydia was adamant that such signatories should be checked as genuine, dispatching Rev. Steinthal in this regard, and reminded canvassers that both signatures and addresses must be in the same handwriting. Her eagerness to include working women was reflected in her letter to Professor Jack, when she asked him to get his maidservant to sign: 'They are a class of person particularly liable to suffer by the operation of the existing law if they have saved a few pounds in service and they are tempted to marry a man who may turn out a drunken or a tyrannical husband.'[10]

The petition, sent by Becker to Westminster in two halves to reduce the cost of postage, was presented in parliament by Jacob Bright on 10 June 1868, accompanied by a speech which included individual cases provided by Lydia in a letter. That of the shopkeeper was typical:

> A woman, well off and in a good business as a shopkeeper, married. In about a year there was some disagreement between the couple. The husband sold off his wife's stock in trade and her household furniture (these had been her property before marriage) put all the money in his pocket and went away to America, leaving his wife entirely destitute. She laid her case before a magistrate, but was of course informed that there was no remedy as the husband had not exceeded his legal powers.

Lydia was immensely proud of her contribution and deduced that 'I may be said to have made my first appearance in earnest by proxy in the House of Commons!' She also made a personal appeal to Bright and included an apology for her own strong feelings on the sufferings of women:

> We have no representatives in Parliament and your brother [John Bright] says the House of Commons never yet passed a measure because it was just. That shows what we have to look for. Please to forgive this little outburst. Of course I ought to [be] able to see women suffering without any disposition to indignation but it is not always easy to maintain serenity. Speak for us on Wednesday. A man may say on behalf of women what women cannot say. I hope for much from you.[11]

The overlap with the suffrage campaign is very obvious and there was much co-operation and sympathy between the two movements. But Becker was determined from the start that the suffrage cause and the married women's property issue must remain separate, as her letter to Elizabeth Wolstenholme demonstrated: 'It will not do to mix the committees, so if you do determine on having one [a meeting], please make it either p.m. or an evening meeting as usual ...' She feared that those opposed to a reform of the property laws might abandon the suffrage cause if the two became too close. This cut both ways, however, as Jessie Boucherett pointed out 'There are many people who would help the MWP [Married Women's Property] Bill who dislike Miss Becker's views and these are repelled by her name.'[12]

Becker's poor opinion of the organisation of the married women's property campaign was possibly another factor in her desire to keep it separate from the suffrage campaign. She wrote to Elizabeth Wolstenholme pointing out the weaknesses of the committee, and wanting to get 'fresh blood' into the movement: 'We must settle our organisation on a better basis.' They arranged to meet to discuss the situation at Lydia's father's house in Grove Street. Although she had confidence in some members, who were 'honourable and high-minded women' whose 'hearts are in the work', others left much to be desired. In May 1868, as they tried to find a secretary for the Manchester group, Lydia's frustration was evident. She dismissed several candidates as too busy, and suggested the French Philippine Kyllmann 'if we cannot find an Englishwoman with sufficient public spirit to undertake the work. I do feel indignant that women should be so stupid and dead in the matter.'[13]

In early June, Elizabeth Wolstenholme sent Becker proposals for the formation of an official fully fledged society for the married women's property movement. The latter was, perhaps insensitively, very critical of her friend's attempts and somewhat patronising in her advice:

> I have looked more carefully over your proposals, which seem to me to be somewhat indistinct. I cannot grasp a definite idea from them. Compare your proposals with the constitution of our [Suffrage] Society, which I enclose, and you will see what I mean. You make no provision for the government of the Society. Who appoints the committee? Are they to be self appointed? You see in our Society we begin at the beginning – First we have a general meeting of the Society – this appoints an Executive Committee. It holds office during a year and the Executive Committee appoints its own officers.
>
> Now the London Society is organised on a totally different basis. There the Executive committee is a self-elected irresponsible body. It appoints the general committee and admits members to the Society, but neither the general committee, nor the body of the members, has the slightest control over the Executive.
>
> Either of these plans is intelligible – in the one case the Society at large, in the other the Executive Committee, is the supreme governing power, but in your plan I find … no source of power, no supreme court of appeal …

Advising Elizabeth to 'rest on your oars' and take stock before rushing ahead, she warned: 'Just review your forces – see how many persons you have on whom you can reckon for work. It is very easy to build a society on paper, but the real thing grows very slowly …' [14] Later she suggested a biblical motto for the society, 'Give her the fruit of her hands', though for the rather cynical reason that 'it would be delightfully orthodox to sail under scriptural colours – We could then accuse our opponents of flying in the face of the Bible! – and it might serve to convince some people that we were not proposing anything immoral!'[15]

The high hopes for a reform of married women's property laws were dashed when in 1870 'the parliamentary mountain brought forth a mouse'. Although the Married Women's Property Bill drafted by Richard

Pankhurst passed the Commons with ease at 131 to 33 votes, in the Lords it was held up for a year. In the *WSJ* Lydia had foreseen danger to the bill: 'We fear that this invitation is somewhat like that addressed by the spider to the fly and that if the Bill comes down again alive out of the Lords' "little parlour" it will have the heart taken out of it.'[16] She was right. The peers accepted that some measure was needed to protect poor women but raised objections to helping wealthy ones.[17] In effect their committee tore the Commons' bill to shreds, replacing fourteen of the seventeen clauses, and amending the three that were left. The bill was approved and sent back to the Commons; it protected the earnings of women, which might have an impact on poorer, working women, but would affect very few of the wealthy ones. Money saved before the Act was not recognised as a woman's property unless it had been invested in specific ways, such as in a savings bank. Even earnings were not automatically protected: a woman had to apply specifically for this. Lydia informed the NAPSS that there was little practical value in the protections on offer because bankers objected to taking deposits or honouring cheques without a husband's permission. The Act made a wife liable to support her husband and children, but Elizabeth Wolstenholme and Lydia Becker objected that a wife should not have to support her husband, rather she should be supported in recompense for her household services. Wolstenholme also argued that she should not be responsible for the maintenance of children, who were still legally recognised as only belonging to their father. The best that can be said of the Act was that it did establish the principle that in some circumstances married women should own and control their own property, and Wolstenholme and Becker accepted that it was 'an important concession to the growing sentiment of justice'.

Despite this they were clearly determined to fight on, pointing out in a joint letter to *The Times* that the Act was so complicated that it was 'unintelligible without a lawyer'.[18] The *WSJ* focused on clarifying and explaining it, and Lydia developed a deep knowledge of the law as it pertained to women, using the *Journal* to give legal advice in response to queries from individual women. Further bills were presented in 1872 and 1873. The latter would have included provisions found in the original bill of 1870 to secure to married women all property acquired before and after marriage, with the same rights and responsibilities as unmarried women. However, it ran out of time in the committee stage.[19]

My dear Aunt

I think you will be rather surprised to receive a letter from me, but I at (last) formed the resolution of sending one. I hope you are quite well, how are little Mary and Emma, how soon are you going to the new house I hope you will be successful there. I like reddish very much, our coughs are much better, the change of air I suppose has done them good. we have a fine cherry tree opposite our nursery window, and I dare say you will think the cherries in danger of being plucked. we too a very large pear tree on the house and cart loads of pears have been got off it. I think it will be fine fun gathering the pears when they are ripe. Mamma Mary Maria and I send our loves to you. I had almost forgot to tell you that a little wren is building close to the nursery outer door. I cannot make this a very long letter because it is the first I have ever written, so I will add no more but that I am your affectionate niece

Lydia E Becker
April 14 reddish Mills
1836

Mrs H Duckhouse
Wornbrook

1. Lydia Becker's first letter, age 9. (*Image courtesy of the LSE Women's Library*)

2. Moorside House. (*Photograph taken by the author, courtesy of Kelly-Anne and Heath Groves*)

3. Lydia Becker. (*Image courtesy of Manchester Libraries and Archives*)

4. Richard Pankhurst 1893. (*Image courtesy of Manchester Libraries and Archives*)

5. Manchester Free Trade Hall c1865. (*Image courtesy of Manchester Libraries and Archives*)

6. Jacob Bright, 1876. (*Image courtesy of Manchester Libraries and Archives*)

7. Manchester Town Hall, Mayor's Parlour where the MNSWS held its meetings. (*Image courtesy of Manchester Libraries and Archives*)

8. Lily Maxwell. (*Image courtesy of Manchester Libraries and Archives*)

9. Clementia Taylor. (*Image courtesy of LSE Library*)

10. Elizabeth Wolstenholme Elmy. (*Image courtesy of LSE Library*)

11. Mangling done here. (*Image courtesy of Chetham's Library, Manchester*)

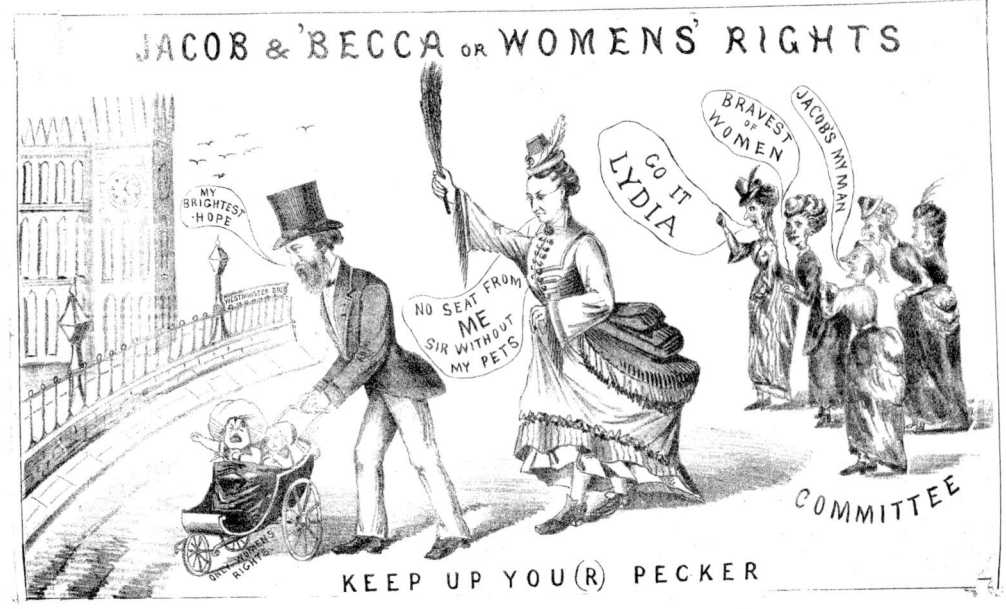

12. Jacob and Becca, 1870. (*Image courtesy of Chetham's Library, Manchester*)

PUNCH, OR THE LONDON CHARIVARI.—MAY 28, 1870.

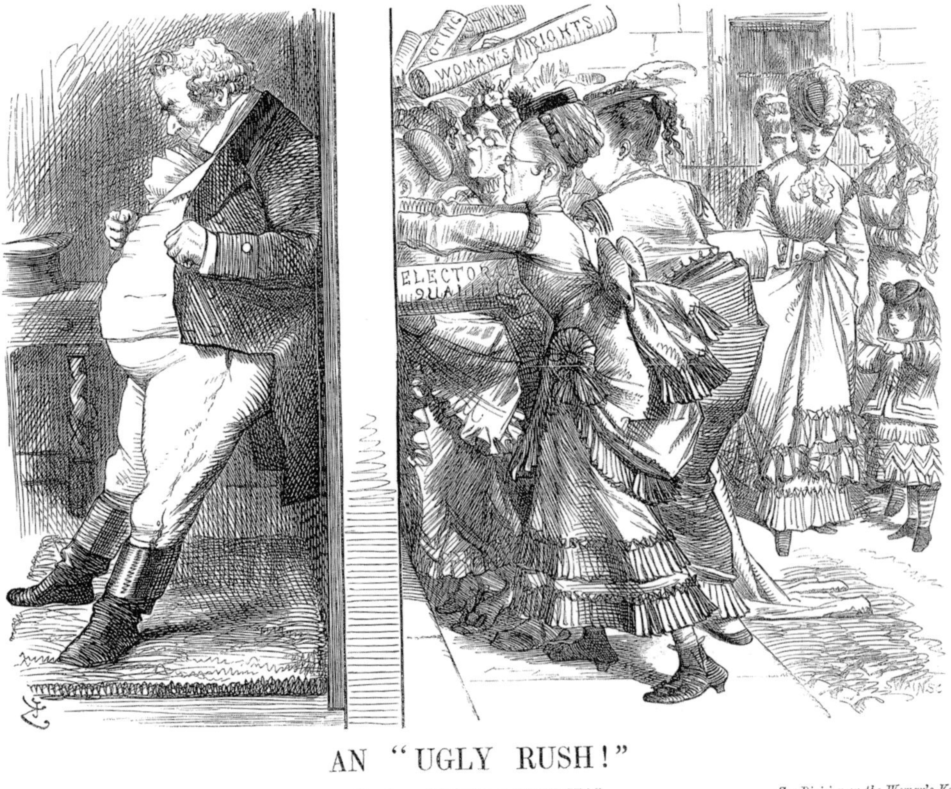

AN "UGLY RUSH!"

MR. BULL. "NOT IF I KNOW IT!"

See Division on the Woman's Vote Bill.

13. 'An Ugly Rush'. (*John Bull resists the suffragists, 1870. Courtesy of Heritage Images*)

14. Josephine Butler. (*Image courtesy of LSE Library*)

15. John Stuart Mill and Helen Taylor. (*Image courtesy of LSE Library*)

16. Helen Blackburn. (*Image courtesy of the Mistress and Fellows, Girton College, Cambridge*)

17. Portrait of Caroline Ashurst Biggs by Elizabeth Guinness, 1897. (*Image courtesy of the Mistress and Fellows, Girton College, Cambridge*)

18. Frances Power Cobbe.
(*Image courtesy of LSE Library*)

19. Priscilla Bright McLaren.
(*Image courtesy of LSE Library*)

20. Lydia Becker in 1873. (*Image courtesy of Oldham Local Studies and Archives*)

21. Hanover Square Meeting, London. (*Image courtesy of LSE Library*)

22. Emmeline Pankhurst c.1880.
(*Image courtesy of LSE Library*)

23. Millicent Garrett Fawcett.
(*Image courtesy of LSE Library*)

24. The great prize fight, election 1876. (*Image courtesy of Chetham's Library, Manchester*)

25. In at the finish. Cartoon. (*Image courtesy of Chetham's Library, Manchester*)

26. City steeplechase, election 1876. (*Image courtesy of Chetham's Library, Manchester*)

27. Lydia squares up to John Bright, *Fun*, 24 May 1876. (*Image courtesy of the George A. Smathers Library, University of Florida, Gainesville, Florida, USA*)

28. Central Board School, Manchester, 1885. (*Author's own copy*)

29. Lydia in 1889, 'poured' into her black silk dress. A photograph in the possession of Helen Blackburn. (*Image courtesy of the Mistress and Fellows, Girton College, Cambridge*)

30. Posthumous portrait (1897) of Becker by Elizabeth Guinness, on a cupboard belonging to Helen Blackburn. (*Image courtesy of the Mistress and Fellows, Girton College, Cambridge*)

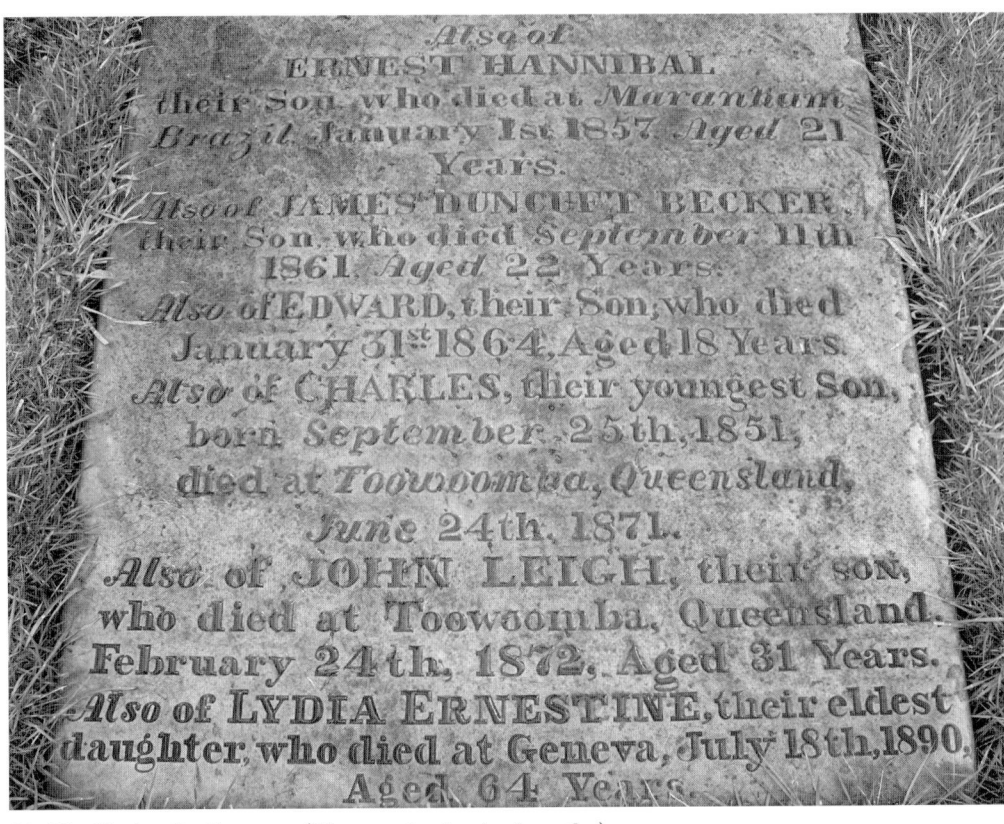

31. The Becker family grave. (*Photograph taken by the author*)

It took a further decade to achieve their goals, and there were turbulent waters in the intervening period. It may have been, as Holcombe points out, that the 1870 Act had taken the momentum out of the fight. That the very supportive NAPSS was suffering a decline at this time was probably also a factor. There were also serious disputes about the direction and nature of the campaign, compounded by a moral threat to the reputation of the women's movement. In 1874, Elizabeth Wolstenholme had to resign from the committee and Lydia Becker, along with Frances Power Cobbe and others, also left.

Maureen Wright, Wolstenholme's biographer, records that relations between Lydia Becker and Elizabeth Wolstenholme had been very close up to this point. Lydia admired her colleague's gritty stance on many issues and described her as the 'moving spirit' of the women's movement. It had been Wolstenholme who encouraged the publication of Lydia's first women's suffrage article, and invited her to the February 1867 meeting of the Manchester committee. She was happy to hand over the secretaryship to this keen recruit so that she could develop her own work in education.[20] By her own account she and Lydia had exchanged 'many hundreds' of letters between 1869 and 1874 and a 'deep private friendship ... enriched their public labours'. Wolstenholme was psychologically fragile and Lydia tried to offer support and comfort, quickly becoming a trusted confidante, such as during a spell of some sort of mental illness which Elizabeth experienced in November 1868. In a letter which began 'My darling friend' Lydia expressed deep distress at her friend's serious condition, and was feeling guilty that she may have exacerbated it by criticising her preoccupation with matters other than the suffrage:

> I ought to have known that what you did must always be the wisest and best thing that could be done. I never thought you had begun to care less for our cause. I only thought in my blindness that you were turning more special attention to the nearer and smaller thing.

It may not have been completely helpful that Lydia expressed her belief that 'all diseases are physical', and advised 'care and judicious management of yourself' with the adoption of an occupation which would not burden Elizabeth with anxiety, such as writing her father's life story.[21]

However, Lydia's support as treasurer of the Married Women's Property committee had always been secondary to her commitment to the enfranchisement of women; she warned her friend against devoting too much time to the 'branch' issue of married women's property: 'The married women's property law – is <u>one branch</u> of the general woman question – the franchise goes to the <u>roots</u> of the matter.'[22] In an article published on 1 January 1872 she rehearsed the full argument, which showed how the many social ills which women suffered were not addressed because all the laws were made and executed by men, who were elected by men.[23] She pronounced that: 'The sufferings and wrongs of women will never be considered worthy of attention by the legislature until they are in possession of the suffrage.' And, in uncharacteristically dramatic terms, that: 'The franchise is needed as a protection for women from the uncontrolled dominion of the savage passions of men.' She was even more convinced that the suffrage should take precedence by 1874, when in her letter of 1 March she cited figures to prove that, in the wake of the 1870 Married Women's Property Act, the suffrage issue was by far the more strongly supported of the two in the Commons and the Cabinet. Her conclusion was clear: 'that is an unmistakeable indication of which question is the right one to push while the present government retain office … I think the best plan [for the married women's property campaign] would be pay off our liabilities and rest on our oars' [again!].[24]

There were also strategic differences about the inclusion of married women in the fight for women's suffrage which spilled over into the committee for married women's property.[25] Although Lydia was aware that married women were just as keen on gaining the vote as single women, and believed that the vote should be given to all adults, and to women on the same terms as men, she was very much a pragmatist on the issue of married women's votes. In 1874, an irreversible rift arose between Becker and Wolstenholme when the former reluctantly agreed with the demand of its presenter, William Forsyth MP, that the Women's Disabilities Bill should specifically exclude married women. She argued against Elizabeth that 'in no respect, in her mind, was the enfranchisement of married women feasible' because of the traditional (coverture) status of wives. Her friend's view was that Lydia was 'weak-kneed'. It must have been a severe blow to both women that they were on different sides of the argument.[26]

There were other factors in the rift. In 1874, Elizabeth Wolstenholme, living unmarried (in any socially recognised sense) with Ben Elmy, at the age of 40 found herself pregnant. This caused, in the later description of

Sylvia Pankhurst, 'a fluttering in the dovecote' as the moral reputation of the campaign was at stake. Ursula Bright supported Wolstenholme's continuation on the committee, in the face of huge opposition led by Irish campaigner, Isabella Tod, and Manchester minister Samuel Steinthal, but persuaded the couple to marry in the Kensington Registry Office on 12 October 1874. In spite of this, the argument still raged, and Lydia Becker brought down the wrath of the Brights on her own head: 'It was poor Miss Becker who was the chief object of her [Ursula's] anger, and the chief cause was her having suggested the searching of the registry to ascertain whether the marriage had really taken place.'[27] Lydia and Isabella were alone in voting this time to remove Elizabeth from the committee. Lydia was deeply hurt and resigned as treasurer of the Married Women's Property committee, along with Frances Power Cobbe and the Ashworth sisters. Their friendship foundered, and never recovered. Elizabeth recalled that this was 'both "a grief" and a lifelong disappointment'.[28]

Nevertheless, Lydia continued to fight the married women's corner when the opportunity arose; in 1880 at the NAPSS she joined the discussion to object to the idea that a woman should be made liable for the joint household expenses, presumably on the usual grounds that she had already contributed to the household through her labour as a wife. At the same time she dismissed the 1870 Act as 'null' and contended that neither husband nor wife should be able to will away all their property from each other.[29]

At last, in 1882 the Married Women's Property Act finally gave women the right to their property, both inherited and earned. Hailed in the *WSJ* as 'the Magna Carta for women', it was a corollary of the ongoing legal reforms, particularly of the Judicature Act of 1873 which rationalised the legal system, but it did not remove the doctrine of coverture explicitly.[30] Nevertheless, this measure gave ammunition to the 'antis': they could now argue that a major grievance had been removed and that therefore the franchise was less crucial to women. It also had an impact on the women's suffrage campaign because now there would be married women, as well as single ones and widows, who fulfilled the property qualifications to vote, but were still prevented from doing so under the rules of coverture. This had already become highly contentious, and was destined to split the women's suffrage movement. But for now the reaction was mainly positive and at the MNSWS AGM of 1882 Lydia recognised that this was an Act of 'unprecedented magnitude' which would 'give a strong impetus to the movement for equal justice to women in every department of personal and political rights'. She stated firmly that it went 'farther than any Bill which has ever yet been before Parliament in recognising the independent personality of a married woman'.[31]

Working women

Lydia Becker developed a strong commitment to working people, with a sense of the 'electric stimulus of the sight of crowds' as expressed in a conversation with Frances Power Cobbe in the late 1880s:

> 'Do you know,' she [Becker] said, 'that the great tide of people rushing through Parliament Street [London], and all the flood of life and business eddying below our windows there, are essential to me? I could not bear to sit and work in your quiet rooms.' 'Then,' I [Power Cobbe] said, 'you are like Tennyson's youth, who longed to be
>
> > In among the throngs of men.
> > You feel, as you look on them, –
> > Men, my brothers! men, the workers! ever working something new,
> > What they have done but then earnest of the things they shall do.'
>
> 'Yes, yes!' she said, 'that is *just* my feeling!'[32]

It was in particular to the women of that class that she turned her attentions across many aspects of their lives. The accusation of later campaigners and some historians that all the early feminists were interested only in the rights of middle-class women is patently unfair when her record is examined. As has been seen, from the start Becker addressed audiences from amongst the working class on political issues, and she fought especially hard for the benefit of poor girls in education as a member of the Manchester School Board.[33] Never one to miss an opportunity to rally support for what she considered the key to all women's grievances, as early as 1868 Lydia was eager to win supporters for women's suffrage amongst working-class women. She wrote to Sarah Anne Jackson, a friend who was not a suffragist, expressing delight that Miss Jackson's maid, Charlotte, was in favour of the Cause:

> Nothing is so encouraging to persons engaged in promoting great questions, as to feel that they are supported by the masses of the people for whom they are labouring. I look upon Charlotte as a representative woman – and when the 'woman question' presents itself to my mind – I do not think of the elegant ornaments of drawing rooms, but of the toiling thousands, many millions of my countrywomen – to whom life is no pleasant holiday matter but a stern reality whose austerities we are trying to soften. Fantastic notions about 'woman-sphere' are unknown in a world where women gain their own bread by their own labour.[34]

Like other feminists of the period, such as Lady Emilia Dilke, Jessie Boucherett and Helen Blackburn, she took an interest in the practical realities of the lives of women at work, supporting attempts to band together in benefit societies and unions, campaigning about conditions and wages, and backing women's attempts to resist the limitations imposed by 'protective' legislation.[35] Along with other feminists, she had sympathies with the temperance movement, hugely popular with the 'respectable' working classes, reasoning that

> Women among the labouring classes suffer very much from the effects of drunkenness among men ... I am not an advocate of the 'Alliance' [United Kingdom Alliance for the Suppression of the Traffic in all Intoxicating Liquors] myself but the organisation here is very favourable to women's suffrage.[36]

Frances Power Cobbe had pointed out that a key factor in violence against wives was 'Drink' in her pamphlet on 'Wife Torture' and Becker approached this issue in practical ways.[37] At the Manchester Royal Jubilee Exhibition in 1887, she found time to complain through the *Manchester Courier* letters page about the failure to provide easily accessible tea in the gardens, contrasting this with the facility with which visitors could buy alcohol: 'Should the committee continue to prohibit the sale of tea and promote the consumption of intoxicating drink in the gardens, they will cause the outdoor part of the entertainment at least to have a character not contemplated by the public of Manchester ...'[38]

She also was particularly favourable towards the co-operative movement because she saw it as a means to help women towards economic independence. This was a view shared by others in the feminist movement, and in 1883 it found expression in the Women's Co-operative Guild, which made the improvement of the condition of women one of its stated aims.[39] Well before this, Lydia was active in attempts to engage women in co-operation. In July 1868 Richard Pankhurst had suggested that a clothing warehouse be set up on such principles, with the participation of women. Lydia decided that this would play to their strengths:

> There is nothing like buying and selling, for making money, and women and buy and sell very well – there is nothing either laborious, or 'unfeminine' in either process. Most of the other plans for promoting 'employment of women' seem to contemplate pursuits requiring bodily labours – handicrafts – the most irksome and least remunerative of all occupations.[40]

Lydia asked him to detail his plans, and tried to enlist the help of her uncle in the project, but it had to be abandoned through lack of resources. Yet they did not give up; at Eccles in January 1871 Becker spoke at a co-operative soirée, encouraging men to persuade women to join and demanding that women should be included on management committees:

> I look on the question of co-operation as a very wide one … I think that if men desire to increase the number of their members of this society they will encourage their wives to become shareholders and have the shares in their own name – there would be a great desire within them to become members of the Society. There is a great charm in a little property … Any person who is a member of this Society is raised in his own esteem, and whatever difference there is in men and women there is none in this respect.[41]

Women-only enterprises were also regarded by feminists as a means to promote female employment. A meeting was held on 16 December 1868 in the Memorial Hall on Albert Square, when an American resident in Manchester, Mr C.W. Felt, demonstrated a new system of typesetting, for which he employed women. The chair was taken by Rev. Samuel Steinthal, and also present were others from the MNSWS, notably Dr Pankhurst and Lydia Becker. Lydia did not, it seems, speak at the meeting, but was clearly there to show her support for the idea of training women to work in a useful trade which had hitherto been male-only.

Indeed, there were many male printworkers in the audience who were not in sympathy with the idea of extending the employment to women, concerned as they were that the trade would be classified as less skilled and that their pay would be undercut.[42] Thirty women were later put into training as typesetters, with a view to their employment in printing the *WSJ*, although in the end a threat of strike action by the local printers union forced the initiative to be abandoned. Lydia recognised from this and similar experiences a significant point with regard to trade unions: 'The Trade Unions are as a rule opposed to the labour of women in many departments of industry in which they are perfectly capable of engaging if they were allowed.'[43]

The following week, the Manchester press was reporting the foundation of a Female Employees Association, presided over by Mr Parr, representing the firm of Kendal, Milne and Co. Joseph Lomas had called the meeting, at which Lydia showed her support. He explained that the situation of saleswomen, milliners, and unemployed shop assistants needed amelioration. Members would pay a subscription, and receive financial help in the case of sickness or unemployment, as well as medical help. There was even a plan to use any surplus which might accrue to establish a home for 'aged and diseased members.' He proposed that a 'directorate of ladies' be established to run the society, and visit unemployed members. Lydia, however, disapproved, arguing that she had no faith in ladies' committees, and even that they were 'objectionable institutions'. She said that 'Men and women alone were not so wise as men and women together.' She successfully suggested that the Warehousemen and Clerks' Association, on which the new body was modelled, be approached with a view to incorporation. Meanwhile, the new organisation progressed, and when on 7 April its committee was announced, Lydia Becker headed a list otherwise composed entirely of men. It is not known whether she was content with this arrangement.[44]

In her support for trade unions, Becker was somewhat outside the mainstream of feminist activity in this era. And whilst it has been posited that Victorian middle-class feminists were blind to the fact that it was the class structure itself which was part of the oppression of poor women, it can be argued that she was very much aware that their situation was different to that of their middle-class sisters, even if she did not consciously blame their troubles on the limitations imposed by social class.[45] It is a clear example of her interest in the plight of working-class women and children that at the BAAS in 1871 Lydia spoke about their employment, and based much of what she said on her research into the condition of Lancashire and Cheshire factory workers. She had acquired statistics from an employer which showed that three-quarters of his workforce were women, and concluded that 'the wealth of Lancashire was very largely supported by the labour of women'. Pointing out that women were invariably paid less than men for the same work, she gave a detailed breakdown of the pay scales. This disparity was justified by contemporaries on the grounds either that men were stronger and so achieved more, or that male occupations were more skilled.

Not that the higher rate of male wages necessarily benefited their wives and children. Lydia had spoken to women employees and learnt that it was normal for wives to have to waylay their husbands on payday to get their wages before they reached the pub. In addition, she had also discovered that in Congleton, a silk town where children could legally work from the age of 11, 'if they were to take the children between 11 and 13 years of age from the mills, the whole trade of Congleton would be destroyed'. She claimed 'It was considered good policy for a man to marry early and have a large family because then he could play and live upon the earnings of his family.'[46] All this she cited in a forcefully expressed argument for fairer treatment of women in the mills; it gave rise to considerable hostile discussion at the conference, but the speech publicised the plight of female factory workers when it was reported in the press.

In 1876, Lydia continued to support women's trade unions. She attended a meeting of the newly formed Society of Sewing Machine Workers on 18 July in the Temperance Hall on Grosvenor Street, Manchester, chaired by Mr Hodgson Pratt of the Women's Protective and Provident League in London. She moved a resolution to promote the organisation and spread its membership among the workers of the city because 'If [the potentially 500 workers were] organised into a compact body, they would command respect, both from their employers and their fellow-workers, both in their own and other trades.' Describing them as 'pioneers' she urged the new union not to be discouraged in walking a novel path, especially as 'In most things, but more especially in public life, women had much greater difficulties than men.' She pointed out also that there was much public sympathy for improving the condition of women and the wages of sempstresses (seamstresses). She acknowledged, however, that 'there was not quite so strong an agreement as to the means by which to attain that end'. She reported that one Manchester firm had given notice that they would not employ any woman who joined the union, but Lydia argued that the women needed to convince the employers that 'no mischief would arise from the organisation'. She referred to the famous *Song of the Shirt* by Thomas Hood, which had appeared in *Punch,* and its impact on the whole country in raising sympathy for the seamstresses, so that 'they might be sure that there was still a great desire that women sempstresses should not be ground down'. Still true to her belief in mixed-gender bodies, she called for a middle-class committee of ladies and gentlemen to help the society, but ended with the affirmation that 'she thought the women had enough determination to do the work themselves'.[47]

Lydia's views on working women were influenced no doubt by the lectures she attended at the NAPSS most years. In 1877, she heard and discussed a paper read by Miss Busson: 'Should the labour of women in factories be regulated by legislation?' The message of the lecture was that legislation concerning women was passed partly due to the objections of working men to any competition from women in the labour market. She illustrated her argument by pointing out that there was no proposal for legislation for the 'millions of female domestic servants who had longer hours and more severe labour than very many working men'.[48] Lydia elaborated on this theme at the 1878 Domestic Economy Congress, held in Manchester, when she put it that

> The best way to raise the quality of women's work is to cultivate the intelligence and raise the status of the workers, to place domestic service on the same level as service in factories and workshops, and to reward it not only with wages adequate to the work performed but with a recognition of such work as a necessary and worthy occupation, by which women helped to maintain their families, and earn for themselves an honourable and independent livelihood.[49]

In taking this stance, Lydia was unusual in the ranks of the feminists; as middle-class campaigners, few of them had personal knowledge of the life of a working woman, and there was relatively little disquiet amongst them about the plight of those women who were in service in their own households.⁵⁰ Perhaps the experience of a loss of income in her youth had opened her eyes more than most of her peers'.⁵¹

Following up her support for better conditions, Lydia addressed meetings agitating for shorter hours, such as that for shop assistants (who were said to be working up to eighty hours a week) presided over by Bishop Fraser of Manchester in Hulme Town Hall in April 1880, when a weekly half-day holiday was called for. Lydia had done her homework, and had clearly talked to the workers themselves, so she offered some practical suggestions: that the assistants should be provided with seats when 'disengaged', have longer and more regular times for meals, and benefit from later opening times (currently 8 a.m.). On the other hand, she warned the assistants to try to 'suit the convenience of all parties' or else they might alienate the support which they currently had from the general public.⁵²

As well as the issue of how best to organise women into trade unions, another aspect of feminist engagement was with the thorny issue of legislation aimed ostensibly at protecting, against their will, the well-being and moral standing of women at work. Lydia was called upon with other feminists to support women workers in the collieries of Cumberland, when women employed above ground were gathering all around the country. At a 'large and enthusiastic' meeting at Whitehaven in April 1886, resolutions were passed protesting at laws proposed by the Lib-Lab MP Thomas Burt, a miner and trade union leader, to prohibit the employment of women at the pit-head. The opponents of the legislation contended that it would prevent women working in jobs at the 'pit-brow' which were better paid and less onerous than alternative jobs open to women in other places of work. As the principal speaker, Becker backed a petition to be sent to the Home Secretary, which was also supported by the local MP, Cavendish Bentinck. She gave her views in the *WSJ:* 'I have observed that wherever any attack is made upon the liberties of women two things are done by their opponents: they first begin to blacken the character of the women; then they contend that the proposed legislation is for their good.'⁵³

On 17 May, a high-powered deputation from Lancashire, Cumberland and South Wales met with the Home Secretary. It included twenty pit-brow women who were asked to speak up in their own cause. Lydia went with them, along with colleagues in the women's movement; the words of Josephine Butler reflected Lydia's view that 'The industries at present open to women were far too much restricted, and ... not only would great hardship be inflicted on many hundreds of working women, but an evil precedent would be set.'[54] But not all feminists, particularly in the early twentieth century, were against such protective legislation and Sylvia Pankhurst found fault with this approach in *The Suffragette Movement* and criticised Becker (though not Josephine Butler) for her part in such campaigns:

> In opposing all legislation intended for the protection of women in industry... she expended the energies which Elizabeth Wolstenholme, Ursula Bright and Josephine Butler devoted to securing positive reforms. In women like these, on the one hand, and in Lydia Becker on the other, were embodied the two main tendencies which strove to control the women's movement throughout its history.[55]

Lydia continued to campaign for working women right up to her final year; her leader in the December 1889 edition of the *WSJ* included a substantial discussion of the unfair settlement of a strike by male and female operatives in Forfar jute factories, by which the men achieved a pay rise, but the women were to continue working at the old rates. Lydia's judgement was that:

> The case affords another illustration of the danger incurred by women who make sacrifices in order to enter into industrial or political warfare in partnership with men without the power and protection of the Parliamentary franchise.[56]

It may be that at times Lydia Becker failed to take full account of the need for some protective laws; feminist campaigners have been accused of failing to grasp the realities of the lives of working-class women. Indeed she naively wrote on one occasion that 'women of the lower classes have nearly as good a chance of maintaining themselves in an independent position as men, at least in the manufacturing districts ... A *great lady* or a *factory woman* are independent persons – personages – the women of the middle classes are *nobodies* ...'[57] Her view was obviously coloured by her own middle-class experience, but it was certainly tempered over time by the first-hand knowledge of the lives of working-class women which she gained through her work on the Manchester School Board and her interviews with factory women, seamstresses and other working women. Claims that she and her colleagues made no attempt to reach out the working classes are unfair. In fact, it was in defence of the rights of working-class women that she first became involved in the Vigilance Association, formally established, at least initially, to guard against government interference to the detriment of women's working and civil rights.

The Contagious Diseases Acts and the Vigilance Association

One of the spurs to create such an organisation was the passage of the Contagious Diseases Acts in 1864, 1866 and 1869.[58] These Acts were passed in association with others to prevent diseases in cattle, but related in this case to women. Initiated by fears about the spread of sexually transmitted diseases amongst men in the armed forces, the Acts allowed police in garrison and naval towns to arrest any woman merely suspected of being a prostitute, which might extend to any working-class woman. She would be forcibly given an internal examination, and if found to be infected would be subjected to treatment in a 'lock' hospital. Such was the outrage amongst both male and female feminists that a campaign was begun to repeal the laws, under the auspices of the National Association for the Repeal of the Contagious Diseases Acts. This was an all-male body, as the indelicacy of the subject was thought to be unsuitable for respectable women to participate; the women, under the leadership of Elizabeth Wolstenholme Elmy and the charismatic Josephine Butler, therefore set up their own Ladies National Association.

Although she was treasurer of the committee of this association, which had its Manchester office in the same building as the MNSWS at 28 Jackson's Row, Lydia Becker did not engage in the agitation against the Contagious Diseases Acts as fully as she did in other campaigns; her priorities lay elsewhere. She feared that support for women's suffrage and education would be lost by such an involvement; many people, notably J.S. Mill and Helen Taylor, thought it was best left to men, and that women should not sully their reputations by dealing with such unsavoury matters. Nevertheless, Lydia did sign the Ladies' Appeal and Protest on 31 December 1869.[59] Furthermore, on 16 November 1870 she helped to organise, in Manchester's Free Trade Hall, a big national demonstration for working men and women against the Contagious Diseases Acts. It was completely ignored in the national press.⁶⁰

There existed a warm but sometimes fraught affection between Lydia and Josephine Butler, who was the campaign's most prominent leader. It was characterised by profound admiration on Lydia's part; she described Butler as 'a truly noble woman', who displayed a

> vivid and far-reaching sympathy with all forms of human suffering which is the great secret of her influence ... she maintains that it is not the disappointed and the personally unlucky women who feel most keenly the disadvantageous position of their sex – rather though the happiest who are most induced to exert themselves for the benefit of those less fortunate, and she is an example of her own theory.⁶¹

They did not work easily together; where Lydia was a rationalist and did not wholly support the idea of separate spheres, Butler was very religious and believed in traditional male and female roles being upheld. As time went on Butler found Lydia harder to please; the latter clearly became impatient with her friend's frequent illness. Though encouraging Butler to take a holiday in July 1871, a year later she was proving a hard taskmaster, as Josephine complained:

> The Jackson's Row Committee was <u>extremely</u> angry with them [her Birmingham friends, who encouraged her to take a break] for meddling with <u>their servant</u> and I feared I was never to hear the last of it. My holiday was very short ... I am I hope working hard enough now to satisfy the Becker.⁶²

Although Lydia accompanied a large deputation of 200 men and women who lobbied Home Secretary Bruce in July 1871, and indeed was one of a handful of women to speak up, her involvement became increasingly irksome to Butler:

> Our movement [for repeal of the Contagious Diseases Acts] needs to be revived, or rather to be started afresh on a wholly new footing in Manchester. It has been overshadowed there from the hour of its birth, on the one hand by the strong shadow of Miss Becker, and on the other by that of Mrs Hume Rothery, well-meaning but

injudicious 'screaming' woman. The only religious people who have taken it up are twaddly half-believing unitarians ...

I cannot work in Manchester free of Miss Becker and others whose support on our repeal platform does not aid the cause ... [the cause] has been taken up too much as a political and too little as a moral and religious question ... The advocacy of Miss Becker and other supporters of the Women's Suffrage movement, has prejudiced quiet people against the movement in Manchester. It wants new blood.[63]

By 1873, Lydia's contributions had been limited to veiled support in the *WSJ* and appearances at Ladies National Association meetings, such as their Manchester AGM on 3 December 1877.

One effect of the association was to forge a bond of solidarity between middle- and working-class women, and this gave rise to a new committee for Amending the Law in Points Injurious to Women which became in 1872 the Vigilance Association for the Defence of Personal Rights. It was set up by Elizabeth Wolstenholme Elmy as secretary, Lydia Becker as treasurer (until 1875) and Josephine Butler. Its aim was to uphold equality before the law, irrespective of gender or class, which clearly linked with Lydia's defence of the rights of working women, and her support of trade unionism amongst them. It also lobbied parliament, and its first campaign, publicised in the *WSJ* and in speeches which enraged the magistrates, focused on the case of a Fanny Goss, who was ultimately found to have committed infanticide and suicide. Fanny lived with her brother, the rector of Kingsland in Herefordshire. When the body of a murdered baby was discovered in a drain, a 'medical examination' of Miss Goss was ordered by the coroner, to which she refused to submit. She had to lock herself in her room to prevent it being forcibly inflicted, and there she committed suicide. The coroner ordered a compulsory 'personal examination' of all the women in the household to check which had given birth, even though after death it was found that Miss Goss was undoubtedly the mother. The association consulted lawyers, and the Home Secretary was urged to intervene to protect women from the abuse and exceeding of their powers by coroners.[64]

The association went on to espouse other very specifically female issues; baby-farming, the responsibilities of fathers, the rights of wives to maintenance, wife-sales, and the legal position of mothers. Through the *WSJ*, Lydia attacked the contemporary idea that women were in some way property, and waged campaigns against sexual violence, collecting statistics on cases of assault, and deriding the attitudes of the courts in imposing small fines or brief imprisonments for such offences.

In the mid-1880s, the Vigilance Association was re-formed, galvanised by a 'moral panic' about child prostitution. This time Lydia Becker did not feature in its leadership or its campaigns.[65] Perhaps this was because she was busy rebuilding the women's suffrage campaign after a major setback in 1884.[66] Moreover, the Vigilance Association began to focus strongly on moral regeneration and was increasingly dominated by purity groups wanting to suppress what they considered obscene literature (including works on birth control), music halls, and nude statuary; such issues never preoccupied Becker. In any case, one of the fears of male legislators was that a female electorate might foist upon them policies from the agenda of the purity lobby; Lydia would hardly wish to be associated with a creed which could be so damaging to the suffrage campaign, although that did not prevent her colleague, Millicent Fawcett, along with other feminists, from taking a prominent role.[67]

Lydia's participation in more than one women's campaign was typical of the nineteenth-century feminist movement. There were so many issues which demanded attention that most activists were engaged in several at any one time. As the century wore on, reform was achieved in the rights of married women to property, divorce and their children; the campaigns of women at work gained better conditions and greater freedoms; and poor women were freed from fear of arrest by the repeal of the Contagious Diseases Acts. Women had even been given the right to vote in local elections. By the time Lydia Becker died in 1890, therefore, the other main issues on which women had taken a stand had to some degree been resolved; the right to vote in national elections was now the most outstanding remaining battle, and the one which proved most difficult to win.

Chapter 7

Local Government and the Isle of Man Franchise

Although attaining women's suffrage in national elections was proving more elusive than had been hoped, in 1869 there was a quiet and almost unremarked revolution in local government when the 1869 Municipal Corporations Act gave the vote in local elections to some women.[1] It meant that, henceforth, women householders had the right to elect municipal councils. This might appear contradictory to a modern audience, but in the later nineteenth century the business of the local authorities was perceived as an extension of women's sphere, dealing as it did with the poor, health, education and similar social matters. Parliament considered these less important than matters which still dominated national affairs such as taxation, law and order, imperial and foreign policy, and defence.

Moreover, parliament was reminded that this was a modest change, as the ratio of women to men voters was relatively low at, for example, 1:6 in Manchester and 1:7 in Bristol. The number of women was also kept low by a decision in Queen's Bench in 1872 to exclude married women, some of whom might have expected to qualify under the Married Women's Property Act of 1870. This was occasioned when a male candidate in Sunderland was defeated by one vote, so he challenged the right of two married women to vote, and won.[2] However, the proportion of women grew over time and by the end of the century they made up about 17 per cent of the municipal electorate. This rendered them sufficiently numerous to be taken seriously, but not numerous enough to be seen as a threat to male power. Whilst parliament may not have understood the potential of this development, the suffragists certainly did, and had high hopes that it would act as a pilot and unlock the door to women's suffrage in national affairs too.

This was particularly the case after 1881, once the Isle of Man parliament, known as the Tynwald, implemented a major electoral reform, enfranchising not only more men but also women on the same terms. This caused great excitement amongst the suffragists, whose hopes of the coming Third Reform Act at Westminster were raised considerably.

The Municipal Corporations Act, 1869

It was Lydia Becker who suggested to Jacob Bright MP that the Municipal Corporations Bill might be amended to include women. She may well have been influenced by the fact that a certain Miss Jessie Goodwin managed to exercise a vote in the municipal elections in Manchester in December 1867; Lydia had been delighted to read about it in the morning paper, and noted that this proved women wanted the franchise, and that it had elicited 'the hearty approval of their townsmen'.[3] Nevertheless, she appreciated the importance of proceeding discreetly so as not to raise alarm amongst the opponents of women's suffrage. Indeed, Bright slipped in the amendment in the small hours of the morning, presumably in the hopes that it would get through 'under the radar'. Lydia wrote to Jessie Boucherett on 3 May 1869:

> It is quite likely we may yet have a fight this session, not on the Parliamentary, but on the *municipal* franchise. Mr Hibbert, MP for Oldham, has a bill giving it to every *male* occupier who has resided a year in a borough ... an amendment will be moved in committee to leave out the word *male*. Mr Jacob Bright said if he could find half a dozen men on our side willing to support him, he would run the risk of the trial ... Mr Hibbert is quite agreeable to the amendment. Altogether I feel quite encouraged, for I really think it may be carried. It will be a grand step towards the Parliamentary franchise. But we must be very quiet until notice is actually given of the amendment, and then we must work for it, as hard as we can.[4]

The government decided to back the amendment and it was passed in the Commons 'without a dissentient word'. Lydia was jubilant and wrote to Barbara Bodichon on 9 June reporting the 'very great victory'. However, it still had to get through that most Conservative body, the House of Lords. Accordingly, Lydia wrote to the Marquess of Salisbury, requesting his support on the measure. It is a surprising fact that his lordship, who was in many ways the most conservative of politicians, was avowedly sympathetic to the women's cause. Lydia followed the line that Jacob Bright had taken in proposing the amendment, that it would in fact restore to women in boroughs an ancient right which had been taken away by the Municipal Corporations Act of 1835, which only gave the right to vote to 'male persons'. Or in places which were not incorporated boroughs it would protect ancient rights women still had. She hoped to appeal to Salisbury's conservative instincts: 'I would earnestly invoke your support of a measure which is at once liberal in restoring their vote to classes which have been disfranchised, and conservative of existing rights.'

She gave the example of Birkdale Park, near Southport, to illustrate the point. This district had not adopted the Act of 1835 because of its potential impact on its voters; of the 290 ratepayers, a third would have been disenfranchised because they were women, and the person with the largest assessment and therefore with the largest number of votes at twelve, was a woman. Had Birkdale Park become a municipal corporation she would have lost all her votes, 'and the franchise given to a poor cottager, of which the largest ratepayer had been deprived'. Arguments in defence of the rights of property always appealed to the Lords; the amendment was allowed to stand and the bill became law.

Manchester had become a municipal corporation in 1838, and women were therefore not able to vote there from that date until 1869. To counter perennial arguments that women were not interested in voting, Lydia gathered statistics on their participation in the municipal elections which followed in November 1869. She believed that women had voted in greater proportion to their numbers than men, and there were some notable displays of eagerness to participate. In one ward, a woman elector 'set her heart' on being the first at the poll. Lydia drew the lesson for Henry Bruce, the Liberal Home Secretary, that

> electoral privileges are very earnestly prized by women. The removal of the disabilities with regard to the Parliamentary vote, which is the natural sequence of the removal of municipal disabilities, would undoubtedly be followed by a manifestation of the value attached to these privileges, and I venture to express a most earnest hope that a Liberal Government will be found willing to declare that free government is the privilege of all Her Majesty's subjects.[5]

As Patricia Hollis explains, the system of local government as it developed after 1869 was extremely confused with regard to women.[6] Parliament preferred to avoid making law, but to deal with each case as it arose. From 1869, single women ratepayers could vote for all local government bodies, and a few married women ratepayers had the vote for some things, like parish vestries and Poor Law boards. Each type of local authority had different qualifications for its candidates. In some places it was easier for a woman to be a candidate than a voter; on school boards, any woman could be a candidate but only single women ratepayers could vote. For borough councils single women ratepayers could vote but not stand; married women could do neither. Whenever there was confusion and a woman's right to vote or stand was challenged, the case ended up in court, and judges were always strongly impressed by women's Common Law disabilities, and not at all by their offer of service for the common good, so they usually found against the women.[7]

One concern about women voting was how they would fare in the rough atmosphere of the polling stations. In Ardwick, Manchester, there was the scandal that some of the women had been plied with drink in a pub before being taken to vote. By contrast, in Bury the ladies were helped to avoid a huge crowd around the polling booth by being given a separate entrance and 'shown every consideration' which included policemen proffering their umbrellas, and even the roughest men making way for them to cast their votes.[8] The issue of behaviour at polling stations was finally addressed, however, by further legislation which in 1872 introduced the secret ballot, and in 1883 was effective in preventing bribery.

There were limits to the expansion of women's role in local government, however. When in 1888 Lord Salisbury's Conservative government established county councils, initially with provision for women both to vote and stand for election, this met with opposition because it was argued that such councils were more like parliament, in that they were party-orientated, had greater resources than other local government bodies and were involved in important issues such as wage rates and housebuilding. It is likely also that this bill met such opposition, in contrast to that of 1869, because by 1888 those against women's suffrage had become a more organised force, alert to any possible breach in the defences of male privilege. In the end, there was some confusion and a few women were actually elected to office, but this was overruled in court and women became ineligible to stand until 1907, though they could nominate male candidates earlier.

The political education of women for municipal elections

As local government and the opportunities it presented evolved, it occurred to Lydia that women were inevitably inexperienced in matters of politics, and that even the process of registering and voting would be difficult and off-putting in this male-orientated, public arena. Therefore, in October 1878 she held the first of many women's meetings, on this occasion in Manchester St Luke's ward, speaking on 'The Duties and Responsibilities of the Municipal Vote'.[9] The candidates for the ward attended, which gave the meeting especial weight, as it was a chance for women to put their own questions to them. This initiative appears to have been Lydia's alone and there was no apparent involvement from the MNSWS, though her efforts were noted in AGMs.

To a 'densely crowded' hall Lydia explained why their votes mattered, as 1,000 of the 5,134 electors in the ward. She reminded them that those elected would have influence over institutions like bath and wash-houses and free libraries, and over issues such as temperance. She accordingly urged women to 'ask those gentlemen who sought their suffrage if they were prepared to do what they could in their municipal capacity to improve the condition of the people.' She also encouraged them to think about laws which could specifically affect the lot of women, citing the current bills to legalise marriage with a deceased wife's sister and for extending the parliamentary franchise to women. Reminding them that they had a vote at school board elections, she suggested they should think about questions relating to the board and form opinions; she believed that 'a good staff of intelligent women officers was the right staff to visit the mothers of children and see that the latter attended regularly at school' but she had not yet managed to persuade the men about this because they were 'too many for her ("Hear, hear," and laughter) … she hoped … that the women electors of Manchester would find another lady to go to the Board with her.' She was so successful in rousing the women that when questions were put 'the meeting became somewhat disorderly'.

In advance of the council elections for 1879, Lydia repeated this success and started with a meeting in St Michael's ward, the largest and poorest in the city, to persuade women to vote.[10] Cards were issued inviting women electors to attend, but on this occasion the meeting was gatecrashed by a large group of men who filled up all the seats before the women could gain entrance, and not all of the men were sympathetic to this approach to their womenfolk. As Lydia entered the room she was received 'with mingled cheers and hooting'. Both the candidates in the forthcoming municipal election had been invited to attend to explain their views, but only the Liberal, Councillor Brown, had actually been brave enough to turn up. The whole meeting was disorderly, despite the best efforts of Alderman Worthington in the chair. Lydia's own appeals for a 'fair, patient and impartial hearing' went ignored, despite three attempts to speak. The uproar was continuous, and at times so intense that the speakers sat down. The crowd heckled, cracked jokes and sang *Rule Britannia*, generally treating the occasion as one for hilarity. At one point the 'cheers and ironical laughter' so offended two ladies near the door that 'they forcibly ejected a gentleman of lean aspect who was indulging in eccentric cachinnations [sic] in one corner of the room, while some of the ladies on the platform warmly applauded the act and frantically waved an approval with their pocket handkerchiefs.' The attitude of many men, and indeed some women, was that the idea of women in politics was not to be taken seriously, but was an opportunity to poke fun and a matter of great entertainment. Indeed, the *Manchester Courier* called this a 'discreditable, if somewhat amusing spectacle'. Jessie Craigen, the working-class campaigner who was thereafter employed by Becker, had accompanied her; she was unimpressed and sarcastically commented that 'she had been greatly edified by her first experience of a Manchester public meeting'. Nevertheless, undaunted at further such meetings, when Jessie spoke, according to Lydia she 'held the meeting enchained by her grand voice and her strong and witty words'.[11]

At the end of the gathering, Lydia called another meeting for the next night which would be strictly limited to women. Between 700 and 800 working women and shopkeepers attended this very successful event, demonstrating that, despite the roughs, there were plenty in that audience who genuinely wanted to hear what Lydia and the other speakers had to say. The local press compared the 'superior intelligence and self-control of the women' to the 'rowdiness of the men the preceding evening'.[12] Unphased by the experience in St Michael's, further women's meetings were called in other wards of the city.

The immense value that Lydia placed upon this work was clear in a letter she penned to Priscilla McLaren in Edinburgh:

> Manchester, Oct 25, 1879
> We have had such a meeting that I must write and tell you of it – the room, which will seat 600 or 700, was quite full of women only, all seemingly electors – all poor working women – How they listened – how they cheered – how strong and intelligent an interest they took in what was said to them. It would have done your heart good to see –
>
> It has been a new life to me to know and feel the strength there is in those women – when many fall away from us and leaders desert us; but in those women there is a force which, gathered together, led, organized and made manifest, is enough to lead us to victory.[13]

In an article that same year, she stated plainly the wider import of female participation in local government:

> Men in this country obtained parliamentary representation in and through local government. They used the power they had, and they obtained more extended power. We urge women to follow their example – to take an interest in the local affairs in which they have a legal right to be represented, to make their votes felt as a power which must be recognized by all who would govern such affairs, and to be ready to fill personally such offices as they are liable to be nominated for, and to seek those positions to which they are eligible for election … Political freedom begins for women, as it began for men, with freedom in local government. It rests with women to pursue the advantage that has been won, and to advance from the position that has been conceded to them in local representation to that which is the goal of our efforts – the concession of the right to a share in the representation of our common country.[14]

When the MNSWS held its AGM on 12 November 1879, it was reported that at the special meetings held for women electors the candidates had been questioned 'as to whether they would support a petition from the council in favour of giving the Parliamentary vote for women, and in all cases they agreed to do so, and expressed their adhesion to the principle of women's suffrage'.[15] Such women's meetings, all addressed by Lydia Becker alongside a variety of other speakers, continued to be held before municipal elections into the 1880s. Not only were they valuable in furnishing women voters with a political education but they also kept the issue of women's suffrage in the public eye, consistently encouraging women to question candidates on their views with regard to the matter, and not to vote for those who were opposed. That they had considerable obstacles to overcome in the way of feminine timidity and reserve is suggested by Lydia's urging them to get out and vote, and 'not to stay at home until the agents of the candidates waited upon them'. But the fact that they could expect to be so approached indicated that candidates were aware of the importance of the female vote in municipal elections.[16]

Indeed, the fear some felt at Becker's influence over women led a certain 'Verax' to write to the Tory *Manchester Courier* on 14 February 1883 at the time of a New Cross Ward election, about her influence:

> Sir, – I see by an advertisement that the 'Radicals' have put their 'favourite agitator', Miss Becker, in motion to secure women's support, if possible, on behalf of the 'Radical' and 'Free Thinker' candidate. I think it is high time that the ratepayers of New Cross (and indeed every other ward) should know that Miss Becker is the paid agent of the Radicals for the purpose of carrying on this agitation among the female electors in the various wards, and that is the reason she only 'crops up' at municipal elections. The women electors of New Cross Ward would do well to ask themselves the question, 'What has Miss Becker done for us?' You never hear of her labouring amongst the poor, needy, and afflicted of her sex, or lending a hand in any way whatever to assist in improving their position, in fact, she has not done one single act to benefit them, and, therefore, has no claim whatever to the attention of the electors of New Cross Ward. I hope at the coming meeting of the women electors of New Cross Ward, that they will let Miss Becker clearly understand that they don't want her interference in this election.

The objection seems to have been voicing the view that Lydia had failed to help women by the means which were conventionally acceptable, such as charitable works and practical caring. Indeed, a letter by 'A voter' a few days later was more explicit in opining that 'If Miss Becker would instruct her lady friends in domestic duties, it might save newspaper remarks on bad cooking and the moral degradation of women and girls.' That she was active in political and educational matters was a cause of unease, and gave rise to what may be considered some very unfair criticism.[17]

By contrast there were men who thought that the role of women in local politics should be extended; a candidate in New Islington, Mr Wilkinson, at one of the women's meetings convened by Becker, expressed the belief that there should be women on the Manchester Council. He had noticed that women 'had great business capacity' and their role of housekeeping honed in them the very skills they would need to 'make first-rate town councillors'. He went on to suggest that 'some day they should get hold of Miss Becker, and send her there'. Both he and the Conservative candidate could see no reason why women electors in the municipality should not also have the parliamentary vote.[18]

In the end, the suffragists were misguided in believing that local political power would inevitably and speedily lead on to a vote in national elections, but there can be no doubt that what Lydia Becker and Jacob Bright achieved in this field helped to persuade many that women were capable of exercising a vote responsibly. Women were now also given the opportunity to serve on important local bodies in cities such as Manchester, demonstrating irrefutably their capacity to contribute to wider society. Lydia and women like her who appeared on school or Poor Law boards were undermining the concept of separate spheres, and effecting a quiet revolution in attitudes to the place of women in society.[19]

The Isle of Man franchise

Almost half a century before women in most of the UK gained the vote on the same terms as men, the Isle of Man parliament, the Tynwald, voted to enfranchise women alongside men in elections for the House of Keys, the lower house. Lydia Becker and Alice Scatcherd of Leeds were instrumental in this groundbreaking change, which passed into law with remarkable ease, when compared to the angst and heart-searching over the same issue elsewhere in the UK. It occurred as part of a general move to democratise the existing system, in which very few ordinary inhabitants were enfranchised, and the women's vote was added to the bill presented for consideration.

The government of the Isle of Man, consisting of a governor, an upper house known as the Council, a lower house called the Keys, and the bishop and judge named the Deemsters, was able to enact its own laws and impose its own taxes. The system pre-dated parliament by hundreds of years, but the original voting system of the Keys was abrogated in the fifteenth century and a system of co-option replaced it until 1866. In that year, it was agreed that the Keys would again be elected every seven years; the right to vote was based on property, but by the end of the 1870s it was felt that this was too restrictive, and so in 1880 there was a move to revise the system in favour of a male householder franchise.

Lydia and Alice visited the island in August 1880 and held a series of five well-attended meetings which were reported sympathetically in the Manx press. Becker's reputation had gone before her; at a meeting of the Douglas Town Mission in 1875 there had been mention that in their evangelising 'Fault had … been found with the fact that women had been allowed to teach and preach in the Bethel [chapel]', but the chairman went on to defend the women:

> If they had been where St Paul was, they would there have seen that the women there were allowed to show no feature except the eyes, but if St Paul had lived in these days, he would probably have thought and taught differently with regard to women than he had done, and if he had seen and heard such women as Miss Lydia Becker, and Mrs Dr Garrett [Elizabeth Garrett Anderson, the first woman to qualify as a doctor in Britain], he would, no doubt, have held out the right hand of fellowship to them.[20]

Moreover, women's suffrage meetings in England were reported in the Manx press; that held in St George's Hall in Langham Place, London, on 13 May 1876 is a case in point. Lydia proposed 'That this meeting hereby records its approval of the assimilation of the conditions of the Parliamentary to those of Municipal franchise, in so far as regards the disabilities of the sex, and pledges itself to support the principle by every constitutional means.' The paper went on to report her speech in favour of the resolution:

> Referring to the speech of Mr John Bright [brother of the suffragist, Jacob] against the Women's Suffrage Bill, she held that it was unjust and ungenerous and untrue to assume that their claim for the suffrage was based upon hostility, real or assumed, between the sexes.[21]

So it was that by 1878 Lydia's name was a byword as a champion of women's rights in the Isle of Man, and when the Laxey branch of the

Royal Manx Union Henpecked Club celebrated its anniversary in the mountains of Lonan in March, it was remarked in the press that: 'There is every probability that, if Miss Lydia Becker was to come to Lonan and inspect the roll [of members], she would find that *Women's Rights* are there supreme, and the men, bowing to necessity, rejoicing in being henpecked.'[22] She also came in for other customary mockery by satirical writers; the same newspaper went on in September to report that at a festival of skating and bicycling a ladies' race was won 'easily' by 'Miss Becker (scratch)' who was awarded a gold locket.[23]

On 31 July 1880, it was publicised that there were to be addresses by Lydia Becker and Alice Scatcherd in support of the claims of women ratepayers to the parliamentary franchise at Douglas on 4 and 6 August. These were followed up by meetings in Ramsey, Castletown and Peel. Admission was free, to encourage as large a turnout as possible. The visitors addressed packed and sympathetic meetings, beginning in the Masonic Hall on 4 August, when Alice chaired and Lydia was the main speaker; they reversed this on 6 August. The former explained that it had been Lydia's idea to 'hold a series of meetings in some of the leading watering places of the kingdom' during the quieter summer months, and they had already visited Llandudno and other venues. She gave her colleague a great build-up: 'Since the formation of the Society, Miss Becker had been the heart, soul and brain of the movement ...'[24]

Lydia began by focusing on the different positions of unenfranchised men and women; whilst men had no vote because they lacked property, women were debarred and 'declared by law to be incapable of possessing it'. She cited the case of John Bright's sister, the suffragist Priscilla McLaren, who was denied a vote, when a felon in Pentonville prison was allowed one. She caused amusement when she compared women to 'lunatics':

> A lunatic was allowed to vote during a lucid interval, if, during such interval, he could remember the names of the candidates. That was the law: but the law did not admit that a woman ever had a lucid interval – (laughter) – and thus women were, in respect to the Parliamentary franchise, reduced below the level of criminals and lunatics.

Indeed, in answer to a question, she mentioned that she had personal experience of how acute this issue could be when in the election for South-

East Lancashire 'she had not a vote, while nearly every man, no matter how low in the social scale or in intelligence, enjoyed this privilege'.

She also marshalled what were by now the usual arguments. She cited the unfairness of taxation without representation and the fact that women had the municipal franchise and had proved themselves more than equal to its effective use. More unusually, she put it that it was more challenging to vote in a municipal election because it required technical knowledge of sanitation and water supply whilst parliamentary elections did not. She concluded by pointing out that the disenfranchisement of women was bad for the whole of society because it deprived the system of that area of knowledge and expertise peculiar to women.

Lydia also sought to reassure by estimating that giving women a UK parliamentary vote on the same terms as men would enfranchise only about half a million women, as compared to the existing 3 million male voters. She appealed to the audience's sense of fair play by showing the disadvantages inherent in women's position in society; girls received only 1 per cent of the spending raised for educational purposes; there were no girls' traditional grammar schools; women's work, such as baking or sewing, was undervalued and underpaid. There was some discussion of party leaders amongst the audience when Lydia pointed out that Gladstone, the great leader of the Liberals, had not acted on his observation that 'the law of England was too much for men, and too little for women.' She argued that it was not a party question – all could support women's suffrage. A week later, Lydia wrote to the *Isle of Man Times* to clarify her view on Gladstone, who had been referring in his comment to other laws on women's rights, not to the parliamentary franchise. She claimed to believe that Gladstone genuinely wanted to amend the laws, but was powerless to do so because women lacked the political power to back him. It seems unlikely that this was truly her assessment of Gladstone's position, but she had by now grasped that party politics were a major obstacle.

She went on to discuss the disadvantages of married women under the current laws, passed by MPs elected by men; how until only a decade ago abandoned wives had no rights over their own earnings, and they had no say in what should happen to their children. She countered arguments that women lacked the education to vote by pointing out that it was men who had hindered women from educational opportunities by controlling the money and the power to offer such opportunities. Although she conceded that women could not fight in the army, she pointed out that most men did not actually fight, but paid taxes so that others could do so. The idea that women were too emotional to vote was dismissed; indeed she argued that 'it would be a very good thing for society if some of the emotions by which men were actuated and influenced were replaced by the softening and refining emotions of women.'

She called on the patriotism of the Manx: 'What a great thing it would be for this ancient kingdom of Man if it should be the first to give to women the right of exercising the franchise.' This was something that only they could do for themselves, but she ended with a rousing call for men and women to 'go forth hand in hand together to make the world better than they found it'. For those unable to attend, the speeches were reported sympathetically and in detail by the local press.[25]

When a women's suffrage amendment to the proposals for reform was put forward in the Keys by Richard Sherwood, omitting 'male' so that qualified women might vote, it was carried by 16 votes to 3. This would have admitted to the franchise male and female owners of rural property valued at £8 a year, occupiers of property at £12 a year, and owners and occupiers of urban property of £8 in value. The bill had to be approved by the Council, however, and there was some reluctance amongst them about admitting women. They proposed a more restricted measure by limiting the vote to all owners of property worth £4 annually, and excluding all female occupiers and lodgers. After further wrangling, which included an offer from the Keys to make the qualification for women occupiers £20 a year whilst it would still be only £12 for men, in the end it was settled that the women occupiers would be dropped, in the interests of achieving suffrage for women owners. This was under protest on the part of the Keys, who openly stated that they had given in 'simply to secure the partial concession, rather than lose the whole; and that their opinion as to the equal rights of males and females remained unaltered'.[26] This received the royal assent and became law on 31 January 1881. Gratifyingly for the suffragists, within a short time the right to vote was in any case also extended to women occupiers. Even before this, in early December 1880, the MNSWS at its AGM celebrated this success, recalling the efforts of Becker and Scatcherd and congratulating by name all the members of the House of Keys.[27]

This was indeed a remarkable development for the women's suffrage movement, and before the first election under the new regime on 19 March 1881 a letter appeared in the *Isle of Man Times* from Becker and Scatcherd.[28] They congratulated the women of the island on 'the proud position you occupy as being the first women within Her Majesty's dominions whose rights as Parliamentary electors have been recognised and legally secured'. Going on optimistically to hail this as 'an earnest of the coming recognition of the same principle in the next electoral Act for the United Kingdom', the letter emphasised that 'The eyes of the friends and opponents of the movement all over the world are bent on you, watching with eager interest the result of the great experiment of women's suffrage in the election … which you are now about to afford.' It was hoped that the Isle of Man would 'demonstrate the fitness of women for the exercise of political rights …'

To encourage them further, every one of the 1,000 enfranchised women received a letter from Lydia Becker and Alice Scatcherd congratulating her on her new status.[29] It stated that every woman on the register must vote and use her best judgement in her choice, considering particularly the cause of good government, and the promotion of measures to improve the condition of the people and to amend laws injurious to women. It continued even more prescriptively to cite such laws: the exclusion from voting of women occupiers in the Isle of Man, married women's property rights, female education, and industrial rights.

Becker and Scatcherd had clearly even thought about suggesting the names of candidates Manx female voters should support but had resisted that temptation, considering that just having to win the votes of 'good and thoughtful women' would have 'an ennobling influence' on the candidates. The worthy intention was that the addition of the women voters would not just be an increase in numbers but would lead to 'the infusion into political life of those higher morals and spiritual influences which it is the mission of women to diffuse in family and social life'. In short, the new voters were to 'regard the exercise of this privilege as a most solemn and sacred duty'.[30]

Manx women accordingly showed a keenness to vote and impressed with their decisiveness and efficiency.[31] Accordingly, in Glenfalba Richard Sherwood received the votes of all the women of that sheading (constituency) and was head of the poll, as was another prominent proponent of women's suffrage, Mr Stephen in Douglas; what women thought and whom they supported was immediately recognised to be significant.

Although the Isle of Man may be regarded as a sideshow, irrelevant to the UK Parliament, for the suffrage campaigners it had a wider significance, in that it demonstrated how they could achieve their aims where there was a will in the legislature to change the constitution. It allowed women to reinforce what they had already shown in the municipal elections: that they were keen to vote and did so thoughtfully. And it demonstrated that hitching a women's suffrage amendment to government electoral reform legislation could be the most effective way to gain the vote for women. At Westminster, proposals were in the offing under Gladstone's second ministry (in the first half of the 1880s), to extend the vote to men in the rural areas on the same terms as it had been given to men in boroughs in 1867. The National Society for Women's Suffrage became convinced that this was their great opportunity. Surely, they reasoned, the government could not enfranchise uneducated male farm labourers without also granting the vote to the educated female owners of the land on which they worked?

Chapter 8

A Woman in a Man's World: the Manchester School Board

In 1870, Gladstone's great Education Act, known as Forster's Act, enshrined in law the crucial and novel principle that government had a responsibility for the education of children. It provided that rate-funded school boards should be elected in all areas. They would make provision where necessary for children's schooling up to the age of 12, alongside the existing institutions which were largely run by religious bodies, notably the Church of England (National Schools) and non-conformist churches (British Schools). The Act caused a storm of controversy; it was unsatisfactory to campaigners such as the National Education League, who had hoped for free, compulsory and non-sectarian education. It was equally unacceptable to non-conformists, who resented the favourable treatment, especially in terms of finance, which would be afforded to those schools run by the established church. Nevertheless, it proved to be the foundation stone of the modern education system.

Moreover, the Act allowed women not only to vote for but also to sit on the new school boards. Feminists seized the opportunity to extend the scope of their activities and enhance their status. The school boards were a popular focus of their votes, and they showed considerable political sophistication in using the franchise tactically on occasion. Those who put themselves forward as candidates sometimes met resistance from local party machines, but when they demonstrated how a vote could be split they had to be taken seriously, and their electoral experience and confidence developed. By the end of the decade, there were seventy women on school boards across the country. Once in office, they took responsibility for policy, raising local rates, inspecting conditions, and pioneering innovations such as free school meals and the waiving of fees for very poor children. Women became expert, holding seminars and attending conferences, bringing back best practice from other boards, writing learned papers on education, and giving information to government committees of enquiry.[1]

Lydia Becker was elected to the Manchester School Board in November 1870 and remained in harness until her death in 1890. Her work on this body was by no means secondary to her role as a suffrage campaigner: for instance, the AGM of the MNSWS in 1873 had to be postponed by a month because of her preoccupation with the school board elections. The opinion of the *Manchester Times* on 26 November was that 'As a member of the Manchester School Board she has achieved a conspicuous and influential position which elevates her work and her words into a matter of undeniable public importance.'[2]

Although educational reformer Emily Davies was elected onto a London school board (Greenwich), as was Dr Elizabeth Garrett (Marylebone), neither of them really engaged in depth with the role.[3] Lydia Becker was ploughing a lone furrow away from the main thrust of feminist agitation in the sphere of education. The leading educational campaigners focused their main efforts on private schools and higher education provision for middle-class girls.[4] Becker, on the other hand, made it her special mission to press for the improvement of provision for working-class girls in board schools, and for their inclusion in an academic curriculum which would allow them to excel and gain higher qualifications. She was not completely alone in her preoccupations; Helen Taylor, stepdaughter of J.S. Mill, joined a London school board in 1876 and campaigned consistently for changes which Lydia would have endorsed: free and compulsory education, an end to corporal punishment, and the provision of school meals and clothing for needy children. Sadly, however, their relationship had foundered on the issue of strategy in the suffrage campaign, and they appear never to have repaired the rift which had opened up between them in the later 1860s.[5]

As the only woman on the Manchester Board, Becker must have found herself in an isolated position, requiring considerable strength of character. She was not, however, a stranger to such challenges. In September 1869, she had been noted as the only woman amongst ninety prominent men listed as members of the newly formed National Education League, which originated in Birmingham.[6] By the end of October, Lydia and nineteen men had formed the executive committee of a Manchester and Salford branch of the league. This may not have been as lonely as it sounds, as other members of the committee were friends in the MNSWS, notably Reverend Samuel Steinthal and Dr Borchardt.[7] League policies included the compulsion of local authorities to provide and fund sufficient schooling for all children in their districts, and to ensure that education provided on the rates should be unsectarian, free and compulsory. It was with this as her agenda that Lydia put herself forward as a school board candidate in Manchester in 1870.

School Board elections

School board seats generated the most tension of all local elections; on average there were only about a quarter of the number of seats that were available on the town council, so they were few and prestigious. This was the case for Manchester, which had a school board of fifteen, as compared to the council's forty-eight. In general it is believed that women voters favoured women candidates, as did working men, the clergy, doctors and philanthropists.[8] The seats were not based on the ward system, but each voter had as many votes as there were seats, so this meant that organisation was required for any interest group (often religious or non-sectarian) to win a working majority.

On 24 November 1870, Lydia Becker became the first woman in the country to be elected to a school board. Her work on the Manchester Board reflected her lifelong love of education and the development of children, first manifested in her role as surrogate mother to her own siblings. When she offered herself as a candidate there can be no doubt that she was sincerely compassionate towards children, but she was also alive to the politics of the situation, and she used a most effective strategy by showing how a woman would complement the male influences on the new body. In her manifesto, she admitted that her goal of compulsory attendance for all children was going to be difficult to achieve 'owing to the miserable condition of vast numbers of children'. Moreover, whereas male candidates stressed the importance of a proper academic education, the formation of character, preventing the creation of criminals, and in some cases the avoidance of sectarianism, Lydia carefully focused on the accepted feminine ideals of compassion and nurturing. Reminding readers that many children were malnourished, she continued 'I consider that it … will be the duty of any Board which makes such attendance compulsory to see that the children are sent to school properly washed, dressed and fed.' The final paragraph of the manifesto summed up her approach:

> Electors of Manchester, – You are now about to choose a body to whose care will be given the interests of the most utterly weak and destitute section of the community ... Should you think fit to confide a share of this sacred charge to my hands, I should accept it in a spirit of deep responsibility, and earnestly endeavour so to discharge it that the little boys and the still more helpless little girls of this great city might not in after years have cause to regret the choice you had made.[9]

Thirty-nine men and one woman stood for election to the fifteen places on the board. It was noted that the polling was much more orderly than was often the case in parliamentary or municipal elections, and also that 'the number of women voters ... was very much greater in proportion than at any of the municipal elections in which they have hitherto enjoyed the privilege of the suffrage.' However, less than half of the ratepayers voted. At the top of the poll, with well over 54, 000 votes, was the Catholic Canon Toole, followed by his Catholic colleague, George Richardson, a solicitor; they had benefited from the large Irish vote in New Cross and St Michael's wards. It was also remarked that in the wards where the Catholic candidates did well, so too did the five successful Church of England candidates. Lydia came a respectable ninth with 15,249 votes, pretty evenly distributed across the city. It was acknowledged that 'Miss Becker's large score is largely, but not altogether, owing to the exercise of the cumulated voting of women electors in her favour.' The lowest of the successful candidates was Oliver Heywood, the banker and philanthropist who polled 7,902.[10]

It may be that Lydia's showing could have been better, had she expressed support for religious teaching in the proposed new schools. Although she received some criticism in 1870 because she lacked formal educational experience, such a capability in itself was insufficient to garner support; Elizabeth Wolstenholme, a highly experienced teacher, failed to gain election in Congleton. Significantly, Elizabeth believed this was due to her not being a church candidate. By contrast, Elizabeth Garrett Anderson and Emily Davies in London topped the polls, having both expressed support for religious teaching and Bible reading. Moreover, Becker's campaign was low key; she held no meetings, gave no public speeches, gathered no committee to support her, and made a last-minute electoral address. She did not ally herself with any political grouping, and her election expenses were minimal. It was perhaps, therefore, surprising that her showing was as good as it was.[11]

Her success was noted in London, when *The Observer* described Lydia's achievement as 'a distinct triumph', and added 'we can hardly see how it can be helped as a strictly logical inference that a person qualified to sit on a school board is also qualified to exercise the franchise, or even to legislate if returned by the electors.'[12] This would have been music to the ears of suffragists, and it has even been claimed, with some justification, that in fact women stood for school boards purely to break barriers against women in public life, and thereby to move inexorably towards enfranchisement in national politics.[13] Nevertheless, the article went on to remind readers that education might be considered a particularly appropriate arena for females, and hoped the women would use their triumph 'with modesty and moderation'. It pointed out sententiously that 'To cross the Rubicon is not, after all, to capture Rome.' Indeed, Lydia faced attack from influential quarters, not least from the newly appointed Bishop of Manchester, James Fraser, who disapproved of women on school boards and opined that

> Home seemed to be the woman's proper place … and he could not welcome any attempts by which women sought to intrude upon functions that did not belong to them. When he saw ladies thrusting themselves in all directions into the domains of politics and medicine, he was reminded of the Athenian council in one of the plays of Aristophanes, where the ladies, presuming to take in hand affairs of state, found that they made a mess of them …[14]

Lydia took advantage of a conference for 'ladies connected with various school boards' in London to meet like-minded women, in June 1874. They heard papers on attendance, drill for girls, the teaching of health matters, kindergartens, and needlework in girls' schools (probably not Lydia's favourite topic, as will be shown), as well as on 'the voluntary assistance of lady school visitors', which was a bone of contention on the Manchester Board. The upshot was the formation of an association for school board ladies, which played its part in providing mutual support.[15]

The triennial election for the Manchester School Board was particularly contentious in 1879. It looked likely that the election would be contested on religious grounds. At a meeting (in which she was significantly lumped in as an honorary 'gentleman' in press reports, which was not unusual), Lydia pointed out that a contest was worth the cost in both money and effort if there was some issue at stake on which voters should have a say. She expressed the hope that those standing for election were doing so, not on party or personal grounds but because they hoped to provide 'an efficient education for the people'. In this she was pointedly singling out the church party, which was putting up an excessive number of candidates, and resisting attempts to be dissuaded. The election had to go ahead.

Lydia was nominated as a member of the unsectarian group, now based in the Liberal Manchester Reform Club.[16] At a meeting in the Co-operative Hall in Downing Street, the unsectarian candidates met their supporters, and each said their piece about where they felt the school board now stood. Becker's opinion for the electors was that 'It was well to have a good representation of parties on the school board because it afforded a guarantee that a matter would be looked at from every point of view.' Her hope was that the electors would choose the existing board members as they had achieved so much. She compared the board to 'soldiers in the field' fighting against ignorance and vice, and 'The weapons with which they had to combat that enemy were educated, thoroughly instructed girls and boys.' Her view of board schools and their relationship to voluntary (church) schools demonstrated that she was not doctrinaire in the methods she favoured to achieve her goal of universal education:

> The board schools were the arsenals where those good weapons were furnished, and she was far more concerned to find that those schools should be in good order, and those weapons well burnished, than that any number of inferior private arsenals should be commenced. If voluntary schools were doing good work she would not oppose them because she believed a little competition was healthy.[17]

At the last board meeting before the contested election, the members paid tribute to the chairman, Herbert Birley; despite his position as a churchman, Lydia recognised his skill in the chair, saying that 'whatever might have been the differences of opinion amongst themselves, they all unanimously respected the chairman.'[18]

A meeting of women electors for the school board was held in support of the unsectarian candidates at Chorlton-upon-Medlock Town Hall. In her address, Lydia pointed out that the 10,000 women voters in the city controlled 150,000 votes, and she wanted to impress on her audience the power this bestowed. She encouraged the return of the existing board members, arguing that the churchmen already in post would safeguard the interests of churchwomen, and a similar case for the Catholics. But she did ask those who favoured the unsectarians to vote for her and the others of her group. She pointed out that she had recently been arguing in board meetings that women officers, such as school visitors, were essential, especially if the board was to have due consideration for the feelings of women and children. She hoped to carry on, and win, that fight.[19]

In dense fog, voting took place to select fifteen members out of a final twenty-two who were standing. There was some confusion; some voters went to the wrong polling stations and others, who were unsure where to go, did not vote at all. There was widespread tactical voting, and the six unsectarian candidates agreed with the four Catholics to instruct their voters as to how to allot their fifteen votes. Because there was a secret ballot, there was nervousness as to how effective this would be.[20] In a low turnout of under 36 per cent, the vote produced a board of six (previously five) unsectarians, five churchmen (previously seven) and four (previously three) Catholics.[21] Despite the slight change of emphasis on the board, in a speech to the Bradford Liberal Club Lydia expressed the view that the election had vindicated the work of the Manchester School Board up to this time, which had 'pledged to the purpose for which it was elected'.[22] It was also a personal vindication for Lydia of all her hard work; at 22,692 votes she came second only to Herbert Birley who gained 25,171 votes.[23] A prominent Manchester Liberal, Robert Leake, acknowledged her worth when he wrote to Becker asking her permission to present a £75 scholarship to the board under the name of the 'Becker scholarship'. He explained:

> It may then be some slight evidence of the high esteem in which you are held by me and by thousands of your fellow-citizens, who have witnessed your work as a member of the School Board, and your

constant endeavours to raise the social and political condition of the whole nation by the elevation of its better-half – your own sex.

Lydia, who was handed the letter just before a meeting with a request that the clerk read it out, was taken aback and clearly somewhat embarrassed; she asked that the name of the award be considered later, but Leake's suggestion was eventually adopted.[24]

It is notable that much of Lydia's support came from the working classes. She was proud of what the board had achieved and in December addressed the St George's Working Men's Reform Club on a variety of political issues, including the fact that, due to the work of the Manchester School Board over nine years, there were a great many more children in education. Despite her middle-class background, she spoke to them in a practical and easy manner, and was perceived to be disinterested and 'true'. According to Lilias Ashworth Hallett in 1890, it was reported by canvassers in the school board elections that 'the working men always say they must keep some of their votes for Lydia'. Indeed, so popular was she that she once laughingly declared that she was far more the representative for Manchester than any of the MPs because far more electors voted for her than for any of them.[25]

Every three years, Becker received nominations to stand for re-election from both men and women. For example, in 1882 her nominators were Edward Potter, calico printer, and Richard Hankinson, solicitor, but also Charlotte Tinsley, confectioner, Mary Sterland, shop keeper, Lucy Woodhead, spinster, and her relative and assistant in the suffrage society, Sarah Backhouse, clerk.[26] Thus she continued to be elected for the rest of her life, a popular and respected member both within and outside the board.

At the Ducie Avenue Higher Grade Board Schools prize-giving Lydia reminded the audience (and posterity) about the extent of the board's work:

> She supposed that many of her hearers were electors, and that they might possibly have paid some attention to the deliberations which took place on the board. What she desired to point out was that what they saw in the newspapers with regard to the discussions at the board meetings, and more especially what they saw as to differences of opinion among the members, really represented a very small proportion of the work done by the board.[27]

The inauguration and operation of the Manchester School Board

In 1869, a parliamentary survey of education in Manchester had horrified the city authorities, and was the impetus which led the city to be the first to elect a school board.[28] The educational census showed that Manchester had a shortfall of educational places of 8,000. Although this was lower than other cities because Manchester had a strong voluntary sector, the census also showed that attendance was very irregular, and the child population was expanding faster than the provision. There was harmonious agreement, therefore, to receive and support existing schools, to build new ones, and to adopt a liberal curriculum. Those elected to the Manchester School Board were people who had already shown an interest in the education of children, and they must have met together with great excitement that they were about to launch a groundbreaking initiative which would dramatically alter the prospects of the poor children of the city.

The first meeting of the Manchester School Board on 15 December 1870 began with the town clerk explaining its powers to the new body, and proceeded to the election of a chairman and deputy.[29] For the former, Herbert Birley, cotton magnate, was selected, even though he was also chair of the Salford Board. He was of the 'church' party – those who favoured sectarian religious instruction in schools – and his success was due to the support of that group. Lydia, although nominally brought up in the Church of England, voted for his 'unsectarian' rival, Oliver Heywood. Her favoured candidate as deputy, the radical Dr John Watts, also lost out to Conservative and church party man W. Romaine Callender. Under Birley's chairmanship the board proved a very proactive body with a national reputation; its members were progressive in educational matters, sympathetic to the plight of children, but religiously conservative in supporting the voluntary schools and religious teaching in board schools. They agreed that, unless inappropriate, they would keep their meetings open to the press. However, attempts by Lydia to open up its committees for school management and general purposes to press scrutiny were unsuccessful.[30] Even so, at a poorly attended meeting of the board she later managed to get a resolution passed in July 1875 to allow ratepayers into board meetings, but the numbers were limited to four due to a shortage of space.[31]

As the discussions proceeded, it is clear that Lydia Becker was determined to be as vocal as the rest of the board, and was not proposing to be the modest and retiring feminine presence they might have expected.[32] When appointing the officers there was discussion about whether to pay the secretary, a full-time position, as much as a handsome £500. Lydia supported a lesser amount of £300 because she argued that the office should be held by someone committed to the work, not out for money. The board was to meet monthly with a quorum of seven. Lydia again spoke up pointing out that once a month was the statutory minimum and might seem to suggest that the board was doing 'the least possible work'. The town clerk explained that there had to be a monthly meeting but that the board could hold additional, interim ones.

There was lengthy discussion about whether the board should immediately make school attendance compulsory, but it was objected that in some areas there was, as yet, insufficient provision to allow all the children to attend school. Lydia asserted that it was desirable to bring in this by-law as soon as possible, so that it could be enforced as and when provision became adequate. Fortunately, the board was agreed on the principle that compulsory attendance was desirable, but again the vote went against Lydia and they decided to await returns which were being gathered on the state of existing educational provision. The meeting ended with the appointment of a sub-committee to look into the reception of existing schools under the board's umbrella, and the whole committee was to seek out suitable offices where they might be based.

As the year drew to a close, William Birch gave notice that at the next meeting, on 4 January 1871, he would move a series of resolutions to divide Manchester into five areas, each of which would have three board members allotted to it. These were to organise house-to-house visits to ascertain numbers and details of school-age children, educational provision and attendance in their area. They would also meet with educational providers to discuss co-operation with the board. Children not attending school would be called on and the visitor would 'expostulate with the parents' and if they were still obdurate, they would be reported to the board. Provision would, however, be made to pay the fees of children whose parents could not afford them. Lydia Becker was appointed with Canon Toole and Mr Birch himself, to Hulme district.[33]

By April the following year, the board was meeting in offices at 28 Cross Street and discussing the urgent need for an 'industrial school' for children liable to become embroiled in crime, as well as 'beadles' to find accommodation for street children and to help hapless widowed mothers deal with recalcitrant sons. Whilst the children at issue were thought to be mainly boys, it was also admitted that there was a problem of the entrapment in brothels of girls as young as 12. Despite the fears of Canon Toole as to safety of the 'hands in which children might be placed', Lydia voted, this time successfully, in favour of temporary provision being made until the new industrial school could be constructed.[34]

Initially, Lydia found the school board egalitarian, and in January 1871 had reported 'In this case complete equality has been attained. There is no room for that condescending permission to associate with them in their pursuits which men display under show of deference to a lady.'[35] However, as she began to campaign on educational issues she considered important, she met disapproval and resistance. Although she was put on several committees, notably the Rota and the Industrial Schools committees, she never appeared on the Finance, Parliamentary Bill or Technical Education committees. The board tried to channel her into 'female' areas such as the Girls' Manual Instruction committee and the Free Breakfast sub-committee. She only chaired meetings on two known occasions; at the By-Laws Rota committee on 21 March 1872, when only three members were present, and the Industrial Schools committee in 1881, when only she and Mr Cooper were present. Her expertise in areas such as parliamentary matters and science was largely ignored, and her femininity was raised as an objection to her participation in a discussion on criminal activities late at night in Manchester streets; this was not a suitable subject for a woman. But she did have allies, particularly the radical Dr John Watts. In the *WSJ*, Lydia wrote how he 'was sure she held her own ... extremely well', and how he believed she 'sometimes opened the eyes of his colleagues to facts which would not be visible to them if they had not a lady with them'. She encountered a small suffragist group on the board; several members were also in the MNSWS, notably John Watts himself, and some signed a petition that female membership of school boards 'renders anomalous' the parliamentary disabilities of women.[36]

At the end of its first year, the board received the report of a committee made up of Lydia Becker, Canon Toole, Dr Watts, Mr Birch and Mr Callender on the proposed 'scheme of education'. This provided for existing schools' transfer to the board, how board schools should be established and organised, and what they should teach. Each of the committee members added a number of caveats to the findings, and it reflected the complexity of their task that they clearly could not agree on many fundamental aspects. Lydia objected to a recommendation for separate sex schools because 'grave moral evils to both sexes, and serious intellectual disadvantages to girls, arise from the separate system of education.' She also disagreed with provisions for religious instruction, which were included by the church supporters. It was agreed (against the vote of Lydia and two others) that this would all be discussed without reporters present. There was also a dispute within the board about access to its records and statistics, with church supporters attempting to make it difficult for the unsectarian Dr McKerrow to get hold of information he wanted to use in agitation against denominational schools. On this occasion, Lydia's proposal to make quarterly returns showing the numbers of children sent to schools, along with attendances and fees, was successful. It seems that in a letter after the meeting, Canon Toole claimed that Lydia was put up to this by Dr McKerrow, but both of them strongly denied this claim.[37]

After the secret meeting, a final discussion was held by the board to which the press were admitted. Lydia took the opportunity to explain why she felt the education of girls in separate schools was so deficient:

> She showed by statistical returns that at the present time the proportion of girls who received instruction in what are known as extra subjects, such as geography, history, grammar, singing by note, drawing etc., is very small as compared with the proportion of boys; and she believed the reason was that girls were excluded from those schools [i.e. boys' schools] where thoroughly trained teachers able to teach the extra subjects were employed.

When it came to a vote, she had only the support of Alderman Rumney; the rest of the board agreed with Canon Toole that mixed schools were undesirable 'on grounds of propriety and morality'. Becker was also in a minority on the issue of opposing religious instruction in board schools.

She was forceful in objecting 'entirely to the School Board ... having anything to do with religious instruction ...' However, the church group was victorious on this issue.[38]

Despite her gender, Lydia took on some duties which hitherto had been the province of men, and on 2 April 1871 attended the annual examination in the Manchester Jews' School in Derby Street near Cheetham Hill Road. It was the first of many such occasions. The school educated both Jewish and non-Jewish children in an unsectarian manner and Lydia had the opportunity to examine some of the pupils and 'expressed her high sense of the efficiency with which the teaching was conducted'.[39]

A momentous day for the Manchester School Board was 11 June 1874, when the very first of three new elementary schools was opened in Vine Street, Hulme, with the attendance of the mayor and mayoress and several of the board, including Lydia Becker. They spoke in support of the auspicious occasion, and Lydia said that the presence of the mayor showed that the education of children was 'a matter for ... public concern'. The institution would accommodate 500 children or more. In addition, there were new schools in Every Street in Ancoats (1,000) and in Chester Street in Ardwick (800).[40] When these latter were inaugurated in 1875, Lydia attended both ceremonies on the same day, the representatives of the board travelling between them by omnibus; at the Every Street inauguration she made her first full public address at a school opening.[41] In some ways, the triumph was particularly hers, along with Dr Watts'. The proponents of voluntary (religious) schools had tried to slow up the progress of the Every Street school by challenging the choice of architect by the unsectarian board members, but Lydia and Watts pushed forward the project by requesting his designs.[42] She appears to have taken similar interest in the actual construction of other board schools, notably the Central Higher Grade School opened in 1884 by A.J. Mundella, vice-president of the government education committee.[43] In this case, she unsuccessfully advocated that the board should seek professional assistance with the school plans, which might suggest some worrying corner-cutting in building standards.

In February 1877, she was allowed to lay the memorial stone of the new board schools for girls on Burgess Street, Harpurhey, and spoke of the 'deep sense of honour' which the board had done her by inviting her to lay the stone, as it was the first by a lady. She went on to explain that although highly gratified to be involved in the great work of educating girls, she wanted to make it clear that she was also very interested in the education of boys as 'the education of boys was of just as much importance to women as the education of girls: for were not boys to be their husbands, and fathers, and brothers, and sons?'[44] Her role was also soon extended to presiding at prize-givings. All these occasions gave her an opportunity to speak about her educational aspirations and beliefs.

Over the years, Lydia acquired considerable influence on the board, and was acknowledged as second only to Birley himself, as judged by the elections of 1879 and 1882. She furthered its work in innumerable ways, even down to supporting the installation of a telephone in its offices in 1883. Despite the views of one writer, who in 1890 after her death described her as 'a strong-minded' woman 'too masterful for School Board colleagues', her work was done quietly, in an unthreatening manner, with assiduity, attention to detail and reliability.[45] She had needed to be forceful as the lone woman on the board, and was in some ways very typical of the women elected to school boards: individualistic, unmarried, educated (in her case, self-educated) and formidable. Everyone agreed that her achievements were immense and invaluable, and her male colleagues recognised that she was the best known of them 'to the world at large'.[46]

Fees and attendance

A prerequisite for any kind of success was that children should be in school, and the board had its work cut out to ensure that there was sufficient provision, in the right places, of the appropriate nature and at affordable costs to parents and ratepayers. It then had to begin the difficult task of persuading, cajoling and enforcing school attendance on reluctant families.

One reason for poor attendance was a lack of compulsion combined with the requirement for parents to pay school fees. The voluntary schools had long remitted the fees of very poor children, and the board continued and extended this policy. In 1871 it was a matter of discussion, and Lydia was concerned that the board was not directing help effectively:

> She had been most thoroughly dissatisfied with the plans adopted by the board in regard to the payment of fees. She thought that they had

> operated very disastrously in Manchester ... they were pauperising the people, and ... by fixing an arbitrary scale of poverty they were offering temptations to imposition ... [47]

She felt that, although some parents took advantage of the system, some children were absent from school because the fees and the remittances were not properly targeted. In October 1872, on her initiative, it was agreed that the level of family income at which fees should be remitted was to be much higher than hitherto. She justified this by the fact that with the approach of winter more of a family income would have to be used for fires, food and clothing, and families might not be able also to pay for schooling.[48] Two years later, Manchester at £2,405 and Salford at £1,323 were spending more on remitting fees than the rest of the country put together; the next two authorities were Liverpool at £824 and Bristol at £386.[49] Indeed, in 1889 at the prize evening of the Birley Street Board School in New Islington, Becker expressed the opinion that remittances could go too far:

> She looked with some alarm on the prospect of going too far in providing education for the children of the people at the public expense. She thought there ought to be a certain minimum of necessary instruction which ought to be provided at the public expense, but when they came to what she might call the luxuries of education she thought that parents should be encouraged to pay for them ... She thought that parents should pay for and provide so far as they could out of their own wages and earnings for the education of their children, just as they were bound to provide for their clothing and food ... [50]

In July 1871, the board was re-drafting the by-laws for the seventh time, and Lydia raised another issue which she considered vital for consideration. She moved that, contrary to previous practice, which had provided for a fee of 3*d* a week for mixed schools and girls' schools and 4*d* for boys' schools, all schools for children of 6 to 12 should charge a fee of 4*d* per pupil; for infants' schools the fee would be 2*d*. According to the *Manchester Times* she expressly stated that she was aiming to defend the interests of girls. She also pointed out that it would mean that the Wesleyan schools, which were mixed, would not be unfairly disadvantaged as compared to the single-sex schools run by other denominations. She hinted at her own inclination in favour of mixed schools because they offered more opportunity for girls to study the academic subjects provided for the boys. However, Mr Cooper suggested an amendment to pay the usual 4*d* for boys but 3*d* for girls, arguing that the education of girls cost less than that of boys, especially as the salary of a mistress was two-thirds that of a master. In the end, despite her contention that if less were paid for the girls they would be 'pushed out' of any mixed schools, the committee voted to set the fees at 4*d* for boys, 3*d* for girls and 3*d* for infants up to 6 years old.[51]

With regard to attendance itself, there was a multiplicity of factors to address; many children were half-time mill workers, others were hawking in the streets. Often they were earning money essential to the survival of themselves and their family. Lydia at first may have been somewhat naive in her explanation of this issue: 'the duty of parents to provide for their children of tender years is not generally recognised by the very poor; and the contrary practice of making them work for their bread is lamentably frequent.' Children, often girls, were also drafted in to care for siblings: 'Houses have to be kept in order, babies have to be nursed, fathers' dinners have to be taken, etc. Girls are kept from school to do these things, and when there are no girls, boys are frequently detained for these purposes.'[52]

Nevertheless, Manchester passed by-laws requiring children up to the age of 13 to attend school (in London the age was initially 11).[53] At Lydia's Attendance committee her eyes were opened to the realities of poverty, as parents pleaded the case for their children having to work. She responded with attempts to find novel solutions and took an interest in part-time education for working children. In 1874, she proposed that there should be an experimental half-timers' school, offering the same curriculum both morning and afternoon, to cast the net as widely as possible. She was especially concerned with this because a lot of the half-time pupils were girls. The idea was already in operation in Copenhagen where a correspondent of hers had seen it successfully applied. Lydia was fully alive to the realities of the situation:

> She (Miss Becker) thought that anyone who attended the meetings of the rota committee must have found themselves painfully perplexed with the domestic difficulties of the mothers ... which, she thought,

were perhaps not given quite sufficient consideration by the hon. gentlemen in London who devised the act which this board had to put in force.

After discussion, the matter was left for the General Purposes committee to investigate.[54] Lydia, meanwhile, continued to think up schemes to help with the reorganisation of domestic arrangements, such as the childcare of younger siblings. She also tried to prevent parents from being hounded by the courts for their children's non-attendance. And she often confessed herself baffled as to how the intractable issue of feeding a family without children's wages might be resolved.

On the other hand, she believed the board did not help the situation by accepting 50 per cent attendance as satisfactory, as this gave the impression that full-time schooling was unimportant and unnecessary.[55] She was accordingly keen to clamp down on non-attenders who pretended illness, and in December 1876 the board agreed to her proposal that it should be considered whether medical certificates be required 'where sickness is alleged as the cause for irregular attendance at school'. The cost of such a certificate, at a shilling, was a huge issue, and an indignant letter by 'AN ELECTOR' to the *Manchester Courier* protested that her idea was unreasonable and likely to cause ill-will, showing that she and the board were out of touch with people to whom a shilling was a large sum, ending 'I would just remind the magnates, that when they sit in solemn conclave again, making such arbitrary laws, that they may carry their high-handed work too far.'[56] Lydia was surely cognisant that 1 shilling was a huge amount, but her intention was perhaps to deter and punish those who were tempted to keep their children away unnecessarily. Her sympathy with well-intentioned parents was clear from her statement to the board in 1883 when she declared that 'However poor and low people were they were anxious to give their children the benefit of education.'[57]

Chapter 9

Aspects of Becker's School Board Career

Whilst she was a committed member of the school board, proving to be a popular candidate at almost all elections and inspiring faith particularly in working-class voters, Lydia's career was distinguished especially by her close interest in several aspects of the board's work. In particular, she was notable for her views on educational methods, her focus on equal education for the very poor and for girls, her desire to limit the influence of religion in board schools, her attempts to support and regulate Manchester's specialist schools, and the campaign to achieve high-class training and fair remuneration for women teachers.

Philosophy and approaches to education

In view of her keen interest in her own education and in that of her siblings, it is not surprising that Lydia developed a belief in the importance of education and of effective teaching. Moreover, she was eager to share her ideas and took the opportunities offered by her work on the school board to spread them. A tea in aid of the City Road Congregational Church's new day school was one such occasion, when she stated 'She was very much afraid … that in many cases children attending schools were not very happy, and that the teaching was not very intelligent.' Her enlightened idea was that 'Teaching should be a mutual pleasure to the teacher and the child', and she sounded even more idealistic when she opined 'Wherever there were stupid, dull children, who did not attend to their lessons, the fault lay with the teachers …' She hoped that eventually every school would be 'a little paradise' for children. This laudable goal would be achieved by allowing the pupils a choice in the subjects studied, and ensuring that education was aimed at 'the acquisition of information, the cultivation of habits of observation and reasoning, and the application of the knowledge and reasoning so acquired to the general purposes of life'.[1]

She was also concerned about excessive pressure on teachers and pupils to achieve, which led the former to see the latter 'in the mere light of scholastic material'. The corollary of this was that 'She was very strongly of opinion that home lessons [homework] should be dispensed with as far as was possible ... and that they ought never to be enforced where the parents felt that the child had quite enough work at school.'[2]

Lydia had developed a scheme for the teaching of reading, based on her own experiences, and demonstrated a knowledge of the latest theories:

> I have a young sister [Esther] who was 4 years old in August 1858. On January 1st 1857 I began to teach her to read, she not knowing a letter. I predicted that on the 1st of June, she would be able to read any English book that was placed before her ... I gave her a lesson every day, and long before that time she could read quite well ... I believe that any child can acquire the art of reading <u>perfectly</u> ... without consciousness of the mechanism of letters, syllables etc. So as to take in a whole sentence at a <u>glance</u> without having to go over every word ... and this practice can only be attained by letting children have <u>books</u> which excite their imagination ...[3]

Her sister Esther recalled that Lydia acquired her ideas from the Swinton Schools, where a phonic method had been introduced by Sir James Kay Shuttleworth, and explained Lydia's feelings on the current system:

> She must say that from the very bottom of her heart she pitied the poor little children taught to read under the irrational mode at present in vogue, of teaching them by spelling ... She had taught many children to read, and the alphabet was the last thing she taught them.

In 1878, she developed this theme further in a letter to the *Manchester Guardian*, explaining the advantages of the 'phonic' method, in which only a few characters were taught to begin with, and those as sounds. She recommended the phonic reading books which included graduated stages, but accounted for the failure to adopt her system with the contention that 'it requires more intelligence, patience and care in the first lessons, both on the part of the teacher and pupil than the old plan.'[4]

Also key to Becker's philosophy was her belief in mixed schools and classes, which she argued would be more economical than the current separation of the sexes above infant level. This was in line with her contention that girls should be taught the same subjects as boys. Equally importantly, she believed that the current system of separating the sexes 'taught boys to disparage girls', and argued that 'a boy would respect a woman more if he had been accustomed to sit side by side with her in his class.'[5] She reached out to parents and others outside the board in an attempt to convince them that there was no impropriety in mixed education: 'she did not see why it was more likely that young men and young women should misbehave when they were studying in the science classes than when they were together with their families.'[6]

The methods and uses of punishment exercised Lydia too. In 1877, the board had to confront the issue of the use of corporal punishment in their schools in City Road and Hamer Street, and to what extent it may have been improperly applied. She appears to have modified her views to some extent on the issue of who was to blame for recalcitrant pupils; although she stated that the board 'set their faces against arbitrary punishment in their schools', she went on, half tongue-in-cheek, to admit that 'Children were very provoking animals – (laughter) – as all who had large families or many brothers and sisters were aware; and it was with the greatest difficulty that one's temper and nerves could be kept in order. (Laughter.)'[7]

At the NAPSS conference of 1880, she also mentioned that she was not against the use of whipping on 'juvenile delinquents', that is, outside the school setting, as long as it was carried out by a public official.[8] Nevertheless, she was strongly opposed to corporal punishment in education in any circumstances, as evidenced in her address to the Manchester District Teachers' Union on 2 November 1878. She 'could not for a moment entertain the idea that it was necessary to have corporal punishment in schools for some children. If a teacher could not teach a child without beating it, it simply showed the incompetency of the teacher.'[9]

It can be said that in some ways Becker was in sympathy with the prevailing view that education for the working classes was about creating biddable citizens. However, when taken in the context of her own rebellion against social norms, the speech she made in 1879 may be taken to reflect her genuine desire to create a happy and law-abiding civil society. In a further ten years she believed all the children in Manchester would have been brought under regular systematic instruction ... It was something to take children and accustom them to regular habits – to inspire them with pride in their schools, with a wish to do right, and a wish to succeed; and she believed that when they had had the experience of a whole generation of people growing up under these influences, they would have a very different condition of things ... for, after all, the great hindrances to progress and happiness were not so much wilful violation of law as ignorance of what that law was, and consequences of the violation of it.[10]

Commensurate with a belief in education for all children, whatever their social status, Lydia understood that education could not succeed without attention to the general well-being of children and their families. She took a particular interest in the welfare of the poorest slum children, for instance petitioning the council not to salt the roads, to prevent damage to their bare feet. She blamed a degree of parental failing on the public house, where some men spent their wages, leaving their families in rags.[11] Accordingly, as a keen advocate of temperance, she on occasion asked the board to petition parliament not to 'sanction any extension of the hours during which intoxicating liquors may be sold'.[12] She recognised the realities of poverty, and when, in 1873, the Manchester Board pioneered schemes for feeding malnourished children, Lydia took it upon herself to check and taste the school meals provided.[13] She was active on the Free Breakfast committee from 1879, which received grudging support from the board; provision was limited to bread and coffee when the weather was very severe, and only the very poorest children benefited. Becker managed to broaden the variety of drinks offered, and by 1880 the board was giving soup dinners to a hundred children on alternate days in the winter. Progress was slow, however, and even by 1887, breakfasts were only provided at ten board schools and free meals at a mere five.[14]

She especially sought ways to send the street hawkers and beggars, many of whom were desperately poor Irish immigrants, to ragged schools in the city, in an effort to furnish them with the tools to escape dire poverty. On her initial election to the board, she had been invited to the inaugural meeting of the Salford Queen St Ragged Schools, and took a lead in encouraging the board to adopt them in the hope of enhancing their provision. This institution, out of charitable funds, educated up to 600 children in a kindergarten during the day, and held adult 'instructive entertainments' in the evenings.[15] Lydia, moreover, expressed a desire in March 1880 to abandon the term 'ragged school', when she attended the annual meeting of the Barrow Street Ragged School in Salford. She pointed out that rags were 'an accident' and should not be accepted and enshrined in the name of any school. She did not believe Manchester or Salford needed to have a ragged class among them and called for 'an amendment of the laws to bring parental responsibility more directly home to every man and woman in the land'.[16]

Lydia was always very careful to stress that the education offered to both boys and girls in board schools should be academic; this was the basis of her lifelong argument against girls spending time learning needlework. When there was discussion at a meeting on the teaching of cookery in Manchester, she was quick to reject a suggestion by the speaker that it should be done through the board schools in lessons for the girls. She stated quite categorically that 'The board schools were not intended to be technical schools in which children were to be taught the occupations by which they would have to earn their living, but to cultivate their faculties generally.'[17]

Pushing very hard for science to be taught in Manchester Board Schools, in 1879 Becker proposed herself for co-option onto the snappily named BAAS 'Committee on the Manner in which Rudimentary Science should be taught, and how Examinations should be held therein, in Elementary Schools'. The committee had been set up to influence public opinion and the government to improve and extend the teaching of science. At the BAAS conference of 1883 she argued 'warmly' that 'useless' subjects like grammar and needlework should be abolished in favour of lessons on 'the principles which underlay their [the children's] daily lives'.[18] Learning was to be by experience, as Lydia demonstrated through her knowledge of astronomy:

> Children should be <u>shown</u> the sky moving round the earth and carrying the sun, moon and stars along with it, and the moon and planets creeping backwards along the surface[?], they ought not to be bewildered with 'information' till they have seen and thoroughly taken in the actual appearances in the sky.[19]

She remained on the committee for ten years, and was able to make new and distinguished contacts, most notably Sir Henry Roscoe of Owens College. Her influence was extended when, for the 1887 BAAS conference at Manchester, Lydia was also appointed to the Local Government committee.[20]

Her attitude to the importance of science education was at times almost evangelical in its scope. In her article 'On the Study of Science by Women' she put the case that the universe was governed by laws which it was the duty of scientists to discover, and when everything was known, the miseries of human life could be eradicated:

> Every step gained in advance reveals something which can be turned to account in ameliorating the hardships and discomforts of life, and promoting the happiness of mankind. With complete knowledge of the conditions under which we live ... we might hope to see most of the evils that afflict our race entirely disappear ... The greater the number of minds that are impressed with this belief, the greater the encouragement that will be given to the inquirer, and the greater the probability and the proximity of success.

Her point was that, with women involved in the great endeavour, the pace of progress would be more than doubled in a humankind which was all pulling in the same direction, where men and women would share the same 'deep and intense sympathy in their noblest aims and aspirations'.[21]

The education of girls

The position of some feminists like Emily Davies and Lydia Becker, with regard to the education of middle-class girls in the second half of the nineteenth century, was that it should mirror as closely as possible that offered to their brothers.[22] Thus in the private sector, female education became more academic and rigorous. It is, therefore, all the more ironic that, as the state began to take an interest in the education of the working classes, boys were offered academic subjects whereas the curriculum for girls was increasingly focused on preparing them for domestic duties, either in their own home or as servants.[23] Fully in keeping with her beliefs about the complementary roles of the sexes, from the start Becker particularly fought the corner of girls, demanding 'for my own sex an equal share in these [educational] advantages in order to attain that end after which we are all striving – namely that the whole people shall be educated'. She was aware that she faced prejudice which was 'so deeply ingrained as almost to reduce to despair those whose own intellects and whose instincts taught them to claim essential and intellectual equality for all human beings'.[24] This came, not least, from the highly esteemed chairman of the board, Herbert Birley, who proved a difficult challenge. In her manifesto as a candidate Lydia marked herself out as a defender of the interests of girls when she stated 'Experience has proved that the education of girls cannot be properly regulated, and that it has never been adequately cared for, by corporate bodies consisting only of men.'[25] As in other areas of her activities, she believed that mixed committees of men and women would best serve the interests of those concerned.

In 1871, when appointed to the Scheme of Education committee by the board, she made recommendations which included large, mixed schools of at least 500 children. These would be better suited to teaching expensive science courses, and would give girls access to scientific equipment. She also suggested the schools should teach history, geography, algebra and geometry, and recommended swimming as healthy exercise, though this was 'not considered advisable' by some of her colleagues. Sadly, this attempt to broaden access to include girls was defeated by 10 to 2 with Herbert Birley and Canon Toole leading the opposition to her proposals; mixed schools were immoral.[26]

One major reason for the inequality in educational provision was, as has been seen, the structure of the fees. Girls' fees were fixed at only 3*d* (as compared to 4*d* for boys) and mistresses were paid less than masters, receiving poorer academic training. As a result, the total amount contributed in Manchester in one year for girls' education was just over £508, whereas boys were funded to the tune of £978.[27] On 20 December 1871, Becker presented the prizes at the girls' school and infant department of the Miles Platting Institute and gave the address. She regretted that the future mothers of the country were less advantaged than the future fathers, especially in view of the universal acknowledgement of the importance of a mother's influence on her children. She put it that the schools should be common to both sexes, as statistics showed that girls' intellectual attainment in Manchester was well below that of boys. She considered that, if girls were educated alongside boys, they would receive instruction in more academic subjects, such as geography and science. To fears about morality she responded that 'there could be no conceivable condition under which boys and girls could associate with so much advantage and little danger as when they were engaged in their studies under careful superintendence.'

What her audience made of these suggestions is not known, but it is not surprising that there was widespread resistance to her ideas in view of the strength of feeling about the separate spheres of male and female.[28] On occasion she was able to achieve her co-educational goals by the back door; in March 1874 the board discussed the Ashley Lane School, where 72 boys were taught in a large room and 125 girls in a much smaller one; the school managers had suggested that some older girls should therefore join the boys at a cost of £40–50, and this was approved by the Manchester Board. [29]

The education of girls in Manchester was also the theme of three lectures Lydia delivered in the early 1870s at the BAAS, attempting to challenge prejudice against an academic education for females.[30] Using statistics to show the variety of subjects studied by boys whilst girls studied needlework instead, Lydia advocated that the needlework should be replaced with other subjects, such as physiology and health education. Despite this, in 1877 the Department of Education introduced a 'Needlework Code', which even extended the needlework curriculum, and called for intricate and detailed work which was, in any case, irrelevant to the needs of a working-class home. Becker supported the London School Board in resisting this, describing it as 'a specimen of masculine legislation in women's sphere'. She managed to get the Manchester Board to write to the Education Department, demanding that 'My Lords will explain what they mean by "counter hemming" as required by the schedule.'[31] Predictably, the Department was deaf to protests and proceeded to give more generous grants to schools which focused on needlework, to the detriment of other subjects..

The committee established by the BAAS to oversee the teaching of science in schools, in which Becker's specific remit was to oversee the interests of girls in relation to government inspections of science in elementary schools, achieved little for them. By 1888, the committee pointed to an actual decline in science in girls' schools, and in particular that needlework was gradually replacing geography.[32] Of course, the ultimate justification for this was that girls were destined for domestic service in the homes of the middle classes, the biggest employer of working-class women, and the education on offer would prepare them for it. At the Domestic Economy Congress in Manchester in 1878, Lydia challenged this notion strongly. Startlingly, she even proposed that boys and girls should both study some domestic skills. Again though, it was a frustrating battle; in the same year, the Education Department made domestic economy compulsory for girls.[33] Her belief in academic education for women was further demonstrated in 1880 at the Women's Education Union when she argued against that body involving itself in girls' technical education because this might detract from its core mission of promoting academic education for women.[34]

Not only was girls' education lacking in quality, in Becker's view, but there was a deficiency in the amount of provision for them. In 'On the Attendance and Education of Girls in Manchester', presented to the BAAS in 1872, she pointed out that the accommodation for boys in Manchester schools was in excess by 2,399 places, whereas that for girls was deficient by some 2,379 places.[35] Moreover, there was evidence that their attendance was not enforced as rigorously as that of boys. In August 1872, at her instigation, the board agreed to enquire as to how and why the percentage of orders of attendance for girls issued but not enforced was 15.7 per cent, in contrast to 13 per cent for boys. Lydia cited attendance percentages at 75.77 for boys and 67.15 for girls, which she hoped the board would agree was unsatisfactory.[36] In January 1875, the attendance required of boys was 75 per cent, whereas for girls it was still only 60 per cent.[37] However, the board did agree to set a target of 80 per cent for both sexes.[38]

When the board awarded exhibitions at Roby Street Schools in 1876, Lydia took the opportunity to point out the way the system was failing girls. All the exhibitions were won by boys, though two girls did gain certificates of merit. Lydia lamented the small proportion of schools who had sent in candidates, and especially the low numbers of girls, which she believed 'showed that the girls' education had not been sufficiently attended to …' She quoted the experience of the Scarborough School Board, where a girl had won first prize ahead of all the boys: 'It appeared therefore that the Scarborough School Board and schools could teach and educate girls equally as well as boys, and she hoped the Manchester School Board would set that object before them.'[39]

When eventually evening classes for boys were piloted by the board in 1887, Lydia had as usual to make a case for the same opportunity being offered to girls, indeed the unsectarians had proposed evening schools as early 1874 as a partial solution for half-timers, many of whom were female. But in 1887 it was predictably objected that mixed education was not acceptable, and there the discussion rested.[40] Her tactic of a patient wearing down, and almost infinitesimal progress, must have been stressful and frustrating for a woman of such passionate commitment.

She met with resistance at all levels. In 1877, when laying the foundation stone of the girls' school in Harpurhey, she set out the feminist position, describing how a male friend who was head of an Oxford college had written to her asking 'If all this education goes on, who will wash my shirts?' Lydia, responding perhaps with irony but in a manner tailored to her hearers' preoccupations, declared that an educated woman with 'a little knowledge of elementary chemistry' would wash shirts much better than 'ignorant, untidy, uncultivated women'. It was also on this occasion that she first pithily expressed her more revolutionary (and therefore famous) view that boys too should receive education in domestic duties: 'if she had her way, every boy in Manchester should be taught to darn his own socks and cook his own chops'.[41] Yet she did not completely favour a uniform education; when it came to exercise, she scored an own goal at the board meeting of September 1879 when she objected to the introduction of dumb-bells in girls' drill, which elicited the comment from Mr Broadfield that 'he quite agreed with Miss Becker that it was no more possible to expect uniformity in the physical education of boys and girls than in their mental education. (Laughter.)'[42]

A significant development in 1877 was the establishment at Sale Moor of an industrial school for 100 girls under the auspices of both the Manchester and Salford School Boards. Although the boys' industrial school at Ardwick had contained fifty or so places for girls, it was deemed necessary for them to have separate provision. Lydia, newly appointed to the Industrial Schools committee of the board, addressed the meeting at the school's inauguration, but what she said was not thought worthy of report in the press. On visiting it later, the school came under her criticism for unlighted cells, a lack of furniture and toys, and the fact that it was preparing its pupils for a life in domestic service.[43] In an attempt to find examples of 'best practice' Lydia travelled around the country visiting similar establishments, and was notably impressed by those at York and Chelsea because they gave individual care and thought. The Good Shepherd Home at Leytonstone was praised for providing access to a farm and 'motherly' supervision.[44]

However, there were some young girls who were even less fortunate than those in 'penal institutions' like this. In the later 1880s, there was considerable social concern about young girls in brothels; the chief constable of Manchester had said that there were forty-two such girls known in the city. The board proposed that those over 10 years old should be punished by the Rota committee for non-attendance in school, but Lydia urged that they should instead be removed from the brothels and went so far as to inspect two houses in Greenheys where 130 girls could be housed at the expense of the board. Unfortunately, she was obliged to go to London as part of her suffrage work at this point, and the rest of the board deferred such rash expenditure.[45]

For the more able pupils, there was some progress. Much like other feminists in the educational field, notably Emily Davies, Becker accepted male academic values in external examinations, since they were the only ones on offer. She was influential in setting up several exhibitions, and from 1878, girls were successful. This was both a scholastic triumph, and a psychological breakthrough, reinforced when in 1881 two girls gained first-class honours in Practical Chemistry in the exams in the Manchester Central Higher Grade Schools.[46] Matters continued to improve gradually, and in 1882 when the board awarded its annual scholarships Lydia was quick to congratulate girls 'upon the high position they had taken in the examinations', but added pointedly 'especially so when they knew that the girls did not possess the same opportunities as the boys for study'.[47]

She was always aware of the prejudices and priorities of society with regard to the education of girls, and managed to knit her desire for their academic advancement with more traditional aims. At the presentation of the Queen's prizes in the science and art exams in the Manchester Road Schools she developed a theme which she had proposed earlier:

> Miss Lydia Becker said she was glad to know that in many instances the women of Manchester had shown their appreciation of the science and art classes. (Hear, hear.) No fewer than 14 women students had received prizes on the present occasion, and she noticed that their successes were chiefly in chemistry and mathematics.

Well mathematics would not hinder a woman in making a pudding. (Laughter.) Geometry might help her in cutting out a garment or arranging her furniture. There was no department of household work in which was not applied science of some kind, and the woman who wished to do household work in the most efficient, and quickest, and economical manner would be greatly helped by the science taught in their classes. (Applause.)[48]

She was delighted that at the BAAS conference in 1888 she was able to say with great pride that in Manchester schools, girls were now being given a 'chemical education', which she urged other places to emulate.[49]

Becker was more in line with other feminists when she took a great interest in the private Manchester High School for Girls, which had been founded in 1874 with funds from public subscription by the Manchester Society for Promoting the Education of Women, of which she was a member.[50] Along with Birley and others on the Manchester School Board, Becker became a trustee and attended their annual meeting at the end of October 1880. She was keen to see the High School do for the city's girls what the Grammar School did for the boys, by offering scholarships for the most able elementary school pupils, but believed it would require a more central location or 'at least four good schools in every quarter of the town'.

She reminded the governors that there were sums available from the Hulme Trust, a local charity, which gave such a disproportionate amount to boys that the girls received only 'a most beggarly pittance, which she really wondered the men of Manchester were not ashamed of offering to their townswomen and daughters'.[51] She expressed the view that girls' high schools, like those for boys, should be endowed and not self-supporting, and colourfully appealed to the 'chivalry of men':

> Knights in former days went forth with spear and shield and, as they were now told, underwent wonderful adventures on behalf of fair damsels, and she now asked the knights of the present day to go forth with their bank notes and gold to deliver fair damsels from the stronghold of ignorance in which some of them were immured.

Despite her petitions, which were supported by the school board, the fund opted to build a new boys' school, with no less than 300 places, immediately. For three years there would be a yearly payment of £500 to the existing Manchester High School for Girls, which was not endowed as the Boys' Grammar was. If it did become permanently endowed within five years the governors would be able to apply for a permanent appropriation of the Hulme Trust funds. In the event that this did not happen, a girls' 'Hulme Grammar School' would be established in five years, and it would be for not less than 200 pupils. Maths would not be taught, and the mistresses would be paid less than the masters at the boys' school. At both schools there were bursaries to remit fees, but the boys would also be offered ten scholarships of £15 per annum. Rubbing salt into the wound, the girls' tuition fees would be £6–12 per annum as compared to the boys' £5–10. The upshot was that the Hulme Charity would furnish a total of £3,500 yearly for boys, and £500 for girls. The girls' school would be governed by fifteen men with three women – too few to 'secure to women an effective voice in the regulation of the education of their own sex'.[52]

Becker addressed further the issue of curriculum in such schools, and opined that there was no place for domestic economy in high schools. Perhaps based on her own painful early difficulties, she made a forceful plea against obligatory study of the pianoforte, cruelly imposed on girls who did not wish it, dramatically likening the practice involved to 'a treadmill – which was not only torture to themselves, but also to those who had to teach them. (Hear, hear.)' She broadened this idea at the NAPSS in May the following year when she recommended that parents be allowed to select and limit the subjects taught to their daughters in high schools, in order to avoid excessive pressure on students.[53]

Although not an active campaigner for women's higher education in the way of Emily Davies and Emily Shirreff, (a founder-member of the National Union for the Improvement of Education for Women of all Classes), Lydia did uphold the principle when the opportunity arose. At the BAAS conference, she attended a lecture by Shirreff on the subject, and in the discussion revealed further her philosophy of women's education. She argued with Shirreff's point that the country's wealth was created by men, since 'women had assisted to create that wealth'. She referred to her own lack of formal education and hoped that future women would have the opportunities she had missed: 'She considered that it was necessary for the happiness of the world that the women should be as well educated as the men, inasmuch as a woman unequal in education could not be a companion to a man.'[54]

At a lecture by Professor Roscoe of Owens College on 1 April 1878 on 'The Condensation of Gases' in the Albert Square Memorial Hall, she challenged him about the lack of access for women students to the college. She had already been signatory to a memorial to Owens College which the Manchester Association for Promoting the Education of Women had submitted. The professor patronisingly claimed he would be glad to see ladies at his lectures, but 'they must remember that he did not always lecture on the liquefaction of gases, nor at a convenient hour in the evening'. He went on to explain that his lectures started at 9.30 a.m. when 'in winter the mornings were often very dark and wet. Ladies would have to go through the arduous undertaking of regular attendance every morning …' He disingenuously claimed that 'It would be a pleasure to him to receive ladies if it could only be managed; but circumstances were against the idea, and he could not at present hold out any hope as to their admission.' Lydia's fury and exasperation can only be guessed at.[55]

Religious controversies

When the Manchester School Board was set up, there was no scheme of religious instruction, but as time wore on, religious controversy became a major theme of their meetings between the 'church party' (both Church of England and Catholic) and 'unsectarians'. Lydia Becker, although on the side of the unsectarians, in February 1872 declared that she was not at all hostile towards sectarian schools, which 'had done a great deal of good'. Nevertheless, she argued that a by-law should be rescinded which allowed the payment of fees to denominational schools to continue indefinitely. She contended that the Manchester Board should maintain an option to pay or cease to pay the fees of poor children in such schools. Her reasoning, in line with a policy adopted by the National Education League, was that sectarian schools were set up, not primarily for the purpose of education, but to propagate a particular religious agenda. She did not condemn such objects *per se*, but in her usual analytical way perceived that such a purpose was not commensurate with the aims of a school board. 'She desired to see all schools supported by the Board built for the purpose of education, and education solely. She desired to see all schools maintained on the rates, managed by the Board which was elected by the ratepayers.' Although she agreed with the interim measure of the board paying fees for poor children in denominational schools, she did not want this to be 'prejudicial to the erection of Board schools'. The fear was that if religious schools were supported out of the rates through the payment of fees for poor children, then religious bodies would continue to build schools and the board would not have the mandate or the wherewithal to build their own non-sectarian schools. The church party successfully opposed her resolution, however, and their contention throughout was that it was not in the ratepayers' interests to build new board schools when there was already sufficient accommodation in sectarian schools.[56]

On visiting the Lombard Street school with the chair of the School Management committee in 1873 she made her antipathy to sectarian education in board schools even clearer when she requested the removal of scriptural mottoes from the walls, seeing them as a reinforcement of religious doctrine, and claiming that they might frighten the children. A row ensued in the board, Alderman Lamb claiming that she had said she wanted the words 'God is love' to be removed, which she denied. Lydia refused to withdraw her opinions, and in exasperation referred to the 'raw head and bloody bones' meaning (presumably referring to the Crucifixion) behind some of the mottoes. Letters appeared in the press on the controversy, but in the end Lydia, supported by the Lombard Street schoolmistress, Marion Bayley, was cleared of Lamb's accusation; she in turn apologised for any offence she might have caused. The churchmen were indeed highly offended, and exploited the incident against Becker in the triennial election of the board, resulting in her being placed, unusually, second from bottom of those elected in the poll. Nevertheless she had succeeded in putting religious instruction on the agenda as a subject like any other, open to question and needing justification.[57]

By early 1874, the church party had drawn up for board schools a highly detailed scheme of compulsory religious instruction based on Anglican tenets which proved anathema to the unsectarians on the board. Although there was a conscience clause which allowed parents to withdraw their children from religious classes, Lydia objected that pupil teachers, who were an essential part of elementary education, would not be able to withdraw, which meant that those from Catholic or Unitarian backgrounds would be forced to resign their posts. She also reiterated the views she shared with Dr Watts that a board school was not the place for compulsory religious teaching, and that in a secular world they need not defer to religion to make good, moral members of society. She and Watts were the only outright opponents when it came to a vote, and the church party was able to impose the new regime.[58]

The public debate on religion in schools reached a peak at board elections, and in particular in that of 1882. Lydia found time to post cards, all handwritten, to the 9,000 women voters in Manchester, appealing to them to support the unsectarian candidates who 'will care for the interests of the children and endeavour to serve you to the best of their power'. Despite the public furore, there seems to have been some agreement within the board that the work of the church party's Herbert Birley as chairman had poured oil on troubled waters, and at the last meeting before the 1882 election he was fulsomely praised, by all sides. Lydia, for example, stated that

> They had worked harmoniously together. There had been no serious dissensions on matters of policy, and that was in a great measure to be attributed to Mr Birley. (Hear, hear.) She hoped the next board, at the end of its three years' duty, might have as pleasant a reminiscence.[59]

The placings in this election favoured the unsectarian group, but they were still outnumbered. Although the very popular Birley as usual topped the poll, Becker was second and was followed by the five other unsectarian candidates. They were still over-matched by six churchmen, and three Catholics.[60]

By the mid-1880s, the Manchester School Board had opened numerous new schools, and a major row developed over whether the board schools, cheaper to attend than the voluntary schools, were poaching children to the detriment of the latter. There were recriminations and resignations from the church party, and letters appeared in the press accusing the board of spending money opening schools where there was already sufficient provision for all children by the voluntary sector. Lydia particularly came under fire. This may have been somewhat unfair. Although a member of the unsectarian group, Lydia was always keen to show that she was not completely hostile to voluntary church schools; when distributing the prizes at the Strawberry Road British (non-conformist) Schools in Pendleton she claimed that 'a wholesome competition was generated between voluntary school managers and the managers of board schools

...' and she interpreted this as a favourable pressure on both types of school. She also expressed a typical view of the time that it was better that people, in this instance of a religious disposition, were active in their own interest, rather than waiting for the authorities to provide for them.[61]

By the late 1880s, there was some debate as to her thinking on religious teaching. In a letter to the *Manchester Courier* of 24 October 1888, the pro-church (and suffragist) Nicolai Schou, also a member of the board, wrote: 'Miss Becker ... has, unless I am much mistaken, changed her former views, and now favours religious teaching ... There are accordingly differences of opinion among the Unsectarians as to the advisability of religious teaching in our board schools.' This was denied by Joseph Nunn, who, in response, claimed that Lydia 'would banish the Bible entirely from the schools ...'[62] It appears that her view was, to the end, somewhat anomalous.

Special groups

Even before the formation of the Manchester School Board, Lydia Becker had demonstrated a desire to open up educational opportunities to those with particular talents or needs. In March 1870, for example, the proposal to establish examinations in French and German by the Council of the Union of Lancashire and Cheshire Institutes was discussed at a town hall meeting. The exams were to be open to both girls and boys attending day or evening classes in the Manchester area, but Lydia spoke up to clarify that they were indeed open to 'all-comers'.[63]

A meeting was held in Manchester Town Hall on 5 October 1880 expressly to discuss the treatment of another group which exercised the conscience of the Manchester School Board: juvenile offenders and street hawkers. The first resolution was that legislation was urgently required to ensure that young offenders should not be sent to common gaols and should be detained separately from adult criminals at all times. Lydia was in full agreement with this proposal. The second resolution, put forward by the Bishop of Manchester, failed to meet with her approval, however. He suggested that there should also be laws, similar to those in Scotland, to prevent young children from hawking in the streets 'at untimely hours'. She argued that existing measures were gradually having an impact on the crime figures (which she quoted) and that they should be given more time. She feared the measure Bishop Fraser favoured would be used to oppress the deserving poor and prevent children from earning a living:

> It was an unhappy fact that many families in Manchester were not possessed of a sufficient income to provide for their wants, and the great mass of the children had to learn to work for their own living, and the best way in which they could do that was by engaging in casual employment.

On this occasion, Lydia's arguments failed and both resolutions were passed. [64]

Reflecting her interest in the matter, she was included on a committee of the school board, appointed with the specific remit of considering a letter from the Home Secretary on offenders. It merely produced the same recommendations as the town hall meeting. And again, Lydia was in disagreement with the criminalisation of child street hawkers; she preferred instead to look at powers to prosecute parents for sending their children out into the streets at untimely hours and mis-spending the money they earned (on drink). She pointed out that earning money honestly should not be punished:

> To make the honest earning of money by a child under 12 years of age illegal, and to enact that a child so earning money should be liable to be taken up by a policeman and lodged in a place of detention – in other words, liable to receive exactly the same treatment as a child caught stealing – would be a grave injustice and injury to honest but poor or unfortunate children, and would tend to create an impression in their minds that stealing was no more a crime than selling a paper after eight o'clock on a summer evening. In her opinion children under 12 years of age were in some cases so poor that the money they earned by street hawking was necessary for their support ... She thought that children, if discouraged by law from attempting to earn money, might not in after years be as industrious and self-reliant as if their efforts to do so had received no such check.

She broadened her point by contending that laws should be limited to the repression of crime, and 'legislation which was aimed at regulating the habits of the people and prescribing their actions and their hours of labour was unsound in principle and dangerous in practice ...' This reflected her philosophy with regard to other groups in society, notable the women pit-brow workers. But her voice, demonstrating an empathy with the children and families concerned, was a lone one, and the report was unanimously adopted.[65]

Nevertheless, the Manchester Board also perceived the need for care to be combined with schooling and training; they accordingly established the industrial boarding schools for boys (and later girls) liable to fall foul of the law because they had no home or effective parental supervision; many of them were street hawkers. The rationale for not allowing the children to go home at night (which similar London establishments did) was explained by Lydia at the NAPSS conference in 1880. She argued that, if the schools were feeding hungry children, they would attend, but if the school was 'penal', and subjected the children to hard discipline, as was the case with the industrial schools, they would not attend; children who boarded were therefore automatically under the school's control.[66] Considerable care was exercised to ensure that the children 'committed' to such schools were in fact in need of very strict supervision, as the case of Thomas Gleave revealed. The boy was apprehended by the beadle, James Power, but Lydia argued that the case of the mother and her son had not been fully presented before the magistrate and that he had been wrongly assigned to the industrial school. Her contention was not accepted by the board committee, but the discussions took up six pages of their minutes.[67]

Becker was especially vigilant in visiting these schools, as there were reports of cruelty in the London reformatories. In November 1881, there was much discussion about the inadequacy of the inspection of industrial schools in the light of such reports, especially with regard to the poor quality of intellectual education on the training ship, *Clio*, moored in the Menai Straits, where Manchester sent some of the most recalcitrant boys. It was one of three training ships under the supervision of the board, and Lydia inspected all of them, the *Clio*, the *Wellesley* and the *Formidable*. On the *Clio*, she found four boys under loss of dinner punishment, which she modified to one. Although the physical condition of the pupils was satisfactory, the living quarters were too crowded and the children's uniform not sufficiently smart. She advised a further inspection in the winter to check on conditions in that season.[68]

Lydia, on the Industrial Schools committee under the chairmanship of Dr John Watts, reminded the board that 'She had herself paid considerable personal attention to the schools in Manchester, in connection with which she and Dr Watts represented the board, and thought she was tolerably well acquainted with the management of them.' She went on to explain that the teachers and managers had a very difficult task to control children 'of the wildest and most unruly classes … suddenly, from a wild liberty, placed under discipline which would be irksome and trying even to the best-disciplined children'. She felt that, although cruelty must be condemned, under the circumstances it was no surprise that there was disorder 'and that the managers and teachers found it difficult to keep their tempers and resorted to unusual modes of correction'. She also found fault with the authorities of the Education Department at Westminster because teachers could not get their 'parchments' by teaching in an industrial school, so the best ones went into elementary education. She ended with a plea for the long-suffering industrial school teachers to be rewarded for undertaking 'that most difficult and most thankless, yet most important, duty', of teaching the most challenging children.[69]

Female staffing – board officials and teachers

Lydia Becker was very keen for women to be involved at all levels in the work of the school board. She would no doubt have welcomed another woman member on the board itself, and at one stage tried to encourage Mrs Roby, a suffragist, to put herself forward for election, but to no avail. She also favoured the idea of women inspectors whom she thought might be recruited from amongst the ranks of governesses; she took this so far as to accompany Josephine Butler and Elizabeth Wolstenholme in May 1871 to approach William Forster, the government minister responsible for the 1870 Education Act, on the matter. His suggestion that women could be appointed as an experiment for the infants and lower standards only did not satisfy the redoubtable trio. Indeed Lydia consistently commended the notion of an open inspectorate, to ensure the proper running of schools, and 'trusted that schoolmistresses as well as schoolmasters would have a chance in connection with it'.[70]

There were other positions which might also be suitable for women. In August 1871, Lydia instigated a discussion in the board with a view to appointing women visitors to call on the poor in their homes and check on attendance. Mr Birley objected that the board offices did not have proper accommodation for females – though quite how Lydia had got on was apparently not considered. Perhaps more indicative of his objections was his further comment that 'he thought it would be very undesirable to have them there'. Lydia appealed for a fair trial of women visitors, arguing that the difficulties suggested were 'purely imaginary', and at the succeeding meeting this was agreed.[71] It was not until 1874 that it was suggested that the board advertise for three male visitors and one female. Lydia lobbied for more women because 'If two women were appointed they would protect and strengthen and help each other in their work ... and ... there was much work in connection with the Board which women could do more efficiently than men.' Again, objections to men and women visitors sharing accommodation, and the fear that women would be 'savagely and brutally treated' by those they were visiting, meant that the trial still did not run.[72] The first woman visitor was finally appointed in 1882 in Manchester to enquire into special cases, working with the industrial schools; a small but significant victory in the face of opposition from the influential Canon Toole.[73]

Lydia took the opportunity of the Manchester School Board's move to spacious new offices in Deansgate to raise the issue of women officials again in 1889, when she suggested that the work of attendance officers would be enhanced by the appointment of two or three women, who 'would be able to go to the homes of the children with a better insight into the matter than the men'. This time, the committee agreed – another step forward was achieved.[74]

Whilst most feminists were preoccupied with the quality of education available to middle-class girls, Lydia focused on the training of the teachers of the working class, which was very limited and patchy. A large proportion were ex-pupil teachers, apprenticed on leaving school themselves, and learning 'on the job'. She argued that training leading to qualifications should be essential requirements for the educators of both boys and girls. Her especial attention was reserved for the female staff who presided over the education of girls. The pay of male and female teachers was dramatically different – the former receiving £120 a year, the latter £80.[75] A pay rise in 1882 was the occasion for Lydia to call for 'a nearer approximation of the salaries of the mistresses to those of the masters'.[76] It was always argued that pay reflected the respective qualities of the male and female teachers, but Lydia was ever quick to point out that this difference was attributable to lack of training and opportunities for the women.

She had expressed strong opinions on the matter from as early as 1868, when she wrote drily to Richard Pankhurst that schoolmistresses did the work of three persons in one – teaching, maintaining a household, and running a school: 'a kind of trinity in unity, as incomprehensible as it is objectionable. It tends to be of the "weaker sex" to be capable of such an achievement.'[77] In her address to the BAAS at Edinburgh in 1871, she tackled the issue head on and argued that women were prevented from applying for the best-paid teaching positions because they were reserved for the teachers of boys, and only men were thought capable of teaching boys. She argued that on the contrary 'women make excellent teachers of boys', and that the laws of supply and demand should be allowed to operate irrespective of gender.[78] Moreover, at the Domestic Science Congress of 1878 she put forward the idea that women should be more extensively employed throughout the whole system, as teachers in mixed and high schools, and as inspectors.[79]

The *Manchester Courier* in its report of the board meeting of 25 September 1882 employed the rather peevish sub-title 'Another "Woman's Rights" Grievance' to recount her attempts to improve the opportunities for female teachers. The programme of evening classes for ex-pupil teachers proposed to the board included two classes in mathematics for male teachers, but none for the female ones. She pointed out that mathematics was 'a most admirable mental training' and should therefore be open to both sexes. Whilst there were two classes of arithmetic for women, she argued that it was unjust that they were not allowed to develop their intellects to a higher level. She tried unsuccessfully to pre-empt the objection that females had not demanded such classes by arguing that in the board's experience of providing schools, supply had preceded demand, and the same was true in this case. Her proposal that night-school classes in mathematics be offered to female ex-pupil teachers was met with objections that there were other similar classes open to the females; the ones the board had arranged were specifically aimed at allowing the (male) teachers to gain particular certificates open only to men. They believed, they said indignantly, that 'no single instance could be quoted in which they had neglected, purposely or unwittingly, the wants of the girls of Manchester, whether in the elementary schools or in the evening classes.' Lydia, apparently realising that she had riled the rest of the board too far, decided that discretion was the better part of valour, and agreed that the fault lay more with the Department of Education, who laid down the criteria for male and female teaching qualifications, but still argued that Manchester should see that the standards required of both sexes were the same, and should put pressure on the government accordingly. However, she agreed to withdraw her resolution.[80]

Eventually, pupil-teacher centres were established to train advanced students, which were developed to link with Owens College, Manchester's higher education establishment, later to become the Victoria University of Manchester. In May 1889, an important meeting was held between the Manchester and Salford School Boards and the council of Owens College to discuss the training of elementary school teachers. It was agreed that the college would set up a day training college for such teachers, and the boards would provide 'practising schools'. The provision was only for male educators.[81]

Sometimes the teachers themselves caused consternation and there were attempts to regulate their behaviour. In 1883, the more puritanical board members were in high dudgeon about 'an epidemic of dancing' in Ardwick board schools by the 'upper teachers'. This was reported to have taken place after hours, but to have gone on late into the night at St Matthew's National Schools. Other board members defended the fun as harmless and even beneficial, and Lydia went so far as to advocate that dancing should be 'spread more amongst young people than it was'. The killjoys were strongly outvoted.[82]

Lydia even tried to set up a trade union for female educators. In March 1881, she attended the AGM of the charitable Manchester Governesses' Institution and Home, where eighty ladies had resided in the preceding year. Expressing the view that bodies like the institution should not be reliant on the charity of the community she demanded: 'Surely women engaged in [educating children] ought to receive sufficient remuneration to enable them to provide a comfortable home for themselves.' She proposed that the committee of the institution extend their operations to the many female elementary teachers, and form 'a sort of trades union'. By means of a small contribution from the numerous women educators in Manchester, many more would be able to participate in the benefits of such an organisation.[83]

In spite of many disagreements, notably on religion and gender, the Manchester School Board by 1902 had opened forty board schools, adopted twenty-six voluntary schools and established six higher grade and science schools. Teachers were being trained to a higher level than ever before. Lydia Becker played a considerable role in all these achievements, and perhaps most rewarding of all for her was the access to science and other academic subjects offered to some girls. She was a 'hands-on' member of the board and her interest in children and their education was genuinely and deeply felt. It was by no means only a vehicle for extending the scope of feminist involvement in wider society. The road had been hard, and particularly so in the early 1880s, when the demands of her political work meant that her attendance (at 61 per cent between 1879 and 1882, for instance) came into question. Although there was still much to be done to achieve gender equality in education, she had kept the issue to the fore, and, as in many other areas, had laid the groundwork for future generations to build on.

On her death in 1890, Lydia was replaced on the Manchester Board by another woman, Rachel, wife of the editor of the *Manchester Guardian* C.P. Scott, but the Manchester Board was obdurate in its resistance to the idea that girls deserved the same rigorous intellectual development as boys. Rachel Scott found herself excluded from the Technical sub-committee, and put on the Girls' Manual sub-committee which dealt with a domestic curriculum for girls. Even Emmeline Pankhurst, elected to the board from 1900 until its abolition in 1903, was unable to effect an improvement in the status and salaries of women teachers.[84] But the achievement of one Manchester woman, Margaret Lee, was emblematic of a sea-change in education which would bear fruit and testify to the ultimate success of Lydia's endeavours. Lee, a former board school pupil who had won a scholarship to Manchester High School for Girls, went on to Girton College, Cambridge, and in the year of Lydia's death gained the position of twenty-seventh Wrangler in the Cambridge Mathematical Tripos.[85] Nor was Lydia forgotten in higher education; by the 1920s, the University of Manchester was offering a £35 scholarship for women under her name.

Chapter 10

The Bills for the Removal of the Electoral Disabilities of Women, 1870–80

In 1870, excited and encouraged by the granting of the municipal vote the previous year, many suffrage campaigners were naively optimistic that it would not be long before the national vote was also extended to women. The 'antis', as the opposition came to be known, were not yet organised into any kind of coherent group, and their arguments were easily countered and exposed as prejudice rather than a rational position. Queen Victoria herself, a notable 'anti', was not slow to give her views on the matter; when Lady Amberley, the president of the Bristol Society, gave a public address on the 1870 women's suffrage bill in Stroud, the queen condemned suffragists:

> The Queen is most anxious to enlist every one who can speak or write to join in checking this mad, wicked folly of 'Women's Rights', with all its attendant horrors, on which her poor feeble sex is bent, forgetting every sense of womanly feeling and propriety. Lady ____ [Amberley] ought to get a GOOD WHIPPING.[1]

The suffragists believed, however, that they had merely to convince sufficient individual MPs through logic and persuasion for parliament to legislate and include women in the electoral system. The policy, therefore, was to keep up the meetings and speeches, petitions to government and lobbying of candidates, MPs and local councils for their support. Lydia Becker was amongst those who led the way in answering the arguments of the 'antis', keeping track of parliamentary voting patterns and planning the next move. This was something very novel for MPs, who had hitherto been used to dealing with women as mostly submissive lesser beings. The opposition often fell back on insult and personal abuse 'largely consisting of irrelevances, buffoonries [sic] and coarseness passing the bounds of decency'.[2]

However, there were in fact immense obstacles, which became greater as time went on, and Lydia and her colleagues had it borne in upon them that the fight would be long and hard. The plan in 1867 had been to use an existing government reform bill as a vehicle, but campaigners accepted that they had to work a lot harder at preparing the ground amongst MPs and the Lords if they wanted such an amendment to succeed. The problem was that there was no prospect of another such bill until the early 1880s, but inaction would be demoralising. It was therefore resolved to attempt to gain women's suffrage by means of a private members' bill.

Such laws were difficult to achieve, and it became harder to do so as the executive increasingly dominated the parliamentary agenda. The *Manchester Evening News* pointed this out in no uncertain terms: 'The question is far from ripe for legislation; other matters with much more pressing claims await the action of Parliament; and Government has a great heap of business to dispose of before it can propose to deal with female aspirants to the electoral privileges.'[3]

Moreover, party whips became more powerful over their MPs, who were less likely to step out of line. If the campaigners had managed to persuade the party in power to adopt their bill, it would have stood a much better chance, but the party leaders were not willing to do so. Gladstone, hugely dominant over the Liberal Party, was essentially not in favour of women's suffrage; although there was sympathy amongst his MPs, they followed his lead and did not vote in sufficient numbers to get a bill passed. Disraeli, from 1868 to 1881 leader of the Conservatives, was in favour, but most of his party were not. In any case, on both sides of the House there was a fear that enfranchised, propertied women would vote for the opposition, and also a widespread apprehension that, if women began to dictate the agenda, there might be an overweening drive against the sexual double standard and male mores and values.[4]

Even if the Commons had passed a suffrage bill, there was still the issue of the House of Lords, which had the power to prevent almost any bill becoming law. It was overwhelmingly dominated at this time by the Conservatives, and notoriously obstructive with regard to reform; the Liberals found the Lords a perennial problem when they were in government. When it came down to it, in the 1870s the suffragists believed that if they argued strongly enough they could win their case; but they failed to take realistic account of the power of party politics.

In addition, whilst their task was increasing in difficulty with the growing power of leaders, whips and government, the anti-suffragist opposition was also becoming more organised and vocal in both parliament and the country at large. What is more, social and economic changes were alleviating many of the grievances which underpinned the campaign for many women; women had made headway in rights in education, work, property, custody of children, and participation in local government. Although Lydia avowedly felt that social rights were secondary to political ones, this was not a position shared by all women. Indeed, other feminist leaders, in particular Elizabeth Wolstenholme Elmy and Josephine Butler, on occasion expressed disagreement with her in this view. Keeping up the momentum became a challenge by the later 1870s, and it took a Lydia Becker to spearhead the effort needed, working with feminists all over the country. With the exception of 1874, they saw to it that the matter was debated in parliament every year in this decade.

The Bill of 1870

At the start of the decade, Richard Pankhurst drew up a bill for presentation to the Commons by Jacob Bright and Sir Charles Dilke. Around the country, meetings were held to reinforce and publicise the efforts in parliament, and Becker and her colleagues in Manchester wrote directly to MPs and local bodies to canvass support. The other regional societies were encouraged to do likewise. This was a gargantuan task: not only did they send handwritten missives to major councils like that of Manchester but also to local boards such as Accrington in Lancashire. The response was varied: Manchester's council voted by 42 to 12 to support the bill, whereas Accrington Local Board were said to have received Lydia's letter with hilarity.[5]

The bill was designed so that, in the case of all laws relating to the registration of voters, wherever words importing the masculine gender were used, women would also be included. This would give a vote to women on the same terms as men; that is, if they were householders with the same value of property. It received its second reading on 4 May 1870, but disappointingly the government refused to back it, although promising neutrality. Bright showed that he was alive to the difficulties faced by private members' bills, and tried to play down the impact of his proposals by showing that the number of women to be enfranchised was relatively low. The highest proportion of women to men was in Bath at 1 to 3.8, but in general Manchester was more typical at 1 to 6.

This was regarded in some quarters as disingenuous because once women had the vote, why should they not become MPs too? Whilst many of those opposed went out of their way to protest that they did not regard women as inferior, it was the doctrine of separate spheres on which they took their stand. An equally telling argument was that by asking for the franchise for female householders the bill implicitly excluded married women, who were disqualified by the law of coverture. Some opponents in parliament objected particularly to the bill because the wives and mothers were excluded. Bright justified this as the only practical approach in the present circumstances of the law.[6]

Despite all this, the second reading was carried in the Commons by 125 votes to 91, which was hugely encouraging and gave rise to the belief that the bill would become law. Ursula Bright described to Josephine Butler the delight of the ladies watching in the gallery:

> Mrs McLaren ([Priscilla,] Mr Bright's sister) sank upon Mrs Peter [Mentia] Taylor's breast, and Mrs Peter Taylor sobbed! Miss Becker stood bolt upright like a statue with hands clasped in a dumb ecstasy of joy. Then a lady behind clapped her hands and at once a minion in office rushed in to tell her there must be no noise!'[7]

However, at the committee stage the great leader of the Liberal government, William Gladstone, pronounced his view:

> I think I may say, for most of my colleagues as well as for myself, that we felt something more than surprise – that we felt disappointment – at the result arrived at on Wednesday last. We do not attempt to limit the freedom of any one on such a subject, either within the official body or elsewhere; but undoubtedly it is an opinion prevailing among us – and one which I for one strongly entertain, in common with all those now sitting near me – that it would be a very great mistake to carry this Bill into law.[8]

The dominance of the Liberal leader was clear when the next vote rejected the bill 220 to 94, and the *WSJ* was quick to point out that Gladstone had done the opposite of allowing his colleagues to vote freely, and had used his influence to ensure that the bill failed. This may not have been a total surprise; as early as 1868 Lydia had noted his opposition, and in a letter to Miss Robertson called him 'the Arch Enemy' who had spoken in his campaign with 'open contempt'.[9] Later she developed this: 'since he fears to trust women with political power it would seem as if he doubted their being "flesh and blood".'

This was true of others who argued against women's suffrage. In July 1870, the *WSJ* reported the parliamentary debate in full; one opponent had claimed that if the House allowed the bill 'it would be as if the Knight of La Mancha [Don Quixote], the impersonation of chivalrous regard for women, had desired to reduce Dulcinea to the level of an ordinary mortal'. Lydia replied in like kind:

> If we remember rightly the story of the Knight of La Mancha, the fair Dulcinea was in fact a washerwoman, and we think that if she had put in a claim for an advance of wages, an extra bunch of garlic for her pottage, or even as an aid to the amelioration of her lot, for such a modicum of political privilege as the constitution of Spain accorded to Sancho Panza [Quixote's servant], it would have been a very unsatisfactory reply if she had been told that to grant her demands would reduce her to the level of an ordinary mortal, and that chivalrous regard for women forbade that she should be taken down from the high pedestal on which she was placed. To us it appears that the notions regarding women entertained by the opponents of the Bill resemble very closely those of the Knight of La Mancha. They decline to regard women as ordinary mortals, they place them on an ideal pedestal, invest them with imaginary attributes, and base their arguments on the assumption that women are exempted from the rough trials and burdens of life. They refuse to recognise the real Dulcinea at her wash-tub, they see only the ideal creation of the crazy knight's disordered brain.[10]

It was in such erudite, cogent and clever disputation that Lydia put her trust. When the bill failed it was immediately decided to try again the following year, even though it is obvious with hindsight that a similar situation was likely to arise; the campaigners did not yet see clearly the nature of the beast with which they were wrestling. It may be argued that Lydia in particular did not learn quickly to recognise it. In March 1872, this blind spot was summed up in a report in the *Manchester Times* of her speech to the Salford Liberal Association:

> It was said by many that the enfranchisement of women would be disastrous to the Liberal Party. To her mind it appeared that the

interests of the Liberal Party were secondary to the advance of Liberal principles. She believed that the great Liberal Party could make no greater mistake than to sacrifice something distinctly in the way of principle for the sake of keeping it in office.

Gladstone was particularly slippery and avoided engaging in dialogue with Becker and her colleagues; he ignored their demands, gave ambiguous replies, and turned away deputations, notably in 1871 when 100 women turned up to present a memorial. In the same year, he seemed to be coming round to the idea of female suffrage, in that he left the House before the vote on the bill and so abstained by default, and the Manchester committee thought that 'the principle of the enfranchisement of women has been accepted in its integrity by leading statesmen on both sides of the House of Commons.'[11] But he had done enough in his party to ensure that the bill failed by 220 votes to 151. One way or another Gladstone ensured the defeat in the Commons of every Women's Disabilities Bill, even though at the 1873 Liberal conference in Leeds, which was addressed by suffragists Jane Cobden and Helen Bright Clark, the delegates voted to support women's suffrage.[12] Support in the Commons peaked in the same year, when 157 MPs voted in favour, but it was not enough.

In the following years, the attempt to pass further such bills was repeated without success. Meanwhile, in 1874 the movement suffered even more serious setbacks; the defeat of Jacob Bright in Manchester in a general election, and a huge internal row over the issue of married women.

1874: Readjustments and compromises – married women and the franchise.

The defeat of Jacob Bright in the general election of 1874 necessitated finding the support of another MP to put forward the Women's Disabilities Bill of 1875; the choice, proposed by the London Society, fell upon William Forsyth, Conservative MP for Marylebone. He immediately insisted that the bill should explicitly exclude women who were married; they had indeed been effectively cut out in previous bills because of the law of coverture, but this was now to be made integral to the suffrage proposals offered to parliament. Despite the support of Tory papers like the *Manchester Courier*, which called this a 'wise discretion', and argued that 'a bill which proposed to give the suffrage to married women would be laughed at', the movement itself was riven with conflict over this policy.[13] Forsyth was at pains to explain to the NSWS that some people had assumed that the previous format would allow married women to vote because they had not been explicitly excluded. Whilst he was not personally under that illusion, he was not in favour of enfranchising married women and therefore it seemed sensible to him to make it crystal clear that it was definitely not on the table.[14]

The issue for the NSWS, however, was that some, particularly in the more radical Manchester Society, very much wanted married women to be able to vote and were working to remove all the limitations imposed upon married women by the law of coverture, including their electoral disabilities. Unfortunately, Forsyth's insistence on specifically excluding married women not only split the suffragists themselves, notably setting Jacob and Ursula Bright, Elizabeth Wolstenholme Elmy and Richard Pankhurst against him, but also alienated some of the parliamentary Liberal support the Women's Disabilities bills had garnered in previous votes. It was impossible to please all sides.

Initially, Becker had been against Forsyth's proposal. In 1868, she had strongly put the case for including married women in the agitation for female suffrage to Professor Jack of the Natural Philosophy Department at Owens College, Manchester:

> Suppose I had been in the habit of exercising the right [to vote], and a suitor, also in possession of it, were to ask me in marriage, I should not feel that perfect justice would be done to me – if the act of marriage were to deprive me of my cherished right, while it left the man in possession of his intact. I should think he proposed to me a very unfair bargain and if the exigencies of the case, or my love for him induced me to accept it the sense of injustice would tend to embitter the marriage relations and endanger domestic peace ... The proposition that marriage ought to disenfranchise one sex and not the other, seems to me logically untenable ... [15]

She argued against Forsyth that Bright's bill had been carefully and purposefully drafted to avoid objections both from those who supported suffrage for married women and those who did not support it. She proposed that they should limit themselves strictly to the disabilities of *sex* and leave the marriage question alone; the common law disabilities of married women effectively precluded them from the exercise of the franchise anyway.[16] Eventually, she was persuaded to countenance the proposal as a step in the right direction; it would, after all, enfranchise 800,000 women. She was not alone, being supported by Lilias Ashworth, with whom she was increasingly allied at this time, and by up and coming campaigner, Millicent Garrett Fawcett, who indeed expressed personal reservations about giving the vote to married women at all, given the imbalance of power in many marriages.[17] However, Lydia's decision put her in extremely bad odour with those who were intransigent in their opposition to the modification and ended her friendship with Elizabeth Wolstenholme in particular.[18] Later commentators, notably Sylvia Pankhurst, classed her as one of the more conservative suffragists as a result, and her reputation was permanently damaged. According to Sylvia, the support which Becker gave to Forsyth's bill was commensurate with the view of the majority of the executive of the Central Committee, whom she described as 'the more retrograde elements in London'.[19]

It was amongst Conservatives in particular that there was a fear that married women might eventually be enfranchised, and according to the Tory *Manchester Courier* this was a major stumbling block: 'When Miss Becker can give some guarantee that such speeches [advocating a vote for married women] will not be repeated … she may take it for granted that the day of her complete triumph is at hand.'[20] The fear was that enfranchising married women would put women in the majority in the electorate, and ultimately it might threaten the institution of marriage as husband and wife might disagree about how to vote and thereby might irretrievably damage their marriage. It must have been most frustrating for Becker that opponents on the one hand accused her of dishonesty, claiming that her stance was one of expediency, and not of conviction, and that therefore she would not stop at the franchise for unmarried women and widows. Yet on the other hand it was argued that married women were much better fitted to be enfranchised than women who had not fulfilled the female role of marriage and motherhood, and, as this was impossible due to coverture, no women should be included within the electorate.

The later 1870s – further bills and campaigns

In 1875, the first formal resistance to women's suffrage arose when, in response to the Women's Disabilities Bill of that year, the Parliamentary Committee for the Protection of the Integrity of the Franchise was established by, amongst others, Edward Leatham, Lord Randolph Churchill, and Manchester MP Thomas Bazley (who had changed sides). Edward Leatham put it crudely: 'is it any proof because a woman happens to have failed, from one cause or another, in the role of her own sex [marriage], that she can adequately discharge the more difficult and less congenial part of man?' He was backed up by P.B. Smollett, who used the exclusion of married women as grounds to object to the bill of 1875, saying 'Under this Bill, elderly virgins, widows, a large class of the demi-monde and kept women ... would be admitted to the franchise, while the married women of England – mothers who formed the mainstay of the nation – were rigidly excluded.'[21]

It was noted that such a move by opponents was very unusual; William Forsyth pointed out that 'except in the case of Catholic Emancipation [1829], he had never heard of a society got up to oppose a claim of political rights.' Lydia opted for a positive interpretation of this development:

> Your committee venture to regard as a testimony to the strength of their position, the circumstance that the opponents of the measure appear to be so greatly alarmed at the progress of the question that they have deemed it necessary to form an Association of Peers, Members of Parliament, and other influential persons, for the purpose of resisting the claims of women to the suffrage.[22]

Lydia faced ruthless tactics: Edward Leatham, MP for Huddersfield, was reported to have boasted in parliament that he had a petition from 6,000 of his constituents against the bill; this was repeated in the reprint of his speech submitted to the *WSJ*. Lydia had already pointed out to him that this was an error and that the petition was actually in favour. He blamed a reporter for the 'mistake', but it was too late and the damage was done.[23] There was clear evidence that Lydia Becker was getting under the skin of those who wanted to uphold the status quo; in meeting after meeting in the mid-1870s she was mentioned, reviled or ridiculed, most often at Conservative gatherings around Manchester, such as at the Free Trade

Hall on 7 February 1876, on 25 March 1876 in Newton Heath and on 8 April 1876 in Burnley.[24] On the back of such 'anti' agitation, attempts were made to undermine existing, ancient and hitherto unchallenged rights of women to vote in vestry elections for churchwardens. Lydia was quick to re-assert the right in a letter to the press, fearing that women ratepayers might be deterred from exercising their rights in municipal elections, or that those in charge might prevent them from doing so. The 'anti' fight-back was powerful and the vigilance required to counter it must have been exhausting.[25]

The following years of the decade seem to have seen a dip in some aspects of support for the movement; there were fewer petitions and signatories; the Manchester Society organised fewer meetings, claiming that they were choosing quality over quantity; public gatherings were supplemented with much less ambitious 'drawing-room meetings'. On the other hand, the *WSJ* seems to have been doing very well right through to at least 1878. In 1876 the amalgamation of the Manchester and Yorkshire societies took place. Their leaders, Becker and Alice Scatcherd, had already been working closely together. It may well be that this move was intended to lessen costs and pool resources, although it could also be argued that Lydia was taking advantage of the situation to unite the movement much more closely under the lead of Manchester, in keeping with her ambition from the start. Indeed, by 1883 Priscilla Bright McLaren was commenting that 'Miss Becker keeps Mrs Scatcherd in the background.'[26]

Crucially, the Women's Disabilities Bill of 1876 was defeated again when the very prestigious Liberal voice of John Bright, Jacob's more famous brother, was raised against it. This must have been an awkward family event; Jacob had recovered his seat in a by-election and was therefore the proposer of the bill, minus the clauses excluding married women. His brother's speech was believed to have swung opinion, and at the AGM of the MNSWS that year John was blamed for the defeat of the bill. The only saving grace was that in Lydia's optimistic opinion this was arguably the 'best yet' debate on the topic.[27] John and Jacob's sister, the suffragist Priscilla Bright McLaren wrote an agitated letter on the subject to her MP son, Charles. She described a missive from her sister-in-law Ursula Bright (wife of Jacob) criticising Lydia Becker for putting too much pressure on Jacob in forcing him to present 'her Bills'. Priscilla was also critical of her brother, John's, stance, which had aroused hostility towards the bill from the influential Dunckley, editor of the *Manchester Times*. Moreover, she did not exonerate Ursula herself from blame for the pressure put upon Jacob:

> I have a letter from Aunt Urlie [Ursula Bright] this morning ... telling how insulted she and Uncle Jacob were by Miss Becker's conduct about her Bills – and telling what dreadful pressure is put upon Jacob by his constituents against the Suffrage Bill and how a word from her would have prevented his taking it and how his life would have been 5 yrs longer had he <u>not</u> taken it, and how he won't have it longer than this year and how she will advise him to this – and telling what a fearful sacrifice he has made etc. – which is indeed too true – and I look up at my brother John's likeness and wonder how such a noble looking head can have made all this disturbance for if <u>he</u> had been for us, Dunckely [sic] wld never have played the renegade. I pity uncle Jacob, she says he threatens to withdraw from the Manchester committee – <u>she</u> no doubt encouraging him to feel all this indignation.[28]

At the AGM of the NSWS in London on 13 May 1876, Lydia made an important speech which addressed particularly John Bright's arguments against women's suffrage. He was a staunch campaigner for male universal suffrage, and Lydia turned his own arguments against him by comparing women with unenfranchised men. She proposed that if he believed, as he implied, that 'the present possessors of political power have the sole right to possess it', then 'This is very unlike the doctrines we are accustomed to hear from Mr Bright.' Bright's claim that the Women's Disabilities Bill was based on 'an assumed hostility between the sexes' was dismissed, and further she went on to put it that

> Mr Bright has had some experience of warfare of this kind. He has been persistently accused of a desire to set class against class. No one has suffered more than he from the kind of misrepresentation against which we now protest. Of all living men he should have been the last to steal this base weapon from the armoury of his adversaries, and to hurl it, not against strangers to himself in aims, in sympathies, and in blood, but against those of his fellow-citizens who are aspirants

for the privileges which he has taught them to value, which he has spent his life in enforcing, against women of his household and his home.[29]

By contrast, the support of Benjamin Disraeli, leader of the Conservative party, was fulsomely recognised in Lydia's report to the MNSWS AGM in November; he had stated his belief in women's suffrage as early as 1867 and had voted for it consistently ever since. In the run up to the introduction of the Women's Disabilities Bill of 1877, a large deputation of suffragists from England and Ireland met with Sir Stafford Northcote, the Chancellor of the Exchequer, in the hope that the Disraeli government might adopt the bill. The spokespersons were Lady Hannah Gore Langton and Miss Ashworth, from the south-west, along with Lydia Becker. Despite his own sympathies, and that of several Conservative leaders, including the prime minister himself, the response was one heard so often: 'He dissented entirely from those who opposed the bill on the ground that women were not qualified to exercise the franchise; but he had considerable doubt whether so large and important a change was one that should be adopted without much more consideration.'[30]

The bill was even less successful than previous ones, as in its second reading 'the opponents of the measure burst into tumultuous uproar' and 'the purpose was formed of preventing a vote'. As a result, the usual voting statistics could not be collated, but in her report to the MNSWS AGM Lydia opined that the numbers in favour would have 'shown no diminution'. She cited, as usual, the names who had promised support as a result of her copious correspondence with MPs. More excitingly, she also introduced the notion that a new reform bill, to enfranchise agricultural workers, was in the offing if the Liberals were returned to power at the next election, and that the suffragists must begin to prepare: 'The moment when the doors of the Constitution are being opened to admit a new class of voters would be a favourable one for pressing the claims of any excluded class …'[31] So supporters were urged to continue the pressure through meetings and petitions, and the fight went on unabated.

It was now led in the Commons by MP for Liskeard, Leonard Courtney, as Jacob Bright had fulfilled Priscilla McLaren's fears and declared himself 'unable to continue the charge of the Bill in the House of Commons'. He and his wife had ceased contributing financially and otherwise to the

Manchester Society, due to a developing rift over the failure specifically to include married women. In 1878, the bill was discussed in a Conservative-dominated Commons seriously and at length, but to no avail; the government, including Prime Minister Disraeli, were significantly notable by their absence, and it was voted down in the second reading by 219 to 140. At the MNSWS AGM, Lydia took heart in her report from the fact that the number of MPs in favour had remained steady, despite an organised campaign against the bill by the 'antis' under Mr Bouverie.[32]

She noted the opportunity offered by the forthcoming municipal elections for women to exercise their electoral power and to question candidates about their views on women's parliamentary suffrage. Courtney himself congratulated Manchester on its leadership:

> It was in Manchester that they met with the most energetic and indefatigable supporters of the cause. It was from Manchester that the largest number of petitions had been sent, and Manchester was the centre of activity which, if it could be imitated in anything like the same degree, their ultimate success would be much nearer.

He went on to put the case that earlier reform campaigns had only succeeded when resort had been made to violence, or the situation had become so catastrophic that the government was forced to act, citing Catholic Emancipation (1829), the Great Reform Act (1832), Corn Law Repeal (1846), the Second Reform Act (1867) and the Irish Fenian attack on Clerkenwell Prison (1867). But he perhaps reassuringly conceded that 'their indefatigable and honorary secretary would scarcely lead any band of women to pull down park railings [as in 1867] and he did not believe there would be any attempt made to blow up any prison ...'[33] And presumably, the few women who were withholding taxes around this time, as a protest to being taxed without representation, did not present any real threat to the exchequer.[34] In this vein Courtney was unconsciously echoing Lydia's own opinion expressed privately in 1867 that it would take violent action to change the situation, and presaging by many years the policies adopted by the extremists of the WSPU (the suffragettes).

It had been decided by the 1879 session to focus on raising support for an amendment to the anticipated reform legislation on the county franchise, so Courtney introduced a resolution, rather than a bill in March 1879. He made it crystal clear that it was about granting the parliamentary franchise only to those women included in the municipal and other local franchises; this implied the exclusion of married women, but the Forsyth clause specifically excluding them had been dropped. He was keen to cite examples in the USA and the British Midlands of how allowing women to vote had 'elevate[d] the character of the active politicians and induce[d] different parties to bring forward their best men'. He stressed how the moral character of politically educated women would allow them to raise 'a race of patriots equal to the famous men of the reigns of Elizabeth and Anne'.[35] The Conservative-dominated Commons were unconvinced and the majority against rose to 114.

In her Manchester Society AGM report of that year, Lydia put the best spin possible on it by claiming that support was nevertheless growing amongst the general public. She focused on the coming 1880 general election, exhorting all members to challenge candidates as to their views on women's suffrage. Leonard Courtney could not hide his disappointment that 'Some of their friends had become lukewarm, or had fallen away, whilst the enemy appeared to be as energetic as ever …' He counselled perseverance and patience, and even hinted that when eventually women had the vote on the same terms as men, it might then be thought appropriate to enfranchise married women too.[36] At the end of the meeting, Alderman Abel Heywood, Father of the Manchester Corporation, made a prescient suggestion:

> He said that the agitation should be shortened, if possible; some means ought to be adopted … in order that the question of women's suffrage should become not a question of crotchets but a national question … Petitions had been signed by many women, but that was not sufficient. They wanted larger demonstrations of women. But in order to advance that question, he saw no other way than of attaching it to the great party in the State [the Liberals] that had for generations supported the greatest and grandest for extending the rights of mankind.[37]

The principle of a non-party organisation was sacrosanct to Lydia and her allies, however, and despite growing calls from elements within the suffrage movement for affiliation with the Liberals she doggedly clung to the non-partisan approach which had been pursued for the previous thirteen years.

The determination and assiduity of the women's movement led by Lydia Becker in the 1870s cannot be faulted, but by the end of the decade voices were being raised proposing alternative strategies, in particular that married women should be explicitly included in the Women's Disabilities bills, and that the movement should ally with one political party, namely the Liberals. They had spent ten years battering away, with little to show for it in terms of success where it really mattered: in parliament. It may be true that opinion in the country had moved on but the only way that this would be reflected in the legislature would be to harness the party political system. Lydia Becker was not prepared to move in that direction. Instead she grabbed what she perceived to be a golden opportunity to approach the matter differently by hitching an amendment to the Reform Act which Gladstone's second Liberal government, elected in 1880, was expected to bring in. From 1880 until the passage of the Act in 1884 the suffragists went all out in an attempt to secure their goal. However, they underestimated the immense status and control of the 'Grand Old Man' over his party. Meanwhile, significantly for the future, at the end of 1880 a new member appeared on the Manchester executive committee in the person of the young Emmeline Pankhurst.

Chapter 11

Lydia in London: The Third Reform Act and its Aftermath

In the 1880s, possible new approaches to campaigning presented themselves, and there were critics within the suffrage movement, echoed by historians, who advocated a fresh look at strategy. One suggestion, voiced at the time by the Liberal MP Sir Charles Dilke, is that they could have joined the growing ranks of radical Liberals and socialists who were demanding universal suffrage, and gained a popular, working-class movement in their support. Sandra Stanley Holton has argued that in the twentieth century it was the alliance of the NUWSS with the new socialist Labour Party in the cause of universal suffrage which ultimately won some women the vote, alongside men in 1918.[1] However, when the issue is examined from the perspective of 1880, it is not clear-cut. Although Lydia was a believer ultimately in universal suffrage, she and her colleagues were well aware that this would have been a very extreme position.[2] The vote was generally regarded as a privilege, dependent on responsibility in society and a stake in the wealth of the nation. It was not seen as a right by any but the most radical. Joining that company might well have alienated far more people of the political class of all parties than it would have persuaded. It would have especially alienated Conservative supporters and indeed the party leadership, to whom Becker and others were beginning to turn in the 1880s. This was exemplified in the case of lifelong Conservative Frances Power Cobbe, who regarded the working class as a threat to British values and political stability.[3] Even more importantly, such an alliance would have entailed the abandonment of political feminism as a discrete movement.

This was also the problem with the second proposed strategic change: that they should hitch their wagon by affiliation to one or other of the main parties, probably the Liberals, so that they would not have to rely on private members' bills and trying to find a formula to please all parties.

This was a view which, at the time, found strong support within the movement. Lydia held staunchly to the view that the women's cause should not become party political; some of the most prominent suffragists, such as Jessie Boucherett, Frances Power Cobbe and Emily Davies were Conservatives, whereas until the mid-1880s she, like the Brights, the Pankhursts and the Fawcetts, was a Liberal. She did not want to alienate any potential support by alliance to one party. Moreover, which party would it be? The Conservative leaders were ostensibly supportive but never actually did anything to help women get the vote when they were in power; their rank and file were thought to be mainly hostile, though that was changing in the 1880s. The Liberals as a party were generally in favour of women's suffrage, but of course Gladstone had already proved himself a stumbling block, and the House of Lords, notoriously hostile to reform, regularly opposed (and could halt) Liberal government legislation, or indeed any reform they considered too radical. The time would come when a new Labour Party would force the re-alignment of politics and enable the alliance of feminism and working-class interests, but that configuration did not arise for another thirty years.[4]

The women's suffragists, it is also claimed, could even so have done more to garner working-class support by abandoning the intimidating and inconveniently timed drawing-room meetings which they allegedly favoured. The criticism that the female suffragists focused only on drawing-room meetings and did not address the issues of working-class women is patently unfair with regard to the Manchester suffragists, and Lydia Becker in particular.[5] Large evening meetings with free entry were made as accessible as possible to working-class women. Becker's work to meet and involve them in the election of 1868 and the municipal political process is well documented, and she would have concurred with the contention that more ordinary women needed to be included in the ongoing national campaign; she encouraged them to challenge candidates as to their position on women's votes and issues in both local and national elections. She was also aware of her own limitations in appealing to them as a rather academic woman of the middle class, but she employed as speakers women like Jessie Craigen and the Stockport silk weaver Mrs Winbolt with exactly that issue in mind, and with some success.[6] That they did not succeed in mobilising large numbers of working-class women in support of the franchise campaign may have been a disappointment, but it was unsurprising in view of the limitations on the time and freedom of such women. And they did succeed in mobilising ordinary women to vote in all the elections for which they became eligible.

Against this background, Lydia Becker continued to strive tirelessly for the Cause, from 1881 mainly in London itself, initially as secretary to the London committee, then from 1884 as the parliamentary agent for the campaign. Her dominance, so evident in Manchester, now became a feature of the London Society too; it was a cause for celebration for some but frustration for others. So great was the opposition to her from some quarters, that from 1884 onwards she faced attempts to oust her from her position of power, even by erstwhile friends like Ursula Bright. When these failed, secessions followed. The long-standing argument within the movement, about whether to include married women in their demands, became more acute. This and the issue of political affiliation caused damaging splits within its ranks in the later part of the decade, leading to the establishment of new organisations, notably the breakaway Central National Society for Women's Suffrage, and the Women's Franchise League. When the fortunes of the campaign were particularly low in 1889, the opponents of women's suffrage dealt it a forceful blow when over a hundred women, many of them prominent, issued their 'Protest' in a direct challenge to the Cause.

In the first half of the decade, however, the focus of all campaigners was on the long-anticipated Third Reform Act, the first major revision of the electorate since 1867, and a new opportunity to persuade the government to allow a women's suffrage amendment. Lydia Becker was not alone in her excitement and determination to make the most of this opportunity, and the invitation from London to take a lead in the suffrage movement from the capital endowed her with huge influence, of which she took full advantage.

London secretary and parliamentary lobbyist

The election of a Liberal government in 1880 gave the suffragists fresh hope. Matters began auspiciously, if symbolically, in some areas; during the election itself in Manchester, South-East Lancashire, Oldham and elsewhere some women had managed to register, and indeed in Manchester had voted, to prove a point.[7] The Liberals had campaigned on a policy to enfranchise working-class men in the counties, on the same terms as those in the towns had already been enfranchised by the Conservatives in 1867. The proposed Third Reform Bill offered the women's suffragists the prospect of a different approach from the private members' bills which had been tried and failed in the 1870s; a great opportunity to persuade the government to allow a women's suffrage amendment, as had been unsuccessfully attempted by John Stuart Mill in 1867. As this time it was the Liberal Party which was in power, and there were many MPs amongst them who were favourable, the suffragists were hopeful of greater success. *The Times* commented 'when the time ... arrives for a great re-casting of the electoral scheme, the case of the women may be thrown into the crucible with the rest.'[8] Prime Minister William Gladstone was, however, effectively an 'anti'. With inordinate influence over his party and regarded by Liberal radicals as a 'shibboleth', he prevented the adoption of many progressive policies.

Lydia made the object clear: 'Our place is to make ours a part of that measure, and to take advantage of the opening of the door by others to get in ourselves.'[9] This approach seemed even more hopeful when in 1881 Lydia and Alice Scatcherd persuaded the Tynwald to add women's suffrage to an electoral reform bill in the Isle of Man, thereby giving women on the island the vote.[10] The suffrage societies organised petitions and large meetings of women, at which Lydia frequently spoke, to support the amendment to include women in the rest of the UK. The first of these was the Grand National Demonstration of Women in the Manchester Free Trade Hall on 3 February 1880, which was emulated by the other major suffrage societies.[11] Resolutions in support of women's suffrage were also passed at gatherings of both the main political parties. Lydia, together with Jessie Craigen and Alice Scatcherd, took on a huge number of meetings in Manchester, the Isle of Man, London and other parts of England. She was not going to let any opportunity slip.

Against this background the London Society invited Lydia Becker, by now acknowledged to be the leading expert in parliamentary procedure and lobbying, to become general secretary to the NSWS in the London and Central District, and prepare the ground in parliament.[12] Perhaps the most significant battle of Lydia's suffragist career was about to begin in the capital, and in her person it could be said that the suffrage movement did at last have a leading personality who was acknowledged by both Manchester and London.

She had come a great distance from the naivety of her early career in campaigning, when she had wondered whether Jacob Bright, after only a year in the House, would get a ministry in Gladstone's 1868 cabinet. She had been put in her place on that occasion:

> he told me I must be either joking or ignorant of the routine in such matters – for a seat in the cabinet will not be afforded to anyone who had been so short a time in Parliament as himself, and he would not accept a subordinate office, which would make him responsible for a policy which he had no share in deciding.[13]

Yet, she was now widely known for her understanding of the arcane rules of parliament and accordingly was sounded out in February 1881 by London's Laura McLaren, the daughter of Lydia's old allies in Salford, the Pochins, and daughter-in-law to Priscilla and Duncan McLaren:

> With your intimate knowledge of the political work which lies before us, you will quickly see all the bearings of this proposal ... the strong feeling we all have in favour of uniting our forces under the leadership of one whose political ability and talent we have always recognised. It appears there is a waste of force in having two centres of political action, and although the energy of Manchester is powerfully felt in the country, still as all Parliamentary business must be transacted in London, it is here we need the powerful head to act promptly ... The movement is your pet child which you have seen grow up from infancy and whose welfare is nearest your heart.[14]

Although Lydia was still to continue as secretary to the Manchester Society, she was expected to move to London and take charge of the office during the parliamentary session. McLaren acknowledged the significance of Manchester in the movement, but stated that leadership really should rest with London. 'While *you* remain in Manchester it [London] can never have proper authority to manage the political business of the movement as it should ...'[15] Not everyone in the capital was delighted with the decision to approach her. Laura McLaren wrote to Helen Taylor

> You will see by the summons to a special meeting that the sub-committee has reported in favour of the appointment of Miss Becker as secretary ... the feeling in favour of the course we propose was so strong that no dissenting voice was raised. I think it will be carried by a very large majority if not unanimously at the special meeting ... I must express my great regret that the course now taken has not the sanction of your approval. Your active support and assistance has been invaluable to the Committee and it is only with pain that we do what you consider unwise.[16]

Lydia agreed to an initial trial period of a year, and accepted a consideration of £200 per annum, which was intended to cover her living and travel costs, though it was recognised that, as in Manchester, she offered her services 'as a free gift to the cause'. She was to have clerical help in the offices of both the London and the Manchester societies, and would spend a few days each month in Manchester, to enable her to continue her suffrage and school board work in the city. She was expected to increase the income of the London Society from its current £1,500 a year, and encouraged to combine the financial resources of both London and Manchester for the parliamentary work.[17]

After further discussions and an interview in London, work began on 2 April. Lydia lodged, according to the census of that year, at 15 Langham Street, Marylebone, interestingly classifying herself as 'Member Manchester School Board'. With the assistance of a Miss Tourraine, and the addition in 1883 of a Miss Moore as organising agent, she very quickly established herself as a well-known and respected figure in the Westminster lobbies. Her attendance at London executive committee meetings became regular, and on the odd occasions when she did not attend she usually sent a letter to be read out giving reports or making proposals to be considered. Even on such occasions, she was deputed to take action, such as ensuring resolutions were placed on the order book of the House of Commons or using her influence to encourage trade unions to support women's suffrage.[18]

To keep the momentum going, every year in the 1880s resolutions or private bills supporting female suffrage were introduced into parliament. They were constantly stymied by the control of the government over parliamentary time, which meant that they were effectively blocked.

So the key strategy from 1880 was that every franchise bill should be accompanied by a women's suffrage amendment; the Irish Borough Franchise Bill of 1880, a bill against corrupt electoral practices and one to amend the 1872 Ballot Act were all targeted. In the event, these bills were withdrawn before discussion in the Commons could take place.[19]

The movement's first parliamentary spokesman under this new plan was Hugh Mason, MP for Ashton-under-Lyne, who was approached by Becker and the Manchester Society when Leonard Courtney's acceptance of a post in the new Liberal administration precluded his continuance as leader of the women's suffrage campaign in the House. However, Mason did not offer unalloyed commitment as he had already promised his backing for a Boiler Explosions Bill; the women had to play second fiddle to the boilers![20] As London secretary, Lydia was every bit as active rallying the forces as she was in Manchester; in June 1882, for instance, she wrote to Priscilla Bright McLaren asking her to come to the House of Commons to meet MPs to discuss the proposed suffrage amendments. Unable to attend, Priscilla asked her MP son Charles to take up the cudgels on her behalf and rally their parliamentary friends.[21] When Mason finally presented a resolution to parliament on 6 July 1883 the voting was 'the most favourable' since 1870 at 116 in favour and 132 against; the margin was now reduced to only 16 and the number of opponents had fallen by 87 since the last vote in 1879. The auspices were thought at last to be promising and excitement mounted in the women's suffrage camp.[22]

The Third Reform Act, 1884

As the Gladstone government moved towards the introduction of the reform bill to enfranchise male agricultural workers, nine huge women's demonstrations were organised in London and other key cities. Lydia was keen to control events, which no doubt aroused hostility in the Central Committee; hostility which grew as the 1880s went on. She did not always trust other women to act in a way that she felt was appropriate, and was perturbed to learn that the Mid-Somerset association was sending some representatives to the big reform conference in Leeds in October 1883. Her letter to Anna Maria Priestman, president of the Bristol association, explained that she feared they might mess up the work of Birmingham

Unitarian minister Dr Henry Crosskey, who was to present a resolution on women's suffrage:

> All depends now on the prudence and self-control of the delegates – you know how ready men are to catch out the slightest thing in a woman that they think strange. I do very earnestly wish that the women delegates would have the self-denial to limit themselves to <u>voting</u> ... There is every reason to believe that the resolution will be carried. The only thing that is likely to cause a defeat is some untoward incident which might turn the current of feeling and set the mind of the conference the wrong way. A dozen men might make mistakes in speaking and it would do us no harm but the least thing said by a women and taken amiss might be fatal to our purpose.[23]

Helen Priestman Bright Clark, the suffragist daughter of 'anti', John Bright, reported that the Manchester committee had been 'wire-pulling' to prevent the appointment of herself and others as delegates to the Leeds conference. She attributed this to contrariness, linked to a rejection of political affiliation, on Lydia's part: 'I concluded it might be because as Miss Becker could not go as a Liberal, she wishes no other woman to go.' Later she noted 'Somebody has succeeded in frightening away all the women except us four who resolutely refused to be frightened.' There were nine delegates in the end, including Helen Clark, Alice Scatcherd and Jane Cobden.[24]

Meanwhile, town councils were lobbied to show support, many of them with success. Prominent women, including Florence Nightingale, Millicent Fawcett (wife of MP and Postmaster General Henry Fawcett) and Lady Verney, signed a letter sent to every MP. Liberal organisations, notably the National Reform Union, the National Liberal Federation and the Counties' Liberal Union, voted overwhelmingly, with 'a perfect forest of hands' in favour. A hundred and ten Liberal MPs signed a memorial supporting women's suffrage, which was presented to Gladstone. By contrast with all this effort, the women pointed out that there was minimal agitation from the male objects of the reform bill, the agricultural workers.[25]

Later in 1883, Hugh Mason resigned as the parliamentary leader for the movement due to illness. At this critical juncture, a special meeting of the Central Committee was convened for 22 January 1884 at which

Lydia announced the Manchester committee's desire to ask Jacob Bright to resume this role. Sandra Stanley Holton has posited that Lydia, supported by Jacob's niece Lilias Ashworth Hallett, worked against his reinstatement. This represented a dramatic change in her attitude towards him since the 1870s, no doubt accounted for by their disagreement over married women.[26] In any case, Jacob had told Priscilla Bright McLaren, his sister, that on no account would he again take up the question in parliament, 'unless there was absolutely no one else who would do it'. This reluctance was probably due in part to battle-fatigue combined with the antipathy between him and Becker, and to a growing determination on his part, and maybe even more importantly that of his wife, Ursula, that married women should be specifically included in any women's suffrage legislation.[27] Becker and many on the Central Committee favoured the appointment of William Sproston Caine, Liberal MP for Scarborough. She wrote in this vein to Millicent Fawcett, clearly already an ally, four days before the meeting:

> Shall you be able to be present at the meeting on 22nd? Up to now the overwhelming majority seems in favour of Mr Caine. I feel that we are in a _most_ critical conjuncture and that our success or failure depends on a wise choice of a leader.

The committee agreed unanimously to approach Caine, but in the event he declined this dubious honour.[28] So it was on William Woodall, Liberal MP for Stoke, that the mantle fell. He agreed to present an amendment to the government franchise bill, proposing that 'words importing the masculine gender should include women', thus not specifically excluding or including married women. Sandra Stanley Holton notes that the suffrage movement was by now 'almost paralyzed' by internal divisions.[29]

So when, in March 1884, Liberal suffragist women wrote to the prime minister asking for his backing, his private secretary, perhaps aware of the disarray in the women's camp, replied in a most discouraging tone:

> He is most unwilling to cause disappointment to yourself and your friends, whose title to be heard he fully recognises; and he can assure you that the difficulty of complying with a request so referred does not proceed from any want of appreciating the importance of your representation, or of the question itself – His fear is that any attempt

to enlarge by material changes the provisions of the Franchise Bill now before Parliament might endanger the whole measure.[30]

With her official position in London, Lydia's clout was considerable. She reported, to the approval of the committee, 'that she had issued a whip [presumably to all the sympathetic MPs] on April 1st when Mr Woodall was to speak in the Franchise Debate'.[31] On 10 June 1884, Woodall finally moved his amendment, but it was completely squashed by Gladstone in colourful naval metaphor:

> The cargo which the vessel [the Reform Bill] carries is, in our opinion, a cargo as large as she can safely carry ... women's suffrage would overweight the ship ... With regard to the proposal to introduce it into this Bill, I offer it the strongest opposition in my power, and I must disclaim and renounce all responsibility for the measure should my honourable friend succeed in inducing the Commons to adopt the amendment.[32]

A furious debate ensued in the Commons on 12 June, and Lydia Becker called an emergency meeting of the Central Committee. Jacob Bright had pledged that if the amendment were withdrawn, he would introduce another. In the event it remained and was defeated in the Commons by 271 votes to 135. When the reform bill was thrown out by the Lords, the government re-introduced it, but no women's amendment was put forward. It passed, enfranchising an estimated 6 million men.

The suffragists had calculated that if all MPs voted with their conscience their amendment would pass with a majority of seventy-two. Conservative supporters of the amendment, numbering as many as ninety-six, aimed to embarrass Gladstone's Liberal government, and also hoped that the propertied women who would be enfranchised might vote Conservative and prove a counterweight to the enfranchised agricultural labourers, who were expected to vote Liberal. But fear of the Grand Old Man's displeasure led 104 Liberals to break their pledges, 'and flung them in the faces of the women of the country apparently without any sense of shame or compunction. Such is the pie-crust nature of MPs' promises when given to the politically impotent.'[33] Indeed Becker and her colleagues referred to this event as 'the great betrayal' and in her letters to Lydia, Frances Power Cobbe referred to Gladstone as 'the arch-enemy' and claimed 'Gladstone has been our ruin.'³⁴ Elizabeth Wolstenholme Elmy later expressed the opinion that *'Women* have every reason to hate and despise Gladstone's memory' and that he was 'the main cause of the long delay of our Suffrage victory'. In the *WSJ*, Becker thundered: 'This injustice will reign for ever as a blot on the escutcheon of the professed Liberal Parliament elected in 1880, and on that of the prime minister.'³⁵

However, the suffragist belief that this was a great opportunity missed has been questioned. It is claimed that they never convincingly converted enough Liberals for Gladstone to be able to take any other course than the one he chose. His government had been voted in on a mandate to enfranchise the agricultural workers, and therefore he could not endanger his reform act.³⁶ Moreover, many parliamentary Liberals were hopeful of gaining the support of newly enfranchised agricultural workers, whereas it could not be predicted which way propertied women might vote, and this may have weighed against support of the amendment when the time came to commit themselves. Although Gladstone had suggested that he would abandon the bill if the amendment were carried, this was probably a bluff, as he could ill afford to alienate the radical wing of the Liberal Party. His contention that the women's amendment would lead the Conservative-dominated House of Lords to vote down the whole bill was plausible; in the event, they only accepted the bill as he presented it when he agreed to a redistribution of seats, which would mitigate the worst effects on the Conservative party of admitting poor rural men, expected to vote Liberal, to the electorate. Becker's attempts, in her MNSWS annual report of 1885, to show that the Lords would have voted a women's suffrage amendment through are unconvincing, based as they were only on 'the tone of debate' and 'indications of opinion'.³⁷

Many suffragists, middle class and well educated, took exception to the fact that the Third Reform Act gave a vote to ill-educated working men, effectively rendering the position of women relatively even worse than before. Farm labourers could vote, whereas the 30,000 female tenant farmers who employed them could not. This was not likely to change soon; the legislation was intended to settle the electoral system for at least a generation by tidying up perceived anomalies. For the suffragists, the most glaring of those anomalies had been ignored and thereby accentuated. With hindsight, later suffragists identified this as the moment to revolt. Theresa Billington-Greig, writing in 1911 when suffragette militancy was making a great stir, thought they had missed an opportunity:

> The special work to which the older Suffrage Societies devoted themselves was the work of creating a majority sufficient to pass a suffrage measure. As I have shown elsewhere, it completed this task in the early 'eighties of the last century; at this time it had created its voting machine ... Mr Gladstone ... stepped in and stopped the machine. This was the moment for revolt.[38]

However, this begs the question of whether such an approach would have helped or actually created more opposition. In any case, this was not yet the mindset of even the most radical activists; the Pankhursts themselves were still loyal committee members of the MNSWS at this point, and the strongest direct action which any suffragist took was, in a very few cases, to withhold taxes.[39]

So it was back to the old strategy when, in November 1884, Woodall brought in the Parliamentary Franchise (Extension to Women) Bill with the controversial clause which specifically excluded married women. It was symptomatic of the state of the suffrage campaign that Alice Scatcherd, Becker's old ally over many years, confided to Anna Maria Priestman 'I feel as though Miss Becker were at the bottom of this.' As usual, the bill was unsuccessful.[40]

Parliamentary Agent

Historians have argued that in the second half of the 1880s the women's suffrage movement entered the doldrums, and there is some justification to this view. There was indeed a decline in support in the country as splits and confusions in the leadership became acute. The suffragists fell back on regular attempts to pass a private members' bill. Frustratingly, despite their strong belief that there was a majority in the Commons in favour, progress was consistently blocked by deferments and adjournments as the time was diverted into government business.

Meanwhile, Manchester had largely ceased to be the engine driving the campaign when Lydia moved to London, and there was discontent in the committee there. On 25 June 1884, the Central Committee received a letter from John P. Thomasson, a member of both committees.[41] He expressed his dissatisfaction with the arrangement whereby Lydia Becker was secretary to both, and asserted that 'many members of the Central are equally dissatisfied'. It is not clear from the minutes what the reasons were for this unhappiness, but in the case of the Manchester Society it may well be that Lydia's constant presence in London was proving irksome, bearing in mind her hitherto huge contribution to their efforts. In addition, her apparent opposition to Jacob Bright as the Commons' standard bearer for women's suffrage in 1883, when he was the chosen candidate of the Manchester committee for that role, may have aggravated the sense that she was no longer working in the interests of the committee there. Moreover, the failure of 1884 may have undermined Lydia's position, and there was also some discontent in London at her overweening power in the Central Committee, and her methods, as became increasingly clear, were not always to the taste of the powers that be in the London Society.

It was agreed to consider the matter at the next Central Committee meeting on 2 July; Lydia did not attend because she was the object of the deliberations, but the turnout otherwise was exceptionally full. She was supported by a resolution proposed by Millicent Fawcett, now a member of the executive committee, to nominate her again for the secretaryship after the AGM. However, the chairman, Mr Hopwood, submitted a copy of a resolution from the Manchester committee putting it that the dual secretaryship was not in the interests of the movement and requesting Becker 'to consider the advisability of reverting to the sole secretaryship of Manchester'. Mr Thomasson then proposed to amend Fawcett's motion to say that the Central Committee was willing for Lydia to revert to 'the sole secretaryship of the Manchester Society'. This was voted down 13 to 7, and it was noted in the minutes that the Bristol Society had passed a motion supporting that of Mrs Fawcett to reappoint Becker as secretary for the London and Central Committee.

A compromise was reached, however, when Laura McLaren proposed another amendment that Lydia be 'nominated as Parliamentary Secretary of the Central Committee, and that the London members of the Central be requested to form themselves into a separate Committee with a separate Secretary to undertake the district work of the London division'. This was carried by 15 to 11 and was later passed as a substantive resolution on the proposal of Millicent Fawcett.[42] It had the effect, in theory at least, of lessening Lydia's burden by hiving off the parliamentary side of her duties, and leaving the other aspects of the secretaryship in London for others to fulfil, initially Florence Balgarnie.

So Lydia continued to work in the capital, as Priscilla Bright McLaren, who had reservations about her, wrote to her sister around this time:

> I do not grudge Miss Becker her journey to America [for the BAAS conference in Canada]. I hope it will do her good and liberalize her mind – but Lilly [Lilias Ashworth Hallett, Priscilla's niece] and she will be more knit together than ever ... There is such a power in London in form of L.B. – that I can only see that rigour and faithfulness and courage on the part of the Committee can keep matters right.[43]

Priscilla, though still feeling a 'tender sympathy and affection' for her, referred to the closeness of Becker and Lilias as the 'Dual Combine', and regarded it as a negative and destructive influence in the movement.[44]

In October, a conference was planned for delegates of the Central and Manchester committees to meet up to plan future co-operation, an event which was being facilitated by Lydia Becker. The Central Committee sent Millicent Fawcett, and a special meeting on 24 October met to hear her report. Fawcett was also proposing that Lydia should be awarded £50 a year by the Manchester committee as editor of the *WSJ*, and £250 a year as 'a salary' as secretary to the Central Committee only. The Central Committee voted 12 to 8 in favour.

However, the issue was not so easily resolved; at the end of October Lydia wrote to the Central Committee explaining that Manchester had given her an ultimatum that she must choose between the two committees, and she had felt that her 'native city' had first claim on her services because of the 'political and personal ties' which bound her to it. She, therefore, would be tendering her resignation after the Manchester AGM, and this later occurred. The Central Committee reluctantly accepted her resignation and hoped 'that the cause may long have the benefit of her labour and experience'.[45]

Her resignation turned out to be very temporary, however, as there were strong elements in London, notably Laura McLaren, who felt that Lydia's presence was essential to the suffrage efforts in parliament. The exact circumstances are unclear, but Becker, despite the reservations of Manchester, ploughed on in London, and it seems that the two societies had come to some pecuniary arrangement by which the Central Committee paid an agreed sum to the Manchester committee in return for her services.[46]

By August 1885, she was back on the Central Committee as their parliamentary agent, and still a power to be reckoned with. The committee minutes for January 1888 to March 1889 reveal just how prominent Lydia was; she had her own regular and substantial slots in the meetings to report on parliamentary matters and the activities of the Manchester committee.[47] Priscilla McLaren wrote to Helen Taylor about her concerns on 21 January 1888: 'I am greatly concerned to see how a few women rule there [London] – and often by beating up votes in a way that I do not approve of.'

But perhaps Lydia, under pressure in adverse circumstances, did not feel her position to be as secure as it appeared. Priscilla went on to criticise her role in preventing delegates from going to a Washington conference proposed by American suffragists Susan B. Anthony and Elizabeth Cady Stanton to set up an international suffrage organisation. When Lydia was approached about it by Stanton 'a very unpleasant interview' ensued. Sandra Stanley Holton has suggested that the origin of this strange attitude was that Lydia was fearful of losing her power, and perceived that the proposed organisation might enable her erstwhile friend and ally, Ursula Bright, to take over the leadership of the British suffrage movement.[48] Priscilla advocated that a few women of high status in the movement should go 'and thus defeat the few women who would rule the whole body'. So she, Ursula Bright, and Margaret Bright Lucas agreed to establish an international organisation based in the United States, and in 1888 the proposed Washington conference went ahead.[49]

After the high hopes had been dashed in 1884, there were many challenges to the suffrage campaign. It had become an uphill task to rally enthusiasm and the Manchester Society's income, for instance, declined from the £2,000 plus a year it had reached in the mid-1870s. In spite of an upbeat MNSWS annual report which claimed that a majority of candidates for the forthcoming general election in 1885 were favourable, other support began to fall away.[50] Leonard Courtney, who had led the suffrage cause in the Commons up to 1880, voiced this clearly in November 1885: 'I cannot, I really cannot come to Manchester [for a meeting on14th?]. I feel as if after the election I should like not to speak for you. The number of candidates pledged to the cause is insignificant. With best wishes ...'[51]

Moreover, there were now alternative roles for women in political life, which to some extent took the sting out of their lack of representation through the ballot box. Opportunities at a municipal level continued to expand as their electoral experience grew. Women were admitted to boards of guardians as well as to school boards, becoming adept in the management of local affairs, including policy and finance. Then from 1883 the Corrupt and Illegal Practices Act had capped the spending permitted on electoral campaigns. As a result, election candidates and their agents resorted to recruiting volunteers to carry out the routine operations of campaigning, and many of those who responded were women. They came from right across the political spectrum, and the parties developed their role by opening up the Conservative Primrose League to women in 1884, and establishing, in 1887, the Women's Liberal Federation.[52]

Although the Primrose League had no policy on women's rights, and was dominated by 'antis' like Lord Randolph Churchill, it embodied a prime example of the law of unforeseen consequences, as its activities brought women into the political arena and educated them in its ways. Moreover, the League became an advertisement for the political acumen of women, extended party organisation into middle- and working-class districts, and was perceived to be an antidote to the influence of radicalism and socialism. The Women's Liberal Federation was much more overtly political and, after considerable wrangling, in 1892 it officially espoused the women's cause. On both sides of the political scale, women became the indispensable 'foot soldiers' of political campaigns. They gained a political education by the back door, and for some this was sufficient involvement.

In an attempt to revive the flagging fortunes of the women's suffrage campaign, suffragist leaders such as Becker and Millicent Fawcett began to focus more on winning over the Conservative party from 1884. They had no faith in Gladstone, still the Liberal leader, and his party continued to follow him rather than their own beliefs when it came to women's suffrage. Moreover, in 1886 the Liberals were weakened by a serious split over the issue of Home Rule for Ireland. The election of that year which brought in a Conservative government saw the return of a large number of suffragist MPs, and they added to their numbers in the subsequent years, reaching an estimated 365 members by 1889.[53] In addition, in November 1887 the National Union of Conservative and Constitutional Associations adopted a resolution in favour of women's householder suffrage and Lord Salisbury, Conservative prime minister from1886 to 1892, endorsed this in speeches in 1888. Sadly, this meant little in practice; it remained the case that neither party was prepared to espouse the Cause as official policy, and the suffragists had learnt the hard way that private members' bills were ineffectual.

In 1887, to strengthen and unify support, liaise with the Central Committee, and narrow the points of contact, a cross-party parliamentary organisation of seventy-one pro-suffrage MPs, was formed with Becker's backing.[54] The non-party nature of the body was reflected in its two secretaries, Tory Captain Edwards-Heathcote, MP for Staffordshire, and Liberal Walter McLaren, MP for Cheshire. It first met in committee room fourteen on 15 June 1887, and held meetings to which Lydia was not admitted; she had to wait outside the room to receive the minutes, which is indicative of the limits on her influence in the corridors of power. In these years, the government had even tighter control of parliamentary time, and did not allow women's suffrage bills to be put forward; the government of Ireland, and Irish Home Rule in particular, became the issue of the day. This was reflected in a letter of July 1887 from Walter McLaren to Becker, in which he suggested that a memorial she was circulating to MPs for signatures might benefit from being sent to battle-weary Irish Nationalist members, keen to challenge the government from whatever angle seemed useful:

> W[illiam] Woodall greatly doubts the wisdom of sending the circular to Members who are not known to be favourable to W[omen's] S[uffrage] … I think you should in any case send to all the Irish Nationalists because they are likely to sign in order to 'have a day' on some other subject than Ireland.[55]

Attempting to keep the feminist cause on the agenda, when the Central Committee, chaired by Woodall, met in the same month in Westminster Town Hall, it drew up a loyal address for the golden jubilee of Queen Victoria, despite the fact that she was well known to be an opponent of the women's movement. Making the best of it, the address congratulated the monarch on all the laws passed under her auspices which had benefited women's lives, such as the Married Women's Property Acts. It also attempted a little persuasion when it mentioned the extension of the local and the Isle of Man franchise to women, hinting that the same had not yet been granted to all women in her realm. It pointedly noted that the queen herself had not been subject to the discrimination which other women suffered when she was allowed to ascend the throne, and that she had very ably managed herself to combine feminine duties with a political role. Lydia Becker was one of the two Manchester signatories and Millicent Fawcett headed the list of those from the Central Committee.[56]

By contrast with the Conservatives, Liberal supporters in the same year failed to get women's suffrage into the National Liberal Federation programme. This was due in large part to the inner turmoils of the party, occasioned by Gladstone's decision to adopt the policy of Home Rule for Ireland. Many Liberals felt that the bitter split which had resulted was a much more important issue than whether women should vote. Even the suffragists themselves fell into one or other of the two camps; Lydia Becker, Millicent Fawcett and Priscilla McLaren became 'Liberal Unionists' in opposition to Gladstone's mainstream policy, fearing that it was the start of a break-up of the British Empire.

This developed in Lydia into a commitment to Conservatism, which, as well as expressing her resentment of Gladstone, may have been also linked to a strong antipathy towards the internationalist doctrines of socialism, which were spreading amongst not only the working classes, but also some parts of the middle classes. At the BAAS conference of 1888, George Bernard Shaw read a paper on the new creed, and it was reported that 'Miss Lydia Becker felt sure that the women of England would never adopt these felonious doctrines.'[57]

When the Liberal Unionists joined forces with the Conservative party, Lydia was amongst the nominators of Captain Rose, Conservative candidate for Stretford in the County Council elections in 1889, and graced the platform at his election meeting, speaking up for the women electors. Indeed, she went further than this, stating quite categorically that she was there as a supporter of the Conservative and Unionist government. She expressed regret that she was 'in the opposite camp to many good friends and colleagues with whom she had fought in many elections' but explained that she had entered the party political fray because 'in her judgement the present political crisis of the country was great, and the great questions

Lydia in London: The Third Reform Act and its Aftermath

relating to the dismemberment of the Empire were to her paramount'. She regarded it as vital 'to support those who maintained the integrity of the Empire and the honour of the English flag'. She shared in this the sentiments of Millicent Fawcett, who helped to found the Women's Liberal Unionist Association in 1888; they may have been influenced by a feminist tendency, notable in the work of Frances Power Cobbe and Josephine Butler for instance, associating the British Empire with the propagation of Western values which supported the freedom of women.[58]

In any case, Lydia had long exhibited conservative tendencies in supporting the monarchical system, though for feminist reasons, at least initially. Writing in 1868 to the American Susan B. Anthony, she had ended with a comparison of how historically it was only under monarchies that 'great women politicians' had emerged, citing 'Anne of Bretagne, Catherine of Russia, Catherine de Medici and Elizabeth of England'. She was quite clear that 'republican institutions are a hindrance' to the advancement of women. In 1887, she was accordingly included on the Manchester committee to organise a jubilee gift of money to the queen from the women of Britain. She wrote to the press to publicise this collection, noting Victoria's fifty-year burden of 'the toils and troubles of public life' and also how as a wife, mother, widow and ruler she had 'held up a bright and spotless example to her own and all other nations'.[59] And all this despite the queen's own continuing antipathy to the women's suffrage cause.

Splits in the movement

All was not well in the suffrage movement, and by the end of 1888 there had again been talk of Lydia giving up her post in London. In recognition of the dominance of party politics, there was a growing lobby in favour of allowing the Women's Liberal Federation to affiliate with the NSWS, thus putting the Cause firmly in the Liberal camp. Suffragists like Lydia who opposed this feared that women's suffrage would be subsumed into general Liberal Party policies, which would destroy the suffrage movement's claim to non-party status and inevitably alienate those of other political persuasions.[60]

Just how strongly wedded to this position she still was had become apparent in 1883, when Richard Pankhurst had stood for parliament as a Liberal in a Manchester by-election. Despite her earlier feelings of powerful admiration, his wife Emmeline's appeal to Lydia Becker for her support did not bear fruit. Becker's reluctance was partly due to Richard's radicalism; he advocated the abolition not only of the aristocracy, but also of the monarchy, which as has been seen was an object of Lydia's admiration. Her resolute adherence to a non-partisan approach by the suffrage campaign was also demonstrated by her comment that the 'extreme radical' Dr Pankhurst, and the 'staunch Conservative' Mr Houldsworth both believed in women's suffrage, and that therefore the Cause would be supported whoever won. The question must also arise as to whether Becker was more affected than she would admit by his siding against her over the issue of married women in the Women's Disabilities bills, and by his ultimately choosing the impossibly beautiful and young Emmeline as a wife. The latter was furious with Becker, according to the testimony of their daughter, Sylvia:

> She [Emmeline] seethed with bitter resentment against his opponents, still more against those whom he had aided and who now refused to aid him in return. She rushed impulsively to the Women's Suffrage Society, asking an official declaration in his favour and the active support of its members. The stern, impassive Miss Becker received her with a cold refusal: the Society could not go out of its way to support Dr P: he was a 'fire-brand,' Becker declared.[61]

Conservative Frances Power Cobbe wrote from retirement in her home in Wales in December 1888 to express her disquiet about a suggestion which had come to her ears that Lydia might resign over the issue of affiliation, although she 'was obliged to admit that the double work of both Manchester and London was too great for <u>any</u> one person'. It seems that Lydia may even have mooted the idea of retiring from the suffrage battle altogether, owing to opposition within the movement. Her friend continued:

> But that you should be lost to the whole cause of women suffrage would be a matter of far deeper moment, and speaking for myself (and I am sure for the majority of our supporters) I should count such an event as nothing short of calamity.
>
> I know nothing whatever of ... the opposition to you of which I grieve to hear. But I think I am a fairly competent judge of your

masterly literary work in the suffrage journal and of the estimate in which your abilities are held by the outside public. Nothing I think would give our opponents more satisfaction than to learn that as a result of dissentions our party had lost your services. It would be in my judgement, as unwise to put you aside at this juncture as for a man going into battle to put his right hand behind his back.[62]

Lydia was re-elected parliamentary agent in the Central Committee, but after much wrangling December saw a decisive split. From the start, Lydia perceived the actions of those who wanted to challenge the status quo as underhand. In her *WSJ* account of a preliminary meeting in November to discuss proposed new rules for the committee which would allow political affiliation, Lydia noted that replies from other societies outside London were ignored, as they 'lay on the table unopened, while the rules were under consideration'.[63] There appears to have been a desire to keep her away from the crucial meeting of 12 December, as indicated in her letter to Miss Balgarnie, the secretary of the Central Committee, whom she notified of her intention to attend, despite the secretary's 'difficulty'.[64] Finally, the highly contentious meeting of 12 December lasted over three hours. The result was that the majority, which included the Jacob Brights, the Pankhursts, the Thomassons, Priscilla McLaren, Rev. Steinthal and Alice Scatcherd, broke away from Millicent Fawcett, Lydia Becker and others who wanted to remain unaffiliated to any political party.[65]

The split can only have caused confusion, not least because of the names adopted. The rebels formed the 'Central National Society for Women's Suffrage', known as the Parliament Street group due to the location of their offices. The existing Central Committee of the National Society for Women's Suffrage, was referred to as the College Street group. Parliament Street particularly welcomed Liberal affiliation, and sixty-eight Women's Liberal Associations became affiliated accordingly.

This was the end of Lydia's official position as parliamentary agent to the new Central Committee, whose minutes record a letter making this clear written early in the new year (1889) on their behalf by Walter McLaren. It seems that Lydia had chosen to vacate the Parliament Street office she had occupied by virtue of her role, which led the Central National Society for Women's Suffrage to assume that she had severed her connection with it 'and had resolved no longer to remain Parliamentary Agent under it'. They acknowledged her 'valuable services' but pointed out that they would no longer pay the Manchester committee for her services from the end of 1888. The letter also stated that, unbeknownst to them, Becker had advised the Manchester committee to repudiate William Woodall, who was proving ineffectual as the suffrage leader in parliament, and that was another reason why they could not retain her.[66] At the same time, the new committee resolved to cease its subscription to the *WSJ*.[67] This did not, however, mean an end to her activities in London and she continued as assiduously as ever working on parliament in an unofficial capacity.

On 19 December 1888, College Street issued a detailed explanation of their objections to the new dispensation. They pointed out that it took away power from the local associations, and admitted to the general council delegates from societies which had other purposes than women's suffrage, and that therefore the Cause would be subsumed in other agendas. The new rules were characterised as 'menacing', and those who were keeping to the old rules wanted 'to have no party *shibboleth*, but to welcome the help of all who will keep the women's suffrage barque to the front'.[68] The College Street group thus remained politically neutral, and Becker continued as its secretary, with other high-powered feminists including Millicent Fawcett, Frances Power Cobbe, Jessie Boucherett, Lilias Ashworth Hallett, Emily Davies, Caroline Biggs and Helen Blackburn. In her annual MNSWS report, Lydia's view was predictably one-sided:

> Many members of the Committee, and most of the Societies which had heretofore worked in association with it, disapproved of the new departure and resolved to continue the Central Committee on the old lines and with the old constitution.

But she could not hide the fact that many in the large societies, including some in Manchester, supported the new group, and only the Manchester, Bristol, Dublin and Belfast committees associated themselves with the old dispensation.[69]

Such fragmentation can only have caused disillusion in the membership, and subscriptions saw a serious decline. The break was bitter, and Lydia referred to her own committee as 'the real Central Committee' and the rivals as the 'extreme left'.[70] Nevertheless, her report of events in the *WSJ* placed a characteristically positive spin on the split and used lively analogies drawn from her scientific background. She hoped that the two bodies would co-operate in friendly rivalry:

> The division of the 'Central Committee' into two organisations may be regarded as an evidence of redundant energy in that section of the Women's Suffrage Society which has hitherto existed under that name. There are some living organisms in the animal world which increase by fission. The observer perceives an animalcule, perhaps moving a little slowly, as if conscious of some difficulty in progression. The two extremities of the creature now show signs of wanting to go in different directions. In a few minutes he looks again, and lo! instead of one, he beholds two organisms, each instinct [sic] with new life. Thus, the Central Committee, having divided into two parts, represents two organisms, each seeking new adherents, each gathering in its harvest in its own separate field, and each, we trust, destined to add its quota to the forces which will bring nearer the accomplishment of the object of the society.[71]

The splits continued, and in 1889 an arguably even more serious breach occurred in the nationwide NSWS over the perennially thorny issue of married women and the vote. The second Married Women's Property Act of 1882, which had given married women control of their own property, had not removed other aspects of coverture; married women were still legally dependent on their husbands. In effect, giving the vote to women on the same terms as men, or as municipal electors, two of the bases on which it had been demanded, still left married women unrepresented. Indeed, the up and coming suffragist leader, Millicent Fawcett, argued that wives should not be enfranchised because of the effects on home life 'which have not been adequately considered'. She considered it undesirable also because, as married women were obliged by law to obey their husbands, the effect would be to give the men an extra vote, so 'it seems inexpedient to allow political independence (which would only be nominal) to precede actual independence.' She believed that the single women could 'virtually' represent all women. This played into the hands of the 'antis' who derided single women.[72]

Becker was opposed also by strong elements in the movement; in 1884, Ursula Bright, had contended pointedly that Woodall's amendment would enfranchise prostitutes but not respectable married women.[73] This time the rebels, led by Elizabeth Wolstenholme Elmy, who demanded that married women should be immediately and *explicitly* included in the demands for women's suffrage, formed a separate organisation, the Women's Franchise League. She was joined by others who had long worked with Lydia Becker; Alice Scatcherd, Clementia and Peter Taylor, Josephine and George Butler, Emmeline and Richard Pankhurst, and Ursula and Jacob Bright. Lydia continued to be supported by the more conservative suffragists, notably Millicent Fawcett, but her isolation from her old friends was clear. As with earlier splits, there was no love lost between the two groups; the Women's Franchise League referred to their rivals as 'the Spinster Suffrage party'.[74]

There were no further debates on women's suffrage in parliament until 1892, despite attempts to introduce bills. This was partly because their spokesman in the House, William Woodall, left something to be desired in terms of his management of parliamentary procedure, which meant that the women's suffrage issue was easily evaded by unsympathetic governments of whatever complexion. In December 1888, the Manchester committee had apparently recently decided on agitation to replace Woodall with some other MP as the leader of the suffrage group in the Commons.[75] Edinburgh's Priscilla Bright McLaren agreed, fearing Woodall was too weak to manage the task as he had proved 'very pliable in his leadership' and 'too much of a Christian to take any plan connected with war'. She was keen that her son Charles should have the chance to present the bill but, probably due to the split over political affiliation, she was 'afraid Miss Becker might get Manchester to move against any of our family taking it'.[76] There was clearly a division between Becker and McLaren, with Priscilla's niece, Lilias Ashworth Hallett, siding with the former. On 4 April 1888, Priscilla had inveighed against their high-handed attitude to fellow suffrage workers:

> It is most disgraceful the way Miss Becker and Lilly are treating all the suffrage workers. To think of that great Council with some of our best women at it being absolutely ground [?] in the Journal [*WSJ*] and Miss Becker has agreed to advertise a great W.S. meeting which is to be held in L.Pool on the 20th at which Walter [McLaren, her son] is to speak – our most faithful friend in the House – and Mrs Sherbrook the Lady who has chiefly got it up says Miss B. has thrown every difficulty in the way – these women seem to me jealous of any new workers.[77]

Nevertheless, in 1889 there was a widespread belief, shared by Lydia, that the make-up of parliament meant that the women's suffrage bill would succeed. Woodall applied for parliamentary time, but blundered by selecting a day during the Easter recess. In an attempt to retrieve the situation, he and other parliamentary supporters of the women's cause over-optimistically asked the government to curtail the recess. In the *WSJ*, Lydia was unusually scathing about his error, and opined that it was 'not surprising that the Government did not see their way to interpose to help Mr Woodall out of the pitfall into which he had stumbled'.[78] Then suffragist MP Walter McLaren withdrew from the second place he had secured in the ballot; the first place was held by an anti-suffragist – for a bill on dried fruit. McLaren too got the sharp end of Lydia's pen. She was further angered when Jacob Bright refused to support Woodall's bill because married women were still not included, and said he would rather 'wait ten years for a Woman's Suffrage Bill rather than support Woodall'. It must have seemed that, whether by accident or design, the campaign was faltering disastrously, and it was just at this point that opponents of women's suffrage gathered their forces and made a major and concerted attack.

Backlash

The backlash was all the more powerful because it came from prominent women; this was the first large-scale formal expression of female hostility. Organised by writers Louise Creighton and Mrs Humphry Ward, 104 of them signed a letter headed 'An Appeal Against Women's Suffrage', printed in June 1889 in the journal *Nineteenth Century*.[79] It described the extension of the vote to women as 'a measure distasteful to the great majority of the women of the country – unnecessary – and mischievous both to themselves and to the State'. Signatories included four duchesses, a countess, twelve ladies of Girton College, poet Christina Rossetti, Beatrice Potter (later Webb) and the actress Ellen Terry. This was followed up by a petition of 2,000 signatures, which was published in August.

Both the Parliament Street and the College Street groups were galvanised into action and circulated a call for signatures in favour of women's suffrage. In a fortnight, the suffragists had gathered 2,000 names, of which an initial 600 of the most significant and influential women were published in the July edition of the *Nineteenth Century*, together with a reply by Millicent Fawcett and Emilia Dilke.[80] Lydia Becker added to this an article, later reprinted as a pamphlet, in the *Manchester Guardian*.[81] She put her usual positive light on the opposition's protest, claiming that it was 'a sign of progress ... a testimony to the strength of the movement for the enfranchisement of women'. She has received some support in this view from Brian Harrison, who points out that the Women's Appeal was partly drawn up in response to the fear that the sympathetic Conservative PM, the Marquess of Salisbury, in an era of increasing socialism, might find that religious and class factors meant that it was in the interests of his party to support the enfranchisement of a small number of propertied women. Conservative anti-suffragist women were alarmed by the sympathy the suffrage movement seemed to be gathering in the party. Moreover, Lord Salisbury sat in the House of Lords and might exercise considerable influence in that body if he chose.[82]

There was much that was striking in Lydia's article, arguing that 'antis' ignored the great body of respectable independent women. It was her point about prostitutes which showed she was still in many ways a radical, and not a social conservative, as some suffragettes later tried to paint her. She began conventionally by singling prostitutes out as 'unfortunate beings whom they [men] maintain in a condition of degradation'. But she was much more challenging of contemporary attitudes in her contention that giving the vote to the prostitute would be to raise her 'from under the feet of the partner of her sin, and to place her as a political equal at his side'. The result would be a moral strengthening of the community.

The backlash was in fact far less dangerous than might originally have appeared. Ironically, the leading female 'antis' were less active than they might have been because it was difficult for women who did not believe they should engage in the male world of parliamentary politics to campaign effectively.[83] Moreover, many of the male Conservative rank and file were increasingly sympathetic to women's suffrage and voted regularly at conferences of the National Union of Conservative and Constitutional Associations in favour of women's household suffrage.

On the other hand, despite their grit and resilience, and the headway they were making at grass-roots level, the suffragists seemed little nearer to their goal of gaining votes for women. Under Becker's leadership they had plugged away for two decades, bit by bit moving parliament towards an acceptance that women's suffrage was a serious topic for debate, then on to a realisation that it would eventually become a reality, willingly in the case of many MPs, and grudgingly for others. There was an ingredient lacking though, and that was party will; until it was present, women's emancipation could not come to pass. It was to take further hard campaigning, some of it violent, social and political upheavals across Britain, a new party representing labour, and a world war before the conditions would be right.

Chapter 12

Death and Legacy

Lydia Becker died far from home, friends and family. She had travelled to Europe alone except for a maid, demonstrating her independence of spirit, and perhaps the relative isolation of her position by this date. She had embarked in search of a cure in July 1890, but the origins of her final illness are to be found in the preceding years when she was clearly weakened by the stresses and strains of controversy and enmity. From early in 1888, her colleagues had been concerned at her frailty and lack of energy, which was much more prolonged than the other illnesses she had suffered periodically in the wake of major campaigns. Helen Blackburn, a close co-worker, put her indisposition down to depression resulting from the arguments and divisions in the suffrage camp: 'She took all these troublesome matters as part of the incidents of political work, to be met passively and impersonally, but the depression of the time fell with special heaviness on a leader of her sympathetic nature.'[1] Despite a strong public face, she was suffering from a painful condition which hindered her mobility:

> She to the last appeared strong and vigorous, and by no means looked so old as she really was. She was present at the May meeting of the School Board, but for some months before that she had been suffering from a rheumatic affection, which affected her power of walking, and she had been compelled to use a stick, while, when she came down to the city from her residence in Shrewsbury street ... she did so usually in a cab.[2]

By the winter of 1889, she was 'almost entirely confined to her house', the little terrace where she had lived since her father's demise in 1877. In January 1890, she wrote to Herbert Birley that she would be unable to attend the school board for three months; she did reappear in April, but only to request a further three-month leave of absence, which was granted.[3] Meanwhile, she continued to do her work on the *WSJ* from home, and friends visited her to keep her occupied, often with games of chess.[4]

A sudden and lonely death

When her condition worsened, she decided to try a rest-cure in Bath and set off in the spring of 1890 to be treated by a Dr Spender in her lodgings at 8 Queen's Square. Continuing there with her usual voluminous correspondence, her letters seemed cheerful, but realistic. To the Central Committee she wrote:

> It is with great regret that I have to report the serious indisposition that disables me from attending at the office and from active work of all kinds. I am suffering from what the doctors call *rheumatoid arthritis* or *osteoarthritis* which cripples my limbs and undermines my strength. My physician says he can give me no hope of effective cure, but he advises me to devote a year to measures for the restoration of my health as far as it can be effected. He thinks I might return home for a while in a few weeks but of course nothing can be settled until it is seen how the cure progresses here. Since I have been here I have had the letters forwarded as usual so that the correspondence has gone on much the same as under ordinary circumstances when I am in London. It is not detrimental to me to continue this work – quite the contrary, as the post is something to work at day by day and my health and spirits would suffer if I were deprived altogether of my usual interests and occupations.[5]

She characteristically concerned herself with the finances of the committee, the parliamentary programme, and future policy.

As she improved to some extent, she decided in early June to travel to Aix-les-Bains in France for further treatment, leaving the editorship of the precious *Journal* in the capable hands of her colleague, Helen Blackburn. On her way to the Channel port she called in on friends in London, and even attended a meeting of the College Street committee before going to Waterloo Station for the onward journey. She was still described as being in a 'crippled state' and friends were concerned that this was a 'serious journey' for her. 'Her immense courage making light of all difficulties', she set off accompanied only by a maid, Annie Purchase, who had very possibly been hired for the occasion as a companion.[6] However, her letters from the French spa were reassuring, telling of steady improvement, which allowed walks, excursions to the lake and drives in the mountains. She continued to take an avid interest in matters at home and wrote about the academic success of Philippa Fawcett, daughter of Millicent:

> I have had English papers every day, and so keep fully in touch with all home interest. What a triumph for Philippa Fawcett at Cambridge! That is just one of those instances which strike the public mind, and do more for the cause of women, at a stroke, that the labours of others for years ... If there could be a renewal of the proposal to admit women to degrees at Cambridge, I think for very shame they could no longer refuse. The general public will refuse to believe it just, that a woman should be excluded from the honours she has so justly gained.[7]

Deciding to take a trip to Chamonix in the Savoy Alps via Annecy, where she spent a week, on 6 July she arrived at St Gervais-les-Bains. From there she wrote an upbeat missive to her Manchester secretary and relative, Sarah Backhouse:

> Just arrived here and find your welcome letter and budget of newspapers, which I regard as a famished lion might look at a bone, after having no news for some days. You must have thought I was lost, and so indeed I have been for the last two days – stuck at the bottom of a deep, damp hole from which escape seemed hard.

She continued to describe the journey in detail, and had clearly enjoyed the beauty of the scenery. The 'deep, damp hole' was the site of the spa at St Gervais, at the bottom of a narrow ravine, which was not conducive to recovery as 'The place struck a damp chill into my very bones.' And then the weather deteriorated and torrential rain kept her there for longer than she had planned. She admitted that she had been imprudent and would 'never be so foolish again', having caught a cold from the experience. Six days later she was still in good spirits and making plans for extending the work in London, and debating whether to settle permanently there as 'I believe there is more to be done for the cause in London than anywhere else just now.'[8]

A further missive on 15 July showed that she was still engaged with suffrage matters, planning a report for the *Journal* on the Central Committee AGM. But alarm bells rang for some when she mentioned that she had been disabled for three days by a severe sore throat, was unable to take solid food, and had to 'use the pen as an instrument of conversation and communication'. Also worrying was that there was no doctor nearby and she was being treated by the local pharmacist 'who has practised medicine and has treated me very skilfully'. Although the weather was fine, she was confined to her room. She was still confident of making a recovery, and was being attended by an English mother and daughter who 'are very sympathetic and often come to see me, which is cheering. It would have been very dreary to be ill alone among foreigners.'[9] Interestingly, there is no mention of the maid, and Lydia does not seem to have gained much advantage or comfort from that quarter, although the details of her last hours furnished by Blackburn must have come from her servant as it seems they were alone together at the end.

There were poignant missives from Lydia in the post which arrived after her demise, such as the postcard sent to Sarah Backhouse on Wednesday, 16 July.[10] She was still at St Gervais in the Hôtel de Mont Blanc, uncharacteristically complaining that she was very poorly and miserable. It arrived on Saturday, the day following her death. Despite being clearly very ill, in great pain and plagued by nightmares about her travels, the redoubtable Lydia continued to fret about the women's cause. On 17 July she sent another postcard, which arrived on the Sunday morning, giving minute directions for the proofs of the speeches at the Central Committee meeting and expressing some optimism for a recovery. She related how the pharmacist was visiting her as often as three times a day, and had brought in a Doctor Bonnefoy from Sallanches, who had given her stronger remedies.[11]

On 18 July, the medical men pronounced her improved, and she expected to be taking food in two days, asking for papers to be sent to her whilst she convalesced. Almost immediately after writing she took a turn for the worse, and the doctor recommended that she travel the 40 miles to Geneva to see a specialist. She resolved to do so, but first telegraphed to her brothers, Arthur and Wilfred, to come to her there: 'Am dangerously ill of diptheria: come at once.' Setting off with her maid, unable to speak she wrote 'I shall not live to get there'. Blackburn reported on the dreadful five-hour carriage ride:

> It was one of her maxims in life, that if we had but one day to live, we should try to make it as bright as we could, and she was true to her rule to the end: even on that terrible drive she took enjoyment in the glorious scenery they were passing through, pointing to some of its beauties.[12]

Although she did reach Geneva, the doctor was not at home and after a two-hour search for accommodation, apparently being refused entry at several lodgings because she looked so ill, she was admitted to the Clinique Juillard. A doctor eventually saw her and recommended that the only possible measure would be an operation, possibly indicating a tracheotomy. Having taken some tea, Lydia died sitting in a chair, on Friday, 18 July 1890. At 1 a.m. the next morning her brother Wilfred received a telegram from the maid which said: 'Come at once: poor Miss Becker is gone for ever.' A later message from the doctor said baldly 'Mademoiselle Becker est mort[e].'[13] Wilfred telegraphed back that if Lydia had expressed a wish to be brought back to Manchester for burial this should be fulfilled, but it seems she had not. A desire in her draft will that she should be buried in the family grave at Altham was qualified in the probate copy by 'should I die within Great Britain'.[14] Priscilla Bright McLaren expressed the view of many:

> One would have liked that she should have been buried in English soil, and near her native city. The men of Manchester appreciated the remarkable woman who had dwelt in their midst; but I have heard her say her friends were more amongst the working men than amongst the richer merchants. I trust the working men will show their appreciation of her memory by insisting that the object of her life's work shall be realised; for what Manchester wills the House of Commons, under whatever party rule, must obey.[15]

Wilfred and his brother Arthur set off as soon as they received the telegram. They arrived in Geneva in time to bury Lydia in the cemetery of St George on Monday, 21 July. She was afterwards commemorated (with her age given incorrectly as 64) on the family gravestone in Altham churchyard.[16]

At the end she attracted personal tributes even from recent acquaintances. On 5 August 1890, in the Hôtel du Mont Blanc at St Germain-les-Bains, a letter was penned to Wilfred Becker by Mr A. Courtney Tagart relating how he and his mother had not been aware of Lydia's prominence in public life until they read an account published by the *Manchester Guardian*, sent to them by her brother.

> We all thought Miss Becker wonderfully bright and clever and fully appreciate [sic] her, but she must have been singularly modest, for

one would not have guessed that she was so distinguished a lady. Hers was indeed a valuable life and I can well understand the great grief of her family at her sudden illness and death.[17]

Lydia's will provided for the eventuality of her death in Britain as well as abroad, and for the re-assignment of bequests should several other people pre-decease her, which implies that it was not written when she was at death's door, but at some earlier point; indeed in her extant papers there is a draft of the will in her own hand.[18] She must have had this with her in her luggage because the witnesses were Dr Bonnefoy and Annie Purchase, her maid who accompanied her throughout. By the time she sent for her brothers, she was patently seriously ill, and probably in any case past the point of being able to write a will.

To confuse matters, it was signed and dated for 19 July, which was the day after her death. The probate affidavit corrected this: 'This Will bearing date the nineteenth day of July 1890 but in fact executed on the eighteenth day of July 1890 was proved at Manchester on the 6th day of September 1890.' She appointed her two brothers executors with full powers and chose to leave all her possessions to members of her family; there was no reference to the suffragists as such.

Bequests included money and furniture, pictures and silver plate to Arthur and Wilfred, as well as 'the ring in memory of Sarah Thorpe' to Arthur and 'the turntable mourning ring' to Wilfred. Lydia's sisters also benefited; Louisa Withington was to have 'my Gold Albert chain with cross pencil case' and Jessie Charlotte Withington, Louisa's daughter (and in view of the nature of the bequest possibly also Lydia's goddaughter), 'my silver spoon King's pattern given me by my Godmother and aunt Sophia'. Esther, perhaps singled out for a more valuable gift as a loyal supporter in her political activities, received a diamond ring with three stones. Then Mary Henderson, Esther Becker and Victoria Crompton received the rest of her jewellery, her 'wearing apparel' and carpets, curtains, glass and china to share between them. Arthur and Wilfred were given the dubious honour of arbitrating if they could not agree on how to divide these spoils. Mary, Esther and Victoria were also left the residue of the estate, but in the case that they all died before Lydia, it would go to Arthur and Wilfred. In the wider family the Backhouses also featured; like Esther, they had been supporters, and Sarah Maria Backhouse was Lydia's assistant secretary in Manchester. Sarah and

Newton Backhouse 'or Brookhouse' got her 'sovereign' purse and her gold compass respectively. Valued at just over £2,000 in her personal estate, perhaps the equivalent of around £165,000 today, it is clear that by the end of her life Lydia, having long struggled to live and campaign, was comfortably off.

The sad corollary to this was an auction in December 1890 of household goods, most of which had belonged to Miss Lydia Becker. They comprised the contents of a typical over-full Victorian middle-class home, including pianos, china, glass and silver, kitchen equipment, 'a wringing machine', and 'an assortment of Bohemian Glassware ... suitable for Christmas presents', as well as a diamond ring and three diamond studs.[19]

Political legacy

<u>Lydia E. Becker, July 19th 1890</u>

Like lightning, a word
Speeds over the sea;
And some, who have heard,
Are weeping with me.

It says: We may see,
In this world, no more
A vision of thee,
On sea or on shore;

That ne'er may we hear
Thy counsels again;
Or feel thou art near
In sunshine or rain.

So tender and strong,
So faithful and true,
Thou wast all along;
Yet few of us knew

How gentle thy hand,
How tender thy heart;
How firm to withstand,
Yet swift to impart.

God bless thee, dear Friend;
And give thee great store
Of peace without end,
And joy evermore!
ETA[20]

The lamentations back in England in response to the news of Lydia Becker's death were fulsome and heartfelt, particularly those expressed by her colleagues and supporters. They all agreed that they had lost a leader of 'immeasurable' worth who inspired and led the movement. Despite their differences with her with regard to policy, the executive committee of the Parliament Street Central National Society for Women's Suffrage adopted a resolution recording their sense of her 'many invaluable qualities, her clear intellectual powers, her wholehearted and persistent devotion to duty, her courage and hopefulness in times of difficulty, and her zealous labour for the cause which in her death has, indeed sustained an irreparable loss'. Her own College Street Central Committee of the National Society were no less fulsome in their regret at her passing; 'we are deprived of her sagacious counsels and devoted services to the cause of Women's Suffrage and other movements for the advancement of women.'[21] Helen Blackburn received letters from all over the country expressing dismay, and recorded the most notable sentiments in her account of Becker's life.

Yet there were hints that she was felt to have left her best years behind. References were made to 'the mental flights she was able to take in her best days' and the view that 'she was the leader of the vanguard at the beginning and the chief supporter of it through all its first difficult years'.[22] This was certainly a reflection of the divisions and controversies which had dominated the movement in the last half-decade. In relation to this, it is interesting that in the memorial issue of the *WSJ* of August 1890 the tributes published were overwhelmingly from those based outside Manchester: Millicent Garrett Fawcett, Leonard Courtney, Priscilla Bright McLaren, Lilias Ashworth Hallett, Jessie Boucherett, and Frances Power Cobbe. Only Robert Adamson as the Manchester treasurer represented her home city. The northern feminists who had been her closest comrades and friends – Elizabeth Wolstenholme Elmy, Josephine Butler, Alice Scatcherd, Emmeline and Richard Pankhurst, Jacob and Ursula Bright – were conspicuous by their absence.[23]

Although, according to Blackburn, Lydia, in her last days in England, had said 'The movement has got far beyond depending on any individual', those left behind found it very hard to overcome the sudden absence of their leader; 'the loss of her guiding spirit lay heavily on the work everywhere.' The Manchester committee was 'paralyzed' and the Central Committee 'suffered grievously by the absence of her political acumen and knowledge of Parliamentary procedure'.[24] The *WSJ* did not continue beyond the commemorative issue of August 1890, and was replaced for some years only by occasional papers, and articles in the *Englishwoman's Review*.

There was widespread appreciation beyond the organisation of what she had achieved. The local press was generous in its plaudits; the *Manchester Guardian* afforded a sympathetic appraisal of her life, and even the Tory *Manchester Courier* was full of praise for this recent recruit to Conservatism:

> She was one of the pioneers of the movement for woman's suffrage, and bravely championed the cause during the years of universal opposition and derision through which it had to elbow its way. As an eloquent, logical, entertaining speaker, she took part in public meetings ... Twenty years ago the movement had got so far that most politicians knew there was a small body of men and women who were seeking the emancipation of the female sex. But very few then contemplated the idea, except to look upon it as a wild and foolish dream. Now the principle is practically conceded, and Miss Becker lived to see the triumph of her life work, although the parliamentary franchise has not yet been granted.
>
> In speaking Miss Becker was deliberative, and occasionally very caustic, at the same time possessing a great fund of humour, which she turned to good advantage. She used most cogent arguments, and possessed a power of criticism which enabled her to say, in a very pleasant and courteous manner things which from other speakers, less practised, would have given offence on many occasions. Her utterances, which at all times gave evidence of deep thought, were listened to with the greatest attention, not only at the meetings of the School Board, but wherever she went. A pleasant looking lady, who dressed well, she had yet a strong individuality, and her genial

voice and characteristic personality will be seriously missed in Manchester.²⁵

Whilst in Britain her loss was 'felt by a very wide circle to be almost a personal one', there was also international dismay. The Women's Suffrage Council of Adelaide, South Australia, was typical; it forwarded a resolution to the Central Committee of the NSWS expressing deep regret at her death, which would be a loss to the women's suffrage movement felt 'throughout the world'.²⁶ In Helen Blackburn's words: 'To members of Parliament, to the general public, to workers in the Colonies and United States, and indeed in every place where the question was alive, Miss Becker had been the visible head of the British movement.'²⁷

Undeniably, Lydia Becker had raised women's consciousness, united them, helped support laws which gave them more rights, and had fulfilled a pioneering role in national politics and local government. The MNSWS executive issued a statement which summed up the importance of her work:

> With the movement in this country for extending the political rights of citizenship to women, Miss Becker's name will continue to be in the future, as it has been in the past, inseparably and most intimately associated. Even her untimely death, before the final achievement of the success towards which she had so largely contributed, will not deprive her of her well-deserved fame.²⁸

Indeed there was a strong sense that her work was on the verge of achieving its goal; Leonard Courtney wrote:

> So Miss Becker has left us with her work unfulfilled after the end had been within reach. That it cannot be long delayed is the faith her friends hold in quiet and confident strength; that when it comes Miss Becker will be entitled to a great share in the result they know; but it must remain a fond regret that she did not live to share the reward of earnest and thorough work pursued with unwavering zeal and with a single regard to the cause of the welfare of women.²⁹

He elaborated on this in his memorial of Becker:

> As far as political calculation could be assured, a House of Commons had been elected, the majority of whose members were ready to

> confer on women the right to vote in parliamentary elections on the conditions which entitled men to the franchise, and there was a reasonable confidence that the House of Lords would confirm and complete the decision of the Commons ... an idealist in her aims, a realist in her appreciation and management of means ... she was faithful to the one object that was supreme over all divisions, and her faithfulness was not devoid of recompense. She saw women voting in municipal elections, in the elections of School Boards, and in the elections of County Councils.

He even went on to compare her to St Paul when he alluded to the controversies she sometimes caused within the women's movement:

> Miss Becker sometimes failed in following the most difficult of all the Apostle's social precepts. Differences from time to time arose, hard to compose. There were secessions and reunion, and then again separation. The Apostle himself, despite his precept, went through sharp contentions, and had to agree to a severance of activity.[30]

This was a huge compliment, when it is considered in what exalted regard St Paul is held in the Christian faith, indeed as its founder and first great theologian. Like Paul, Lydia wanted her band of campaigners to 'love one another', working together for the greater good of the Cause. Also like Paul she demanded commitment and compliance from supporters, and thereby caused opposition and division, losing several close friends over the course of her campaigning.[31]

After the initial shock of Lydia's death, the work was taken up again and progress continued. One of the first priorities of the Manchester committee was to launch an appeal for funds to make up a long-standing deficit, which by the end of October 1890 still stood at over £100.[32] In the mid-1890s, a large number of MPs were returned who in their manifestoes had pledged support to the suffragist cause, and, as Pugh has pointed out, from 1897 the Commons voted in favour of private members' bills to enfranchise women.[33] Women textile workers in the north, encouraged by the Manchester Society under Eva Gore-Booth and Emmeline Pankhurst, joined the movement in large numbers.[34] And this all before the formation of the WSPU in 1903 and the subsequent adoption of illegal and violent tactics.

The style of nineteenth-century suffragists under Becker's lead had been persistent propaganda and oratory, and the use of constitutional means. Many of their methods were adopted by the twentieth-century suffrage movement. They too used legal precedents to challenge the government and court decisions; they lobbied parliament and presented petitions to ministers. Indeed, they looked back for their models to illustrious heroines of the past, amongst them figures as disparate as Joan of Arc, Florence Nightingale, Josephine Butler, and Lydia Becker herself. Eventually though, an extreme wing of the suffragettes lost patience with the 'moderate' approach and began the dramatic use of 'militant', even violent, tactics. The aim was no longer to persuade but to render political life impossible and thereby force the government to concede women's suffrage. This effectively eclipsed the progress made hitherto, even though that progress had established the preconditions which allowed the suffragettes to claim the limelight.[35]

The question remains as to how and why the early suffragists, foremost among them Lydia Becker, have been forgotten by popular history, even by proud Mancunians! In so far as material and artistic tributes are concerned, those that remain are unremarkable or unnoticed. In Manchester there was discussion of a stone or a marble statue, which was apparently thought to be Lydia's own favoured type of memorial. A committee of suffragists was set up to achieve it. It was led by Maria Atkinson in Manchester and Helen Blackburn in London, and included Priscilla Bright McLaren in Edinburgh, and the future suffragist leader, Millicent Fawcett.[36] Their efforts came to nothing. A bust only was sculpted by Joseph Swynnerton, who was the husband of another suffragist friend and artist, Annie Swynnerton; it was exhibited at the Manchester Autumn Exhibition of 1897.[37] The 1907 NUWSS (suffragists) procession in London, popularly known as the 'Mud March', saw the Manchester Society bearing a banner to commemorate Lydia. Presented by Margaret Ashton and created by the Artists' League for Women's Suffrage, it was inscribed with the words of Whitman: 'Pioneers! Oh, Pioneers!'[38] The whereabouts of these works is now unknown.

What does remain today are a few portraits. That painted by a friend and fellow suffragist Susan Isabel Dacre two years before Lydia's death, according to 'A friend' in the letters column of the *Manchester Courier* 'strikingly characteristic', was at one stage intended to be hung in a public building in Manchester, but until recently has been hidden away in the stores of Manchester Art Gallery.[39] A further portrait by Sarah Elizabeth Guinness, on a panel in a bookcase which belonged to Helen Blackburn, survives in the collection of Girton College, Cambridge. Several photographs such as that held by Manchester Central Library complete the physical commemorations.

It has been pointed out that the disappearance of Becker's reputation was remarkably swift, and it began with the national press. Apart from the Manchester papers, Lydia had few obituaries; that in *The Times* was brief, low key and hidden away in the middle of a column. Her career as 'the well-known advocate of women's suffrage' took up a mere four understated lines in a twenty-three-line paragraph: 'When in later life she emerged from retirement, initiated discussions of "woman's rights" at the British Association, and distinguished herself as a platform speaker, her success was surprising only to those who had no previous acquaintance with her.'[40]

Later, with the advent of the flamboyant and newsworthy suffragettes, the law-abiding suffrage campaigners who preceded them, and indeed the contemporary suffragists led by Millicent Fawcett and women's rights campaigners in other fields, were overshadowed. The mere fact of a woman addressing an audience was no longer remarkable or interesting. What the press wanted was a new 'militancy' to spice up its pages; at its most extreme this included the destruction of paintings, the desecration of golf courses, arson, and self-sacrifice through imprisonment and hunger strikes. Furthermore, the Edwardian movement managed to mobilise working-class women in a way that Victorian feminists had not, so that its impact on grass-roots society was much greater and therefore more threatening than anything early feminism had presented.[41]

Laura Mayhall has further pointed out that after the First World War there was a 'fetishization of militancy' by those suffragettes who had been active in violent resistance to the state. The pre-war period was memorialised and narrowed down to violence against property, arrest, imprisonment, hunger strike and force feeding, excluding other aspects of protest such as tax resistance or petitioning. In this version of the narrative, Emmeline Pankhurst 'became single-handedly responsible for British women acquiring the vote'. This in turn paved the way for the claim that it was the war itself, and women's war work enthusiastically embraced by many suffragettes, rather than long-term campaigns which began in the 1860s, which were responsible for women's partial enfranchisement in 1918.[42]

The fall-outs and divisions which characterised Becker's leadership also played their part in her obscurity. She had made influential enemies, particularly on the Manchester committee, in favouring an incremental and non-party approach to the campaign for votes, and they were apparently unwilling to perpetuate the memory of a woman whom they regarded as ultimately an obstacle to the women's cause. When the Pankhursts in particular began to dominate the suffrage agenda in the early twentieth century they were adept at controlling the story of the movement, and the achievements of Lydia Becker and her contemporaries were not a significant part of their narrative. Emmeline Pankhurst was (from 1880) very much a junior member of the Manchester committee, and conceded that Becker was her initial inspiration as a campaigner. But in her autobiography, *My Own Story*, when she described the achievements of the early MNSWS she failed to attribute them to anyone by name.[43] Her daughter, Sylvia, in *The Suffragette Movement* went even further; any success in the early years she largely accredited to her beloved father, Richard Pankhurst, and when she did refer to Lydia Becker, it was to criticise her for narrowness and rigidity, dismissing her skills as a thinker and speaker, which is patently unfair. The only early suffragists Sylvia valued were those who had later thrown in their lot with the suffragettes, notably Elizabeth Wolstenholme Elmy who, working alongside the Pankhursts in the WSPU, lived to see some women granted the vote in 1918.[44]

In the early twentieth century the political scene changed considerably. Pre-First World War upheavals sparked not only by women's rights campaigners, but also by strikes amongst the miners and other workers, rebellion in Ireland, and the growth of a socialist Labour Party, were shaking the foundations of the old order. Democratic, even socialist, ideas became widespread, and fear of an alliance of suffragists with Labour concentrated the minds of the old parties. In 1914, the time was ripe for a review of the position of women in the constitution, but war intervened.[45] The war itself was the most powerful agent of social, economic and political convulsions. In 1918, when all men over 21 were enfranchised, women over 30 with property also gained the vote. It was the suffragettes who claimed, and were perceived, to have won this victory for women.

Yet there were several elements in the process of women's enfranchisement which vindicated the strategies of Lydia Becker and the early campaigners. As she had reluctantly accepted and argued would happen, women did not gain the vote on the same terms as men all at once, but by increments; with a first instalment which enfranchised propertied women (whether single or married) over 30, and finally the achievement of parity ten years later. Whilst the twentieth-century movement, notably the NUWSS (suffragists) and the WSPU (suffragettes), had allied with the Liberal Party, disillusion eventually set in; Lydia's fears that affiliation would mean that women's suffrage would be subordinated to other issues proved well founded. As war approached, the NUWSS moved away from Liberalism and closer to the new Labour Party.[46] In the end, it was a coalition government which gave some women the vote in 1918, and a Conservative one which put the women's franchise on equal terms with men a decade later. The cross-party route which Lydia had advocated in the end delivered the vote to women. Moreover, suffragette militancy almost came to an end in 1914, and after 1918 the tactics reverted to the constitutional suffragist methods of campaigning which Lydia, and later Fawcett, had vigorously refined and applied, leading to the 1928 Equal Franchise Act, which was passed with almost no opposition.[47]

It can be posited that the foundations for an alliance between middle- and working-class women had been laid by the feminists of the nineteenth century, through changes in the municipal electoral system which allowed the concerns of women to gain prominence, in campaigns such as those for married and working women's rights, and in establishing throughout new codes of politics, language and behaviour. The employment of working-class women as speakers was a feature of the earlier campaigns and the twentieth-century movement continued and developed this strategy. Philippa Levine has argued that a new sense of female autonomy developed, in which male values and structures, the policy-based organisations and the hierarchies, were shunned. The 'politics of domination' were replaced by 'a pragmatic humanitarianism' and by the early twentieth century there was a sense of 'commonalty' among women, on which the later suffrage movement could build.[48]

In the circumstances of the later nineteenth century, Lydia Becker and the network of fellow feminists she joined pushed the women's cause as far as it could go, and achieved for it an acceptance that it was a valid topic of discussion, and in many circles an understanding that it would eventually gain equal political rights for women. It had started out in the mid-century as one among many grievances and struggles for women's rights; in Lydia's lifetime many of these had been addressed to a considerable degree, and the national franchise was the one glaring gap in reforms which had improved the social, economic, political and legal rights of women. But the conditions for change needed to be present for this bastion of male dominance to be conquered, and Lydia in 1890 handed on the torch to younger souls in the fight, most famously Millicent Fawcett and Emmeline Pankhurst, who would take on her work, make it their own, and bring it to the next stage in its completion.

Indeed there were many parallels between the leadership of Becker and her more famous successors. With Emmeline, Lydia shared a love of clothes and attached great importance to self-presentation by feminist women.[49] And they had far more significant features in common, not least their single-minded passion for the Cause, at the expense of personal relationships. They were both intolerant of dissent and experienced bitter fall-outs with close colleagues. Lydia had privately expressed the view early on that the government seemed only to listen to agitation when it became violent; a tactic put into action by the Pankhursts and some of their supporters.

It has been strongly argued that in fact the franchise was really won by Becker's direct heirs, the suffragists under Millicent Fawcett and her lieutenant Catherine Marshall. Whilst suffragette violence after 1906 served to alienate much public opinion, with the establishment of the NUWSS in 1897 the constitutionalist stance had been revitalised; it is claimed that through their peaceful campaigning, by 1914 the Cause was all but won. Only the intervention of the world war delayed its achievement.[50] Ultimately, all these campaigners inspired huge loyalty by dint of their commitment and achieved considerable strides towards their ultimate goal of women's suffrage on the same terms as men. Where Lydia Becker and the early feminists blazed a trail, Millicent Fawcett, Emmeline Pankhurst and their cohorts forged on to gain success in 1928.

Conclusion

If Lydia Becker had remained in her rural Lancashire backwater, it is likely that she would never have found her métier in the women's movement. She might have remained in a vacuous state of spinsterhood and subjection. As it was, the move to Manchester in middle age brought her into contact with forces hitherto beyond her experience: the political, social and economic maelstrom which was industrial Manchester; the scientific world and its prejudices against women; and the growing community of men and women who refused to accept received wisdom about the role of women in society.

Had Lydia never come to the city and joined those feminists, the movement would probably have been much more sedate and gradualist. As it was, once her eyes were opened to the possibilities for change, she threw herself with prodigious energy into the fight with a spirit which won her both admiring friends and frustrated enemies. She had found a focus and purpose amongst the feminist men and women who were beginning to organise a movement. Becoming the *de facto* leader of the women's suffrage cause, she and her colleagues broke taboos by addressing audiences of both men and women at public meetings, and by personally lobbying in the corridors of power itself, meeting not only MPs but also ministers of the Crown. Her involvement in other feminist campaigns, notably married women's property and working women's rights, was never allowed to supersede her dedication to what she saw as the crucial Cause; the suffrage was the key to solving all women's grievances. In her own life, on the Manchester School Board, she demonstrated in the most practical way how women could hold public positions and excel in them. As a result of all the hard work, the concept of female suffrage ceased to be an excuse for hilarity and ribaldry and became a serious topic for debate in parliament where, by the time of Becker's death, many members accepted that it was not a question of 'if' women were enfranchised, but 'when'.

In the later 1880s, Becker's brand of feminism was less and less comfortable with what had become a new radicalism in the movement; the incrementalism and non-party approach she had adopted was increasingly challenged and undermined. It has been noted how Davies and Cobbe both withdrew from feminist campaigning when it moved away from its early roots; there is every sign that Lydia Becker, had she lived into the 1890s and even more so into the twentieth century, would have reacted in a similar way.[1] Certainly she was vehemently opposed to new ideas such as 'rational dress' although the 'new woman' ethos of the twentieth century would have appealed in other ways, particularly in attitudes to work and education. Her lack of interest in 'purity' suggests that she may have been more tolerant than some of the new sexual attitudes which often attended the concept.[2]

Nevertheless, she decisively rejected the rising cry for affiliation to a political party, usually the Liberals, and although she desired to win the vote for married women she had become convinced that this could not yet be achieved, but that it might be possible for single women.[3] The fact that at the BAAS she spoke out against socialism would indicate that, despite her sympathies with their concept of universal suffrage, she would have been even less open to the idea of affiliation with a socialist Labour Party, which was adopted by the NUWSS in 1912.[4] Indeed, there is strong evidence that Millicent Fawcett, as president of the NUWSS, only accepted it because Labour was the only party formally to espouse the women's vote; it was younger women in the organisation, notably Catherine Marshall and Kathleen Courtney, who had pushed forward this agenda.[5] Making common cause with those 'democratic suffragists' agitating for universal suffrage, although she would have been in sympathy with it, as with the married women's vote, would probably have been rejected by Lydia on the grounds that it was too radical a move to be achieved all at once.[6] It is perhaps true to say that Lydia Becker was always a radical in ambition, but a constitutionalist and moderate in strategy. As it was, her death in 1890 allowed her effectively to leave the stage when she still had much of her influence in the movement, and saved her from even worse heartache than she experienced in her last few years.

Despite Becker's considerable achievement within the feminist movement, she has been largely forgotten by popular history, and her treatment in academic literature is cursory. Mancunians, proud of their city's heritage, fail to recognise her name. In a recent poll to select one of twenty outstanding Manchester women to be the subject of a new statue in the city, Lydia Becker did not even make it to the shortlist of six. Predictably, it was Emmeline Pankhurst, another great daughter of Manchester, who gained the accolade, with an impressive 56 per cent of the final votes cast.[7]

Lydia Becker deserves better than this. She was a dynamic force in a process which is still ongoing today, fighting to change the social and political position of women. Admittedly, even in 1928 when her dream of electoral parity with men was achieved, there was still a very long road ahead in the struggle for full equality. But social, economic and political justice are closer than they ever were, and for that we have to thank her and fellow campaigners of the nineteenth century, just as much as her more famous successors.

It is fitting that Millicent Garrett Fawcett resoundingly recognised Lydia's seminal influence on the tortuous road to equality through the franchise:

> No one had [sic] worked so long, so continuously, and so exclusively to secure this corner stone of political justice for women as she ... She has laboured and others will enter into the fruits of her labours ... the fruits of all labour that are good for anything must necessarily be entered into more fully by succeeding generations than by those who have actually toiled and groaned in producing them ... Miss Becker's life has its crown; for her work has made it easier for those who succeed her to continue her efforts to base the lives of women on truth, justice, and freedom. There cannot be a more perfect measure of success, nor a stronger claim on our gratitude.[8]

Notes

Introduction
1. M[anchester] G[uardian], 22 April 1891, p. 7.
2. Emmeline Pankhurst, *My Own Story* (London, 1914), p. 9.
3. E. Sylvia Pankhurst, *The Suffragette Movement* (London, 1931), pp. 34–5.

Chapter 1: Creation of a Feminist, 1827–67
1. Philippa Levine, *Victorian Feminism, 1850–1900*, (Florida, 2018), p. 12.
2. Cited in Martha Vicinus, *Independent Women: Work and Community for Single Women, 1850–1920* (London, 1985)
3. Joan Perkin, *Women and Marriage in Nineteenth Century England* (London, 1989), pp. 262–3.
4. Vicinus, *Independent Women*, p. 14.
5. Pat Jalland, *Women, Marriage and Politics, 1860–1914*, (Oxford, 1986), p. 256.
6. Olive Banks, *Becoming a Feminist: The Social Origins of 'First Wave' Feminism*, (Brighton, 1986), p. 126.
7. Vicinus, *Independent Women*, p. 32.
8. Barbara Caine, *Victorian Feminists* (Oxford, 1992), p. 128.
9. L[ondon] S[chool of] E[conomics Women's Library] 9/28/B/10.
10. LSE 9/28/14. MG, 21 July 1890, p. 5 reported in Lydia's obituary that the family moved to Sparth House, Enfield, during the building of 'Moorside Cottage, a substantial house on a breezy site'.
11. LSE 9/28/B/11, 13.
12. LSE, 9/28/A/1.
13. Linda Walker, 'Becker, Lydia Ernestine (1827–1890)', O[xford] D[ictionary of] N[ational] Bi[ography], (Oxford University Press, 2004) http://www.oxforddnb.com/view/article/1899, accessed 10 Feb 2017; Helen Blackburn, *Women's Suffrage: A Record of the Women's Suffrage Movement in the British Isles, with Biographical Sketches of Miss Becker*, (London, 1902), p. 28.
14. M[anchester] C[entral] L[ibrary] M50/1/3, 15 October 1868, L[ydia] E[rnestine] B[ecker] to Mr Acworth; Tina Gianquitto, 'Botanical Smuts and Hermaphrodites. Lydia Becker, Darwin's Botany, and Education Reform', *Isis*, vol. 104, no. 2, June 2013, p. 258.
15. MCL M50/1/3, 25 October 1868, LEB to Anne Robertson.
16. Levine, *Victorian Feminism*, p. 96.
17. MCL M50/1/3, 25 October 1868, LEB to Miss Robertson; W[omen's] S[uffrage] J[ournal] August 1890, p. 8.
18. Lancashire Record Office, death certificate, 14 February 1855.
19. LSE 7LEB 1/12; WSJ August 1890, p. 11.

20. It has been tentatively suggested that her ill-health may have been caused by spina bifida or by multiple sclerosis, but insufficient evidence precludes any reliable diagnosis.
21. Indeed, at the very start of their correspondence, on 19 January 1867, Emily Davies commented on Lydia's poor hand: 'I find your hand rather difficult to ready, especially when and i or a t happens not to be dotted or crossed.' See MCL M50/1/2/6. A glance at Lydia's letter book more than proves the point; MCL M50/1/3.
22. LSE 7LEB 1/12.
23. LSE, 7LEB 1/12/1/1. Lydia's letters to various family members from Germany are extensive and provide copious detail of all her activities.
24. WSJ August 1890, p. 4: 'I spent three happy weeks at the Weinberg, and the vineyard in front of the house sloping rapidly down to the Elbe.'
25. Blackburn, pp. 26–8. LSE 7LEB/1/12, 2 October 1844, LEB to Hannibal Becker.
26. Marion Holmes, *Lydia Becker, A Cameo Life-Sketch* (no date), p. 6; LSE 7LEB 1/12.
27. LSE 7LEB1/1.
28. MCL M50/1/3, November 1868, LEB to Leigh Becker.
29. LSE 9/28/A/4, 23 March 1855, LEB to her aunt.
30. LSE 9/28/A/5, 23 December 1858, LEB to her aunt.
31. E. Sylvia Pankhurst, *The Suffragette Movement*, p. 35.
32. *M[anchester] C[ourier]* 1 October 1883, p. 5.
33. MCL M50/1/3, 16 October 1868, LEB to Professor Levi.
34. Caine, *Victorian Feminists*, p. 135.
35. MCL M50/1/3, 22 March 1868, LEB to Professor Jack; Blackburn, p 43.
36. WSJ August 1890, p. 8; discussed in S. Alexander (ed.), *Women's Fabian Tracts* (London, 1988), p. 280, cited in June Marion Balshaw, 'Suffrage, Solidarity and Strife: Political Partnerships and the Women's Movement, 1880–1930', (University of Greenwich, PhD Thesis), p. 43; E. Sylvia Pankhurst, *The Suffragette Movement*, p. 64.
37. GRO.gov.uk Hannibal Leigh Becker, death certificate.
38. Arthur did show support for his sister when he performed at a soirée as part of the AGM of the MNSWS in November 1871: *MGJ*, 8 November 1871, p1.
39. Census 1871; WSJ August 1890, p. 8.
40. MCL M50/1/3, n.d., LEB to Aunt Backhouse; 4 October 1868, LEB to Mrs Alfred Roberts; November 1868, LEB to Leigh Becker.
41. MCL M50/1/3, November 1868.
42. Audrey Kelly, *Lydia Becker and the Cause* (Lancaster, 1992), p. 9; MCL, M50/1/3, no date but in 1868, LEB to Aunt Backhouse.
43. MCL M50/1/3, 17 June1868, LEB to Jacob Bright.
44. LSE 7LEB/1/12.
45. MCL M50/1/3, 21 June 1868, LEB to Elizabeth Wolstenholme.
46. WSJ August 1890, p. 8.
47. MCL M50/1/2/20–24. Jacob was the brother of John Bright, the anti-Corn Law campaigner.
48. MCL M50/1/3, 29 May 1868, LEB to Hannibal Becker.
49. MCL M50/1/3, 25 June 1868, LEB to Mary M Stephens.

50. MCL M50/1/3, 23 November 1868, LEB to Sarah Ann Jackson.
51. 1877 *Slater's Directory for Manchester*, p. 239; 1883 *Slater's Directory for Manchester*, p. 28; MCL M50/1/2/40; Census 1881.
52. WSJ August 1890, p. 11.
53. Blackburn, p. 42.
54. MCL M50/1/3, letter of 18 September 1868.
55. LSE 9/28/A/21, 22, 23. I am indebted to the kindness of Kelly-Anne and Heath Groves for showing me round Moorside and allowing me to take photographs there.
56. LSE 7LEB/1/12.
57. A copy can be seen at LSE 7 LEB1/2.
58. Kelly, *Lydia Becker*, pp. 7–8. It was stated by Jessie Boucherett that she also gave botany lectures in girls' schools; WSJ August 1890, p. 5. The change of language is clearly pointed out in Gianquitto, 'Botanical Smuts and Hermaphrodites', p. 259.
59. LSE 7LEB1/7.
60. Gianquitto, 'Botanical Smuts and Hermaphrodites', p. 256.
61. WSJ August 1890, p. 5.
62. For what follows, see Gianquitto, 'Botanical Smuts and Hermaphrodites', pp. 250–77.
63. Charles Joseph Ashfield, 'On the flora of Preston and the neighbourhood, part IV', *Transactions of the Lancashire and Cheshire Historical Society*, ns, vol. v, 1864–5, p. 181.
64. MCL M50/1/3, 1 June 1868; 16 June 1868, LEB to Mary Johnson.
65. WSJ August 1890, p. 7.
66. Darwin Archive, 22 Dec 1866, see www.darwinproject.ac.uk.
67. The whole address can be found in Blackburn, pp. 31–9.
68. LSE Mill-Taylor Archive, vol. XII, 29, 27 December 1868, LEB to Helen Taylor.
69. Darwin Archive, 30 March 1864.
70. MCL M50/1/3, 31 March 1868, LEB to Jessie Boucherett; 31 March 1868, LEB to Mr J. Plant of the Manchester Anthropological Society; 3 April 1868, LEB to Theodosia Marshall.
71. Barbara Caine, *English Feminism* (Oxford, 1997), pp. 112–7; Josephine Butler, on the other hand, believed that women were by instinct homemakers, and that they should not have the same education or occupations as men. She regarded Davies as 'one of the masculine-aiming women.'
72. MCL M50/1/3, 18 September 1868, LEB to Josephine Butler; 13 September 1868, LEB to Jessie Boucherett; Nov 1868, LEB to Leigh Becker.
73. Cited in Bertrand and Patricia Russell, eds., *The Amberley Papers: The Letters and Diaries of Lord and Lady Amberley*, (London, 1937), vol. 2, p. 335; *The Times*, 22 December 1868, p. 3.
74. MCL M50/1/3 November 1868, LEB to Leigh Becker. See also pp. 248–9.
75. Jack Morrell and Arnold Thackray, *Gentlemen of Science, Early Years of the British Association for the Advancement of Science* (Oxford, 1981), p. 100.
76. Barbara Gates, *Kindred Nature* (Chicago, 1998), pp. 17–18, citing Lydia Becker, 'Is There Any Specific Distinction between Male and Female Intellect?' *Englishwoman's Review*, 8 (1868), pp. 483–91, and 'On the Study of Science by Women,' *Contemporary Review*, 10 (1869), pp. 386–404.
77. Darwin apparently refused to sign the women's suffrage petition in 1867, but his wife probably did as she paid a subscription: MCL M50/1/2/8.

78. MCL M50/1/3, 27 July 1868, LEB to Mary Johnson. The topics were: Some Supposed Differences in the Minds of men and Women in Regard to Educational Necessities (Norwich, 1868), On an Alteration in the Structure of Lychnis Diurnia (Exeter, 1869), On Some Maxims of Political Economy as Applied to the Employment of Women and the Education of Girls (Edinburgh, 1871), the Attendance and education of girls in Manchester (Birmingham, 1872), Practical difficulties in the working of the 1870 Education Act (Belfast, 1874).
79. *The Times*, 10 November 1881, p. 10; *MG* 13 November 1884, p. 5.
80. WSJ August 1890, p. 8.
81. MC 13 September 1876, p. 4; 8 October 1879, p. 6; *The Times* 13 October 1876, p. 8.
82. LSE 9/28/A47.
83. Barbara Leigh Smith Bodichon, 'Reasons For and Against the Enfranchisement of Women', http://purl.dlib.indiana.edu/iudl/vwwp/VAB7059, accessed 05/06/2020.
84. E. Sylvia Pankhurst Papers, Amsterdam, 7, letters from Elizabeth Wolstenholme Elmy, 1 October 1907.
85. MCL M50/1/2/1–17
86. It seems that in fact a Manchester committee had been set up as early as October 1865 by Elizabeth Wolstenholme to gather signatures for the petition to be presented the following year by J.S. Mill. It was made up of Mr Steinthal, Mr and Mrs Max Kyllmann, Mr and Mrs Jacob Bright, Dr Pankhurst, and Miss Wolstenholme herself; E. Sylvia Pankhurst Papers, Amsterdam, 7, letters from Elizabeth Wolstenholme Elmy, 1 October 1907. The meeting of 11 January therefore represented a re-founding of the committee. According to Blackburn, p. 59, those at the meeting of 13 February were: Mrs Winkworth (chair), Mrs Gloyne, Mrs Hume Rothery, Mr and Mrs Kyllmann, Mrs R.R. Moore, Miss Miall, Miss Wilson, Miss Becker, Miss Wolstenholm [sic], and Rev. Samuel Steinthal.
87. MG 7 March 1867, p. 4.
88. MCL M50/1/2/10, 5.
89. MCL M50/1/2/10, 16 February 1867, Emily Davies to LEB; *Contemporary Review*, vol 4 (1867), pp. 307–16.
90. Laura E. Nym Mayhall, *The Militant Suffrage Movement, Citizenship and Resistance in Britain, 1860–1930* (Oxford 2003), p. 4.

Chapter 2: Emergence of the Suffragist Leader, 1867–8
1. Jane Rendall, 'Who was Lily Maxwell? Women's Suffrage and Manchester Politics, 1866–7', in *Votes for Women*, eds. June Purvis and Sandra Stanley Holton (London, 2000), pp. 67–70.
2. MC 4 December 1867, p. 3.
3. *M[anchester] T[imes]*, 7 December 1867, p. 6.
4. Becker herself wrote to Helen Taylor relating this show of approval: LSE Mill-Taylor Archive, vol. XII, 26, 26 November 1867.
5. MCL M50/1/3, 20 May 1868, LEB to Mary Smith of Carlisle; n.d. (?20 May), LEB to Ursula Bright.
6. Before the Great Reform Act of 1832, a few women had been able to vote under the old system; in 1832 the franchise was explicitly limited to men for the first

time. Maxwell's respectability was not quite as perfect as both Bright and Becker appear to have believed as in April 1866 she had been found guilty in the Police Court of cheating her customers using unjust weights and light measures; MC, 14 April 1866, supplement p. 1.
7. Quoted in Jane Rendall, 'Who was Lily Maxwell? Women's suffrage and Manchester politics, 1866–7' in *Votes for Women*, ed. June Purvis and Sandra Stanley Holton (London, 2000), p. 73.
8. MCL M50/1/3, 18 October 1868, LEB to Susan B. Anthony.
9. MCL M50/1/3, 2 May 1868, LEB to Rev W. Hume Rothery; nd (November) LEB to Mr Rusden.
10. Mayhall, *The Militant Suffrage Movement*, p. 14 explains how in 1832 women were widely thought of in the same category as slaves and Catholics, deserving of protection, but not fitted for political power.
11. MCL M50/1/3, 13 October 1868, LEB to Susan B. Anthony.
12. For what follows, see Blackburn, pp. 44–52.
13. See pp. 138–48.
14. The story is fully explained in Blackburn, pp. 53–6.
15. See Caine, *English Feminism*, pp. 104–7; Barbara Caine, *Victorian Feminists*, p. 225.
16. For information about the early campaign in Manchester, see E. Sylvia Pankhurst Papers, 7, Amsterdam, letters from Elizabeth Wolstenholme Elmy. Many years later, during the suffragette agitations, Elizabeth complained that the minute book had gone missing, and supposed that Miss Becker had lost it; see E. Sylvia Pankhurst Papers, Amsterdam, 7, letters from Elizabeth Wolstenholme Elmy letter to Sylvia of 1 October 1907.
17. Blackburn, pp. 59–60.
18. LSE Mill-Taylor Archive, vol. XII, 58, 9 April 1867, Jessie Boucherett to Helen Taylor.
19. Blackburn, p. 61.
20. See p. 81.
21. Cited in Kelly, *Lydia Becker*, p. 19.
22. MCL M50/1/2/10, 17.
23. MCL M50/1/2/20–26.
24. MCL M50/1/3, 16 April 1868, LEB to Sarah Anne Jackson.
25. MCL M50/1/3, 11 August 1868, LEB to Mary Johnson.
26. MCL M50/1/3, 4 October 1868, LEB to Mrs Alfred Roberts.
27. MCL M50/1/3, 4 October 1868, LEB to Mary Johnson; 8 October 1868, LEB to Ursula Bright.
28. In 1885, his wife, Ursula, edited and published his speeches; *O[xford] D[ictionary of] N[ational] B[iography]*, (Oxford University Press, 2004) Jacob Bright, https://doi.org/10.1093/ref:odnb/3418, accessed 19 May 2020.
29. MCL M50/1/3, 24 October 1868, LEB to Ursula Bright; 7 November 1868, LEB to Leigh Becker.
30. MCL M50/1/3, 13 October 1868, LEB to Susan B. Anthony.
31. See fig. 12.
32. Blackburn, pp. 40–1.
33. Mayhall, *The Militant Suffrage Movement*, p. 6.

34. MCL M50/1/3, 2 May 1868, 29 May 1868, LEB to Anne Robertson; 29 May 1868 LEB to Stephen Heelis; 31 March 1868, LEB to Jessie Boucherett.
35. MCL M50/1/3, 28 April 1868, LEB to Esther Becker.
36. MCL M50/1/3, 31 March 1868, LEB to Jessie Boucherett.
37. MCL M50/1/3, 16 June 1868, LEB to Mary Johnson.
38. It seems that Lydia offended Anstey by asking for the view of another lawyer on his findings, which in an apologetic letter to him she argued was to help win over 'the popular mind', and in no way implied uncertainty about his research; MCL M50/1/3, 19 June 1868, LEB to J.C. Anstey.
39. LSE Mill-Taylor Archive, vol. XII, 29, 27 December 1867, LEB to Helen Taylor.
40. MCL M50/1/3, 30 March 1868, LEB to Anne Robertson.
41. MT 15 February 1868, p. 6; MCL M50/1/3, 1 April 1868, LEB to Jessie Boucherett; LSE Mill-Taylor Archive, vol XII, 5, 12 February 1868, LEB to Helen Taylor.
42. MCL M50/1/3, 27 March 1868, LEB to Jacob Bright.
43. MCL M50/1/3, 30 March 1868, LEB to Miss Robertson.
44. MCL M50/1/3, 3 April 1868, LEB to Theodosia Marshall
45. *Burnley Advertiser,* 25 April 1868; MCL M50/1/3, 2 May 1868, LEB to Esther Becker.
46. Quoted in Joan E. Parker, 'Lydia Becker: Pioneer Orator of the Women's Movement', *Manchester Region History Review,* 5, (1991), p. 15, citing *Report of the Public Meeting Held at Manchester, 14th April, 1868* (Manchester, 1868).
47. MCL M50/1/3, 4 April 1868, LEB to Jacob Bright.
48. MCL M50/1/3, 28 April 1868, LEB to Esther Becker.
49. For the Contagious Diseases Acts see pp. 156–9; MCL M50/1/3, 19 October 1868, LEB to Josphine Butler.
50. MCL M50/1/3, 2 May 1868, LEB to Esther Becker; 8 May 1868, LEB to Ursula Bright.
51. MCL M50/1/3, 9 May 1868, LEB to Elizabeth Wolstenholme.
52. MCL M50/1/3, 29 May 1868, LEB to Mary Johnson; 11 July 1868 LEB to Richard Pankhurst.
53. MCL M50/1/3, 8 April 1868, LEB to Sarah Anne Jackson; 9 April 1868, LEB to Jessie Boucherett; 10 June 1868, LEB to Leigh Becker; 15 October 1868, LEB to Mr Acworth.
54. Kelly, *Lydia Becker,* p. 23; MCL M50/1/3 12 April 1868, LEB to Sarah Anne Jackson; 16 April 1868, LEB to Ursula Bright; n.d. and 14 May 1868, LEB to Elizabeth Wolstenholme.
55. MT, 13 June 1868, p. 5.
56. MCL M50/1/3, 14 May 1868, LEB to Ursula Bright; 15 May 1868, LEB to Rev. Steinthal.
57. MCL, M50/1/3, 20 June 1868, LEB to Mary Johnson; 8 July 1868, LEB to Josephine Butler.
58. E. Sylvia Pankhurst Papers, Amsterdam, 340, 24 May 1868.
59. MCL M50/1/3, 20 June 1868, LEB to Richard Pankhurst; 8 July 1868, LEB to Josephine Butler.
60. MCL M50/1/3, 24 May 1868, LEB to Richard Pankhurst; 24 May 1868, LEB to Jessie Boucherett; 20 May 1868, LEB to Elizabeth Wolstenhome; 27 May 1868, LEB to Ursula Bright; 7 June 1868, LEB to Sarah Anne Jackson. Wolstenholme

apparently did not share Lydia's liking for Pankhurst; 4 October 1868, LEB to Mary Johnson.
61. MCL M50/1/3, 10 June 1868, LEB to Leigh Becker.
62. R. Pankhurst, 'The Right of Women to Vote under the Reform Act, 1867', *Fortnightly Review*, 4 (21) 21 September 1868, p. 253.
63. MCL M50/1/3, 11 July 1868, LEB to Ursula Bright.
64. MCL M50/1/3, 11 July 1868, LEB to Richard Pankhurst.
65. MCL M50/1/3, 30 June, 31 May 1868, LEB to Ursula Bright.
66. MCL M50/1/3, 13 September 1868, LEB to Jessie Boucherett.
67. MCL M50/1/3 27 July, 11 August and 13 September 1868, LEB to Mary Johnson.
68. MCL M50/1/3, 18 September 1868, LEB to Jessie Boucherett.
69. MC, 16 September 1868, p. 6; 17 September 1868, p. 3.
70. MCL M50/1/3, 11 July 1868, LEB to Ursula Bright.
71. Pankhurst wrote to Becker that he felt a cessation of the fight at this point would 'wound the honour of the movement'; see E. Sylvia Pankhurst, *The Suffragette Movement*, p. 43.
72. MCL M50/1/3, 15 October 1868, LEB to Ursula Bright.
73. For AGMs see pp. 75–9.
74. LSE Mill-Taylor Archive, vol. XIII, 211, 3 November 1868, Philippine Kyllmann to Helen Taylor.
75. This case caused a serious dispute within the committee over expenses.
76. MC, 29 September 1868, p 5.
77. MC, 14 November 1868, p. 3.
78. MCL M50/1/3, 13 October 1868, LEB to Susan B. Anthony.
79. MCL M50/1/3, 5 October 1868, LEB to Professor F.W. Newman. The allusion is biblical and signifies the repaying of evil with good in order to make one's enemy repent; Proverbs 25: 21–22
80. MC, 10 October 1868, p. 6; See p. 70.
81. MCL M50/1/3, Thursday night, November 1868, LEB to Ursula Bright.
82. MCL M50/1/3, 29 November 1868, LEB to Mary Johnson recounts how the county returned 8 MPs 'to help Disraeli.'
83. MCL M50/1/3, 18 November 1868, LEB to Susan B. Anthony.
84. MCL M50/1/3, 18 November 1868, LEB to Susan B. Anthony.
85. MCL M50/1/3, 13 October 1868, LEB to Susan B. Anthony. In the Report of 1868 she listed the many places all over the country where women had voted; MCL M50/1/4/1, pp. 6–9.
86. MCL M50/1/3, 27 November 1868, LEB to Jessie Boucherett.
87. MCL M50/1/3, 31 May 1868, LEB to Sarah Anne Jackson.

Chapter 3: The Development of the Manchester Society
1. MCL M50/1/4/1, MNSWS 1st Annual Report, p.19.
2. MCL M50/1/4/1–21, Annual Reports of the MNSWS.
3. MCL M50/1/4/7, pp. 3–9, 13–14.
4. MCL M50/1/4/7, pp. 13, 15; M50 1/4/12, p. 8.
5. MCL M50/1/4/1–21, Annual Reports of the MNSWS.
6. MCL M50/1/4/2, p. 15; M50/1/4/5, p. 11; M50/1/4/16, p. 13.
7. University of Nottingham Archives, N Mc 2/105, p. 3. Alice Scatcherd was the wife of a Leeds mill-owner and an ardent suffragist. Sylvia Pankhurst described

her as 'a tall, bony Yorkshire woman … she repudiated as badges of slavery, and refused to wear either a wedding ring or the veil with which every would-be well-dressed woman covered her face in those days … [wearing] staid, unfashionable dress, complete by large, low-heeled, elastic-sided boots'; E. Sylvia Pankhurst, *The Suffragette Movement*, p. 97.
8. MCL M50/1/4/5, p. 16. The society banked with the Manchester and Liverpool District Banking Company on King Street.
9. See pp. 221–3.
10. MCL M50/1/4/3, 27 July 1868, LEB to Mary Johnson.
11. MCL M50/1/3, 17 July 1868.
12. MC 7 November 1874, p. 1.
13. MCL M50/1/4/19, p. 9; 1/4/20, p. 2; 1/4/21, p. 10; 1/4/22, p. 8.
14. Levine, *Victorian Feminism*, p. 85.
15. MCL M50/1/3, November 1868, LEB to Leigh Becker.
16. WSJ August 1890, p. 5.
17. MCL, M50/1/3, 1 June 1868, LEB to Mary Johnson.
18. LSE Mill-Taylor Archive, vol. XIII, 210, 10 March 1868.
19. See pp. 56 and 76–7.
20. MCL M50/1/3, 15 November 1868, LEB to Richard Pankhurst; LSE Mill-Taylor Archive, vol XIII, 216, 8 December 1868, Philippine Kyllmann to Helen Taylor; MCl M50/1/3, 19 October 18668, LEB to Josephine Butler.
21. MCL M50/1/3, 14 November 1868, LEB to Ursula Bright.
22. See LSE Mill-Taylor Archive, vol. XIII, 211–221 and XII, 21 for the whole correspondence.
23. MCL M50/1/3, 14 November 1868, 23 November 1868, LEB to Ursula Bright; 15 November 1868, LEB to Richard Pankhurst.
24. MCL M50/1/3, 26 November 1868, LEB to Rev. Steinthal; Sunday, 22 November 1868, LEB to Elizabeth Wolstenholme; 21 November 1868, LEB to Ursula Bright; 29 November 1868, LEB to Mary Johnson; 29 November 1868, LEB to Ursula Bright.
25. LSE Mill-Taylor Archive, vol. XIII, 216, 8 December 1868.
26. LSE Mill-Taylor Archive, vol. XIII, 217, 22 January 1869.
27. MCL, M50/1/3, 27 July 1868, LEB to Mary Johnson,
28. *Englishwoman's Review*, October 1868, p. 74.
29. MCL, M50/1/3, 21 March 1868, LEB to Mrs E[dward] Kyllmann [Mathilde].
30. The origins of this idea can be found in MCL M50/1/3, 23 May 1868, LEB to Ursula Bright.
31. MCL M50/1/3, 20 May 1868, 25 May 1868, 1 June 1868, 16 June 1868, 4 October 1868, LEB to Mary Johnson.
32. MCL M50/1/3, 7 July 1868, LEB to Mary Johnson.
33. MCL M50/1/3, 15 October 1868, LEB to Ursula Bright.
34. MCL M50/1/3, 25 October 1868, LEB to Miss Robertson.
35. MG 4 November 1868, p. 7.
36. MCL M50/1/3, 19 October1868, 1 November 1868, LEB to Josephine Butler; see p. 57.
37. MCL M50/1/3, 4 October 1868, LEB to Mary Johnson.
38. See pp. 80ff. and pp. 222–3.
39. See pp. 161–3.

40. MCL M50/1/4/2.
41. MCL M50/1/4/2, pp. 8, 13; *MC* 16 December 1869, p. 6.
42. MCL M50/1/4/2, pp. 21–2.
43. *M[anchester] E[vening] N[ews]*, 23 November 1870, p. 3.
44. MT 11 November 1871, p. 7.
45. E. Sylvia Pankhurst Papers, Amsterdam, 7, letter from Elizabeth Wolstenholme Elmy, 1 October 1907.
46. MCL M50/1/2/25, 2 July 1867, LEB to Rev. Steinthal.
47. LSE Mill-Taylor Archive, vol. XIII, 269, 17 June 1867, Mentia Taylor to Helen Taylor.
48. LSE Mill-Taylor Archive, vol. XII, 12, 4 July 1867, LEB to Helen Taylor. The Manchester draft rules had been sent to Taylor at the end of June; 10, 26 June 1867, LEB to Helen Taylor.
49. LSE Mill-Taylor Archive, vol. XII, 3, 30 July 1867, LEB to Helen Taylor.
50. LSE Mill-Taylor Archive, vol. XII, 9, nd; 10, 26 June 1867; 74, 7 June 1867, Jessie Boucherett to Helen Taylor; 13, 12 July 1867 LEB to Helen Taylor; 15, 17 July 1867, LEB to Helen Taylor; 16, 19 July 1867, LEB to Helen Taylor.
51. MCL M50/1/2/27, 8 August 1867, Clementia Taylor to LEB.
52. LSE Mill-Taylor Archive, vol. XII, 20, 12 October 1867, LEB to Helen Taylor.
53. MCL M50/1/4/1, MNSWS Annual Report, 1868, p. 3.
54. LSE Mill-Taylor Archive, vol. XII, 23, 27 October 1867, LEB to Helen Taylor; MCL M50/1/3, 23 May 1868, LEB to Ursula Bright.
55. See Levine, *Victorian Feminism*, pp. 19–20.
56. MCL M50/1/3, n.d. LEB to Ursula Bright; 24 May 1868, LEB to Helen Taylor.
57. See pp. 69–73.
58. LSE Mill-Taylor Archive, vol. XIII, 216, 8 December 1868, Philippine Kyllmann to Helen Taylor.
59. LSE Mill-Taylor Archive, vol. XII, 18, 25 August 1867, LEB to Helen Taylor.
60. LSE Mill-Taylor Archive, vol. XII, 22, 31 October 1868, Helen Taylor to LEB.
61. LSE Mill-Taylor Archive, vol. XII, 24, 3 November 1868, LEB to Helen Taylor.
62. LSE Mill-Taylor Archive, vol. XII, 4, 27 September 1867, LEB to Helen Taylor.
63. LSE Mill-Taylor Archive, vol. XII, 24, 3 November 1867, LEB to Helen Taylor.
64. LSE Mill-Taylor Archive, vol. XII, 28, 23 December 1867; 30, 8 January 1868, LEB to Helen Taylor.
65. MCL M50/1/3, nd, LEB to Ursula Bright.
66. MCL M50/1/3, 28 June 1868, LEB to Ursula Bright.
67. MCL M50/1/3, n.d., 22, 23 May 1868, LEB to Ursula Bright; 24 May 1868, LEB to Helen Taylor; [25?] and 28 June 1868, LEB to Ursula Bright.
68. MCL, M50/1/3, 29 May 1868, LEB to Mary Johnson; 31 May 1868, LEB to Ursula Bright; 29 May 1868, LEB to Clementia Taylor; 27 November 1868, LEB to W.T. Charley, MP for Salford.
69. LSE Mill-Taylor Archive, vol. XIII, 215, 4 December 1868, Helen Taylor to Philippine Kyllmann.
70. This was Lydia's own assessment of the London Society's structure. In an undated document of the later 1860s its rules stated that the executive committee would be appointed annually at a general meeting, but it is not clear what the mechanism for this would be; LSE Mill-Taylor Archive, vol. XIII, 275, 276.
71. Quoted in Caine, *English Feminism*, p. 118.

72. Caine, *English Feminism*, p. 118
73. MCL M50/1/3, 8 June 1868, LEB to Elizabeth Wolstenholme; 31 May 1868, LEB to Ursula Bright.
74. MCL M50/1/3, 13 September 1868, LEB to Jessie Boucherett.
75. The methods of the London committee seemed to have consisted of simply writing to eligible women to urge them to vote; MCL M/50/1/9/1, circular letter of 6 November 1868.
76. MCL M50/1/3, 31 May 1868 LEB to Ursula Bright.
77. MCL, M50/1/3, Tuesday night, LEB to Ursula Bright; 7 June 1868, LEB to Ursula Bright; 19 May 1868, LEB to Mary Johnson.
78. MCL M50/1/3 27 November 1868, LEB to Jessie Boucherett.
79. Mill to T. Hare, 29 May 1870, cited in Parker, 'Lydia Becker: Her Work for Women', PhD Thesis (Manchester, 1990), p. 140.
80. *The Times* 18 January 1872, pp. 6, 10.
81. WSJ, December 1871, p. 131.
82. Caine, *English Feminism*, p. 107.
83. The meeting on 27 April 1876 is another case in point; LSE Central Committee Executive, Minutes, 2LSW/A/1 Box FL 135. She also worked with Mentia Taylor and Elizabeth, Rhoda and Agnes Garrett, and Lady Anna Gore Langton, but there is no evidence that she formed friendly attachments with them. The executive committee minutes are incomplete, and in the period up to Lydia's death cover only 3 February 1875 to 12 April 1877, 19 April 1883 to 17 December 1884, and 4 January 1888 to 13 March 1889.
84. There was a further extension of the concept of co-ordination when in 1876 the Yorkshire Society and the MNSWS joined together in an attempt to streamline the effort in the north of England; *MC* 30 November 1867, p. 6.

Chapter 4: Established leader of the women's suffrage movement, 1868–90
1. E. Pankhurst, *My Own Story*, p. 9. Anthony was, with Elizabeth Cady Stanton, the dynamic and most visible leader of the early US suffrage movement.
2. Martin Pugh, *The March of the Women* (Oxford, 2000), p. 13.
3. Levine, *Victorian Feminism*, pp. 19–20, quoting Lady Frances Balfour.
4. See pp. 80–90.
5. Blackburn, p. 40.
6. See pp. 69–73; LSE, Mill-Taylor Archive, vol. XIII, 215, 4 December 1868; 219, 22 August 1869, Philippine Kyllmann to Helen Taylor. In the latter, Philippine poignantly enclosed photographs of her two little girls.
7. MCL M50/1/3, 26 May 1868, LEB to Elizabeth Wolstenholme.
8. MCL M50/1/3, 11 July 1868, LEB to Richard Pankhurst.
9. MCL M50/1/3, 27 July 1868, LEB to Mary Johnson.
10. MCL M50/1/3, 29 September 1868, LEB to Philippine Kyllmann.
11. MCL M50/1/3, 21 June 1868, LEB to Elizabeth Wolstenholme.
12. MCL M50/1/3, 25 October 1868, LEB to Miss Robertson.
13. LSE 7LEB/1/12.
14. MCL M50/1/3, 8 April 1868, LEB to Sarah Jackson; 19 July 1868, LEB to Josephine Butler.
15. MCL M50/1/3, 9 August 1868, LEB to Sarah Jackson.
16. WSJ August 1890, p. 11; MC 26 October 1885, p. 8.

17. See Joanna M Williams, *Manchester's Radical Mayor: Abel Heywood, the Man who Built the Town Hall* (History Press, 2017), p. 165.
18. MCL M50/1/3, 10 June 1868, LEB to Leigh Becker.
19. MCL M50/1/3, 21 March 1868, w28 April 1868, LEB to Esther Becker; LSE 7LEB/1/12.
20. MCL M50/1/3, 21 March to 29 November 1868, nd, LEB to Esther Becker and Mrs Backhouse; *MT* 26 July 1890; *WSJ* August 1890, p. 11.
21. MCL M50/1/3; E. Sylvia Pankhurst Papers, 7, 1 July 1910, Elizabeth Wolstenholme Elmy to Sylvia Pankhurst.
22. See Cap. 5.
23. Blackburn, p. 39.
24. MCL M50/1/2/32, 28 December 1868, LEB to Francis William Newman.
25. MCL M50/1/3, 20 July 1868, LEB to Elizabeth Wolstenholme; 13 October 1868, 18 November 1868, LEB to Susan B. Anthony.
26. Blackburn, p. 39.
27. MCL, M50/1/3, 7 June 1868, LEB to Sarah Anne Jackson; 21 October 1868, LEB to Theo Marshall.
28. MCL M50/1/3, 30 June 1868, LEB to Ursula Bright.
29. MCL M50/1/3, 9 September 1868, LEB to Jacob Bright.
30. MCL M50/1/3, 7 July 1868, LEB to Mary Johnson.
31. MCL M50/1/3, 20 May and 8 June 1868, LEB to Elizabeth Wolstenholme.
32. MCL M50/1/3, 8 July 1868, 19 October 1868, 1 November 1868, LEB to Josephine Butler; University of Liverpool, JB 1/1 18 November 1873, Josephine Butler to Miss Priestman.
33. MCL, M50/1/3, 4 October 1868, LEB to Mary Johnson.
34. MCL M50/1/3, 27 July 1868, LEB to Mary Johnson. The only other people addressed in such intimate terms at this time were Theo Marshall and Sarah Jackson.
35. WSJ August 1890, pp. 5–6.
36. MCL M50/1/2, 49, 50, 12 and 14 June nd [1885?]. The autobiography was in the event extremely unreliable; Caine, *Victorian Feminists*, pp. 103, 111.
37. WSJ August 1890, p. 9.
38. WSJ August 1890, pp. 5–6, 7–8.
39. See pp. 146–7.
40. See pp. 249–55; Millfield Papers, Box 36, letter of 19 January 1884, cited by Sandra Stanley Holton, "To Educate Women into Rebellion': Elizabeth Cady Stanton and the Creation of a Transatlantic Network of Radical Suffragists', *American Historical Review*, vol. 99, no. 4 (October 1994), p. 1125.
41. WSJ August 1890, pp. 6, 8. She was sympathetic to the anti-vivisection campaign around this time.
42. LSE 9/28/A/13, 31 October 1885; 14, 7 February 1887.
43. Kelly, p. 28; Parker, 'Lydia Becker, Pioneer Orator', p. 15.
44. Pugh, *The March of the Women*, p. 19.
45. Eliza Lynn Linton, 'The Shrieking Sisterhood,' *Saturday Review*, 12 March 1870, pp. 341–2.
46. LSE Mill-Taylor Archive, vol. XII, 19, 10 September 1867, LEB to Helen Taylor.
47. MCL M50/1/3, 17 April 1868, LEB to Sarah Anne Jackson.
48. MCL M50/1/3, 2 May 1868, LEB to Esther Becker.

49. MT 16 April 1869.
50. *Daily Chronicle,* 1 April 1869; *The Gazette,* Local Notes by Spectator, cited in Joan E. Parker, 'Lydia Becker, Her Work for Women', pp. 156–7.
51. Kelly, p. 28.
52. Parker, 'Lydia Becker: Pioneer Orator', p. 20.
53. MCL M50/1/4/2, p. 8. But Mary recorded that the society did not thrive because the local people had 'little time for thought'; Mary Smith, *The Autobiography of Mary Smith, Schoolmistress and Nonconformist, a Fragment of a Life,* (London, 1892), pp. 257–8.
54. Caine, *English Feminists,* p. 118.
55. MCL, M50/1/3, 19 October 1868, LEB to Josephine Butler.
56. For a full discussion see Sandra Stanley Holton, 'Silk dresses and lavender kid gloves: the wayward career of Jessie Craigen working suffragist', *Women's History Review,* 5 (1996), pp. 129–50.
57. For more on this see Holton, 'Jessie Craigen', p. 135.
58. Parker, 'Lydia Becker: Her Work for Women', pp. 169–70.
59. MG 27 October 1880, p. 6.
60. Quoted in Kelly, p. 51.
61. WSJ August 1890, p. 8.
62. LSE 7LEB 1/4; Kelly, p. 44.
63. MG, 24 October 1878, p. 5.
64. Blackburn, p. 148.
65. Blackburn, p. 152.
66. MT, 14 February 1880.
67. MC, 7 February 1880, p. 7.
68. Blackburn, pp. 152–3.
69. Blackburn, pp. 159–61.
70. WSJ January 1879, p. 9.
71. *City Jackdaw,* 31 December 1875, pp. 69–70.
72. LSE, 9/01/1234. See fig. 29.
73. Pugh, *March of the Women,* p. 66.
74. MG 17 February 1925, p. 6.
75. See p. 74.
76. LSE Mill-Taylor Archive, vol. XII, 27, 5 December 1867, LEB to Helen Taylor.
77. Parker, 'Lydia Becker: Her Work for Women', pp. 131–3.
78. MCL M50/1/4/2, p. 8; M50/1/4/7, p. 13.
79. See p. 133.
80. E. Sylvia Pankhurst Papers, 340, 6 June 1869, LEB to Elizabeth Wolstenholme Elmy.
81. WSJ August 1890, p. 3.
82. MCL 50/1/3, 4 October 1868, LEB to Ursula Bright.
83. Ray Strachey, *The Cause, A Short History of the Women's Movement in Great Britain,* (London, 1978), p. 265.
84. Blackburn, pp. 40–1.
85. Pugh, *March of the Women,* p. 16.
86. MT 8 January 1889, p. 6; 12 January 1889, p. 2; MC 12 January 1889, p. 6. She ended with a call to patriotism by citing 'the integrity of the Empire and the honour of the English flag.'

87. See pp. 221–3.
88. MG 30 July 1875, p. 6.
89. See p. 219.
90. See pp. 242ff.
91. Blackburn, p. 174.
92. See pp. 251–4.
93. Christabel Pankhurst, *Unshackled* (London, 1987), p. 26.
94. MC 28 August, 1890, p. 6.
95. MT 6 November 1882, p. 7; cited by Parker, 'Lydia Becker: Her Work for Women', pp.171–2.
96. See figs. 11–13, 24–27.
97. WSJ August 1890, p. 11.
98. Sara Delamont, 'The Contradictions in Ladies' Education' in *The Nineteenth Century Woman*, eds. Sara Delamont and Laura Duffin (London, 1978), p. 145.
99. Levine, *Victorian Feminism*, pp. 21–2.
100. MCL M50/1/3, 25 June 1868, LEB to Mary M. Stephens.
101. LSE 7LEB/2/1/12.
102. MC 9 September 1876, p. 3.
103. MCL M50/1/3, November 1868, LEB to Leigh Becker; Darwin Archive, 13 January 1869.
104. MG 22 September 1877, p. 8.
105. MC 4 October 1877, p. 3.
106. MC 15 September 1888, p. 6. But claims that she defended 'tight lacing' were unfounded. See also Levine, *Victorian Feminism*, p. 113.
107. Reported in MT 3 November 1888, p. 6; WSJ November 1888, p. 107, and MG 21 July 1890, p. 5.
108. WSJ December 1889, p. 147.
109. MC 24 December 1874, p. 6.
110. MG 30 March 1932, p. 7.
111. Caine, *Victorian Feminists*, pp. 4–7.
112. Caine, *Victorian Feminists*, pp. 23–5.
113. Caine, *Victorian Feminists*, p. 77.
114. Caine, *Victorian Feminists*, pp. 113–4.
115. Caine, *Victorian Feminists*, pp. 77, 80.
116. See pp. 4–16 for Becker's early life.
117. See p. 11.
118. Caine, *Victorian Feminists*, p. 119.
119. Caine, *Victorian Feminists*, p. 2.
120. MCL M50/1/3, 17 July 1868, LEB to Richard Pankhurst.
121. Caine, *Victorian Feminists*, p. 80.
122. Blackburn, p. 41.
123. See p. 99.
124. See pp. 101–2.
125. Caine, *Victorian Feminists*, p. 167.
126. Caine, *Victorian Feminists*, p. 78.
127. See pp. 197–204.
128. Caine, *English Feminism*, pp. 127, 111; *Victorian Feminists*, p. 60.
129. See p. 190.

130. See pp.196–7; Caine, *Victorian Feminists*, pp. 171, 176.
131. See p. 136.
132. Caine, *Victorian Feminists*, pp. 229–33.
133. Caine, *Victorian Feminists*, pp. 15–16.
134. Caine, *Victorian Feminists*, pp. 73–4.
135. Caine, *English Feminism*, p. 127; *Victorian Feminists*, pp. 14–15.
136. See pp. 151, 153 for example.
137. Millicent Fawcett is a case in point; Caine, *Victorian Feminists*, p. 225.
138. See pp. 42–3.
139. Caine, *English Feminism*, pp. 102–3; Mayhall, *The Militant Suffrage Movement*, p. 13.
140. Caine, *Victorian Feminists*, pp. 126–7; *English Feminism*, pp. 127–9.
141. Caine, *Victorian Feminists*, pp. 225, 236.
142. See p. 35.
143. Caine, *Victorian Feminists*, pp. 263, 129–30.
144. See p. 159.
145. See pp. 222–3.
146. See p. 248; Caine, *Victorian Feminists*, pp. 264–5; Sandra Stanley Holton, *Feminism and Democracy* (Cambridge 1986), pp.76–90.
147. Pugh, *March of the Women*, p. 66.

Chapter 5: The *Women's Suffrage Journal*, 1870–90
1. MCL M50/1/3, 7 July 1868, LEB to Mary Johnson.
2. MCL M50/1/3, 31 March 1868, LEB to Jessie Boucherett.
3. MCL M50/1/3, 1 June 1868, LEB to Elizabeth Wolstenholme.
4. MCL M50/1/3, 31 March 1868, LEB to Jessie Boucherett; 19 May 1868, LEB to Miss Johnson and Miss Holland.
5. MCL M50/1/3, 14 June 1868, LEB to Jessie Boucherett.
6. MCL M50/1/3, 9 August 1868, LEB to Sarah Anne Jackson.
7. MCL M50/1/3, 13 October 1868, LEB to Susan B. Anthony; 27 November 1868, LEB to Jessie Boucherett.
8. See Levine, *Victorian Feminism*, p. 89.
9. MCL M50/1/3, 11 August 1868, LEB to Mary Johnson.
10. MCL M50/1/3, 4 October 1868, LEB to Mary Johnson.
11. WSJ March 1870, p. 1.
12. E. Pankhurst, *My Own Story*, p. 9.
13. MCL M50/1/3, 22 March 1868, 1 April 1868, LEB to Jessie Boucherett; 11 August 1868, LEB to Mary Johnson.
14. MCL M50/1/3, 11 August 1868, LEB to Mary Johnson.
15. Blackburn, p. 101.
16. MCL M50/1/4/11, p. 11.
17. MT 18 December 1869, p. 5.
18. WSJ July 1889, pp. 94, 98.
19. MCL M50/1/4/21, p. 9.
20. MCL M50/1/4/21, p. 8; M50/1/4/22, p. 5.
21. Holmes, *Lydia Becker*, p. 16.
22. WSJ September 1884, p. 232.
23. WSJ September 1884, pp. 207, 209.

24. WSJ September 1884, pp. 234, 233.
25. Blackburn, p. 102.
26. See p.220.
27. WSJ February 1878, p. 34.
28. WSJ Nov 1878, p. 198; MCL M50/1/2, 42, 25 September 1883, Elizabeth Wolstenholme Elmy to LEB.
29. Quoted in Kelly, pp. 41–2.
30. WSJ December 1870, p. 103; September 1872, p. 121; October 1872, p. 135; November 1872, p. 148.
31. Frances Power Cobbe, 'Wife-torture in England', *Contemporary Review*, vol. 32, (April 1878), pp. 55–87.
32. WSJ July 1878, p. 151; October 1878, p. 165.
33. See for example the 1872 editions.
34. WSJ October 1878, p. 174.
35. WSJ August 1871, p. 83; October 1883, p. 176.
36. WSJ September 1883, p. 169; January 1878, p. 11.
37. MCL M50/1/2/45, 2 March 1885, Mary Carpenter to LEB.
38. WSJ July 1878, p. 98.
39. WSJ February 1874, p. 25.
40. Parker, 'Lydia Becker: Her Work for Women', p. 151.
41. MCL M50/1/4/22, p. 6.
42. WSJ August 1890, p. 1.

Chapter 6: The Women's Movement: a Multiplicity
1. Olive Banks, *Becoming a Feminist*, pp.46, 50, 53.
2. Lee Holcombe, *Wives and Property*, (Toronto, 1983), p. 30.
3. Holcombe, *Wives and Property*, pp. 37–46.
4. Holcombe, *Wives and Property*, pp. 13–17.
5. Holcombe, *Wives and Property*, pp. 57–8, 70, 87.
6. See for instance Caine, *English Feminism*, pp. 91–2.
7. Holcombe, *Wives and Property*, pp. 101–3.
8. Holcombe, *Wives and Property*, pp. 164, 109, 117; MCL M50/1/3, 29 April 1868, LEB to Miss McLaren; 17 May 1868, LEB to Henry Nicol.
9. MCL M50/1/3, 23 May 1868, 26 May 1868, LEB to Elizabeth Wolstenholme; 26 May 1868, LEB to Mrs Taylor; Holcombe, *Wives and Property*, p. 164.
10. MCL M50/1/3, 20 May 1868, LEB to Elizabeth Wolstenholme; n.d. 1868, LEB to Mrs Poole; 2 May 1868, LEB to Professor Jack.
11. MCL, M50/1/3, 7 June 1868, LEB to Jacob Bright; 25 June 1868, LEB to Mary M. Stephens.
12. MCL, M50/1/3, 21 June, 8 June, 10 July 1868, LEB to Elizabeth Wolstenholme; Mill-Taylor Archive, vol. XII, 2 August 1868, 28 May 1868, Jessie Boucherett to Helen Taylor.
13. MCL M50/1/3, 16 May 1868; 20 May 1868; n.d., LEB to Elizabeth Wolstenholme.
14. MCL M50/1/3, 8 June 1868, LEB to Elizabeth Wolstenholme.
15. MCL M50/1/3, 28 July 1868, LEB to Elizabeth Wolstenholme.
16. WSJ July 1870, p. 54.
17. For what follows, see Holcombe, *Wives and Property*, pp. 175–89.
18. *The Times*, 25 August 1870, p. 11.

19. E. Sylvia Pankhurst, *The Suffragette Movement*, pp. 48–9.
20. E. Sylvia Pankhurst Papers, 7, 1 July 1910, Elizabeth Wolstenholme Elmy to Sylvia Pankhurst.
21. MCL M50/1/3/, 26 April 1868; 21 June 1868; 4 November 1868, LEB to Elizabeth Wolstenholme.
22. MCL M50/1/3, 8 June 1868, LEB to Elizabeth Wolstenholme.
23. Lydia E. Becker, 'The Political Disabilities of Women,' printed in Jane Lewis, ed., *Before the Vote was Won* (London, 1987), pp. 118–40.
24. E. Sylvia Pankhurst Papers, 340, 1 March 1874, LEB to Elizabeth Wolstenholme.
25. Holcombe, pp. 184, 186.
26. Maureen Wright, *Elizabeth Wolstenholme Elmy and the Victorian Women's Movement* (Manchester 2011), pp. 92ff.
27. Letter by Isabella Tod, Millfield Papers, Box 22, 8 Dec 1875, quoted in S.S. Holton, 'Free Love and Victorian Feminism,' *Victorian Studies*, vol.37, no. 2 (Winter, 1994), pp. 199–222.
28. MCL M50/1/2/2; Wright, *Elizabeth Wolstenholme Elmy*, pp. 97–107. After this, Elizabeth continued to work for the committee but in an unofficial capacity.
29. MC 8 October 1880, p. 8.
30. WSJ September 1882, p. 131.
31. WSJ December 1882, p. 191; September 1882, pp. 132, 133. Lydia's consistent opposition to the Marriage with a Deceased Wife's Sister Bill, periodically proposed in Parliament from 1842 till its passing in 1907, was due to the continuing inequality in husband-wife relations. She argued that no change in the laws on marriage could take place until equality was achieved; see E. Sylvia Pankhurst Papers, 178, 21 July 1910, Esther Becker to Sylvia Pankhurst.
32. WSJ August 1890, p. 6.
33. See pp. 197–204.
34. MCL M50/1/3 16 April 1868, LEB to Sarah Jackson.
35. Levine, *Victorian Feminism*, p.110.
36. MCL M50/1/3, 20 May 1868, LEB to Mrs Smith of Carlisle.
37. Frances Power Cobbe, 'Wife-Torture in England', *Contemporary Review*, vol. 32, (April, 1878), p. 65.
38. MC 7 May 1887, p. 3.
39. Levine, *Victorian Feminism*, p. 116.
40. E. Sylvia Pankhurst Papers, 340, 17 July 1868, LEB to Richard Pankhurst.
41. MCL M50/1/3, 10 July 1868, LEB to Elizabeth Wolstenholme; *The Observer*, 28 January 1871.
42. MT 18 December 1869, p. 5. This venture is not known to have succeeded.
43. WSJ April 1886, cited in Parker, 'Lydia Becker: Her Work for Women', p. 271; see also Levine, *Victorian Feminism*, p. 108.
44. MEN 24 March 1870, p. 2; MC 24 March 1870, p. 5; MEN 7 April 1870, p. 1; MC 16 April 1870, p. 1.
45. Caine, *English Feminism*, p. 90.
46. MEN 8 August 1871, p. 2, 9 August, p. 2. As early as July 1868 she had already formed the opinion that some men lived off their wives, based on a pamphlet produced by Josephine Butler; MCL M50/1/3, 16 July 1868, LEB to Richard Pankhurst.
47. MC 19 July 1876, p. 5.

48. MC 24 September 1877, p. 5. She also expressed a view in 1873 that women, including servants, wasted a lot of time and effort making clothes and that these items should be mass produced in factories to free up women; *The Times* 24 September 1873, p. 7.
49. MC 29 June 1878, p. 6.
50. Levine, *Victorian Feminism*, p. 123.
51. See p. 10.
52. MC 13 April 1880, p. 4; MT 17 April 1880, p. 6.
53. WSJ May 1886, p. 65–8. See also Levine, *Victorian Feminism*, pp. 119–122.
54. MC 19 April 1886, p. 8, 18 May 1887, p. 8.
55. E. Sylvia Pankhurst, *The Suffragette Movement*, p. 35.
56. WSJ December 1889, p. 147.
57. Blackburn, p. 42.
58. See Levine, *Victorian Feminism, 1850–1900*, (Florida, 2018) pp. 145–6.
59. MCL M50/1/3, 11 July 1868, LEB to Richard Pankhurst; Parker, 'Lydia Becker: Her Work for Women', p. 240.
60. MG 16 November 1870, p. 1; 17 November 1870, p. 8.
61. MCL M50/1/3, 17 July 1868, LEB to Richard Pankhurst.
62. University of Liverpool JB 1/1 Josephine Butler to Miss Priestman, 23 August 1872.
63. *The Times*, 21 July 1871, p. 12; *MT* 7 November 1870, p. 1; University of Liverpool, JB 1/1, 23 September 1872, 23 December 1872, Josephine Butler to H.J. Wilson; 24 December 1872, George Butler to H.J. Wilson.
64. WSJ January 1872, pp. 10–11.
65. Although she was reported to have accompanied Frances Power Cobbe to one of their meetings in the later 1880s, she was seemingly not convinced to join their campaigns; Caine, *Victorian Feminists*, p. 256.
66. See pp. 240–2.
67. Caine, *Victorian Feminists*, pp. 230–3.

Chapter 7: Local Government and the Isle of Man Franchise
1. For what follows, see Pugh, *March of the Women*, pp. 72–7.
2. Patricia Hollis, *Ladies Elect: Women in English Local Government, 1865–1914*, (Oxford, 1987), pp. 32, 6–7, 31.
3. LSE Mill-Taylor Archive, vol. XII, 29, 27 December 1867, LEB to Helen Taylor.
4. Quotes from Blackburn, pp. 91–4.
5. Blackburn, pp. 94–5.
6. Indeed in a Manchester council election in March 1869, a woman had succeeded in getting onto the register and had voted for the unsuccessful candidate in St James's ward, Mr Pennington. Her vote was 'gallantly not objected to'; MC 23 March 1869, p. 5.
7. Hollis, *Ladies Elect*, pp. 43–5.
8. WSJ 1 May 1871, 1 July 1870.
9. MG 24 October 1878, p. 5.
10. MT 25 October 1879, p. 6; MC 25 October 1879, p. 3.
11. For Jessie Craigen, see pp. 105–6.
12. Hollis, *Ladies Elect*, p. 35, citing *WSJ* 1 November 1878, 1 November 1879, and *Englishwoman's Review*, 15 November 1878.
13. Quoted in Joyce Marlow, ed., *Votes for Women* (Virago, 2000), p. 20.

14. Lydia E. Becker, *Rights and Duties of Women in Local Government*, 1879, pp. 349, 353.
15. MC 13 November 1879, p.
16. For example see MG 26 October 1882, p. 6; MC 27 October 1881, p. 6.
17. MC 14 February 1883, p. 2; MC 19 February 1883, p. 3.
18. MC 14 February 1883, p. 5.
19. It should be noted that some anti-suffragist women were in fact beginning to argue that local government and service were included in the sphere of women, concerned as they were with social and educational matters; see Julia Bush, *Women Against the Vote: Female Anti-Suffragism in Britain*, (Oxford, 2007), kindle version, location 289.
20. *I[sle of] M[an] T[imes]*, 16 January 1875, p. 3.
21. IMT, 20 May 1876, p. 3.
22. IMT, 23 March 1878, p. 5.
23. IMT, 28 September 1878, p. 5.
24. IMT 31 July 1880, p. 8; 11 December 1880, p. 5.
25. IMT 7 August 1880, p. 3, 14 August 1880, p. 3.
26. Blackburn, pp. 157–8.
27. IMT 11 December 1880, p. 5.
28. IMT 19 March 1881, p.5.
29. Kelly, p. 46.
30. IMT 19 March 1881, p. 5.
31. Blackburn, pp. 155–8 gives a detailed account.

Chapter 8: The Manchester School Board
1. Hollis, *Ladies Elect*, p. 8.
2. MT 26 November 1873.
3. Levine, *Victorian Feminism*, p. 40.
4. See, for instance, Levine, *Victorian Feminism*, pp. 30 and 40.
5. Philippa Levine, 'Helen Taylor (1831–1907)', *ODNB*, https://doi.org/10.1093/ref:odnb/36431, accessed 19 May 2020. See also pp. 86–7.
6. MC 14 September 1869, p. 8.
7. MT 30 October 1869, p. 7.
8. Hollis, *Ladies Elect*, pp. 33–4.
9. MG 17 November 1870, p. 1.
10. MT 26 November 1870, p. 5.
11. Parker, 'Lydia Becker: Her Work for Women', pp. 295–6.
12. *Observer*, 27 November 1870, p. 5.
13. Hollis, p.47.
14. MG 26 November 1870, p. 8.
15. MC 29 June 1874, p. 8.
16. MC 6 November 1879, p. 6; 8 November 1879, p. 3; Parker, 'Lydia Becker: Her Work for Women', p. 298.
17. MC 10 November 1879, p. 6.
18. MC 14 November 1879, p. 6.
19. MC 11 November 1879, p. 8.
20. MC 15 November 1879, p. 6; *MT* 15 November 1879, p. 5.
21. MC 17 November 1879, p. 4.

22. MT 22 November 1879.
23. MC 17 November 1879, p. 6.
24. MCL M65/1/1/8, School Board Minutes, p. 384, 24 November 1879; MC 25 November 1879, p. 6. The first winner of the prize went on to attend Manchester's Victoria University.
25. WSJ August 1890, p. 4. It is interesting to note that Priscilla McLaren in 1890 recollected Lydia as claiming that 'her friends were more amongst the working men than amongst the richer merchants'. See *WSJ*, August 1890, p. 7.
26. MC 1 November 1882, p. 6.
27. MC 2 October 1888, p. 4.
28. Hollis, p. 142; C.B. Dolton, 'The Manchester School Board', (University of Durham M Ed Thesis, 1959), http://etheses.dur.ac.uk/9818, pp. 25ff.
29. MT 17 December 1870, p. 6.
30. MT 28 February 1874, p. 7.
31. MT 31 July 1875, p. 7.
32. MT 17 December 1870, p. 6.
33. MT 24 December 1870, p. 7.
34. *MT* 1 April 1871, p. 6.
35. WSJ January 1871, p. 1
36. Parker, 'Lydia Becker: Her Work for Women', pp. 305–6; *WSJ* January 1886, p. 2.
37. MT 2 December 1871, pp. 8, 4.
38. MT 23 December 1871, p. 3.
39. MT 8 April 1871, p. 6.
40. MT 13 June 1874, p. 5.
41. MT 17 April 1875, p. 7.
42. MCL, M65/1/9/3, p. 9, Manchester School Board, Site Committee minutes, 25 July 1873.
43. See fig. 28.
44. MC 13 February 1877, p. 1; 19 February 1877, p. 6.
45. *Manchester Faces and Places,* August 1890, p. 169.
46. See Hollis, *Ladies Elect,* pp. 139–45.
47. MT 27 May 1871, p. 3.
48. MEN 29 October 1872, p. 2. *MT* 2 November 1872, p. 2.
49. Dolton, p. 373.
50. MC 13 July 1889, p. 7.
51. MT 1 July 1871, p. 3; MEN 26 June 1871, p. 3.
52. She publicised this issue at the BAAS in 1872; see 'Statistics regarding the attendance and education of girls in the elementary schools of Manchester', *BAAS Report,* 1872, pp. 220–2.
53. Dolton, pp. 50, 57, 77.
54. MC 29 September 1874, p. 6.
55. Lydia E. Becker 'On Some Practical Difficulties in Working the Elementary Education Act, 1870', *BAAS Report,* 1874, p. 192.
56. MT 9 December 1876, p. 6; MC 12 December 1876, p. 7.
57. MC 30 October 1883, p. 6.

Chapter 9: Aspects of Becker's School Board Career
1. WSJ November 1873, p. 157.
2. MG 10 April 1884, p. 6.

3. MCL M50/1/3, 6 October 1868, LEB to Mr Heatherley.
4. LSE 7LEB 1/12; MG 18 January 1878, p. 7.
5. MT 22 April 1871, p. 7.
6. Joan E. Parker, 'Lydia Becker's "School for Science": a Challenge to Domesticity,' *Women's History Review*, (2001), 10:4, p. 640; citing MCL Scrap Book, 2 October 1874, Lydia E. Becker, Prize-giving at Lindley Mechanics Institute.
7. MC 30 October 1877, p. 6.
8. MC 12 October 1880, p. 8.
9. MT 9 November 1878, p. 7.
10. MC 8 December 1879, p. 3.
11. MT 6 March 1880, p. 6.
12. Cited in Parker, 'Lydia Becker: Her Work for Women,' p. 369.
13. MC 1 February 1881, p. 6.
14. Parker, 'Lydia Becker: Her Work for Women,' p. 377. See also Kelly, p. 37.
15. MT 24 December 1870, p. 8.
16. MT 6 March 1880, p. 6.
17. MC 23 October 1880, p. 8.
18. MC 26 September 1883, pp. 5, 3.
19. MCL M50/1/3, 6 October 1868, LEB to Mr Heatherley, in which she details her views on how children learn and should be taught; MG 18 January 1878, p. 7.
20. Parker, 'Lydia Becker's "School for Science"', pp. 636–7.
21. Lydia E. Becker 'On the Study of Science by Women,' *Contemporary Review*, 10, 1868, p. 403.
22. This was not a view shared by all feminists; Josephine Butler, for instance, did not believe that the education of the sexes should be the same; Caine, *Victorian Feminists*, p. 177.
23. Levine, *Victorian Feminism*, pp. 28–9.
24. WSJ September 1871, p. 96; January 1871, p. 1.
25. MG 17 November 1870, p. 1.
26. Parker, 'Lydia Becker's "school for science"', p. 639, citing MCL, Manchester School Board minutes, Scheme of Education Committee, pp. 202–4 and 217–22.
27. Parker, 'Lydia Becker: Her Work for Women', p. 318.
28. MT 23 December 1871, p. 6.
29. MC 24 March 1874, p. 6.
30. These were 'On Some Maxims of Political Economy as Applied to the Employment of Women and the Education of Girls' (Edinburgh 1871), 'On the Attendance and Education of Girls in the Elementary Schools of Manchester' (Birmingham 1872) and 'On Some Practical Difficulties in the Working of the Elementary Education Act' (Belfast 1874).
31. MCL, Manchester School Board minutes, 18 March 1877.
32. MT 28 August 1880, p. 5; Parker, 'Lydia Becker's "School for Science"', p. 641.
33. MG 28 June 1878, p. 7; Parker, op.cit., p. 642.
34. *The Times*, 18 June 1880, p. 10.
35. Lydia E. Becker, 'On the Attendance and Education of Girls in Manchester', *Report of the BAAS*, 1872, pp. 220–2.
36. MEN 27 August 1872, p. 2; MT 31 August 1872, p. 7.
37. MT 1 May 1875, p. 2.
38. Parker, 'Lydia Becker: Her Work for Women', p. 315.

39. MC 25 January 1876, p. 6.
40. MC 1 November 1887, p. 7.
41. MC 19 February 1877, p. 6.
42. On the same occasion she also displayed irritation with bad grammar in board communications; MC 23 September 1879, p. 6.
43. MC 7 July 1877, p. 2; MT 7 July 1877, p. 6; Parker, 'Lydia Becker: Her Work for Women,' p. 373.
44. MCL, M65/1/8/4, p. 7; Parker, 'Lydia Becker: Her Work for Women, ' p. 374.
45. Parker, 'Lydia Becker: Her Work for Women', pp. 375–6.
46. Parker, 'Lydia Becker's "School for Science"', p. 643.
47. MC 27 June 1882, p. 7.
48. MC 10 September 1886, p. 6.
49. MC 10 September 1888, p. 8.
50. I am grateful to Gwen Hobson and Pam Roberts, Archivists of Manchester High School for Girls, for information from the school archives.
51. MC 29 October 1880, p. 6.
52. WSJ August 1879, pp. 141–2.
53. MC 6 October 1879, p. 6; *The Times*, 11 May 1880, p. 6.
54. MG 22 August 1872, p. 7.
55. MT 5 April 1878, p. 6.
56. MT 3 February 1872, p. 8; 30 March 1872, p. 7.
57. MT 1 April 1873, p. 6; MEN 2 April 1873, p. 2; Parker, 'Lydia Becker's "School for Science"', p. 642.
58. MC 31 March 1874, p. 6.
59. MC 10 November 1882, p. 7.
60. MC 14 November 1882, p. 8.
61. MG 10 April 1884, p. 6; MC 5 February 1886, p. 3.
62. MC 24 October 1888, p. 3; 29 October 1888, p. 6; 30 October 1888, p. 6.
63. MT 5 March 1870, p. 7.
64. MC 6 October 1880, p. 6; MT 9 October 1880, p. 7.
65. MC 9 November 1880, p. 6.
66. MC 11 October 1880, p. 8.
67. Dolton, p. 73.
68. Manchester School Board Minutes, ISC, 21 Aug 1879, p. 196.
69. MC 29 November 1881, p. 7.
70. MT 9 November 1878, p. 7.
71. MT 5 August 1871, p. 6; MEN 28 August 1871, p. 3.
72. MT 28 February 1874, p. 7.
73. MC 1 February 1882, p. 3.
74. MC 24 September 1889, p. 6.
75. MEN 20 August 1872, p. 3.
76. MC 29 August 1882, p. 7.
77. MCL M50/1/3, 11 July 1868, LEB to Richard Pankhurst.
78. *Report of the BAAS*, 1872, pp. 201–2.
79. MC 29 June, 1878, p. 6.
80. MC 26 September 1882, p. 7.
81. MC 10 May 1889, p. 5.
82. MC 27 February 1883, p. 6.

83. MC 19 March 1881, p. 10.
84. June Purvis, *Emmeline Pankhurst* (London, 2002), pp. 57–8.
85. WSJ August 1890.

Chapter 10: The Bills for the Removal of the Electoral Disabilities of Women, 1870–80

1. Quoted in Constance Rover, *Women's Suffrage and Party Politics in Britain, 1866–1914,* (London, 1967), p. 34.
2. WSJ June 1871, p. 52.
3. MEN 31 January 1872, p. 2.
4. Levine, *Victorian Feminism*, p. 148.
5. *Accrington Times*, 13 April 1872, cited in R. Strachey, *The Cause, A Short History of the Women's Movement in Great Britain* (London, 1978), p. 265.
6. Hansard 4 May 1870, vol. 201, pp. 194–240.
7. University of Liverpool, JB1/1, Josephine Butler to George Butler, 6 May 1870. She also reported that Lydia Becker looked 'very ill and thin.' By July 1871 she reported that Lydia was 'much better'; ibid., 21 July 1871.
8. Blackburn, pp. 106–7.
9. MCL M50/1/3, 2 May 1868, LEB to Anne Robertson.
10. WSJ July 1870, p. 45.
11. MT 9 March 1872, p. 7; MCL M50/1/4/4, p. 6
12. MCL M50/1/4/4, p. 6. See p. 109.
13. MC 26 June 1874, p. 5.
14. MT 11 July 1874, p. 5.
15. MCL M50/1/3, 22 March 1868, LEB to Professor Jack.
16. Blackburn, pp. 136–8.
17. See p. 253.
18. See p. 146.
19. E. Sylvia Pankhurst, *The Suffragette Movement*, p. 49.
20. MC 29 January 1876, p. 5.
21. Pugh, *March of the Women*, p. 25.
22. *The Times*, 11 November 1875, p. 12; MCL M50/1/4/8, p. 8.
23. MT 8 May 1875, p. 7.
24. MC 8 February 1876, p. 5; 27 March 1876, p. 8; 10 April 1876, p. 6.
25. MG 1 April 1877, p. 2.
26. University of Nottingham Archives N Mc 3/49, p. 6.
27. WSJ May 1876, p. 50.
28. University of Nottingham Archives, N Mc 2/77, pp. 2–3, 10 December 1876.
29. MC 15 May 1876, p. 6.
30. MC 6 June 1877, p. 6.
31. MCL M50/1/4/10, p. 3; MT 10 November 1877, p. 6.
32. MCL M50/1/4/11, p. 3.
33. MC 7 November 1878, p. 6.
34. There was evidence of this tactic in WSJ, from August 1872, p. 115.
35. MG 8 March 1879, p. 8.
36. MCL M50/1/4/12, p. 12; MC 13 November 1879, p. 6.
37. MT 15 November 1879. p. 7.

Chapter 11: Lydia in London: The Third Reform Act, 1884, and its Aftermath

1. Sandra Stanley Holton, *Feminism and Democracy* (Cambridge, 1986), pp. 6–7
2. Mayhall, *The Militant Suffrage Movement*, p. 17, argues that nineteenth century liberal suffragists were not democrats, except for a few 'advanced' liberals like Richard Pankhurst; Becker too was one of their number.
3. Caine, *English Feminism*, p. 126.
4. Holton, *Feminism and Democracy*, pp. 152–3.
5. See for instance Levine, *Victorian Feminism*, p. 70.
6. See Jill Liddington and Jill Norris, *One Hand Tied Behind Us*, (London, 2000), p. 6.
7. *The Times*, 28 April 1880, p. 8.
8. Cited in E. Sylvia Pankhurst, *The Suffragette Movement*, p. 51.
9. Blackburn, p. 149.
10. See p. 172.
11. MC 7 February 1880, p. 7.
12. Laura McLaren of the London committee led the discussions; she is now better known for her development of the Bodnant Garden in North Wales.
13. MCL M50/1/3, 7 November 1868, LEB to Leigh Becker.
14. MCL M50/1/2/38, 17 February 1881, Laura McLaren to LEB.
15. MCL M50/1/2/38, 11 March 1881, Laura McLaren to LEB.
16. LSE Mill-Taylor Archive, vol. XIII, 225, no date, Laura McLaren to Helen Taylor.
17. MCL M50/1/2/40, 11 March 1881, Laura McLaren to LEB.
18. See LSE 2LSW/A/1 Box FL 135 for the executive committee annual reports and minutes.
19. MCL M50/1/4/13, pp. 3–4.
20. MCL M50/1/4/14, pp. 2–3.
21. University of Nottingham Archives N Mc 3/32, pp. 1–2, 4 June 1882.
22. MCL M50/1/4/16, pp. 3–9.
23. LSE 9/28/A/10, 10 October 1883, LEB to Miss Priestman.
24. Holton, *Suffrage Days*, p. 64. Jane Cobden, with Becker and Rev. Steinthal, also attended the National Reform Union conference at Manchester on 25 January 1884, where a resolution in favour of the women's suffrage amendment was carried; MCL M50/1/4/17, pp. 12–14.
25. There had been some rick-burning, but the protests were minimal compared with those which accompanied the Reform Act of 1867.
26. Sandra Stanley Holton, *Suffrage Days*, (London, 1996), p. 66.
27. See pp. 253–4.
28. MCL M50/2/1/19, 18 January 1884, LEB to Millicent Fawcett; LSE 2LSW/A/1 Box FL135, Central Committee Minutes, 24 January 1884.
29. Holton, *Suffrage Days*, pp. 66–7.
30. Quoted in Joyce Marlow, ed., *Votes for Women* (Virago, 2000), p. 24.
31. LSE Central Executive Committee Minutes, 7 June 1883, 6 December 1883, 3 April 1884. 2LSW/A/1, box FL 135.
32. WSJ July 1884, p. 148.
33. MCL M50/1/4/17, pp. 10–11. Holmes, *Lydia Becker*, p. 21.
34. MCL M50/1/2/53, Frances Power Cobbe to LEB.
35. WSJ Sept 1885, p. 139.

36. Brian Harrison, 'Women's Suffrage at Westminster, 1866–1928', in Michael Bentley and John Stevenson eds, *High and Low Politics in Modern Britain* (Oxford, 1983), pp. 97–8.
37. Indeed Lord Denman, apparently off his own bat, introduced a women's suffrage bill in the Lords in 1885 but in July it was defeated thirty-six to eight: MCL M50/1/4/18, pp. 5–6.
38. Theresa Billington-Greig, *The Militant Suffrage Movement*, p. 150.
39. This was regularly recorded for the 1870s in the *WSJ*, as noted by Pugh, *March of the Women*, p. 20.
40. Holton, *Suffrage Days*, p. 67; MCL M50/1/4/17, p. 17.
41. LSE, Central Executive Committee Minutes, 2LSW/A/1, box FL 135, 25 June 1884.
42. LSE, 2LSW/A/1, box FL 135, 2 July 1884; 16 July 1884.
43. University of Nottingham Archives N Mc 3/71, p.6, 12 September 1884, Priscilla McLaren to Margaret Lucas.
44. Holton, *Suffrage Days*, p.66.
45. LSE Central Executive Committee Minutes, 2LSW/A/1, box FL 135, 25 June 1884, 2 July 1884, 9 July 1884, 16 July 1884, 6 August 1884, 24 October 1884, 29 October 1884, 19 November 1884.
46. Central Executive Committee Minutes are missing from 17 December 1884 to 4 January 1888. See also Central Executive Committee Minutes, 2LSW/A/1, box FL 135, 9 January 1889.
47. See for example 2LSW/A/1, box FL 135, 15 February 1888.
48. Sandra Stanley Holton, '"To Educate Women into Rebellion": Elizabeth Cady Stanton and the Creation of a Transatlantic Network of Radical Suffragists', *American Historical Review*, vol. 99, no. 4 (October 1994), p. 1125.
49. Holton, *Suffrage Days*, p. 65; LSE Mill-Taylor Archive, vol. XIII, 238, 21 January 1888, Priscilla McLaren to Helen Taylor.
50. MCL M50/1/4/18, p. 14. Indeed, Becker calculated that 646 election candidates were in favour: 'Your Committee believe that so numerous and representative a body of supporters of one particular proposal is unique in political history.'
51. MCL M50/1/2, 51, 23 Nov 1885, Leonard Courtney to LEB.
52. Linda Walker, 'Party Political Women: A Comparative Study of Liberal Women and the Primrose League, 1890–1914' in Jane Rendall, ed., *Equal or Different*, (London, 1987), pp. 180–8; Patricia Hollis, 'Women in Council: Separate Spheres, Public Space', ibid., pp. 193–5.
53. Pugh, *March of the Women*, p. 68; the estimate was that of the NSWS, which was sometimes rather optimistic in its assessment.
54. MCL M50/1/4/20, pp. 4–8; Blackburn, pp. 173–4.
55. MCL M50/1/2/58, July 1887, Walter McLaren to LEB.
56. WSJ July 1887, p. 77; the other was Robert Adamson, chair of the executive committee of the MNSWS.
57. MC 8 September 1888, p. 6.
58. MT 8 January 1889, p. 6; MC 12 January 1889, p. 6. See Janet Howarth, 'Fawcett, Dame Millicent Garret (1847–1929)', *ODNB*, https://doi.org/10.1093/ref:odnb/33096, accessed 19 May 2020. Also Caine, *English Feminism*, pp. 127–9.
59. MC 11 January 1887, p. 5.
60. Pugh, *March of the Women*, pp. 65–6.

61. E. Sylvia Pankhurst, *The Suffragette Movement*, p. 64.
62. MCL M50/1/2, 63, 3 December [1888], Frances Power Cobbe to LEB.
63. WSJ December 1888, p. 116.
64. E. Sylvia Pankhurst Papers, 340, 12 December 1888, LEB to Miss Balgarnie.
65. E. Sylvia Pankhurst, *The Suffragette Movement*, p. 94, claims that Emmeline joined the London Society specifically to vote in favour of the existing rules, but it seems that in the end she supported the new rules. She also says that Lydia consulted 'her old friend' Richard Pankhurst for legal advice on the whole issue.
66. See pp. 254–5.
67. LSE Central Executive Committee Minutes, 2LSW/A/1, box FL 135, 9 January 1889.
68. *The Times*, 29 December 1888, p. 3.
69. MCL M50/1/4/21, p. 8.
70. WSJ April 1889, p.48.
71. WSJ January 1889, pp. 5–6.
72. Pugh, *March of the Women*, pp. 24–5.
73. See June Hannam, 'Women and Politics' in June Purvis, ed., *Women's History: Britain, 1850–1945* (London, 1997), pp. 281, 283.
74. See Purvis, *Emmeline Pankhurst*, pp. 30–1.
75. LSE Central Executive Committee Minutes, 2LSW/A/1, box FL 135, 9 January 1889.
76. University of Nottingham Archives, N Mc 3/100, p. 2, 16 February 1886.
77. University of Nottingham Archives, N Mc 3/142, pp. 1–2.
78. WSJ May 1889, p. 63.
79. The *Nineteenth Century*, vol. 25, (June 1889), pp. 781–7; Pugh, *March of the Women*, pp. 147–51.
80. Millicent Garrett Fawcett, 'The Appeal Against Female Suffrage: a Reply', the *Nineteenth Century*, (July 1889), pp. 86–96. For a summary and the rejoinder, see *The Times*, 31 July 1889, p. 3.
81. MG 25 June 1889, p. 9.
82. Harrison, 'Women's Suffrage at Westminster', p. 96.
83. See Bush, *Women Against the Vote*, chapter 6, and Brian Harrison, *Separate Spheres: the Opposition to Women's Suffrage in Britain*, (London, 1978), pp. 115–17.

Chapter 12: Death and Legacy
1. For this account, see Blackburn, pp. 181–6. There is evidence that in her final years, Lydia began to research her family history; LSE 9/28/A/50, 51, 52.
2. MC 26 July 1890, p. 6.
3. MCL M65/1/1/28, p. 109.
4. Blackburn, p. 181.
5. Quoted in Kelly, p. 52; see LSE 9/28/A/19 for a letter written from Bath on 5 March 1890.
6. After her death, Lydia's sister Esther, not unnaturally wished to interview the maid, but related that she was not well enough to come when she wrote to her; LSE 9/28/A/65.
7. WSJ August 1890, p. 7. Philippa had been placed high above the male candidates in the mathematical tripos.
8. Blackburn, p. 183.

9. Blackburn, p. 184.
10. MT 26 July 1890, p. 6.
11. Blackburn, pp. 184–5.
12. Blackburn, pp. 185–6.
13. MT 26 July 1890.
14. MC 21 July 1890, p8; Will of Lydia Becker, Manchester Probate Registry, 18/19 July 1890.
15. WSJ August 1890, p. 7.
16. See fig. 31.
17. LSE 9/28/A/63, 5 August 1890, A. Courtney Tagart to Wilfred Becker.
18. Manchester Probate Registry, Will of Lydia Becker, 18/19 July 1890; LSE 9/28/A/57.
19. MC 13 December 1890, p. 12.
20. WSJ August 1890, p. 2. The identity of 'ETA' is unknown.
21. MT 26 July 1890; LSE 9/29/A/60.
22. Blackburn, pp. 186–8; see also Kelly, pp. 54–5.
23. WSJ August 1890, passim.
24. Blackburn, pp. 187–8.
25. MC 21 July 1890, p.8.
26. MC 10 December 1890, p. 6.
27. Blackburn, p. 188.
28. *Manchester Faces and Places,* August 1890, p. 170; MC 11 August 1890, p. 6.
29. WSJ August 1890, p. 3.
30. MC 28 August 1890, p. 6.
31. I am indebted to Rev. Ian Rumsey, Vicar of St Mary the Virgin, Bowdon, for his most helpful insights into this passage.
32. MCL M50/1/4/22, p. 11.
33. Martin Pugh, *The Pankhursts: The History of One Radical Family* (London, 2008), p. 90.
34. Caine, *English Feminism,* p. 156.
35. See Jo Vellacott, *From Liberal to Labour with Women's Suffrage* (McGill-Queen's UP, 1993), p. x.
36. MG 5 February 1891, p. 7.
37. MG 25 July 1907, p. 6; 3 August 1907, p. 8 refers to a marble bust which was offered to Manchester Town Hall by Margaret Ashton, on behalf of subscribers.
38. MG 17 July 1908, p. 8.
39. MG 20 August 1890, p. 7; see front cover.
40. MG 21 July 1890, p. 3; MT 26 July 1890; *The Times,* 21 July 1890, p.9.
41. Caine, *English Feminism,* pp. 156–7, 158–9.
42. Mayhall, *The Militant Suffrage Movement,* pp. 135–8.
43. Emmeline Pankhurst, *My Own Story,* p. 9.
44. See for instance E. Sylvia Pankhurst, *The Suffragette Movement,* pp. 33, 35.
45. Holton, *Feminism and Democracy,* pp. 129–30.
46. Holton, *Feminism and Democracy,* pp. 76–9.
47. Brian Harrison, 'Women's Suffrage at Westminster, 1866–1928', in Michael Bentley and John Stevenson, eds., *High and Low Politics in Modern Britain* (Oxford, 1983), pp. 119–21.
48. Levine, *Victorian Feminism,* pp. 158–61.

49. Martin Pugh, *The Pankhursts*, (London, 2008), pp. 11–12.
50. Jo Vellacott, *From Liberal to Labour with Women's Suffrage: the Story of Catherine Marshall* (McGill-Queen's University Press, 1993), pp. 363, 366.

Conclusion
1. Caine, *Victorian Feminists*, pp. 263, 129–30.
2. See p. 159.
3. See pp. 231–3.
4. Caine, *Victorian Feminists*, pp. 264–5; Sandra Stanley Holton, *Feminism and Democracy* (Cambridge 1986), pp.76–90.
5. Holton, *Feminism and Democracy*, p. 76.
6. Holton, *Feminism and Democracy*, p. 6
7. I am grateful to Andrew Simcock for this information.
8. WSJ August 1890, p. 9.

Select Bibliography

Published sources
Alexander, S., ed., *Women's Fabian Tracts* (London 1988)
Ashfield, Charles Joseph, 'On the flora of Preston and the neighbourhood, part IV' *Transactions of the Lancashire and Cheshire Historical Society*, ns, vol. v, 1864–5, pp. 181–6
Banks, Olive, *Becoming a Feminist: The Social Origins of 'First Wave' Feminism* (Brighton, 1986)
Banks, Olive, *Faces of Feminism* (Oxford, 1981)
Becker, Lydia E., *Directions for Preparing a Petition to the House of Commons* (1869)
Becker, Lydia E., 'Is There Any Specific Distinction between Male and Female Intellect?' *Englishwoman's Review*, 8 (1868), pp. 483–91
Becker, Lydia E., *Liberty, Equality, Fraternity: a Reply to Mr Fitzjames Stephen's Strictures on Mr J.S. Mill's Subjection of Women* (1873)
Becker, Lydia E., 'On Some Maxims of Political Economy as Applied to the Employment of Women and the Education of Girls' *Report of the BAAS* (1871)
Becker, Lydia E., 'On the Attendance and Education of Girls in the Elementary Schools of Manchester' *Report of the BAAS* (1872)
Becker, Lydia E, 'On the Study of Science by Women' *Contemporary Review*, 10 (1869), pp. 386–404.
Becker, Lydia E., 'Reply to the Protest' *Nineteenth Century Review* (June 1889)
Becker, Lydia E., 'On Some Practical Difficulties in the Working of the Elementary Education Act, 1870' *Report of the BAAS* (1874)
Becker, Lydia E., 'Some Supposed Differences in the Minds of Men and Women in Regard to the Educational Necessities' *Report of the BAAS* (1868)
Becker, Lydia E., 'The Political Disabilities of Women' *Westminster Review* (January, 1872), printed in Lewis, Jane, ed., *Before the Vote was Won* (London 1987), pp. 118–40.
Becker, Lydia E., 'Female Suffrage' *Contemporary Review*, vol. 4 (1867), pp. 307–16
Bentley, Michael and Stevenson, John, eds., *High and Low Politics in Modern Britain* (Oxford, 1983)
Billington-Greig, *The Militant Suffrage Movement* (London, 1911)
Blackburn, Helen, *Women's Suffrage: A Record of the Women's Suffrage Movement in the British Isles, with Biographical Sketches of Miss Becker* (London, 1902)
Bodichon, Barbara Leigh Smith, *Reasons for the Enfranchisement of Women* (London, 1866)
Bush, Julia, *Women Against the Vote: Female Anti-Suffragism in Britain* (Oxford, 2007)
Caine, Barbara, *English Feminism* (Oxford, 1997)
Caine, Barbara, *Victorian Feminists* (Oxford, 1992)
Cobbe, Frances Power, 'Wife-Torture in England' *Contemporary Review*, (April, 1878)
Crawford, Elizabeth, *The Women's Suffrage Movement* (London, 2000)

Select Bibliography   305

Delamont, Sarah, and Duffin, Lorna, eds, *The Nineteenth Century Woman* (London, 1978)
Fawcett, Millicent Garrett, *Women's Suffrage: A Short History of a Great Movement* (London, 1911)
Gates, Barbara, *Kindred Nature* (Chicago, 1998)
Gianquitto, Tina, 'Botanical Smuts and Hermaphrodites. Lydia Becker, Darwin's Botany, and Education Reform' *Isis*, vol. 104, no. 2, June 2013, pp. 250–77
Goldman, Lawrence, *Science, Reform, and Politics in Victorian Britain: The Social Science Association 1857–1886* (Cambridge, 2002)
Hamilton, Susan, ' "A crisis in woman's history": Frances Power Cobbe's duties of women and the practice of everyday feminism' *Women's History Review*, 11:4 (2002), pp. 577–93
Harrison, Brian, *Separate Spheres: the Opposition to Women's Suffrage in Britain* (London, 1978)
Holcombe, Lee, *Wives and Property* (Toronto, 1983)
Hollis, Patricia, *Ladies Elect: Women in English Local Government, 1865–1914* (Oxford, 1987)
Holmes, Marion, *Lydia Becker, A Cameo Life-Sketch* (no date)
Holton, Sandra Stanley, 'Free Love and Victorian Feminism', *Victorian Studies*, vol. 37, no. 2 (Winter, 1994), pp. 199–222
Holton, Sandra Stanley, 'Silk dresses and lavender kid gloves: the wayward career of Jessie Craigen, working suffragist' *Women's History Review*, 5 (1996), pp. 129–50
Holton, Sandra Stanley, *Suffrage Days* (London, 1996)
Jalland, Pat, *Women, Marriage and Politics, 1860–1914* (Oxford, 1986)
Joannou, Maroula, and Purvis, June, *The Women's Suffrage Movement: New Feminist Perspectives* (Manchester, 2009)
Jordan, Ellen, *The Women's Movement and Women's Employment in Nineteenth Century Britain* (London, 1999)
Kelly, Audrey, *Lydia Becker and the Cause* (Lancaster, 1992)
Kent, Susan Kingsley, *Sex and Suffrage in Britain, 1860–1914* (London, 1990)
Levine, Philippa, *Victorian Feminism, 1850–1900* (Florida, 2018)
Lewis, Jane, ed., *Before the Vote was Won: Arguments For and Against Women's Suffrage* (London, 1987)
Liddington, Jill and Norris, Jill, *One Hand Tied Behind Us* (London, 2000)
Linton, Eliza Lynn, 'The Shrieking Sisterhood' *Saturday Review*, 12 March 1870.
Manchester Faces and Places (Manchester, 1890)
Marlow, Joyce, ed., *Votes for Women* (Virago, 2000)
Mayhall, Laura E. Nym, *The Militant Suffrage Movement: Citizenship and Resistance in Britain, 1860–1930* (Oxford 2003)
Morrell, Jack and Thackray, *Arnold, Gentleman of Science, Early Years of the British Association for the Advancement of Science* (Oxford, 1981)
Pankhurst, Christabel, *Unshackled* (London, 1987)
Pankhurst, E. Sylvia, *The Suffragette Movement* (London, 1931)
Pankhurst, Emmeline, *My Own Story* (London, 1914)
Pankhurst, Richard, 'The Right of Women to Vote under the Reform Act, 1867' *Fortnightly Review*, 4 (21), September 1868, pp. 250–4
Parker, Joan E., 'Lydia Becker's "School for Science": a Challenge to Domesticity', *Women's History Review*, 2001, 10:4, pp. 629–50

Parker, Joan E., 'Lydia Becker: Pioneer Orator for the Women's Movement' *Manchester Region History Review*, 5 (1991)
Perkin, Joan, *Women and Marriage in Nineteenth Century England* (London, 1989)
Power Cobbe, Frances, 'Wife-Torture in England', *Contemporary Review*, vol.32, (April, 1878)
Pugh, Martin, *Emmeline Pankhurst* (London, 2001)
Pugh, Martin, *The March of the Women* (Oxford, 2000)
Pugh, Martin, *The Pankhursts: The History of One Radical Family* (London, 2008)
Purvis, June and Holton, Sandra Stanley, eds., *Votes for Women* (London 2000)
Purvis, June, *Emmeline Pankhurst* (London, 2002)
Purvis, June, ed. *Women's History: Britain, 1850–1945* (London, 1997)
Rendall, Jane, *Equal or Different: Women's Politics, 1800–1914* (London, 1987)
Rosen, Andrew, *Rise Up, Women! The Militant Campaign for the Women's Social and Political Union, 1903–14* (London, 1974)
Rover, Constance, *Women's Suffrage and Party Politics in Britain, 1866–1914* (London, 1967)
Rubinstein, David, *A Different World for Women: the Life of Millicent Garrett Fawcett* (Ohio, 1991)
Russell, Bertrand and Patricia, eds., *The Amberley Papers: The Letters and Diaries of Lord and Lady Amberley* (London, 1937)
Slater's Directory for Manchester, 1877, 1883
Smith, Harold L, *The British Women's Suffrage Campaign, 1866–1928*, 2nd edition (Harlow, 2007)
Smith, Mary, *The Autobiography of Mary Smith, Schoolmistress and Nonconformist, a Fragment of a Life* (London, 1892)
Strachey, Ray, *The Cause A Short History of the Women's Movement in Great Britain* (London 1978)
Van Wingerden, S.A., *The Women's Suffrage Movement in Britain 1866–1928* (Basingstoke, 1999)
Vicinus, Martha, *Independent Women: Work and Community for Single Women 1850–1920* (London, 1985)
Walker, Linda, 'Lydia Ernestine Becker (1827–1890)' in *The Oxford Dictionary of National Biography* (Oxford, 2004)
Williams, Joanna M., *Manchester's Radical Mayor: Abel Heywood, the Man who Built the Town Hall* (History Press, 2017)
Wright, Maureen, *Elizabeth Wolstenholme Elmy and the Victorian Feminist Movement* (Manchester, 2011)

Unpublished Sources

Balshaw, June Marion, 'Suffrage, Solidarity and Strife: Political Partnerships and the Women's Movement, 1880–1930' University of Greenwich PhD Thesis, 1998
Dingsdale, Ann, 'Generous and Lofty Sympathies: The Kensington Society, the 1866 Women's Suffrage Petition and the Development of Mid-Victorian Feminism', University of Greenwich PhD Thesis, 1995.
Dolton, C.B.,"The Manchester School Board', University of Durham, Masters Thesis, 1959, http://etheses.dur.ac.uk/9818/

Manuscript Sources

Chetham's Library, Manchester, cartoons
General Register Office
International Institute of Social History, Amsterdam, E. Sylvia Pankhurst Papers
London School of Economics, Women's Library, Autograph Letter Collection 9/28
London School of Economics, Women's Library, Central Committee Executive, Minutes, 2LSW/A/1
London School of Economics, Women's Library, Mill-Taylor Archive, vols XII and XIII
London School of Economics, Women's Library, Papers of Lydia Becker 7LEB
Manchester Central Library, School Board M65/1
Manchester Central Library, Women's Suffrage Collection M50
Manchester High School for Girls Archives
Manchester Probate Registry
University of Liverpool Butler Archive, JB1, Papers of Josephine Butler
University of Nottingham Archives, N Mc, Papers of Priscilla Bright McLaren

Newspaper sources

Burnley Advertiser
City Jackdaw
Contemporary Review
Englishwoman's Review
Isle of Man Times
Manchester Courier
Manchester Evening News
Manchester Guardian
Manchester Times
Nineteenth Century Review
The Observer
The Times
Women's Suffrage Journal

Websites

www.ancestry.co.uk
www.britishnewspaperarchive.co.uk
www.darwinproject.ac.uk
www.digital.library.lse.ac.uk
www.findmypast.co.uk
www.flickr.com
https://search.iisg.amsterdam/Record/ARCH01029/ArchiveContentList
https://babel.hathitrust.org
https://tandfonline.com

Index

Alford, Dean 29
Amberley, Lady 216
Anstey, Thomas Chisholm 44, 52, 84, 282
Anthony, Susan Brownell 35–36, 42, 59, 91, 96, 128, 136, 245, 249, 286
Ashfield, Charles Joseph 18
Ashton, Margaret 269, 302

British Association for the Advancement of Science 22–8, 90, 93–4 102–3, 106–7, 116–7, 119, 125, 133, 152, 196–7, 199–200, 203–4, 213, 244, 248, 275, 295
Babington, Charles 18
Backhouse, Sarah 12, 73, 95, 182, 260, 261
Bates, Henry 24
Bazley Thomas 41, 59, 113, 224
Becker, Arthur 12, 261–3, 278
Becker (Backhouse) Charlotte 13, 94, 95
Becker, Ernest Hannibal 4, 5, 13
Becker, Esther 6–7, 9–10, 16, 43, 47, 73, 93–95, 97, 193, 263, 301
Becker, Hannibal Leigh 4–5, 10, 12–14
Becker, John Leigh 5, 8, 16
Becker, (John) Leigh 11–12, 24, 52, 67, 94
Becker, Lydia Ernestine
  becomes a suffragist 27–32
  birth and childhood 4–9
  defence of the rights of working women 148–56
  develops into a renowned orator 102–10
  family relationships 9–15
  feminism 119–26
  foundation of the MNSWS 39–40
  girls' education 197–205
  ideas on universal suffrage 35–6
  industrial schools 210–11
  interest in fashion 116–8
  Isle of Man 168–74
  move to London and the Third Reform Act 233–42
  parliamentary agent for women's suffrage 242–9
  philosophy of education 192–7
  political education of women householders 164–8
  religious beliefs 19–20, 205–8
  ridicule in cartoons 42, 115–6
  scientific interests 16–27
  secretary of the MNSWS 67–75
  struggles with health 7, 49, 259–62
  tactics as leader 110–18
  views on Gladstone and Disraeli 43–4, 240–1
  women teachers and inspectors 211–14
Becker, Mary (née Duncuft) 4–6
Becker, Wilfred 5, 12–13, 261–3
Bentinck, George Cavendish 154
Biggs, Caroline 14, 74, 88, 90, 109, 111, 132–3, 252
Billington-Greig, Theresa 241
Birley, Herbert 180–1, 183, 188, 198, 207, 211
Blackburn, Helen 34, 90, 92, 95–6, 106, 108–9, 130, 132, 252, 258, 259, 261, 266–7, 269, 270
Blackwell, Antoinette Brown 26
Bodichon, Barbara Leigh Smith xiii, 9, 28, 36–7, 132, 139, 161
Borchardt, Dr Louis 28, 40, 76, 177
Boucherett, Jessie 49, 65, 68, 74, 81, 89–90, 97, 101, 127–8, 132, 140, 149, 252, 265

Index 309

Bright, Jacob 13, 28–9, 33–4, 39, 40–3, 45, 55, 58–9, 62–3, 65, 71–2, 78, 79, 85, 89, 96–7, 100, 116, 123, 140, 141, 147, 161–2, 218–9, 222, 226–7, 239–40, 251, 254–5, 265, 280, 281
Bright, John 41–4, 47, 116, 142, 169, 225–6, 238
Bright, Ursula xiv, 14, 34, 39, 48, 50, 55, 57, 62, 69, 7185, 88, 102, 140, 147, 155, 219, 222, 225–6, 233, 245, 253, 265
British Association for the Advancement of Science 22–8, 90, 93–4, 102–3, 106–7, 116–7, 119, 125, 133, 152, 196–7, 199–200, 203–4, 213, 244, 248, 275
Brougham's Act 44
Bruce, Henry 157, 162
Burt, Thomas 154
Butler, George 254
Butler, Josephine xiv, 16, 48, 51–2, 76, 96, 98–9, 105, 119, 121–4, 155–8, 211, 218–9, 249, 265, 269, 279, 292, 296, 298

Carpenter, Mary 136
Central Committee of the National Women's Suffrage Society 80–90, 96, 100–1, 114, 132, 134, 137, 223, 238–40, 242–5, 247–8, 251–3, 259–261, 265–7, 286
Chamberlain, Joseph 136
Charley, William Thomas 78
Chorlton v Lings 56, 78
Chorlton, Thomas 103
Churchill, Lord Randolph 224, 246
Clark, Helen Priestman Bright 109, 221, 238
Clifford, Anne, Countess of Dorset 44
Cobbe, Frances Power xiv, 4, 12–13, 38–9, 54, 66, 79–81, 90, 95, 99, 101, 112, 119–22, 124, 135, 145, 147–9, 231–2, 240, 249–50, 265, 275, 293
Cobden, Jane 109, 221, 238, 299
Cobden, Richard 8
College Street Group 115, 251–2, 255, 259, 265
Conservative Party 13, 38, 42–3, 58–9, 63, 74, 78–9, 99–100, 113, 124, 161–3, 168, 183, 217, 221, 223–4, 227–9, 231–2, 234, 240–1, 246–50, 254, 256, 272
Contagious Diseases Acts xiv, 16, 48, 90, 98–9, 105, 123, 136, 137, 156–9
Corrupt and Illegal Practices Act 246
Counties' Liberal Union 238
Courtney, Leonard 63, 100, 112, 115, 227–9, 111, 237, 245, 262, 265, 267, 275
Craigen, Jessie 105–6, 109, 111, 165, 232, 234
Creighton, Louise 255

Darwin, Charles 17–18, 20–3, 25–6, 117, 120, 279
Davies, Emily xiv, 9, 13, 22, 24, 28–9, 36–7, 39, 74, 116, 119–24, 176, 178, 197, 202, 204, 232, 252, 275, 278–9
Dilke, Sir Charles 79, 218, 231
Dilke, Lady Emilia 149, 256
Disraeli, Benjamin 38, 43, 79, 108, 217, 227–8, 283
Divorce Act (Matrimonial Causes Act) 140
Domestic Economy Congress 153, 200
Dunckley, Henry 128, 226

Edwards-Heathcote, Captain 247
Eliot, George (Mary Ann Evans) 24
Elmy, Elizabeth Wolstenholme xiv, 14, 37–8, 48, 50, 52, 76–7, 80, 95, 97, 99–100, 119, 121, 124, 134, 139–40, 142–7, 155–6, 158, 178, 211, 218, 222–3, 241, 254, 265, 271, 280–1
Englishwoman's Review 74, 94, 127–131, 133, 137, 266

Faithfull, Emily 128
Fawcett, Millicent Garrett xii, xv, 90, 101–2, 115, 119, 121, 123–6, 159, 223, 232, 238–9, 243–4, 246, 248–9, 251–4, 256, 259–60, 265, 269–70, 272–3, 275–6, 290
Female Employees Association 151
Fenians 47, 228
Forster's Education Act 175, 211
Forsyth, William 63, 77, 90, 100, 113, 146, 221–4, 229

Foxdenton Hall, Chadderton 4–5
Fraser, James, bishop of Manchester 154, 179, 209

Garrett Anderson, Elizabeth 3, 122, 169, 176, 178
Girton College Cambridge, 131, 215, 255, 270,
Gladstone, William Ewart 43–4, 46, 57–8, 63, 77, 79, 89, 97, 99, 112–4, 171, 174, 175, 217, 219, 221, 230, 232, 234–5, 237–8, 240–2, 246, 248
Grand National Demonstration of Women 234
Great Reform Act 36, 228, 280
Gurney, Russell 6

Hallett, Lilias Ashworth xiv, 8, 74, 99, 101, 182, 239, 244, 252, 254, 265
Heywood, Abel 229
Heywood, Oliver 178, 183
Hoare, Joseph 24
Hosack, John 54–5,
Hunt, Henry 36

Irish Home Rule 113, 246–8,
Isle of Man 168–74

James, Edward 29, 33
Johnson, Mary 19, 48, 51, 66, 68, 74, 86, 88, 93, 95, 97, 99, 121, 128, 130
Jones, Ernest 76

Karslake, Edward 39, 81
Kensington Society 4, 36, 38
Knight, Anne 36
Kyllmann, Philippine 29, 56–7, 62, 68–72, 76–7, 82–3, 86, 92–3, 142, 280

Labour Party 125, 231–2, 271–2, 275
Ladies' Literary Society 20–1, 69
Ladies' National Association 123, 136, 156, 158
Langton, Lady Hannah Gore 227
Law Amendment Society 139
Leatham, Edward 224
Liberal Party 217, 219–22, 227, 229–30, 231–4, 237–41, 246, 248–50, 272, 275, 299

Liberal Unionists 248–9
Lloyd George, David 110
London Anthropological Institute 26

Manchester Anthropological Society 22
Manchester Committee for the Enfranchisement of Women 38, 42
Manchester Geographical Society 26
Manchester Governesses Institution 214
Manchester High School for Girls 203–4, 215
Manchester Literary and Philosophical Society 20
Manchester National Society for Women's Suffrage 12, 14, 32, 33, 42, 46, 48, 56–7, 61, 73, 75, 80, 82, 93, 94, 102, 106, 118, 129, 132, 148, 150, 156, 164, 166, 172, 176–7, 185, 225, 227–8, 241–2, 245, 252, 267, 271, 278, 286, 300
Manchester Royal Institution 20
Manchester School Board xiv, 106, 122, 148, 155, 175–215, 236, 274,
Married Women's Property Act 134, 138–48, 160, 248, 253,
Martineau, Harriet 9, 89
Mason, Hugh 237–8
Maxwell, Lilly 33–6, 40, 44, 54, 84, 281
McLaren, Charles 225, 237, 254
McLaren, Laura 235, 243–4, 270, 299
McLaren, Priscilla Bright xi, xiv, 6, 12–13, 20, 26, 65, 74–75, 99–101, 105, 107–8, 165, 170, 219, 225, 227, 235, 237, 239, 244–5, 248, 251, 254, 262, 265, 269, 295
McLaren, Walter 247, 251, 254–5
Mill, John Stuart 28, 37–44, 52, 54, 57–9, 65, 70–2, 80–90, 104, 110, 113, 119, 123–4, 129, 140, 156, 176, 234
Moorside House, Altham 5–6, 9–11, 16, 277
Mourning Reform Association 136
Municipal Corporations Act 160–2

National Association for the Promotion of Social Science xiii, 9, 15, 27, 29, 93, 117, 119, 139, 144–5, 147, 153, 194, 204, 210

Index   311

National Education League 175–6, 205
National Liberal Federation 238, 248
National Reform Union 45, 238, 299
National Society for Women's Suffrage 15, 89, 111, 137, 222, 226, 234, 249, 253, 267, 300
National Union of Conservative and Constitutional Associations 247, 256
National Union of Women's Suffrage Societies xii, 125, 231, 269, 272–3, 275
Newman, Francis William 75, 96
Nightingale, Florence 28, 46, 89, 127, 238, 269
Northcote, Sir Stafford 227
Nottingham Philosophical Society 24

Owens College Manchester 197, 205, 214, 222

Pankhurst, Emmeline xi, xiii, 11, 91, 110, 126, 129, 215, 230, 250, 254, 265, 268, 270–1, 273, 276, 301
Pankhurst, Richard Marsden xii, xiv, 5, 11, 29, 44, 46, 50–1, 53, 55–6, 62, 66, 71, 76–7, 79, 93, 100, 120, 123, 131, 140, 143, 150, 213, 218, 222, 249–50, 254, 265, 271, 301
Pankhurst, Sylvia xi, 11–12, 51, 147, 155, 223, 250, 271, 280–1, 283, 301
Parkes, Bessie Rayner 36
Parliament Street Group 115, 251, 265
Parliamentary Franchise (Extension to Women) Bill 242
Persons campaign 13, 42–60, 65, 75–6, 82, 84–6, 88, 99, 102, 127, 129
Pochin, Agnes 46, 53, 103, 235
Pochin, Henry Davis 46, 53, 59, 235
Potter, Beatrice 255
Potter, Thomas 46
Priestman, Anna Maria 237, 242
Primrose League 246

Queen Victoria 47, 216, 247, 249

Ray Society 20
Robertson, Anne 46, 57, 74–5, 96–7, 128, 219

Roscoe, Sir Henry 197, 205
Rossetti, Christina 255
Rothery, Mrs Hume 157, 280
Royal Agricultural Society 135
Royal Geographical Society 25
Rumney, Robert 103, 186
Rylands, Peter 79

Salford Liberal Association 220
Salisbury, Marquess of 161–3, 247, 256
Sandford, Archdeacon 46, 103
Scarisbrick, Lady Anne 57, 77
Scatcherd, Alice xiv, 65, 74, 109, 168, 170, 172–3, 225, 234, 238, 242, 251, 254, 265, 283–4
Scott, Charles Prestwich 215
Scott, Rachel 215
Second Reform Act 74, 80, 129, 228
Shaftesbury, Earl of 6
Shaw, George Bernard 248
Sherwood, Richard 172–3
Shirreff, Emily 204
Slagg, John 115
Smith, Mary 104, 288
Smollett, PB 224
Socialism 125, 246, 248, 256, 275
Somerville, Mary 89
Stanton, Elizabeth Cady 105, 136, 245, 286
Steinthal, Rev. Samuel 26, 29, 39–40, 50, 62, 71, 76, 84–5, 89, 131, 141, 147, 150, 177, 251, 280, 299
Sterling, Frances Mary 109
Strachey, Ray 109
Swynnerton, Joseph 269

Taylor, Clementia (Mentia) 80–1, 85–7, 219, 254, 285–6
Taylor, Helen 38–9, 44–5, 57, 65, 69–70, 72, 80–6, 89–90, 110, 118, 156, 176, 236–7, 245
Taylor, Peter 254,
Third Reform Act 27, 133, 233, 237–42
Thomasson, John P 65–6, 242–3, 251
Tod, Isabella 96, 147
Trade Unions 123, 138, 151–2, 154, 158, 214, 236
Tynwald 160, 168, 234

United Kingdom Alliance for the Suppression of the Traffic of all Intoxicating Liquors 149

Verney, Lady 238
Victoria University of Manchester 214, 295
Vigilance Association 123, 136, 138, 156, 158–9

Wallace, Alfred Russel 18, 25, 27
Ward, Mrs Humphry 255
Wilson, George 45
Wilson, Alice xiv, 45, 50, 57, 102, 129, 280
Wollstonecraft, Mary 36, 119
Women's Electoral Disabilities Bill 79, 89, 128, 134, 146, 216–22, 224–30, 250
Women's Franchise League 115, 233, 254
Women's Liberal Federation 114–5, 246, 249, 251
Women's Liberal Unionist Association 249
Women's Protective and Provident League 152
Women's Social and Political Union xi, xii, 110, 115, 137, 228, 242, 256, 268–72
Women's Suffrage Journal xiv, 79, 90, 95, 100, 111, 118–9, 123, 127–37, 144, 147, 151, 154–5, 158–9, 185, 219–20, 224–5, 241, 244, 251–5, 258, 265–6, 287
Woodall, William 239–40, 242, 247, 252–5